*Ghosts of Home*

# Ghosts of Home

### THE AFTERLIFE OF CZERNOWITZ
### IN JEWISH MEMORY

*Marianne Hirsch and Leo Spitzer*

For Graziella —
with thanks for your
friendship
And with love

Marianne + Leo

Hanover 2010

UNIVERSITY OF CALIFORNIA PRESS

BERKELEY  LOS ANGELES  LONDON

*The publisher gratefully acknowledges the generous contributions to this book provided by the Jewish Studies Endowment Fund of the University of California Press Foundation, which was established by a major gift from the S. Mark Taper Foundation, and by the University Seminars at Columbia University.*

*For Lotte and Carl*

*And for their remarkable generation
of Czernowitzers*

University of California Press, one of the most distinguished
university presses in the United States, enriches lives around the
world by advancing scholarship in the humanities, social sciences,
and natural sciences. Its activities are supported by the UC Press
Foundation and by philanthropic contributions from individuals
and institutions. For more information, visit www.ucpress.edu.

University of California Press
Berkeley and Los Angeles, California

University of California Press, Ltd.
London, England

Library of Congress Cataloging-in-Publication Data
Hirsch, Marianne.
    Ghosts of home : the afterlife of Czernowitz in Jewish memory /
Marianne Hirsch and Leo Spitzer.
        p.       cm.
    Includes bibliographical references and index.
    ISBN 978-0-520-25772-6 (cloth : alk. paper)
    1. Jews—Ukraine—Chernivtsi—History—20th century.
2. Jews—Ukraine—Chernivtsi—Social life and customs—20th
century.    3. Chernivtsi (Ukraine)—Ethnic relations—History—
20th century.    4. Chernivtsi (Ukraine)—History—20th
century.    5. Chernivtsi (Ukraine)—Description and travel.
6. Hirsch, Carl, 1912—Travel—Ukraine—Chernivtsi.    7. Hirsch,
Lotte, 1918—Travel—Ukraine—Chernivtsi.    I. Spitzer, Leo,
1939–    II. Title.

DS135.U42C4533    2009
947.7'6—dc22                                    2009015365

Manufactured in the United States of America
19   18   17   16   15   14   13   12   11   10
10   9   8   7   6   5   4   3   2   1

This book is printed on Cascades Enviro 100, a 100% post consumer waste, recycled, de-inked fiber. FSC recycled certified
and processed chlorine free. It is acid free, Ecologo certified,
and manufactured by BioGas energy.

# CONTENTS

PART THREE
GHOSTS OF HOME, 2006

EPILOGUE, 2008

# ILLUSTRATIONS

## MAPS

## FIGURES

# PREFACE

Czernovitz expelled its Jews, and so did Vienna, Prague, Budapest, and Lemberg. Now these cities live without Jews, and their few descendants, scattered through the world, carry memory like a wonderful gift and a relentless curse.

AHARON APPELFELD
"Buried Homeland"

This is a book about a place that cannot be found in any contemporary atlas, and about a community for whom it remained alive "like a wonderful gift" and "a relentless curse" long after its disappearance. It is a historical account of a German-Jewish Eastern European culture that flourished from the mid-nineteenth century until its shattering and dispersal in the era of the Second World War. But it is also a family and communal memoir spanning three generations that explores the afterlife, in history and memory, of the city of Czernowitz.

Nowadays, of course, Czernowitz is nowhere. As a political entity, it ceased to exist long ago, with the collapse of the Austro-Hungarian Habsburg Empire in 1918. Its name now is Chernivtsi—a city located in the southwestern region of the Republic of the Ukraine, east of the Carpathian Mountains, on the River Pruth, some fifty kilometers north of the present-day border of Romania. After the First World War, when it fell under Romanian authority and became part of Greater Romania, it was called Cernăuţi. Subsequently, under Soviet rule after the Second World War, it was renamed Chernovtsy.

But for many of the surviving Jews who lived there in the decade before the First World War and in the interwar years—now "scattered," as Appelfeld notes, "through the world"—the place forever remained Czernowitz, capital of the outlying Austrian-Habsburg imperial province of the Bukowina, the "Vienna of the East," a city in which (in the words of its most famous poet,

Paul Celan) "human beings and books used to live."[1] For members of these generations, the long imperial connection of Czernowitz to Vienna and their own whole-hearted embrace of the German language, its literature, and the social and cultural standards of the Austro-Germanic world are intimately entwined—a core constituent of their identity. Yiddish certainly remained alive for many of them, as a language spoken in some of their homes and as a predominant language in nearby villages and among urban intellectual proponents of Jewish diaspora nationalism. But, as many of their parents and even grandparents had done, they had accepted the premise inherent in the century-long process of Jewish emancipation and acculturation to Germanic culture that had taken place in lands once ruled by the Habsburgs. One could remain a Jew in religious belief, was the basis of this premise, while also becoming culturally, economically, and politically integrated within the Austro-Habsburg dominant social order. The promise of admission to modernity and cosmopolitanism—of turning away from the poverty, segregation, and what they perceived as the restrictive lifeways of village Jewry—was its motivating assumption. Karl Emil Franzos, the Bukowina's first internationally famed German-language writer, best characterizes the complicated cultural identity of most assimilated Bukowina Jews at the end of the nineteenth century: "I wasn't yet three feet tall, when my father told me: 'Your nationality is neither Polish, nor Ruthenian, nor Jewish—you are German.' But equally often he said, even then: 'According to your faith you are a Jew.'"[2]

Even after the annexation of Czernowitz and the Bukowina into Greater Romania in 1918 and the institution of a policy of "Romanianization," a predominant segment of the Jewish population of the city and region remained devoted to the German language and its culture. Czernowitz, the city, with its Vienna-look-alike center, its Viennese-inspired architecture, avenues, parks, and cafés, largely remained a physical manifestation of this continuing allegiance to, and nostalgic longing for, a bygone Austrian imperial past.

The continuing vitality and strength of this identification is not surprising. It attests to the positive connection so many of Czernowitz's Jews had drawn between Jewish emancipation and assimilation in the imperial Habsburg realm and the significant social, political, and cultural rewards that this process had yielded. Despite the immediate, and the increasingly vehement, anti-Semitic assaults on Jewish emancipation and assimilation that occurred in the imperial core and its periphery in the nineteenth and early twentieth century, citizenship privileges enjoyed by Jews had not been withdrawn. In contrast, for several years after Romania gained control of the area in

1918—indeed, until 1924—the majority of the approximately one hundred thousand Jews in the Bukowina were denied the full citizenship rights which they had enjoyed for decades under Austrian rule.[3] Their new legal definition and exclusion as "foreigners" greatly inhibited their cultural integration and social advancement within the Greater Romania that they now inhabited. In this context, the German language in which they communicated with each other and the Austro-German-Jewish cultural background they shared provided them with an alternative basis of continuing group identity.

It is perhaps this point that is most startling: that even when political reality indicated otherwise, Jews here kept alive an *idea* of a pre–First World War multicultural and multilingual tolerant city and a modern, cosmopolitan culture in which German literature, music, art, and philosophy flourished among a significant majority of their numbers. Instead of the Cernăuţi in which they now lived, they continued to nourish and perpetuate the idea of "Czernowitz" as it had been transmitted to them, physically and in cultural memory. The place where these Jews grew up was thus already haunted by the memory of a lost "world of yesterday" that many of them had actually never experienced but only inherited from parents and grandparents who had enjoyed the benefits of Jewish life under the Habsburgs.[4] If, in their youth they held on to that lost world nostalgically, it was not simply to reconstitute or to mourn what they posited as a better imperial past. It was also one of the ways in which they resisted Romanianization and its increasing social, political, and intellectual restrictions. In this sense, their "resistant nostalgia" reflected what Svetlana Boym has characterized as inherent in all nostalgic constructions: the longing "for a home that no longer exists or has never existed."[5]

At the same time, however, Czernowitz/Cernăuţi was also that place where Jews eventually suffered anti-Semitism, internment in a fascist Romanian-Nazi ghetto, and Soviet occupation. It was where they were forced to wear the yellow "Jew" star, and where a fortunate minority among them, managing to escape deportation, survived the Holocaust. Of the more than sixty thousand Jews who inhabited the city at the start of the Second World War, less than thirty thousand were alive there at its conclusion. When, after the war, the bulk of these survivors left the by then again Soviet-ruled Chernovtsy, they thought it was forever. They knew that the place they had considered their home had now definitively been taken from them. Czernowitz in the Bukowina, now twice lost to Jews, came to persist only as a projection—as an idea physically disconnected from its geographical location and tenuously dependent on the vicissitudes of personal, familial, and cultural memory.

Our primary goal in *Ghosts of Home* is to illuminate the distinct culture of the city of Czernowitz and its Jewish inhabitants during the Habsburg years before the outbreak of the First World War and the afterlife of that urbane cultural ideal over subsequent decades. By focusing on how the inhabitants of this one city constructed their life-worlds over time, we trace the exhilarating promises and shattering disappointments associated with the process of Jewish emancipation and assimilation. Within this objective, moreover, our book engages two relatively unexplored chapters of recent European Jewish history. First, it tells the story of a place and of a Jewish population that was confronted by a largely Romanian-perpetrated Holocaust during the Second World War, facing different structures of persecution and deportation and different possibilities of survival than those characterizing the more thoroughly studied Nazi Judeocide in Poland and other areas of German-occupied Europe. And, second, it considers the positive as well as the negative aspects of the role that the Stalinist Soviet Union played for Jewish refugees from fascism and Nazism: the possibility it offered them for rescue and survival, but also the consequences of its own anti-Semitism, repression, and persecution. Within a larger analytical framework, this work particularizes how Jewish Czernowitz/Cernăuți/Chernovtsy engaged and participated in some of the grand narratives of the European twentieth century: the intensity, the reach, but also the tragedy, of the German-Jewish symbiosis; the encounter between fascism and communism; the rise of Zionism and modern Yiddishism; the displacement of refugees; and the shadow of Holocaust memory on the children and grandchildren of survivors.

Two temporal levels structure our narrative in *Ghosts of Home*. On the level of the past, our book is an account of Jewish Czernowitz and key moments in its history over the course of the past 125 years. On the level of the present, it is fueled by a collaborative quest, reflecting four journeys we made to Ukrainian Chernivtsi—in 1998, 2000, 2006, and 2008—and, during two of these visits, to Transnistria, the region between the Dniester and Bug rivers annexed by Romania in 1941. The first of our trips inspired this project. We made it with Carl and Lotte Hirsch, our parents/parents-in-law, on their first return to the city of their birth since their hurried departure (with false papers) from Soviet-ruled Chernovtsy in 1945. With them as guides and mentors, we searched for physical traces of old Czernowitz and Cernăuți, for material connections to the places, residences, and times that had been so central to their and their fellow exiles' sense of origin and identification.

iarka concentration camp to which David Kessler's father and a number
her Cernăuţi Jews had been deported—a camp whose very existence had
erased from the records and memories of the present-day residents of
izable town near which it had been located.

ur third trip in 2006, the basis for part 3 of this book, reflected a some-
t different intent. This time we went to Chernivtsi, and through Trans-
ria, to participate in a large multigenerational gathering of people who
l either been born in interwar Cernăuţi or who were children and grand-
ldren of Czernowitzers. The group consisted of persons from all over the
rld who had met through the internet on what had, in effect, over the
urse of two or three years become a site in which Czernowitz was actively
ing reconstituted in virtual reality, through extensive contributions and
nline postings of photos, maps, documents, memoirs, recipes, and links to
elevant scholarly and popular materials. This group's passionate interest and
heartfelt effort to discover and rediscover minute details about the history of
a place where many of them had lived only a few childhood years—and from
which some had been deported as very young children—confirmed for us the
unusual nexus between nostalgic and traumatic memory that Czernowitz
elicited among its Jewish survivors and their descendants.

We returned to Chernivtsi again in 2008 to find the city in the midst of
ambitious renovations in preparing to celebrate its six hundredth anniversary. Accompanied by Cornel Fleming from London and again by Florence
Heymann, we went as representatives of the growing Czernowitz-L internet
listserv group that had taken an active part in urging city officials to include
Chernivtsi's Jewish history in the planned commemorations. Bearing images
and objects donated by list members and our own knowledge of Bukowina
history, we came to participate in discussions about the small museum of
Bukowina Jewish history and culture that was in the process of being installed
in two rooms of the former Czernowitz Jewish National House. Except for a
few memorial plaques on buildings formerly inhabited by Jewish writers and
intellectuals, the extensive Jewish contributions to the city had, until that
moment, been forgotten, if not erased from its public face. With the planned
establishment of this tiny museum, Chernivtsi was entering a new phase of
acknowledgment of its layered multicultural past. But the memorial debates
we engaged in only served to demonstrate how fraught the politics of memory
are, and are likely to continue to be in the foreseeable future, in the Ukraine.

The dialogue between the past and present levels of this book raises some
of the key questions that shape our inquiry: How did this small provincial
Habsburg capital produce such a rich and urbane cosmopolitan culture, one

Our first journey could thus be characterized as a [...]
fered in significant respects from other second-gener[...]
to old Jewish Eastern European towns chronicled i[...]
books. We were fortunate to be accompanied by articu[...]
to hear and record accounts they narrated in place as [...]
and videotaped the time-worn but still largely intact str[...]
had been Habsburg-era Czernowitz. Unlike others who h[...]
journeys, moreover, we were not primarily motivated to [...]
Ukraine in search for traces of sites or family members vi[...]
from records by Holocaust destruction. Certainly, as the [...]
of this book reveal, the surprisingly divergent experiences [...]
during the Second World War did come to absorb our int[...]
explorations of the city. Yet, what most fascinated us initia[...]
that its Jewish survivors—even those who had lived throug[...]
and immense suffering in Transnistria—continued to maintair[...]
mit to our postwar generation such strong, positive, nostalgic[...]
a city and culture that had long disappeared in reality, if not in [...]
remembrance, image, and re-creation.

We made our second journey to Chernivtsi in 2000, withou[...]
nying parents, to a city no longer unfamiliar to us. Confident [...]
our bearings, we were now able to act as guides for a cousin, Davi[...]
and a colleague, Florence Heymann—second-generation Czernowi[...]
Marianne, who were visiting the place for the first time.[6] We set of[...]
demic researchers, intent on mining the city's public and private a[...]
and on broadening and deepening our knowledge of Czernowitz/Ce[...]
and its Jewish community for the book we had begun to conceive. Yet [...]
course of our investigations, the ever-darker side of the city and region's [...]
emerged in greater detail. We found material and documentary eviden[...]
old anti-Semitism—Habsburg-era, Romanian, and Soviet—of persecuti[...]
impossible choices, and painful compromises faced by the city's Jews d[...]
ing the fascist and communist periods, of struggles for survival during t[...]
Second World War. And we also found evidence of normality and continu[...]
ity, of kindness and rescue, in these grim historical circumstances. We made
a side trip to Transnistria then, to the region to which Jews from Czernowitz,
the Bukowina, and nearby Bessarabia (now Moldova) were deported, and
where approximately two hundred thousand of them perished. We went in
order to see and to actually make contact with the place that its survivors
had referred to as "the forgotten cemetery." There we also searched for, and
were ultimately able to find, remains of the once notorious Romanian-run

that would remain so vivid and powerful in the imagination of the generation of Jews who came of age in Romanian Cernăuți during the interwar years? What had made their identification with Czernowitz and its Habsburg-era German-cultural appeal so strong as to enable them to preserve and protect their positive memories of the city in the face of devastating negative and traumatic experiences? What role did the Habsburg Empire's multiethnic tolerance, however real or mythic in retrospect, play in the construction of this layered and contradictory memory? How, moreover, did nostalgia for the past and negative memories of anti-Semitic discrimination and persecution coexist and inflect each other in the outlook of the city's Jews, and how were these memories passed down over generations? And how are Jews currently remembered in the Eastern European cities they so actively helped to build before being deported or exiled from them?

To address these questions and illuminate our representation of Czernowitz's past, we rely on a variety of historical and literary source materials. We employ official and private contemporary documents, public and family archival materials, letters, memoirs, photographs, newspapers, essays, poetry, fiction, internet postings, as well as material remnants that we think of as testimonial objects.[7] Central to our approach is the use of oral and video accounts from old Czernowitzers and their offspring—histories and narrations that we collected and taped in the course of our research in the Ukraine, Israel, Austria, Germany, France, and the United States, or that we heard and watched in oral history archives in several places. These materials are more than evidentiary sources for us. They focus our narrative around individual anecdotes, images, and objects that serve as "points of memory" opening small windows to the past.[8] They also enable us to reflect more theoretically on how memory and transmission work both to reveal and to conceal certain traumatic recollections, and how fragmentary, tenuous, and deceptive our access to the past can be. In the effort to capture the effects of the past on the present and of the present on the past and to trace the effects of the "telling" on the witness and listener, our book exemplifies what James Young has called "received history." It explores "both what happened and how it is passed down to us."[9] And in that process it exposes the holes in memory and knowledge that puncture second-generation accounts—accounts motivated by needs and desires that, at times, rely on no more than speculative investment, identification, and invention.

Our own two voices and reflections are certainly present within this book, singly and in dialogue. We write collaboratively, from the perspectives of a literary and cultural critic and of a historian, both active in the emergent field of memory studies. But we would enjoin our readers not to assume that our distinct disciplinary training is reflected in separate sections of this book, or that the "I" we use in different chapters is in any way stable. On the contrary, in the process of writing and rewriting, our voices have often merged and crossed. Our perspectives are those of the Romanian-born daughter of parents who were born and raised and survived the Holocaust in the place they never ceased to call Czernowitz, and of the Bolivian-born son of Austrian refugees who had fled to South America from Hitler's Vienna. Family narratives are important components of *Ghosts of Home,* but this book is not a family chronicle. Instead, we think of it as hybrid in genre—as an intergenerational memoir and an interdisciplinary and self-reflexive work of historical and cultural exploration. It engages many individual voices, including our own, within a web of narratives, recollections, and analyses that connect with each other, and over time, through familial and communal relationships. Such a web of recollections and interconnections, together with our other historical and cultural source materials, allows for the affective side of the afterlife of Czernowitz to emerge in fuller and richer dimensions.

The title of our book, *Ghosts of Home,* highlights this affective aspect of personal, familial, and cultural remembrance. But it also points to the contradictions that shape persistent memories. It evokes the haunting continuity of Czernowitz as place and idea for generations of Jews who survived its political demise—a spectral return emanating both seductive recollections of a lost home and frightening reminders of persecution and displacement. These layers and contradictions, we found, are still remarkably absent from present-day Chernivtsi, a city whose repeated twentieth-century transformations—albeit materially evident in its architecture and urban design—are just beginning to be acknowledged in its cultural landscape. When we first traveled there with Carl and Lotte Hirsch in 1998, visitors like the four of us, searching for traces of this history, appeared like ghostly revenants or haunting reminders of a forgotten world: we unsettled the present by refusing to allow the past to disappear into oblivion. But now, ten years later, this is no longer so. Roots travel has become ever more popular, and the Chernivtsi of 2008 has made space for tourist groups with several new or renovated hotels, new restaurants with translated menus, and English-language city maps. Tour buses pull up on the city's central squares on a regular basis, spewing families of survivors and their descendants from Israel, Western Europe, Australia, and the Americas. What accounts for this dramatic shift? Certainly, the economic evolution of Eastern Europe since the dissolution of the Soviet Union and the increased availability of the internet, with its multiplication of genealogical and cultural sites that disseminate more and more information, have made travel to places of origin easier and thus perhaps also more compelling. But what do these trips to the past actually reveal? What do we find when we identify the streets where our forebears walked, the houses they inhabited, the locations where they suffered mistreatment, deportation, extermination? These, too, are among the central questions propelling our inquiry in *Ghosts of Home*.

⊷ ⊰⊱ ⊶

In our work on this book, we've been most fortunate to have access to the recollections of valuable eyewitnesses and articulate narrators who were born and raised in Czernowitz/Cernăuţi. For their willingness to converse and participate in oral history interviews—many on videotape, hours in length and over the course of several years—we are especially grateful to Carl Hirsch, Lotte Gottfried Hirsch, Lilly Hirsch, Rosa Hirsch Gelber, Moritz Gelber, Rosa Roth Zuckermann, Hedwig and Gottfried (Bubi) Brenner, Polya Dubbs, and Matthias Zwilling. We are also much indebted to Hardy Breier, Sylvia de Swaan, Cornel Fleming, Berti Glaubach, Abraham Kogan, Dori Laub, Arthur Rindner, Andy Rosengarten, Charles Rosner, Martha Rubel Gordey, Ilse Rubel Beral, Jochanan Rywerant, Beate Schwammenthal, Peter Silberbusch, Miriam Taylor, and Yehudit Yerushalmi-Terris. Our book has also been enormously enriched by the invaluable memoirs, some unpublished, by Margit Bartfelt-Feller, Fred Bernard, Martha Blum, Hedwig Brenner, Pearl Fichmann, Ruth Glasberg Gold, Carl Hirsch, Edith Horowitz, Alfred Kittner, Julius Scherzer, Dorothea Sella, Ilana Shmueli, and Zvi Yavetz. And, although we were not able to talk to them about this project, our understanding of Czernowitz and its rich afterlife was also profoundly shaped by our memories of conversations with Jakob (Kubi) Hirsch, Eduard Bong, Friederike (Fritzi) Gottfried Bong, Ruth Kraft, Mischa and Sidonie (Sidy) Flexor, Ita and Marek Singer, Judith and Arthur Kessler, and Judith and Paul Silberbusch.

Over the course of several years, we have profited enormously from discussions and scholarly exchanges with the international community of writers, scholars, and editors who have devoted their intellectual energies to the history, literature, and culture of the Bukowina. We have been inspired and generously guided by Florence Heymann, our best Czernowitzer *copine,* and her beautiful book *Le Crépuscule des lieux: Identités juives de Czernowitz* (The

Dawn of Place: Jewish Identities of Czernowitz). We have learned a great deal from the insights and writings of Othmar Andrée, Aharon Appelfeld, Amy Colin, Andrei Corbea-Hoisie, Sidra deKoven Ezrahi, John Felstiner, Valentina Glajar, Mariana Hausleitner, Radu Ioanid, Helmut Kusdat, Alexandra Laignel-Lavastine, Albert Lichtblau, Ioana Rostoş, Peter Rychlo, Natalya Shevchenko, and Markus Winkler.

As this book makes clear, the memory of Czernowitz reaches across generations, and we have found ourselves among wonderful and generous second-generation companions, informants, and fellow travelers. We particularly wish to acknowledge Alex and Peter Flexor, who shared their memories of the lives of their parents, and David Kessler and Vera Kessler Pollack, who gave us access to the invaluable handwritten memoir and important archive of Arthur Kessler. We are also much indebted to Danny Alon-Ellenbogen, Brigitte Brande, Paul and Michael Brenner, Leah Gelber Chajk, Bracha Gelber Enoch, Eytan and Mark Fichmann, Irene Fishler, David Glynn, Rita Margalit-Shilo, Claude Singer, and Irene Silverblatt.

Felix Zuckermann shuttles masterfully between Czernowitz and Chernivtsi, past and present: he and Marina Zuckermann were our hosts in Chernivtsi on five different occasions, and we are deeply grateful for their colossal hospitality.

Atina Grossman, Barbara Kirshenblatt-Gimblett, Irene Kacandes, Marion Kaplan, and Dana Polan have generously read the manuscript in its entirety and their incisive questions, astute suggestions, and detailed comments have marked this book profoundly.

Along the way, many colleagues, students, and friends have read drafts of these chapters, listened to talks and papers we have given, and discussed questions motivating this book with us. We have benefited greatly from their advice, encouragement, and concrete suggestions. We are enormously appreciative to Lila Abu-Lughod, Sara Bershtel, Pascale Bos, Bella Brodski, Mary Childers, Mary Marshall Clark, Sarah Cole, Sonia Combe, Jane Coppock, Susan Crane, Ann Cvetkovich, Gerd Gemunden, Victoria de Grazia, Judith Greenberg, Farah Jasmine Griffin, Geoffrey Hartman, Saidiya Hartman, Susannah Heschel, Eva Hoffmann, Jean Howard, Martha Howell, Andreas Huyssen, Jennifer James, Alexis Jetter, Temma Kaplan, Mary Kelley, Alice Kessler-Harris, Dorothy Koh, Mirta Kupferminc, Eric Manheimer, Nancy K. Miller, Lorie Novak, Annelise Orleck, Susan Pederson, Marta Peixoto, Griselda Pollock, Jay Prosser, Gail Reimer, Régine Robin, Michael Rothberg, Carol Sanger, Ronnie Scharfman, Joanna Scutts, Pamela Smith, Gabrielle Spiegel, Art Spiegelman, Silvia Spitta, Kate Stanley, Marita Sturken, Susan

Sturm, Susan Rubin Suleiman, Diana Taylor, Monika Totten, Sonali Thakkar, Roxana Verona, Annette Wievorka, Susan Winnett, Janet Wolff, Louise Yelin, James Young, Mariana Zantop, Susanne Zantop, and Froma Zeitlin.

We are also grateful for invitations and editorial suggestions from Robert Abzug, Julia Baker, Zsófia Ban, Marie-Aude Baronian, Betty M. Bayer, Cornelia Brink, Marc Caplan, Laurie Beth Clark, Amy Colin, Jay Geller, Faye Ginsburg, Jonathan Greenberg, Roseanne Kennedy, Adrienne Kertzer, Annette Kuhn, Kirsten McAllister, Alan Mintz, Stephen G. Nichols, Annelies Schulte Nordholt, Sondra Perl, Susannah Radstone, David Roskies, Jan Schmidt, Meir Sternberg, Hedwig Turai, and Johannes von Moltke.

Special thanks go to Jennifer James for her research assistance and to Gail Vernazza for facilitating the preparation of this manuscript. In addition to our wonderful translators in Ukraine, we wish to thank Ofrah Amihai and Andrew Gilkin-Glusinski for their translations from Hebrew and Ukrainian. When Stan Holwitz appeared in our lives, we knew we had found someone who understood our goals and shared our commitments. He has been the most sympathetic of editors throughout, and we are truly grateful to him, as well as Jacqueline Volin and Ellen F. Smith of the University of California Press.

We have been the fortunate recipients of a number of fellowships and grants to support our work on this book. We are most grateful to the John Simon Guggenheim Memorial Foundation, the American Council of Learned Societies, the Liguria Study Center at Bogliasco, the Dickey Center, and the Geisel and Kathe Tappe Vernon Chairs at Dartmouth College. We also express appreciation to the University Seminars at Columbia University for their help in publication. Material in this work benefited from discussion in the University Seminar on Cultural Memory.

Closer to home, our sons, Alex, Oliver, and Gabriel; their partners, Martina, Alanna, and Meghan; as well as our grandchildren, Quinn, Freya, and Chloë, have lovingly cheered and sustained us throughout the writing of this book. In fact, this project began as a personal journey that turned into a work of history and memory—a family trip to Czernowitz that became an act of discovery taking us into the past and across the world. Throughout, our closest guides and mentors have been Lotte and Carl Hirsch. Lotte's textured stories and literary sensibility and Carl's spectacular memory for detail and love of history—the informed and passionate way in which they engaged the turbulences as well as creative energies of the twentieth century—have been invaluable to our research. Their courage and talent for survival continue to be inspiring. In entrusting us with the story of their lives and the lives of their generation they have presented us with the daunting responsibility to do it justice. We are most grateful to them and to our other witnesses for the permission that they have implicitly and explicitly granted us: to write this book from our own perspectives. "I see what you are doing," Carl said to us once, when he read and commented on a chapter draft. "You are telling the story as *you* see it. I would not write it this way, of course. But it's your story now."

## NOTE ON TRANSLATIONS

Unless otherwise indicated, all translations into English are by the authors. Translations of Paul Celan are by John Felstiner.

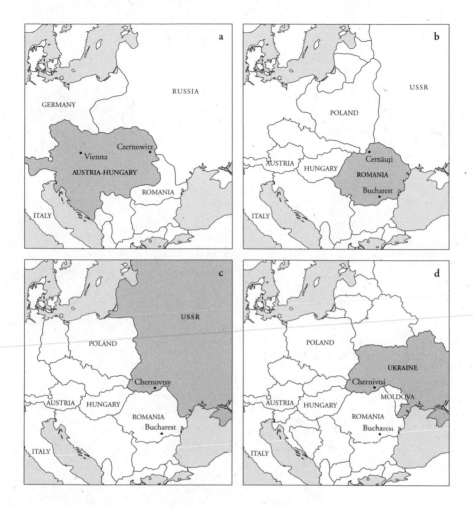

Map 1.  From Czernowitz to Chernivtsi: (a) Czernowitz under the Austro-Hungarian Empire, 1774–1918; (b) Cernăuţi in Romania, 1918–45; (c) Chernovtsy in the USSR, 1945–89; (d) Chernivtsi in the Ukraine, since 1989

———————

# PART ONE

# "We would not have come without you"
## 1998

Figure 1. Lotte Hirsch at the front door of her former Czernowitz home, 1998
(Photograph by Leo Spitzer)

# ONE

# "Where are you from?"

I was born in Czernowitz. The war broke out nine months later.
The Russians bombarded the city. I learned to run before I could
walk. The First World War shoved me one thousand miles to the
west, from Czernowitz to Vienna. The Second World War, which
for me began on March 13, 1938, brought me seven thousand miles
further west, from Vienna to Ecuador. I was a westward moving
Eastern Jew, and I said to myself: two more wars like these and I
will again be back in Czernowitz.

In 1943, in Ecuador, I applied for a travel document for foreigners. Under the rubric "Nationality," the Ecuadorian official filled in
"German." I protested. . . . "Why do you deny being German? After
all, you have an expired German passport!" "It was forced on me,"
I responded. "My homeland was invaded. I am Austrian." The man
looked at me sympathetically and said, "Austria doesn't exist any
longer. Where were you born?" "Let's not get into that," I implored;
"it will only complicate matters."

BENNO WEISER VARON

CHERNIVTSI, UKRAINE, SEPTEMBER 1998

On our first walk through the city once called Czernowitz, a woman stopped
us on the street. She spoke Russian, then switched to Yiddish. Her dyed
light-red hair, with gray roots showing, her heavy makeup, the threadbare
outfit she was wearing, and her worn-out shoes were as striking as the fact
that there were Jews, speaking Yiddish, on the streets of this Ukrainian city.
"Where are you from?" she asked my mother. We were carrying cameras and
looking at maps—obvious tourists—and she no doubt wondered whether
we were from Israel, the United States, or Germany. In response, my mother
emphatically pointed to the ground: "From here, Czernowitzer," she said in

Figure 2. Lotte and Carl Hirsch on Zentraina Square, the former Ringplatz, 1998 (Photograph by Leo Spitzer)

German. It was the first time in my memory that the simple question "Where are you from?" evoked such a brief, clear-cut response from her. Three words: "From *here*, Czernowitzer." Usually it has required a complicated narrative about emigration and diaspora, if not a history and geography lesson. Stunned, I watched my mother reclaim in an instant an identity that I had always connected to a name few people knew—a mythic past place that, I knew, had ceased to exist before I was born.

On that bright, sunny, clear, and crisp early September morning in 1998, Lotte and Carl Hirsch and the two of us, their daughter and son-in-law, were standing in a large tree-lined square, the nexus of seven streets on which, at that hour, relatively little traffic, either human or vehicular, was evident. Two of the square's defining parallel streets were lined with a series of imposing, ornately stuccoed late-nineteenth- and early-twentieth-century buildings in the neo-baroque and Jugendstil styles that had reflected the trends of urban modernism in Vienna, the Habsburg imperial capital on which this city had been modeled. A block-long, windowless Soviet-era wall of reinforced concrete demarcated the square's third side, incongruously fronted by a large, gilded bas-relief crest and an open-air café with red-and-white Coca-Cola sun umbrellas.

CERNĂUŢI — Primăria

Figure 3. Cernăuţi Primăria in a 1920 postcard, recording the Romanianization of the city (bottom), and the Chernivtsi city hall in 1998 (Photograph by Leo Spitzer)

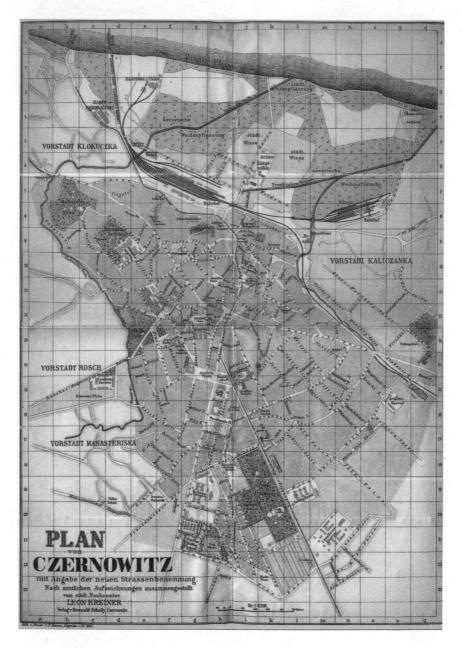

Map 2. Czernowitz city map, early twentieth century

Opposite the wall, on a slightly elevated knoll accessible by some dozen steps, stood a large, impressive, gracefully proportioned neo-baroque building. It was blue-gray, trimmed in white, and highlighted by a large white clock on its top floor and a second clock, black-faced, high on its elegant central tower. Its entrance was guarded by a Ukrainian soldier. Clearly, this was an official structure.

"We are here on the Ringplatz," Carl said to us, "and that is the Rathaus [city hall]. In our time, under the Romanians, it was called the Primăria. But everything looks different. There were no trees planted here. Down there [he pointed toward the café with the Coca-Cola umbrellas] was a large bookstore, Leon König. Here is the Rathausgasse. . . . That is the Herrengasse . . . that, the Liliengasse . . ."

"And that, the Postgasse," Lotte interjected. "And, Carl, what was the street parallel to the Postgasse called?"

"The Hauptstrasse . . . and over here the Russische Gasse."

Lotte nodded, but seemed disappointed. "The Ringplatz is no longer the Ringplatz. It looked much different. It was much larger. They must have built something here. There, the tramway used to run on its tracks. It is all very, very, very changed."

Neither Lotte nor Carl expressed any consciousness that the city tour on which they had begun to lead us, narrated in German, identified the streets and sites by their old German names, as they had been called nearly a century earlier, under the Habsburgs—before Lotte was born. Or that many of these streets and sites—the Ringplatz, Herrengasse, and Liliengasse, for example—were themselves originally intended to mirror the elegance and urbanity of places bearing the same name in Vienna's imperial Ringstrasse complex. Nor did it seem to strike any of us as particularly bizarre that as we explored the city, we were using a photocopy we had brought with us of an early-twentieth-century German-language map of Czernowitz.

THE RETURN

"My feelings about returning to Czernowitz are ambivalent," Carl said to us on September 3, 1998, in the Hotel Maingau in Frankfurt, on the eve of our departure for Ukraine. Although we had not yet envisioned writing about this trip, Leo and I had decided to videotape this conversation with my parents about the expectations they held of their first return to the city they had left more than a half-century earlier. As I listened to the mixture of apprehension and curiosity in their voices, I thought back on the ambivalences that had preceded the decision to undertake the trip in the first place. Whose desires were driving it: my parents' or mine and Leo's? We had left that unresolved, each of us thinking that we were merely going along, not one of us willing to claim responsibility for what might easily turn out to be a truly difficult, if not disastrous, trip.

"Is Czernowitz our *Heimat*?" my father continued, as though reading some of my thoughts:

> The events that took place there—that we lived through—call that into question. The first time we made a visit to Bucharest—in 1968 after our emigration—Paul Roth, a cousin who still lived in Czernowitz came to see us there. And I must admit that I felt so happy that I had not stayed in Czernowitz. The truth of the matter is, we would not have decided to go back there now if it were not for Marianne—because Marianne doesn't have a *Heimat* [home], and we want to show her ours because ours is also in some ways hers.
> We didn't have money there, but we had a very happy childhood. . . . The friendships we made were powerful. They stayed strong through life. We shared experiences and culture. We were like brothers, my Czernowitz friends and I. . . . There are probably not many places in the world that have produced such close fellow feelings among its émigrés. I am curious to see what has become of all of this.

As these comments indicate, Carl and Lotte, like other survivors of deportation or displacement from Czernowitz, continued to be afflicted by affectionate longings for earlier stages and scenes in their own lives, as well as for pleasurable experiences in familiar places and settings in this city of their birth. The strong friendships and close fellow feelings that Carl evoked attest to these positive images and the delight he and Lotte took in their recollection. But I also always knew that their nostalgia for Czernowitz—or Cernăuți, as it later came to be called—was layered. These positive associations with the past were only one aspect of their recall. Like others who had been displaced from their homes and native lands and become refugees or exiles, my parents also carried with them negative and bitter memories of the past—traumatic memories of bad times when they had suffered virulent discrimination and oppression. For them, as well as for the other refugees and exiles among whom I grew up, such negative and traumatic memories were certainly nostalgia's complicating flip side. Geographical and temporal distance and the trauma of exile or expulsion make it difficult to develop an integrated memory of a lost home. Conflicting recollections therefore coexist without being reconciled: the place called "Heimat" contains both "what we lived through, especially in the war years" and the "experiences and culture" that Carl so fondly recalled on the eve of our journey.

In a profound sense, this nostalgic yearning combined with negative and traumatic memories—pleasure and affection layered with bitterness, anger, and aversion—is internalized by the children of the exiles and refugees. We of that "second generation" have peculiar relationships with the places where our families originated and from which they were forcibly removed or displaced. For me and my contemporaries, children of exiled Czernowitzers, Czernowitz has always been a primordial site of origin. Although none of us had ever been there or seen it (or even thought we might ever be able to see it), it was the source of our "native" German linguistic and cultural background, with which we closely identified and, indeed, still identify, although we grew up in Romania, the United States, Canada, Australia, Israel, France, Germany, or Austria. Strangely, the streets, buildings, and natural surroundings of Czernowitz—its theaters, restaurants, parks, rivers, and domestic settings, none of which I had ever myself seen, heard, or smelled—figure more strongly in my own childhood memories and imagination than do the sites and scenes of Timişoara, Romania, where I was born, or Bucharest, where I spent my childhood.

Some of these same places, however, were also the sites of my childhood nightmares of persecution, deportation, and terror. When I began to write about my own early memories and about the phenomenon of personal and cultural memory in general, I needed a special term to refer to the secondary, belated quality of my relationship with times and places that I had never experienced or seen, but which are vivid enough that I feel as though I remember them. My "memory" of Czernowitz, I concluded, is a "postmemory." Mediated by the stories, images, and behaviors among which I grew up, it never added up to a complete picture or linear tale. Its power to overshadow my own memories derives precisely from the layers—both positive and negative—that have been passed down to me unintegrated, conflicting, fragmented, dispersed. As Eva Hoffman writes in her book *After Such Knowledge:* "The formative events of the twentieth century have crucially informed our biographies, threatening sometimes to overshadow and overwhelm our lives."[1]

I grew up in 1950s Bucharest, Romania, within a community of fellow German-speaking exiles from Czernowitz whose tastes, attitudes, behaviors, and stories about a world that had long ceased to exist shaped me profoundly. My desire to visit Czernowitz originated with these encounters and grew in intensity over many years. Although, during my childhood in Romania,

Soviet Chernovtsy was a mere thirty kilometers from the Romanian border, there were severe travel restrictions within the Soviet bloc. To me, at the time, Chernovtsy seemed as remote as if it had been on another continent. After my parents and I emigrated to Austria in 1961 and to the United States in 1962, my parents' city of origin acquired an ever more distant, mythic aura.

It wasn't until the fall of the Berlin Wall and the dissolution of the Soviet Union in 1989 that a trip to western Ukraine began to seem possible. I had heard tapes of a few travel accounts and radio documentaries from Germany, indicating that traces of what Czernowitz once was could still be found in the present-day city of Chernivtsi. On several occasions during the 1990s, Leo and I had suggested a joint visit to Czernowitz to my parents, but even though they went as far as researching travel arrangements and considering potential dates, the trip never materialized. In fact, every time I pursued the subject with them, they seemed either surprised by my interest or noncommittal and even evasive. It wasn't clear to me whether they were afraid of what they might, or might not, find there or were dissuaded by what they perceived to be the practical difficulties of the trip. Austrian Czernowitz, and even Romanian Cernăuţi, had been a provincial capital with excellent rail connections to all of East Central Europe, but Ukrainian Chernivtsi had become a provincial outpost, with inadequate train services and virtually no air connections at all. And yet, I knew that since my parents were in their eighties, and our cousin Rosa Roth Zuckermann, who still lived in Chernivtsi, was close to ninety, the "return" trip I had fantasized we would make *together* would have to happen sooner rather than later.

Throughout the 1990s, moreover, many of my Jewish friends and university colleagues had begun to undertake such "return" journeys to places where their parents and grandparents had lived and from which they had escaped or been deported. Many of these journeys resulted in essays or books, memoirs of their search for ancestral lives that had preceded their own. Since most of these journeys were undertaken belatedly, without parents or grandparents as guides or companions, they were searches driven by archival research and local guidance and by a great deal of desire, curiosity, speculation, and fantasy. I spent many hours talking with fellow travelers to the past and reading their accounts, but I was aware that, unlike them, I still had the opportunity to take such a trip *with* my parents. Moreover, in the early 1990s, I had accompanied Leo on two research trips to Bolivia, the country of his native-Austrian parents' refuge from Nazi persecution. Leo himself had been born in Bolivia, leaving there for the United States at the age of ten: he had his own childhood memories of La Paz and the Austro-German Jewish community there. But the book he wrote about that Andean refuge was not begun until after his mother had died and did not appear until after the death of the uncle who had served as an invaluable witness and informant.[2] His Bolivian quest and the journeys to Eastern Europe of my associates and friends served both as backdrop and as added incentives for my own.

My fantasy of "return" to Czernowitz was not exactly a nostalgic longing for a lost or abandoned Heimat (as my father termed it): how could a place I had never touched, and which my parents left under extreme duress, really be "home"? Nor was it a yearning to recall some better past time in that city, for I had experienced no actual time there at all. Why, then, actually go there? Why make a "return" journey to a place that had been, in Eva Hoffman's words, "home in a way, but . . . also hostile territory?"[3] The more I knew that I wanted to do it, the less I could actually articulate, to my parents or to Leo or to myself, what I hoped to find or do there—beyond, of course, the acts of connecting memory to place, of bringing the memories back to the place. But what exactly would that return accomplish—for me or for the memory I had inherited and, indeed, adopted as my own postmemory? How could I know until I had actually made the trip?

Was it the paragraph I included in my book *Family Frames,* in which I gave up on making the trip, that ultimately changed my parents' minds, or was it Leo's book on his return to Bolivia?[4] At any rate, by spring 1998 a change took place in my parents' wavering attitude, and our trip finally began to take concrete shape. An acquaintance suggested we travel to Lviv, Ukraine, by air via Frankfurt, and from there by car to our destination. A travel agency in New Jersey specializing in Ukrainian journeys procured our visas, arranged for a vehicle and driver to take us to Chernivtsi, and made reservations for us in the one Chernivtsi hotel they could recommend. We paid our fees and sealed our commitment to go.

It is thus that we found ourselves in Frankfurt on September 3, armed with still and video cameras, a guidebook, maps, and lots of single dollar bills stashed in strategic places on our bodies. (Neither charge cards nor travelers' checks could be used in 1998 Chernivtsi; it would be nearly a decade before bank machines would be introduced.) I also brought along a few, to me essential, reading and reference materials: a volume of Paul Celan's poetry and John Felstiner's fascinating book, *Paul Celan: Poet, Survivor, Jew,* about translating Celan into English; some published and unpublished memoirs I had read but wanted to consult further in the place itself (my father's memoir "A Life in the Twentieth Century," Pearl Fichman's manuscript "Before Memories Fade," and Dorothea Sella's volume *Der Ring des Prometheus*);

and an envelope of old photographs we had chosen from Carl and Lotte's albums—pictures of city streets and sites, in particular, but also photos of the two of them, most from the mid- and late-1930s.

In retrospect, I am struck with how unpredictable this journey seemed in comparison to the numerous trips that both my parents and Leo and I had taken on other occasions. We were not crossing the Iron Curtain—that had long been dismantled—but we knew little more about conditions in Ukraine now than we had during its existence. A small exhibition of photos by Roman Vishniac on Jewish life in Ukraine in the mid-1930s, which I had seen in a New York gallery, led me to expect muddy roads in small villages, drab clothing, old people hunched over, made only worse by an additional half century of neglect and destruction. In my imagination, the dominant colors of the place were black, white, gray. In addition, rumors of muggings and petty theft in the Ukraine, as well as U.S. State Department warnings about that country's limited and inadequate medical facilities, increased our anxiety about the trip so visibly that our teen-aged son Gabriel tried hard to dissuade us from making it. And since I still had difficulty explaining why this journey was something I "needed" to do, I was not the most effective advocate for it. Nor could I assuage Gabriel's fears: I had little insight to offer into what traveling in Ukraine might entail. Lacking success with me, he tried to keep Leo home at least but Leo joined me in asserting our "need" to go, without properly explaining or justifying it to a child who would be left at home with family friends and our dog. "What is my need about?" I wrote in my journal. "Recovering a lost world? Experiencing the loss? Or the process of remembering?"

Our fears and lack of familiarity with contemporary Ukraine somehow increased the legendary aura of our destination. At the same time, however, Czernowitz shrank to utter ordinariness after we bought a Lonely Planet guidebook to Russia and consulted its short section on Western Ukraine. Here we found three pages devoted to Chernivtsi, in which the city was written up like any other tourist site in the guidebook—in this case as a site worth visiting for its old Habsburg buildings, its Catholic, Lutheran, and Orthodox churches, its Armenian cathedral, and the palatial buildings, formerly the residence of the Orthodox Metropolitans of Bukowina, which now housed the Jurii Fed'kovych University. The insert map of the city in the guidebook showed street and place names in Ukrainian—its tiny size making it difficult to find correspondences to the Herrengasse or Ringplatz always invoked by my parents. Additionally, the guidebook only mentioned Jews as one among a number of current-day population groups. How disorienting! Somehow it seemed harder for me to see Czernowitz as simply a place like any of the others I had visited in my many travels than to think of it as a place of potential danger, where I might be mugged or hassled and made uncomfortable.

But when we finally did set off on our trip, the flight on Ukraine International Airlines could not have been more ordinary and our arrival in Lviv less eventful. We did have to show and declare all the cash we had brought along for the customs agents, a complicated operation considering how carefully we had hidden it on our bodies and in our clothes. My parents are always nervous around officials, especially if they speak Russian or, as in this case, Ukrainian. I felt a rush to protect them, but I could not speak Ukrainian and had to look to *them* for translations and explanations.

Still, the entry and customs formalities were relatively quick, and when we exited the airport we were happy to be met by Alexei, a tall young man sent by the travel agency to pick us up and drive us to Chernivtsi. He led us to a rickety old VW bus, placed our luggage in its back, and within minutes drove us through the outskirts of Lviv, lined with Soviet-style block apartment buildings, in a southwesterly direction toward our destination. A visit to Lviv's inner city—to what had been the famous Austrian Lemberg and Polish Lvov—was not scheduled until our return from Chernivtsi.

In the VW, my mother, who suffers from occasional car sickness, sat in front, and in just a few minutes, we heard her striking up a conversation with Alexei, the driver, in halting but competent Russian. He seemed delighted that she could communicate with him, and they continued to talk during the entire trip. Occasionally she turned around to check on a vocabulary term with my father or to translate relevant facts about Lviv, the countryside, or Alexei's family for us. Although the trip to Chernivtsi took several long hours, she was animated, engaged, happy.

It was late afternoon when we started out, a clear beautiful, bright early autumn day. The bumpy two-lane road was lined with green fields, small villages with colorful onion domes or pointed church steeples, expansive wheat fields, grazing goats and cows. A few times we had to stop as flocks of brilliantly white geese crossed before our vehicle. The villages certainly did not seem affluent, but they looked neat, with fenced yards and painted houses, nothing like the photographs in the New York exhibit. To me the landscape recalled the countryside from my childhood excursions in Romania, and I took delight in the geese and ducks and the stork nests on top of telephone poles. Carl and Lotte had never been in this area before: it had been part of Galicia, the Bukowina's neighboring province under the Habsburgs that later belonged to Poland rather than Romania. When we reached what had been the former border between Galicia and Bukowina, we took note. Only some thirty kilometers from Cernăuți, during the Second World War this was the boundary between collaborationist Romania and German-occupied Poland: for Jews in my parents' situation at the time, it was the divide between the chance of survival under Romanian rule and almost certain death under the Nazis.

We had now been on the road for over four hours, with one stop at a dilapidated outhouse near a gas station. The only drinks we could buy there were sweet orange sodas. We were parched, hungry, tired, but also excited and full of anticipation. It was dark when we finally drove into Chernivtsi and discovered that the main access road into the city was closed and we would have to make a detour. We circled through newer and older parts of a dark city in which my parents tried hard, but were unable, to recognize any familiar landmarks, although at one point they thought we were passing the central railroad station. They called out street names in German, asking each other whether this, by any chance, was the Siebenbürgerstrasse or the Hauptstrasse. Alexei, a Lviv native, was equally lost and stopped for directions four times, which was not easy since the streets were almost deserted. At one point, we were forced to back up through an entire street. I kept telling myself that a trip to the past was bound to be full of obstacles and wrong turns. Then, after circling for what seemed like hours but was probably not more than thirty minutes, we pulled up in front of an enormous concrete-block building, said good-bye to Alexei, and walked up a large staircase to enter an almost totally dark space. It took minutes for our eyes to adjust, to discern a small lamp at the other end of an expansive empty lobby, and to make our way to the front desk. We had arrived at the Cheremosh Hotel, which we would later jokingly call the Cher et Moche (in French, expensive and ugly).[5]

### ROSA'S BOOKSHELF

Even though it was already quite late, Carl phoned Rosa Roth Zuckermann from the hotel and arranged for us to visit her the next morning. Rosa, Carl's first cousin, daughter of his mother's sister Lotti and her husband, Leon, was nearly ninety years old and the only member of the family who had remained in Chernovtsy after the Soviets took control of the northern Bukowina at the end of the Second World War. She had survived deportation and nearly three years of displacement and misery in Transnistria, where her first husband, young son, and parents all perished from typhus during the bitter-cold winter of 1941. She was married a second time after her return to Chernovtsy, to Martin Zuckermann, a teacher; their son, Felix, was born in 1949. She too became a teacher of languages—first of French, in a school, and then, privately, of German and English. Her husband died in the early 1980s.

I had met Rosa only once before, in 1958, during my childhood in Bucharest, when she and Felix briefly visited our family there. Even though my parents stayed in touch with her by mail in the years following our emigration to the United States, we had not seen each other since that time.

Early the next day, eager for our reunion, we met Felix Zuckermann on the central Ringplatz, where a taxi had dropped us off, and with him we set off to Ulitza Klara Zetkina, the former Pardinigasse, where Rosa had lived for the last fifty years. This residential street, the site of a few villas, small middle-class apartment houses, and humbler residences, all constructed in the first decades of the twentieth century, was now in major disrepair. Its sidewalks were eroded, its pavement torn and potholed, and wild grasses and small bushes grew virtually unhindered within its domain. Rosa, smiling broadly, waved to us from the top-floor window of a small apartment house close to the beginning of the street, welcoming us and beckoning for us to come up to see her.

At the apartment door, she greeted us each joyfully with an embrace and kiss, commenting animatedly on how well we looked and how glad she was that we had come to visit her. A short, full-bodied woman with sparkling, vivid, deep-set dark eyes, wavy gray hair, and a warmly engaging face, Rosa emanated an energy and liveliness that belied her age. Speaking to us in a clear, precisely enunciated German with a slight Bukowina lilt, she invited us into her parlor but then, as we were about to sit down, offered to show us around her apartment. This was the first private residence we would visit in Chernivtsi, and I had been taken aback by the lamentable appearance of the building in which it was located. Like the street it fronted on, her building's entrance yard was rutted and overgrown with bushes, its small public entrance lobby was cluttered and unswept, the hallway and stairwell were dank and dimly lit, with dark green paint peeling from the plaster walls.

Beyond the door of Rosa's apartment, however, a different world began to unfold before our eyes. On a first glance throughout her place, it was as though we had stepped back into another era—as if we were back in the time when Czernowitz was indeed that Austrian provincial capital where "people and books used to live." Certainly the place where she now lived had never been the abode of the very rich: its living spaces were modest in size, graceful but not elegant, with high ceilings, good wooden floors, floor-to-ceiling tiled woodstoves. Yet its less appealing amenities were also apparent: the tiny cold-water bathroom, drippy plumbing, inadequate kitchen stove and refrigeration. The apartment's eclectic furnishings and décor, however, emphatically rose above its structural features and regrettable facilities. Long white lace curtains hung suspended from the ceilings by the windows, enclosing the hominess of this interior. Fresh flowers, in ornate glass vases, decorated various surfaces and shelves. In the bedrooms and parlor, floor and table lamps with ornamental cloth shades supplemented dim ceiling fixtures. Upholstered chairs, of indeterminate vintages, as well as old lacquered-wood tables, large and small but all layered with doilies and knickknacks, covered much of the floor space. The tables' surfaces were barely visible under the piles of books, magazines, and newspapers that threatened to displace the knickknacks. Chests and packed bookshelves lined the walls. And on the walls, shelves, and mantelpieces in all the rooms were pictures of buildings and sights in old Czernowitz and photos in ornate frames—of a much younger Rosa and Felix, of Rosa and Martin Zuckermann, and of Rosa's brothers Arthur, Paul, and Muniu as young men, as well as of various other relatives and acquaintances.

"Come, make yourselves comfortable," Rosa said to us, as we returned to the parlor and she busily cleared books and other reading materials from the surface of a table to make room for cups and saucers. "I can offer you tea with lemon or Nescafé, with a slice of the torte that the mother of one of my pupils baked." Her language pupils, especially the children, were fond of her and affectionate, she explained, and often brought her cakes, flowers, and sweets—"little gifts," as she called them—when they came for their lessons.

The conversation quickly turned from Rosa's queries about our first impressions of the city and the changes it had undergone since Lotte and Carl left to the health and present situation of various close relatives dispersed throughout the world. Leo and I, however, eventually wandered over to one of Rosa's stacked glass-enclosed bookshelves, to which both of us were attracted by the covers of several displayed books and especially by four small souvenir tin and plaster-of-Paris busts of Emperor Franz Joseph and two framed color postcards of Empress Sissy, his wife. Rosa, perhaps noticing my expression of surprise and then amusement as we examined her little imperial pantheon, nodded with a smile: "Yes, I am still a monarchist. I long for those good times. Friends send me these keepsakes from Vienna. And," she added, pointing to a small Israeli flag wedged into a corner of the same shelf, "I remain a Zionist. I have always been a Zionist, never a communist."

The ideological incongruity between her monarchism and her Zionism

Figure 4. Rosa Zuckermann in her apartment (Photograph courtesy of Helmut Kusdat)

seemed not to bother Rosa at all, and neither Leo nor I probed her for additional clarification. But noting our interest in her books, Rosa joined us by the bookcases while we took a look at the works they contained.

The books themselves included the principal German-Jewish Bukowina prewar and postwar writers, as well as some of the traditional texts that shaped their work.[6] As such, Rosa's haphazard-looking library was a testament not only to the vibrancy and persistence of Bukowina's distinct culture but also to its dispersal and dissolution. Most obvious were the collections by Czernowitz authors published recently and, in some cases posthumously, in German and Austrian paperback and hardback editions, as well as some English, French, Russian, and Ukrainian translations of their works: volumes of poetry by Paul Celan and Rose Ausländer and books about them;

the correspondence between Celan and Nelly Sachs; monographs by Selma Meerbaum-Eisinger, Viktor Wittner, and Alfred Kittner; Eliezer Shteynbarg and Itzik Manger in German translation from Yiddish; and the recent anthologies *Fäden ins Nichts gespannt* (Threads Spun into the Void) and *Versunkene Dichtung der Bukowina* (Submerged Poetry of the Bukowina). These books were not shelved but faced outward as if in a bookstore window display, and Celan's and Ausländer's portraits stared at us from a number of covers. Behind and below them were German classics—Goethe, Schiller, Heine, Rilke, Mann, Hauptmann, Keller, Storm—as well as a number of other German-Jewish writers, like the Czernowitz-educated Karl Emil Franzos. Stefan Zweig's *Die Welt von gestern* (The World of Yesterday), his memoir of Habsburg era optimism and post–First World War deterioration and disheartenment, was also displayed face-outward in the bookcase, as though to serve as a comment on its entire contents, as were Lion Feuchtwanger's *Exil* and Marcel Reich-Ranicki's *Mein Leben* (in English, *The Author Himself: The Life of Marcel Reich-Ranicki*). And yet, despite what seemed like an overwhelming emphasis on literature embodying or referring back to a no longer existent Austro-German world of yesterday, there were some Romanian works by Mihai Eminescu and Ion Luca Caragiale, many Russian and Ukrainian titles—by Tolstoy, Dostoevsky, Gogol, Bakunin, Koblyanska—as well as late-twentieth-century German, English, American, and French novels and recent vintage reference works, particularly in German, such as the dictionary *Der große Duden*. And the bookshelves also contained writings on the wartime concentration camps—Viktor Frankl, Bruno Bettelheim, Primo Levi—as well as Israeli fiction in German translation. Books by Amos Oz were prominently in view.

"Those volumes," Rosa indicated, pointing to the classics, "were the books of my youth. My mother knew poetry by Heine, Schiller, and Goethe by heart, and she and my father introduced me to their poems as a young girl. They only had four grades of formal schooling, but they were very well read." As she watched us pick up and leaf through some of the volumes, Rosa continued, "There are only a few specimens like me left here—I mean of old Czernowitzers still speaking German and reading these books. But, you know, I still like Heine better than Celan. Don't you?"

Many, if not most, working- and middle-class Czernowitz Jews of Carl, Lotte, and Rosa's generation grew up with bookshelves such as the one in Rosa's apartment—shelves largely filled with German and German-Jewish classics. In a memoir-essay, Ilana Shmueli, now a resident of Israel, recalls "the beautifully carved mahogany cabinet that stood in the parlor of my parents' house and that was mostly locked. It contained, naturally, the gold-embossed volumes of the classics, new and untouched. There was also a Judaica section, the *History of the Jews* by Grätz, Herzl's *Alt-Neuland* [Old New Land], etc. There was no bible in the house."[7] But the primary contents of Rosa's cabinet, the works of Celan and Ausländer for which Czernowitz is now recognized and remembered (and which, unlike the books in Shmueli's parents' collection, were indeed touched and read), were of more recent vintage. This literature from the period before and after the Second World War—by Czernowitz/Cernăuţi writers and by Czernowitz exiles living in a multilingual diaspora—was written in what has been termed "deterritorialized" German. It was created when German was no longer the official language in the former Bukowina and reflected a stubborn adherence to an Austro-German identity in the face of Romanianization, Sovietization, anti-Semitism, and eventual deportation and exile.

These books, many of which represented the Bukowina literature written in a German best described by Rose Ausländer's image of an "uprooted word"—and many of which are also to be found on my parents' shelves in New Hampshire and Florida—both expressed and embodied the contradictions that had led us here.[8] How, I had always wondered, did the rich, cosmopolitan, multicultural environment of Czernowitz survive its many assaults to produce such a powerful afterlife in its descendants? Is there still a place for it now, in the city itself, or will it forever be relegated to the memories and fantasies of its exiles? What would we, what would my parents, find as we began our explorations?

In a complex way, I realized, the contradictions between "home" and "hostile territory" were indeed the driving forces behind my own ambivalent nostalgia for Czernowitz. I knew that I could not resolve the contradictions, nor did I wish to do so. Still, my parents' own ambivalent nostalgia generated in me the need to repair the ruptured fabric of a painfully discontinuous, fragmentary history. "Returning" to the place with them, finding Rosa and Felix there, surrounded by the literary and cultural objects I recognized from the bookshelves of my own childhood and youth, seemed the first step in a process of reconnection and recovery, in both senses of the word. At the same time, I, like other children of exiles and refugees, had inherited my parents' knowledge of the fragility of place, their suspicion of the notion of home. "Where are you from?" The stranger's question and my mother's unequivocal response from that morning would continue to haunt me throughout those first days in the former Czernowitz.

# TWO

# Vienna of the East

Mother and I speak German. Sometimes it seems to me that the way
Grandfather and Grandmother talk makes Mother uncomfortable,
and that she'd prefer for me not to hear their language. All the
same, I summon up the courage and ask, "What's the language
that Grandfather and Grandmother are speaking?"

"Yiddish," Mother whispers in my ear.

AHARON APPELFELD
*The Story of a Life*

### THE JEWISH CEMETERY, 1998

In the overcast early afternoon of our second day in Chernivtsi we again met
Rosa and Felix, as well as Rosa's friend Matthias Zwilling, and continued
our explorations of the city. Also with us was Othmar Andrée, a German
friend who had come to join us in Chernivtsi to make some connections
between the present city and the past life of Czernowitz Jews, on which he
had begun to do extensive research. In the years after the end of the Second
World War, many Russian-speaking and Yiddish-speaking Jews from other
parts of the Soviet Union and Moldavia had come to settle in Czernowitz.
But Rosa, nearly ninety years old, and Matthias, some ten years her junior,
were among the last of the handful of German-speaking Jews from Lotte and
Carl's generation—old Czernowitzers—who still lived there. They offered to
take Lotte, Carl, Marianne, and me to the Jewish cemetery on Gorechi Hill,
Zelena Street, where, among other things, they would try to help us find the
grave of Carl's father, Markus Hirsch, and those of Carl and Rosa's maternal
grandparents, Yohanan and Chaja Wurmbrand.

As we entered the metal gate of the cemetery, no office or official was in
sight: the place was empty. I was awed by the vastness of this burial ground
and the grandeur of many of its monuments. More than sixty thousand
people are buried here, Matthias Zwilling told us.

Figure 5. Matthias Zwilling, Othmar Andrée, and Carl Hirsch (from left) approach the ceremonial hall at Chernivtsi's Jewish cemetery, 1998 (Photograph by Leo Spitzer)

The cemetery's location, on a gentle rise extending toward an elevated knoll from which the center of Chernivtsi could be viewed in the distance, was stunning. But I was also struck by the decay, neglect, defacement, and wreckage so markedly evident throughout its expanse. The large domed ceremonial building near the entrance, where the dead were once laid out before burial, was an empty shell, with windows and doors ripped from their frames and the interior stripped bare. The building's rusty metal roof was in tatters, with segments lying about on the surrounding bushes and ground outside. Plaster and trimming hung loose or had dropped into piles on the floor; walls, cracked and pocked with holes, were marked with graffiti. Hebrew writing in black lettering with traces of gold-leaf, still visible on one inside wall and high up by the entrance and near the cupola, attested to the opulent detail and rich decor that had adorned this once-elegant structure.

Not far from this ceremonial building, in the section of the grounds closest to the entrance, our guides showed us some of the oldest and most impressive gravestones and monuments in the cemetery. Here were the Habsburg-era family shrines and tombs belonging to prominent individuals and members of Czernowitz's assimilated Jewish elite—industrialists, merchants, bankers, presidents and leaders of the Kultusgemeinde (the Jewish community organization), mayors of Czernowitz, deputies to the Austrian parliament, and university-educated professionals of all sorts. Luttinger, Fechner, Reiss, Rubenstein, Kiesler, Gottlieb, Straucher: these names, as well as those of other Czernowitz Jewish patricians, were engraved here on massive black or gray marble and granite stelae and obelisks, together with memorial captions in German and Hebrew. Sculpted reliefs decorated these graves with Jewish and personal symbols and motifs—candelabra, the Books of Moses, the Cohen hand sign, crowns, birds, lions, the five Hebrew letters *taf, nun, zayin, vet, heh* abbreviating the words "may his/her soul be bound in the bond of eternal life."[1] The epitaphs, some in Gothic lettering, expressed loss and grief in the florid language of lamentation. Emphatically highlighting personal achievement, they marked bourgeois success as well as the possibility of a Jew attaining it:

Hersch Trichter
*Captain of Industry, Member of the Austrian Industrial Advisory Board,*
   *Chamber of Commerce, Municipal Council*
Born 14 April 1860—Died 19 December 1911
*Endowed in Heart and Spirit with Great Gifts, with Your Own Strength*
   *You Forged an Indestructible Legacy for Your Grief-Stricken Family*

*and for the Public. You Remain Unforgettable and Your Memory*
*Will Always Be Blessed. Young in Years You Departed from Us.*
*Rest Peacefully after Such Wonderful, Blessed, Labor!*

Heinrich Feuerstein
*Director of the Bukowiner Brewery Works, A.G.*
*22/1/1865–10/9/1915*
*A Friend of Humanity*
*A Family Bulwark*
*Through Us and Our Offspring*
*His Memory Endures*

Karolina Tittinger
29 Sept. 1850—13 Oct. 1895
*Wife and Mother, Benefactress of the Poor, Beacon among Women of this*
*City in Virtue, Kindness, and Nobility: Loved, Honored, and Mourned*
*by Her Desolate Husband, Her Inconsolable Children, by All Who*
*Encountered Her in Life.*
*May Her Ashes Rest in Peace.*

A few large gravestones were carved to resemble severed tree trunks, symbolizing the tree of life cut short by death and usually used to mark children's graves.

"I have a place reserved for me here," Matthias Zwilling told us matter-of-factly. He pointed to a large black marble Zwilling family headstone on which the name, professional title, and birth and death dates of his mother, father, and two uncles were inscribed in gold lettering. At its very bottom, a small space remained for Matthias's own name. He was the last of the more than 150-year-old Zwilling line in this region of Eastern Europe: engineers, doctors, and scientists who had long been at the peak of the city's professional elite. Rosa then took us to a nearby monument on which her husband and brother's names were carved. "This is where I will be buried," she told us. Amid the other Zuckermanns and Roths on the monument, we were surprised to see the name Lydia Harnik. "Oh, yes," Rosa said animatedly. "Lydia is not a family member, but she and I were lifelong best friends. We were both deported to Transnistria, and we were together during the last half-century in Chernovtsy. I've been inconsolable since she died two years ago. I promised her that we would be buried in the same grave."

We paused for a moment as we took in her explanation. Then Lotte broke the silence. "Lydia Harnik taught me French and English when I was a child,"

Figure 6. Gravestones at Chernivtsi's Jewish cemetery, 1998; note the monument carved in the form of a severed tree trunk, second from left (Photograph by Leo Spitzer)

she said. "And she was my sister's English teacher," added Carl. "Her talent for languages was legendary." Both seemed shaken and saddened by all the familiar names they were encountering and by the cemetery's desolation. We helped them find small stones to place in commemoration on the graves of friends and relatives along our walk.

We were hardly able to penetrate the next sections of the cemetery we came to because of the heavy undergrowth and head-high prickly brush that had enveloped them over the years of neglect. The graves and monuments that remained visible in these sections contrasted significantly with those we had seen in the vicinity of the ceremonial hall. Here were predominantly smaller and more modest, more austere gravestones indicating the humbler economic status of the deceased. Little marble or granite was evident; rather, markers were made of sandstone and limestone, and the weather, combined perhaps with years of exposure to impurities in the air, had scarred, blistered, and deformed many of the names and inscriptions carved into this softer, more vulnerable rock. In several places, it was difficult to discern differences between the monuments shaped like stone tree trunks and the genuine trunks and felled trees that lay close to them. How were we ever going to find Yohanan and Chaja Wurmbrand, or Markus Hirsch's grave, we wondered?

"Except for a few reserved places, this cemetery is now largely filled," Rosa told us. "And the Jewish community has no funds to keep it up. Few of us are left here anyway. Most of the German-speaking Jews whose families are buried here died during the war or emigrated. Many of the Russian Jews who moved here after the war also left for Israel in the last few years." Occasionally, volunteers from other European countries and from overseas come for short periods to clear brush and growth. But in the absence of ongoing maintenance and regular groundskeepers to cut back and control vegetation, nature had managed to unfurl itself with relatively little challenge, covering large areas of this cemetery like a gnarled blanket.

## IMPERIAL SUBJECTS, 1774–1914

Despite the impediments to our mobility, our walk through the Jewish cemetery revealed a great deal about Jewish life and society in this city over the course of some two hundred years. Class background and religious differences, education, individual and communal wealth, the trajectory of Jewish emancipation, assimilation, and acceptance, as well the eventual persecution and dispersion of Jews from this part of Europe—all this and more was reflected on the graves and in the memorials.

The oldest tombs in the cemetery, from its opening year of 1866, held the remains of people born in 1783, nine years after the Austrian Habsburgs had acquired the Bukowina, the northernmost part of the old Moldavian principality, from the Ottoman Empire. Despite their age, the skillful ornamentation on these graves remained sharply visible, although the inscriptions, in Hebrew lettering with no German apparent, had faded into near illegibility. An older Jewish cemetery dating from around 1770—the "Turkish Cemetery"—had existed under Ottoman rule in the heart of the city itself, but it was closed by Habsburg authorities and replaced by the present one. In 1946, the Soviets had built a knitting factory on the site of that older burial ground.[2]

As it was to remain until the Second World War, the Bukowina area of the Ukraine, where Czernowitz and its Jewish cemetery were located, was already a multicultural and multilingual mosaic inhabited by Ruthenians (as Ukrainians were called), Moldavian Romanians, Poles, and Jews when its Ottoman rulers formally ceded it to Austria in the Constantinople Convention of May 1775. For the Austrians, this borderland region, connecting Austria to the imperial possessions in Transylvania (Siebenbürgen) and Galicia, was primarily of strategic importance, and Czernowitz, hilly, naturally protected, and on the River Pruth, became its capital largely for strategic reasons. Given the Bukowina's outlying location and distance from the imperial metropolis of Vienna and the disparate character of its peoples, Austrian Crown officials were interested in populating it and its new capital with a supportive, friendly population, preferably German-speaking, if not ethnically Austro-German. To encourage such changes and to help integrate imperial possessions administratively and, if possible, culturally into the Habsburg imperial core, they made German the official language of the Bukowina—the language of bureaucracy, law, and over time, commerce—and relegated the other native languages to a secondary status.

Almost coincidentally, the Jewish inhabitants of the region, and those who settled there over the course of the nineteenth century, became agents of this centralizing, "Austrianizing," imperial effort. In 1781, the Habsburg emperor Joseph II issued an Edict of Tolerance for the Austrian territories by which, in return for the receipt of a range of civil and economic rights previously denied them, Jews were expected to assimilate to, and readily identify with, the cultural norms and values of the Austro-German metropole. The edict was conceived as one of a series of reforms that would transform the state into a uniform and centralized entity through the modification or elimination of local particularisms and the barriers created by estates, corporations, and denominations. In Austria itself, the edict relieved Jews of the obligation to wear special emblems and distinctive dress, prescribed secular and civic education for their children in German, and required their adoption of German family surnames as well as their use of the German language in business and legal transactions. Jews were now permitted to become artisans and to practice crafts, trades, and professions previously closed to them. They were also encouraged to open factories. Although still maintaining restrictions on their freedom to settle wherever they liked, to own land, and to choose certain vocations, the liberal reforms initiated by the Habsburg emperor recognized the right of Jews to become naturalized subjects and provided them with hope of fuller citizenship privileges and greater equality in the future.

In the Bukowina, the Edict of Tolerance did not become effective law until November 1789, when that region was transferred from its post-Ottoman administration under a military governor to the administrative and political circuit of its adjoining Austrian-ruled province, Galicia. In Czernowitz, however, a state-controlled German-language school was founded in 1784, five years before the legal implementation of the edict, and Jewish children were expected (but not compelled) to attend it. Indeed, for Jewish children, the intended function of this school, like that of other such schools throughout the Habsburg realm, was a culturally transformative one: to provide an alternative to the institutions of traditional Jewish religious learning—the religious elementary schools (*hadarim*) and the Talmudic academies (*yeshivot*)— and to "recast" young Jews through secular education into German-speaking, Austrian-oriented, imperial subjects.

As in colonial and postemancipatory situations in other areas of the world during the nineteenth century, mandated secular education in the Bukowina became an engine not only of assimilation but also of social mobility. "Teachers [from the Austrian metropolis] were the first disseminators of the seeds of this enlightenment [in the Bukowina]," wrote N. M. Gelber. "Thanks to them, a European-oriented core group emerged, even if initially small in size, that would then over time become the advance guard of the Europeanization process."[3] Taught to read, write, speak, and think in the language of the imperial metropolis, Jews were exposed to the literature and views of a world that had previously been denied to all but the wealthiest and most privileged among them. Their spoken or aural knowledge of Yiddish—a fusion language characterized by vocabulary and grammatical structure in large part derived from medieval Germanic dialects—made it relatively easy to learn the "master" tongue. Besides their linguistic and cultural assimilation, however, young Jews, as well as their elders, were also encouraged (if not pressured) to "shed the more conspicuous features of their Jewishness" and to conform more closely with members of the dominant culture in appearance and conduct. *Sich Deutsch kleiden,* for example—to dress in German-style—was presented and encouraged as the model of "acceptable" attire in society, the preferable alternative to the clothing, traditional head and hair coverings, and general outward presentation of unemancipated Jews.[4]

To be sure, Jewish traditionalists, especially in the smaller villages and rural areas of the empire, resisted the prescribed secular education of Jewish youth and the new imperial limitations on the legal autonomy of Jewish communal organizations. In the Bukowina, the strongest opposition to these assimilationist measures came from Orthodox and Hassidic Jews identified with the town of Sadagora, center of the powerful and wealthy dynasty of Sadagora Zaddikim—"wonder rabbis," or holy men who were believed by their followers to possess saintly attributes.[5]

Significant resistance, particularly in the early decades of the nineteenth century, also continued among Orthodox Jews in Czernowitz itself. But younger Jews of the city, who were most exposed to Austro-German cultural influences, increasingly took advantage of the opportunities offered by the newly granted emancipatory rights. Many of them connected assimilation into the German-speaking cultural universe with progressive change and favorably contrasted the enlightened benefits of metropolitan modernity against the economic backwardness and cultural obscurantism that predominated among most people in the region (including some of the more traditionally oriented Jews). Throughout the second half of the nineteenth century, many of these urban Jews who were "Germanized" in language and culture increasingly moved into the bourgeois realm of class society. In Czernowitz especially, they came to view themselves as representatives of the Austro-German *Kulturreich* (cultural realm) and as agents of the Austro-Habsburg imperial mission in the East.

—◦—❖—◦—

Chaja and Yohanan Wurmbrand—whose graves we continued to search for as we tried to make our way through the less-affluent sections of the Czernowitz Jewish cemetery—were not among these modern urban Jews. Maternal grandparents of Carl Hirsch and Rosa Roth Zuckermann, they were both born into Yiddish-speaking, deeply religious families in the village of Neu-

Zuczka, one of the communities in the Sadagora district, in the late 1840s, about the time when young Franz Joseph acceded to the imperial Habsburg throne in Vienna. They died in Cernăuți in the early 1920s, some five years after the emperor's death and not long after the Bukowina became part of Greater Romania. Their lives thus spanned the long reign of Emperor Franz Joseph—decades when the immense social, economic, and political changes linked to modernization and emerging nationalisms affected Jews everywhere within the Habsburg realm.

Little is known about either of the two, or their families, when they still resided in Neu-Zuczka, before the outbreak of the First World War, although both Chaja's and Yohanan's parents had been so pious in their orthodoxy that they emigrated to Palestine in old age in order to die in the Holy Land. They were eventually buried in Tsvat (Safed), in the hills of Galilee. Carl and Rosa also recalled that their grandmother, Chaja, had owned a little store in Neu-Zuczka in which she sold a variety of items. It was there that she earned the income to support her husband—involved in the Orthodox Jewish male prerogative, Talmudic learning—as well as the couple's six children.

"We have no pictures of my grandparents," Carl explained, "because that was not allowed by the very religious Jews like them. But my first memory of them was when I was six, when they came to the Czernowitz train station to meet us after my mother, my sister Lilly, my baby brother Kubi, and I returned from Vienna at the end of World War I. My father was still in the army. We were all going to live in the same two-room apartment in Czernowitz. My grandmother had on a *tichl* [head scarf]—something she always wore—and my grandfather had a beard and *peyes* [side locks]."

"Through them," Carl added, "I learned I was different from many of my neighbors—that I was a Jew. My grandfather never worked, he only studied. He hardly spoke to us, but he hired a tutor for me, to teach me to read Hebrew. Grandfather went to pray regularly in a *stibl,* a small room by his Rebbe's house nearby, and he sometimes took me along on Friday evening and Saturday morning. On Saturday afternoon he and the other men there sang and danced. It all seemed a bit alien to me."

At this point, we had walked to what seemed like the end of a narrowing alleyway to the back of the cemetery. The path led up a hill and expansive views of the city began to emerge behind the thickening brush.

"I am fairly sure that our grandparents' graves are in this back section," Rosa ventured, addressing Carl. "It has been a long time since I've come to see them. The last time must have been in the seventies when your brother Kubi came from Bucharest. We also found your father's grave on that day, but the cemetery was already fairly neglected. So few Jews are left here now. Who is to take care of all this?" she lamented again, as her arm made a sweeping motion over the tall grasses and the impenetrable brush.

We tried another path leading to the back sections and reached yet another cul de sac. Marianne, Felix, and I tried to pull out some grasses and to climb over others. Soon we were entangled in the bramble, surrounded by graves whose markers were barely legible.

"I remember both their funerals," said Carl. "They died soon after my father, and I know that even though I was less than ten years old, I said kaddish [a prayer mourning the dead] on all three occasions. There were a lot of other cousins who could have done it, but it must have been because the grandparents lived with us that I was asked to do it. And then, maybe also because I had already said kaddish for my father, just a little while earlier."

"Chaya and Yohanan belonged to a smaller and less complicated world," Rosa observed. "They were pious and undemanding folk." And yet, even though Carl and Rosa's grandparents had maintained their devout identification with the Jewish lifeways and traditions they had learned in their parental homes and native village community, they certainly did not remain unaffected by the immense societal transformations that occurred during Emperor Franz Joseph's long reign.

Franz Joseph's accession to the throne in 1848 had led to a further expansion of the legal emancipation of Jews in Habsburg lands—a process that culminated in 1867 when Jews were granted full political and legal rights throughout the realm. In the Bukowina—which was separated from Galicia and raised to the position of an autonomous crownland *(Herzogtum)* in 1849—an era of unprecedented growth and prosperity was launched. For the province's inhabitants, fluency in German and an Austro-German cultural identification were invaluable assets for successful participation in the transformation that was taking place. German-speaking "Austrianized" Jews, now legally recognized as Austrian citizens, gained distinct economic and professional advantages over their less assimilated coreligionists. They did so, as well, over ethnic Romanians, Ruthenians, and Poles who had remained less culturally identified with the imperial core—a factor that undoubtedly fed anti-Jewish resentment and fueled the further development of ethnic nationalisms in the region. In practically every sphere of the economy, Jews came to play an active role in the modernization of the Bukowina and especially of Czernowitz, its capital city. In long-distance commerce, they became the wholesale buyers of items imported or manufactured in the Habsburg metropole or in Germany—clothing, shoes, tobacco, printed materials, and diverse

Herrengasse mit Café Habsburg    Hauptstrasse mit Ringplatz

Gruss aus Czernowitz

Figure 7. Greetings from Czernowitz: postcard proudly exhibiting Czernowitz's urban modernity and its two main commercial streets in the early years of the twentieth century (Hirsch-Spitzer archive)

luxury items. As regional middlemen, multilingual in many cases, they helped increase trade with neighboring countries. Their initiatives and capital investment supported the construction of privately owned local short-distance tram and rail transport facilities—passenger as well as freight—carrying utilities crucial to the operation of the industrial and commercial enterprises that bolstered the region's overall economic well-being. They played key roles in the Bukowina's important forestry industry, as forest managers, mill owners, and producers and sellers of furniture and wood items. Taverns, inns, coffeehouses, hotels, breweries, beet sugar factories, mineral-oil refineries, wood-burning-stove plants, building-materials supply yards: these and others were built up, administered, or owned by Czernowitz's German-speaking and Austro-identified Jews.

Jews also invested capital to acquire rural and urban properties after the new laws in 1867 eliminated previous residential restrictions and limitations on their possession of real estate. By 1888 in the Bukowina, 31 out of 141 large estate owners with voting rights in the regional assembly were Jews; by 1910, 42 of the province's large estates were in Jewish hands. In Czernowitz, Jewish entrepreneurs became involved in numerous urban construction projects and

Figure 8. Cernăuți's magnificent Moorish-style temple, ca. 1929 (Hirsch-Spitzer archive)

in efforts to beautify the city. They funded the rebuilding of the Judengasse in the old Jewish quarter after a fire in 1867 destroyed many of its buildings. They built commercial establishments, apartment houses, and private residences in the latest Viennese architectural and decorative styles for members of the growing bourgeoisie. They financed the construction of the Jewish Hospital, the Children's Hospital, and the Jewish Home for the Elderly. A magnificent new Jewish temple was completed in 1877 near the Rathaus and Ringplatz, in the city's new central core. Built in Moorish style as an alternative to the main synagogue in the old Jewish district, it reflected both the architectural tastes and the less orthodox religious practices of upwardly mobile assimilated Jews. A massive, ornate, four-story Jewish National House (Jüdisches Haus), containing the Jewish Community offices and a banquet hall was erected in 1908, next to the Municipal Theater and across from the Chamber of Commerce building.[6]

Together with the layout of new streets, squares, and parks, these new public buildings and private residences helped to transform Czernowitz from a provincial backwater into an attractive Viennese-inspired magnet for visitors and new permanent settlers. By 1900, over 30 percent of the total population of Czernowitz were Jews, some thirty thousand out of approximately eighty-eight thousand inhabitants. By the beginning of the First World War that

Figure 9. A postcard of Czernowitz, showing Theater Square, with the Jewish National House on the right and the Municipal Theater on the left. A statue of Friedrich von Schiller stands in the ornamental circle in front of the theater. (Hirsch-Spitzer archive)

number had risen to nearly forty thousand.[7] Franz Joseph himself visited Czernowitz and the Bukowina province in 1851, 1855, and, again, on Yom Kippur 1880—lavishly celebrated and fondly remembered occasions which, together with the emancipatory laws and liberal reforms implemented in the early decades of his rule, effectively raised his prestige among the region's Jews to a heroic if not adulatory level.

German-speaking Jews, moreover, were increasingly to be found in all the professions—as doctors, lawyers, chemists, journalists, and artists. Their numbers included city mayors and councilors, members of the state parliament, representatives to the Reichsrat (parliament) in Vienna, and judges; teachers and rectors for elementary school (Volksschule), Gymnasium (academic secondary school), and university; as well as members of the police and gendarmerie. Two of the city's police chiefs were Jewish. Even the Habsburg military had Jewish officers from the Bukowina.[8]

As had been true in the first half of the nineteenth century, however, the requisite admission ticket to bourgeois respectability within Austrian imperial culture and society continued to be secular education and fluency in the German language. These requirements were strongly reemphasized and supported with legislation after Franz Joseph became emperor. In 1869 and, especially for the Bukowina, in 1873, laws were passed mandating eight years of school attendance for children between the ages of six and fourteen. At the same time, funding was made available to support existing schools and to establish new ones, both at the elementary and more advanced levels. Not only did Czernowitz benefit from these developments by gaining additional elementary and secondary schools, as well as the Franz Joseph University—founded in 1875 to mark the centenary of Austria's acquisition of the Bukowina from the Ottomans—but smaller towns in the province also received funds to construct and maintain educational institutions.[9]

A qualifying note, however, is imperative here. It is important not to represent Habsburg-era reform measures for Jewish emancipation and assimilation in such an affirmative light that we overlook the less favorable and more ominously negative shadows accompanying them. The lifting of long-standing restrictions against Jews that had begun with the Edict of Tolerance in the 1780s came under attack almost immediately after Joseph's death and was threatened several times afterward by rulers and officials less in sympathy with the potentialities of Jewish integration. Although never successful in stopping the process that led to full citizenship for Jews in the 1860s, reactionary countercurrents remained alive throughout the realm: a potential threat that grew in intensity and vehemence in the final decades of the nineteenth century and before the outbreak of the First World War. Indeed, the centuries-old notion of the "Jew as alien" persisted throughout the emancipation era along with the undercurrent of resentment against Jewish economic and professional advancement. In the 1880s, in Central Europe and the imperial heartland, it was this notion that became the core principle of a new racist, now truly *anti-Semitic* rather than merely *anti-Jewish* ideology. It viewed Jews as a "unique *species* with marked physical and moral characteristics"—as a "race" whose inferiority, according to one of its influential proponents, Eugen Dühring, was immutable, "unchanged and unchangeable."[10] This anti-Semitism, based on a widespread and highly influential ideological premise of the time that viewed races as "distinctively different" and that posited an inherent biological connection between race and human capabilities and behavioral traits, made it possible to maintain that Jews, a "Semitic race," were *by nature* permanently unassimilable into the "true German" or "Aryan" dominant population. Even conversion and baptism could not eradicate the Jews' inherently "inferior" characteristics.[11]

The emergence of this racist anti-Semitism in late Habsburg Austria marked the beginning of a break from the relatively mild anti-Jewish prejudice that had characterized Jewish emancipation throughout the greater part of the nineteenth century. Although the practical consequences of the racist attitudes were initially minor—and reached Czernowitz and the Bukowina some years later than in the Central European heartland—they continued to penetrate the fabric of Austro-German political and social life during the final decades of Habsburg rule. Eventually, they would culminate in the horrors of Nazi genocide.

### ASSIMILATION AND ITS DISCONTENTS

The educational requirements implemented in the early years of Franz Joseph's reign came too late to have a direct bearing on the schooling or cultural outlook of Carl and Rosa's grandparents. Chaja and Yohanan Wurmbrand were already adults when the school reforms became law. Relatively impoverished among Jews, with seemingly few if any of the ambitions that assimilation could help to realize, their personal engagement with cultural Austrianization and with the German language itself remained perfunctory throughout their lives. Nonetheless, the transformations that took place in the era of Franz Joseph affected them profoundly. Progressively, these changes accelerated a generational rift between tradition-bound and assimilated Jews that had begun decades earlier—one reflected in the Wurmbrands' case, as in so many others, in the distance that emerged between their cultural identity and way of life and that of their children.

The generation of Bukowina Jews to which Chaja and Yohanan's six children belonged, including Carl Hirsch's mother, Emma (born Nechume), and Rosa Roth Zuckermann's mother, Lotti (born Leah), was the first to experience the newly required multiyear enrollment in the schools. In the course of their education, each one of the Wurmbrand children learned to speak, read, and write German fluently. Without ever abandoning Yiddish, their mother tongue, they eventually used their fluency in German and the cultural understanding that it carried to advance more confidently within the Austro-bourgeois world that was unfolding before them. All moved away as young adults from Neu-Zucska to city life in Czernowitz or to larger cities in the German-speaking west.

Following her arrival in Czernowitz, Shulamith Wurmbrand chose to be called by her German name, Frieda (Fritzi). She continued her education into the university level, married late, had a son, then divorced, and eventually held a managerial job in a Czernowitz bank. After the First World War, in the post-Habsburg period of Romanianization and the rise of discriminatory and exclusionary practices that called into question the possibility of Jewish acceptance and integration in Europe, she joined Poale Zion, then learned Hebrew well enough to teach it, and became an ardent cultural Zionist.[12] Her sister Nechume—in Czernowitz, Emma—had less formal education and no professional career. In her twenties, Emma married Markus (born Melech) Hirsch, a poor but handsome housepainter who had abandoned Jewish orthodoxy. When Emma and Markus's first son was born in Neu-Zucska (while Emma was visiting her parents), she and her husband registered his name as "Carl"—and not, as her father, Yohanan, had insisted, as "Chaim." Sister Lotti, like Emma, only reached the lower rungs of the bourgeoisie. Yet she raised her four children in German and imparted to them a love of German literature that she had acquired in her four years of schooling. At the same time, she kept a traditional Jewish household on the outskirts of Czernowitz where many of her siblings and their children gathered for the holidays. Sisters Pepi and Bertha married well-to-do businessmen and professionals. Pepi raised three children from two marriages in addition to two stepchildren. Bertha raised two children in Leipzig, Germany, where her husband owned a bindery; they eventually emigrated to Palestine.

Michael (born Moishe), the youngest and only son among the six Wurmbrand siblings, began to write for publication in German for a wider audience even before he first moved to the provincial capital—poetry and short stories that appeared in Czernowitz's German-language newspapers and magazines. In 1906, in his mid-twenties, he published his first book, *Unfruchtbare Seele* (Barren Soul), to excellent reviews and was invited to teach German language and literature in Czernowitz at the Gymnasium level. By 1911, however, after publishing several more books, including dramas and essays that were well received in literary circles in Austria and Germany, he increasingly turned to journalism. Here he eventually made his career and major contribution: as columnist and editor of the *Czernowitzer Allgemeine Zeitung;* as reporter and columnist for German and Austrian newspapers in Copenhagen and Stockholm; as correspondent for the Jewish Telegraphic Agency in Berlin and Prague and editor of its News Bulletins; and ultimately, in New York after the Second World War, as a writer of numerous articles in German on political and social questions for the German-Jewish refugee newspaper *Aufbau*.[13]

In highlighting the assimilationist journey of Jews in the Bukowina and, especially, in Czernowitz during Franz Joseph's long imperial reign—the move "from the *shtetl* to the *Stadt*," as Florence Heymann so aptly characterizes it—it is essential to stress one important, but perhaps easily overlooked, contextual fact.[14] The Austro-Hungarian Habsburg empire, of which the Bukowina was an outlying Eastern European province, was not a nation-state, like its contemporary, the Bismarckian German Reich, but a multiethnic dynastic-state in which Austrians and Austrianized German-speakers were only a privileged minority of the population. In 1910, less than a quarter of the monarchy's inhabitants used German as their principal language. Austro-identified German-speaking Jews in the Habsburg realm at large were thus a minority within a minority—in the most idealized sense, "an anomalous religious community within a privileged nationality," as Fred Sommer has observed.[15]

By 1910 in multiethnic Czernowitz, however, Jews were the largest community (or "national group," as the terminology at the time defined them) of the six principal ones that inhabited the city.[16] Since most, if not all, of the capital's Jews were German-speaking, moreover, their numbers significantly supplemented the non-Jewish Austro-German population linguistically. In effect, this fulfilled one of the goals that had originally stimulated Jewish emancipation in the Austro-Habsburg realm during the reign of Joseph II. In the city of Czernowitz, thanks to its assimilated German-speaking Jews, German moved beyond its privileged status as the language of the rulers to become the language of the majority.

But as significant as the role of Austrianized Jews was, both in this respect and in the overall development of Czernowitz and the Bukowina under Franz Joseph, other groups within the region's multiethnic mosaic were also important contributors to the modernizing transformation that occurred. Although, as Aharon Appelfeld recently observed, "the Jews were the yeast that created the ferment," the majority population of the northern Bukowina throughout this era was Ruthenian (Ukrainian) in primary language and cultural identification.[17] The largest percentage of these, Eastern Orthodox and Greek Catholic in worship, continued to reside in rural areas and in towns and villages surrounding the provincial capital. Many were involved with farm, livestock, and lumber production—but there were also market sellers, skilled and unskilled laborers, craftspeople, and owners of small shops. Many household workers and nannies, like the Cassandra recalled in Gregor von Rezzori's memoir of his childhood in Czernowitz, were from among this group as well.[18] Increasingly, however, during the second half of the nineteenth century, Ruthenians also moved into the bourgeois realm of society through the educational opportunities that Franz Joseph's reforms had established. Although in fewer numbers than their Jewish compatriots, they contributed to the professional ranks as teachers, doctors, engineers, and officials in the city's and region's government and bureaucracy.[19] A similar pattern of involvement existed among the predominantly Catholic and Eastern Orthodox ethnic Poles and Romanians. Sizable segments of both these subcultures remained rooted in traditional rural or village life. A small number of Romanians, related to the pre-Habsburg local aristocracy, owned large landed estates and were involved in lumber sales and wood production. And both ethnic Romanians and Poles also included a substantial urban element in their numbers: manual workers, craftspeople, and small-shop and market traders belonging to a class markedly less affluent than fellow Czernowitzers engaged in larger-scale commerce or in the professions. Yet each of these groups also spawned a significant middle class during this era— Gymnasium- and university-educated individuals whose talents and resources enlivened the arts, strengthened the economy, and appreciably enriched the diverse cultural character of Czernowitz and the region.

On the surface, as many accounts of the last half-century of Habsburg rule in this city indicate, interpersonal relations between members of the various ethnic groups residing in Czernowitz (and between Orthodox and emancipated Jews) were for the most part cordial. Despite lapses—occasional ethnic slurs, insults, misunderstandings—residents of the city did get along quite well. True, they only rarely socialized together across ethnic divisions, even when class background was similar. But they worked with and for each other, bought from and sold to one another, and in numerous everyday practices, culinary as well as material, influenced each other in more ways than they themselves might consciously have recognized or acknowledged.[20] In the less affluent areas of the city especially, it was not unusual for Jewish families and Ukrainian ones to inhabit the same apartment house or to be neighbors living in close proximity. "For hours every day we played soccer in the streets, my friends and I," recalled Carl Hirsch of his early childhood. "Some were Ukrainian boys. The family living above the Flexors was Ukrainian, with two boys who were our close friends. Our landlord was a Pole married to a German woman, not Jewish, very kind to my mother when she was widowed. And it was like that well into the Romanian period. Differences were accepted."

Czernowitz's rich cultural life reflected both this ethnic diversity and the Habsburg monarchy's toleration if not encouragement of bilingual and multilingual cultural production. The region's first cultural journal, *Bucovina*, for example, featuring literary, historical, and political essays, was published in parallel Romanian and German editions. Intellectuals engaged in lively meetings and discussions in literary circles, and organized lectures and musical and artistic events. Interethnic intellectual conversation and debate thrived. At one point, the man who would become Romania's national poet, Mihai Eminescu, and the Jewish Galicia-born writer Karl Emil Franzos, who had lived in Czernowitz from age ten through his Gymnasium years, were classmates in Czernowitz. Eminescu wrote many of his early poems in German, as did the Ukrainian writers Felix Niemchevsi, Osip Jurii Fed'kovych, Alexander Popovich, and Isidor Vorobkevich. Some even adopted German pen names, reflecting not only the external pressure of the dominant ideology, but also perhaps their own desire to assimilate to what was presented to them as a superior and more evolved *Kultur*. Eminescu would later become an ardent Romanian nationalist and would repudiate his early work, while the Ukrainian writers would turn increasingly to Ukrainian language and traditional Ukrainian motifs in their work.[21]

Despite this multiethnic and multicultural diversity, however, through most of the years of Franz Joseph's reign, assimilated Jews in the Bukowina came to regard themselves not only as compatriots of the Austrians, but also as their most loyal partners in safeguarding and representing Austro-German culture and modernity—the "civilized West"—in what many in Vienna and the imperial core regarded as the "barbaric East."[22] Karl Emil Franzos employed the term *Halb-Asien* (semi-Asia) to refer to areas in Galicia, southern Russia, Bessarabia, and Romania where, in his view, people remained ossified in a "backward cultural morass." He drew a sharp contrast between these people and their cultural development and those in *Deutschtum* (Germandom), among whom cultural enlightenment and civilization blossomed. For him, the culture of the classical German humanism of Lessing, Moses Mendelssohn, Goethe, and Schiller, transmitted through the German language, was the ideal toward which peoples of Eastern Europe of all ethnicities and class backgrounds should strive, including orthodox Jewish minorities that still remained in their *shtetl* or ghettoized communities. He looked on Austro-German Czernowitz, with its large German-assimilated Jewish population, as a cultural oasis (*Kulturoase*) within Halb-Asien, a positive model for the potential transformation and development of the entire region.[23]

While Franzos's Germanophilia was no doubt extreme, the polarity he articulated between Austro-German cultural superiority, as represented and enabled through the German language, and the "semi-Asian" cultural backwardness of East-European ethnic "others" was certainly also expressed in the attitudes and actions of many of Czernowitz's German-assimilated Jews. Acceptance, toleration, interaction, and proximity were subtly coun-

Figure 10. "A cultural oasis": the east side of the Ringplatz in the early twentieth century. Elegantly dressed bourgeois Czernowitzers enjoy the newly completed urban ensemble and its modern transportation system. (David Glynn archive)

terbalanced by the attitude of Germanized Jews, that indeed *they,* unlike their Romanian and Ukrainian neighbors—and unlike their less assimilated Yiddish-speaking fellow Jews—were a part of *die Gebildeten:* the cultivated, the refined, the civilized. Class was certainly a factor in this sense of superiority, with degrees of education, professional status, and wealth tangible verification of cultural achievement. But even for poorer assimilated Jews, it was their identification with Austro-German culture and cultural life that mattered: their ability to recite a Heine or Schiller poem by heart, their familiarity with German theater, their conversational knowledge of German literature, their outward presentation of "good" Austro-German taste.

While in hindsight, this display of cultural superiority through "Germanness" might be considered a form of cultural arrogance, or even of Jewish self-hatred, it could just as well be attributed to a provincial and/or ethnic insecurity—as though the sense of belonging and the cultural identity as "civilized" Austrians that Czernowitz's assimilated Jews had so carefully forged could easily be revoked. They needed to repudiate the "others" as "semi-Asians" for fear of slipping into or being relegated to "semi-Asianness" themselves.

During the decades of surging nationalist consciousness in the multinational Habsburg realm that marked virtually the entire span of Franz Joseph's reign, language continued to be recognized as the principal criterion of group identification and identity. In essence, this put Jews in a bind—both those who used German as the primary language of communication and those who still primarily communicated in Yiddish. Legally, from the reign of Maria Theresia (1740–80) until 1880, "mother tongue" (*Muttersprache*) had been the statutory determinant of "national" affiliation in official Habsburg censuses—a determinant that was modified in 1880 to "every-day language" (*Umgangssprache*).[24] In effect, however, under both of these statutory measures (and for the remaining years of the empire), Yiddish failed to gain official recognition as a national language; Jews in Habsburg lands, although granted full rights after 1867 and legally acknowledged as members of the Jewish religious community (*Kultusgemeinde*), were never legally recognized as belonging to an autonomous nation within the multinational realm. Consequently, while individual German-speaking Jews, *as Austrian citizens,* had access to and even potential membership within imperial governmental institutions, including the House of Deputies of the Reichsrat, Jews *collectively* were denied political representation as a national group.

Certainly, given the economic and professional success of Austro-identified Jews in Czernowitz and the vital role they played in the overall development of the region, it is not surprising that so many Jews here viewed the receipt of full Austrian citizenship rights, in combination with cultural assimilation and religious-communal recognition and acceptance, as the best possible of all worlds. And yet, even these assimilated Jews in the relatively tolerant multiethnic city of Czernowitz occasionally found themselves impeded or shunned socially and economically, and their perceptions of barriers to Jewish acceptance could trigger a crisis of identity. Their encounter with anti-Semitism, either indirectly as witnesses or through direct experience of verbal insults or outright discriminatory and exclusionary acts, was perhaps most significant in this regard. But also important was the Habsburg authorities' refusal to recognize Jews as an autonomous nation.

As nationalist passions heightened in Central and Eastern Europe in the years following Franz Joseph's accession to the throne, German-speaking Jews were caught in the ideological and political clash between advocates · of the liberal assimilationist tradition that considered German as a cosmopolitan language, able to transmit German culture and facilitate integration within a German-language universe, and the increasingly vehement believers in a nationalist-exclusivist position that claimed German as the spiritual expression of a German Volk—the articulation of its "race" and nationality.[25] The latter—"true national Germans," in their own pronouncements—defined assimilated Austro-German Jews as outsiders, as distinct "others" who could never be truly incorporated within a German *Volksgemeinschaft*. In its racialized, pseudo-scientific manifestation, this ideological belief provided another foundation for racial anti-Semitism.

The discriminatory and exclusionary anti-Semitic incidents and actions—verbal insults, physical attacks, and impediments to social acceptance—that accompanied and concretized the nationalist-exclusivist position during this era left a number of Jews in Czernowitz and the Bukowina (like in Vienna and other Habsburg imperial centers) in a marginal situation—in a *Zwischenwelt*, a world "in between." Not granted sociocultural recognition as one of the *Völker des Reiches*, yet also not accepted by many German-speaking Austrian gentiles as part of their "nation," some began to question their rightful place within the empire. Where did they in fact belong? Were they *really* German-speaking Austrians, as the law now recognized—equal citizens like other German-speakers from whom they differed only in religious affiliation? Or were they in actuality an autonomous people within the Habsburg realm, as the Magyars, Czechs, Slovaks, Croats, Serbs, Ruthenians, Poles, or Romanians claimed to be—a nationality indeed, with a distinct Jewish cultural and historical identity?

It was language—the very instrument that was used to define "the nation"—that became the core element in various cultural and political responses by Jews to what many among them perceived to be an intensifying anti-Semitic challenge to assimilationist integration. The question of language was also central within responses of a growing number of Jews who came to view emancipation itself and the promise of acceptance and existence in the Diaspora as a failure.

For the majority of Bukowina and Czernowitz Jews until the end of the empire, German remained the predominant language of choice in communication and the acquisition of cultural capital. Ranging broadly across the political and social spectrum, these included political moderates, who believed that anti-Semitic upsurges, exclusions, and brutalities were passing aberrations, as well as democratic socialists and "Golus" or "diaspora nationalists"—those who opposed assimilation and wanted Jews accepted as a culturally and religiously self-directed, if not self-governing, distinct national group within the framework of the Habsburg multinational state.

But many Jewish opponents of assimilation, especially those desiring recognition for Jews as a nation, came to view the language that they had acquired in the process of emancipation (in this case, German) as an inauthentic impediment and threat to the integrity and continuity of Jewish life. There is an irony in this, of course. Even in their opposition to German and other national languages of assimilation, Zionists and diaspora nationalists had absorbed German Romantic notions about the indelible spiritual bond between language and *Volk*—the very same assumptions indeed that were used by German-exclusivist nationalists to keep out "others," especially Jews, and to draw a circle of inclusion around their own. Hebrew and Yiddish were the alternative languages promoted by some of these Jews as the "true" expressions of Jewish nationhood, and each acquired articulate supporters within the Bukowina.

The "Hebraist" movement, as it came to be called, sought the universal adoption of Hebrew as the national language of Jews. It was particularly associated with political Zionists who advocated *aliyah*—the "return" emigration by Jews from the Diaspora to a land of their own, preferably Palestine. It also attracted cultural Zionists, who throughout the first decades of the twentieth century criticized Jewish settlement plans, emphasizing cultural work for Jewish regeneration as a primary focus. And yet, even though the Hebraist position at the turn of the century had gained adherents among a number of Zionist intellectuals in urban centers of Southern Russia, Ukraine, and Galicia, it received relatively little support among the Jewish elites and masses in Czernowitz and the Bukowina. Despite their Hebrew names, for example, members of Czernowitz's Zionist Gymnasium and university student youth organizations Hasmonäa (founded 1891), Zephira (founded 1897), and Hebronia (founded 1904) all remained deeply immersed within a German-language cultural orientation. While taking public positions against assimilation, they paradoxically departed little in purpose from the German-nationalist student fraternities in Vienna on which they were modeled, and expressed no need for Jews to acquire Hebrew as a national language. Only members of Emunah (founded 1903), took up the Hebraist call. They viewed the primary goal of their organization to be the education of a new generation of Zionist leaders, and to achieve this end, they instituted intensive study groups to learn and teach the Hebrew language, study Jewish history and culture, and gain knowledge about Palestine.[26]

On the other hand, the so called Yiddishists, or supporters of what came to be known as the Yiddish Language Movement, perceived the Bukowina and its capital, Czernowitz, as more fertile ground for the development and dissemination of their ideas. At the instigation of Nathan Birnbaum (1864–1937), the Viennese-born champion of diaspora nationalism, and with the active support of Chaim Zhitlovsky, A. M. Evalenko, David Pinski, and other leading Yiddish writers and intellectuals in Europe and the Americas, the first international Yiddish language conference was planned and then held in Czernowitz between August 31 and September 3, 1908.[27]

Yiddish, the everyday language of communication of the vast majority of Jews living in Eastern Europe, had initially begun to acquire new status and dignity with the spread of Hasidism in the latter half of the eighteenth century.[28] Hasidic teachers had recommended its use in personal religious worship, and rebbes had written fables and tales as well as prayers in Yiddish, using Hebrew letters. The effort to gain acceptance for Yiddish in "high" culture circles, however, really only gained impetus in the mid-nineteenth century, after it was used by Austro-German, Russian, and Polish Jewish *maskilim* (emancipated, "Enlightened" Jews) to propagate Enlightenment ideas and culture to the masses. It was then that it began to be developed into a literary language, with a "high" literature of its own, and it was increasingly used in the press, theater, and published discourse.[29]

Birnbaum and some of the most ardent Yiddish advocates felt that a conference was needed, both to help elevate Yiddish above what many critics still called the bumbling jargon of the "wretched rabble" *(Pöbel)* and to gain recognition for it as the binding language of a Jewish nation. Modeled on recently held Zionist congresses, such as the one in Basel in 1897, with attendees from many countries, such a conference could be a vehicle for the standardization of orthography and grammar, which would promote further development of a Yiddish literary, journalistic, and theatrical culture. It could also address the question of the establishment of an institutional network of Yiddish–language schools—sites where Yiddish would be formally taught and its literature studied and propagated.

Czernowitz was selected as the most appropriate place for such an international conference because Birnbaum and the planners, like Karl Emil Franzos before them (although for different reasons), had come to view the city as an oasis within Eastern Europe. They saw it as an ideal microcosm of the multinational character of the Habsburg Empire—a "Jewish-friendly" place that had had a Jewish mayor on several occasions and that had sent a Jew as a representative to the imperial Reichsrat. It was, moreover, located near Russia and Romania, two countries where Yiddish flourished, but where, because of severe government restrictions, such a conference would never have been allowed to convene.

Paradoxically, however, when the conference was held, its actual location within Czernowitz reflected the dismissive attitudes of many of the city's German-oriented Jewish elite toward a language they associated with a way of life they had wished to leave behind. Originally scheduled to take place entirely in the new, elegant Jüdisches Haus, the conference was compelled to move after its opening session to the Musikvereinssaal (philharmonic hall) and then to the Ukrainian House. Allegedly, the orders for this transfer came from Benno Straucher—elected Reichsrat representative, *Tribun des kleinen Mannes* ("Delegate for the Less Privileged"), declared Zionist—and the dominant force within Czernowitz's Austro-German-oriented Jewish community.[30]

Some seventy people, forty of whom were actual voting delegates, attended the conference, including delegates from Russia (Poland), Galicia, Romania, Switzerland, the United States, and the Bukowina. It was also attended by members of Yiddishe Kultur, a student organization founded by Birnbaum in Vienna, and by members of the Czernowitz student groups Hasmonäa and Emunah. Local Czernowitz dignitaries and representatives of the Yiddish-language and general press were present as well. Featured speakers included Birnbaum, as well as a number of the leading contemporary intellectual lights in Yiddish literature and the arts—Sholem Asch (Kozmer/Warsaw), Chaim Zhitlovsky (New York), Matisyohu Mieses (Przemysl), Ester Frumkin (Vilna), Abraham Reisen (Kracow), and Y. L. Peretz (Warsaw). Sholem Aleichem had planned to attend, but fell ill shortly before its opening, and sent his regrets. Mendele Moykher Sforim was invited but did not respond.

The conference's immediate accomplishments were sparse. Its main focus was the resolution introduced by Birnbaum that Yiddish be recognized as "*the* national language of the Jewish people."[31] This position was articulately supported in a major address by Matisyohu Mieses, who established himself during the conference as the leading ideological and linguistic theoretician of the Yiddish-language movement. Taking an extremely combative stance against the Hebraists, Mieses argued that only Yiddish, the living language of *Yidishkeyt* (Judaism), "could protect Jewry from assimilation and shield it from alien attacks."[32]

But opposition, especially from those affiliated with Zionism and with "Bundist" socialism (such as Ester Frumkin), was also strong.[33] A number of Zionist participants argued that Hebrew was truly the "sole bond of Jewish existence," while Yiddish was merely "the necessary language of the Jewish exile," and they, in conjunction with Bundists, managed to attract sufficient support so that eventually a compromise resolution, declaring Yiddish to be, not *the,* but *a* "language of the Jewish nation," was adopted instead of the original one.[34]

In its immediate aftermath, critics dismissed the Czernowitz conference as inconsequential in its practical results. As Emanuel Goldsmith indicates, at the conference's third session, Y. L. Peretz had proposed that the delegates create a permanent central organization, to be headquartered in Czernowitz. Among a long list of objectives, this new organization was intended to help to establish Yiddish schools and libraries throughout Europe; act as center for the publication of Yiddish textbooks and cultural and artistic materials; propagandize for the recognition and attainment of equal rights for the Yiddish language; and call for and plan periodic Yiddishist international conferences to follow up on the first one.[35] Peretz's proposal, however, was significantly watered down by the time it came to a vote. The functions of the new organization were limited to the preparation of the next conference, the publication of the minutes of this one, and the publication of Miese's address, as well as of Sholem Asch's Yiddish translation of the Book of Ruth from the Bible. But no central organization was ever established in Czernowitz, and the proposed projects were not realized. Not until 1931, twenty-three years after the 1908 event, were the proceedings of the First Czernowitz Conference published, in Vilna, by YIVO (Yidisher Visnshaftlekher Institut, or Yiddish Scientific Institute, presently the Institute for Jewish Research).

And yet, despite harsh dismissals by its detractors (the Hebraist Ahad Ha'am mocked the conference as a "Purim-shpil"—Purim play, or farce—and a "betrayal against Hebrew"; others, as "a harmful illusion" and a "mistake"), the longer-range results of the gathering and its symbolic impact throughout Eastern Europe were significant.[36] Many of the goals of YIVO, which was founded in 1925 in Vilna, can be programmatically and intellectually connected to the 1908 conference. In Cernăuți in 1919, young left-leaning, intellectuals—anticipating the dynamic Yiddish language, theater, and literary cultural renaissance of the mid-1920s and early 1930s that developed in the city and surrounding region—founded the Yiddisher Shulferain, a center for Yiddish language instruction, Yiddish literature study, and lectures and seminars.[37] The Shulferain also sponsored summer camps in the countryside for young people in which Yiddish language instruction, theater, and cultural discussion played a central role.

In 1928, for the twentieth anniversary of the conference, Chaim Zhitlovsky, who by this time was recognized as one of the leading thinkers in the modern Yiddish cultural and political arena, published an analysis of the conference he had helped to organize. He honored it as a milestone event. Not only had it served to rid many intellectuals of their prejudice against Yiddish as "jargon" or "bad German," but the "spirit of Czernowitz," as he termed it, had also contributed immensely toward the maturation of the Yiddish language from a mass folk language into a literary one. It had also, through the conference's fostering of a uniform national language, helped assert "the unity of the Jewish people."[38] Thus, having served as the site for the conference, Czernowitz itself, as David Roskies so insightfully noted, became "for Yiddishism what was Basel was to Zionism."[39]

Nowadays, one hundred years later, that "spirit of Czernowitz" associated with the conference remains very much alive. To mark the centenary of this groundbreaking 1908 event, three major international academic gatherings took place: in April 2008 at York University, Toronto, entitled, "Czernowitz at 100: The First Yiddish Language Conference in Historical Perspective"; in October in La Jolla, California, sponsored by the International Association of Yiddish Clubs; and in August in Chernivtsi itself—held at the same venues as the 1908 conference and sponsored by an array of impressive institutions, including the Hebrew University (Jerusalem), the Center for Studies of History and Culture of East European Jews (National University, Kyiv), the Maimonides Academy (Moscow), and the Chernivtsi State University.

### VIENNESE REFUGE, 1914–1918

As we continued our walk through the cemetery, we became increasingly tired and discouraged by alleys of dense undergrowth. We perked up, however, when we came upon a well-cared for grave that resonated with the city's Yiddish history, that of the well-known Yiddish poet and fable-writer of the interwar years Eliezar Shteynbarg, founder of the Yiddisher Shulferain. Shteynbarg's gravestone was beautifully decorated with bas-reliefs of the sun, the moon, stars, flowers, birds, and butterflies—motifs from his tales—as well as of curtains indicating his activity in the Yiddish children's theater. "I heard that when Shteynbarg died in 1932," Matthias Zwilling told us, " the whole town turned up here. Shopkeepers closed their stores to honor him, even though Yiddish was not spoken or read by very many people."

Still searching for Markus Hirsch's grave, we made our way back toward the middle section of the cemetery. On our way there, we noticed several rows of graves of First World War veterans and began to examine them closely.

Markus had been a private in the Austrian army and ultimately a casualty of that war. He died in Czernowitz two years after his demobilization, following a lengthy illness from the complications of tubercular laryngitis probably caused by the gas that had been used in battle during his service in Russia and Italy.

"I don't think he's here among these," Rosa said. "He was a veteran, of course, but he died after the war, so he was buried further over, in another section. I wish we had a way to look this up right now but, as you see, there is no one here keeping records. We might have to make some inquiries. I wish you were staying longer."

It seemed to me that Marianne and I were more eager to find Markus's grave even than Carl was. Carl, who was born in 1912, two years before the start of the war, had hardly known his father. After I came to know Carl and Lotte, I had heard numerous stories about different members of their family, but, for obvious reasons, Markus did not figure vividly in them. Certainly Carl and his siblings had few if any recollections of their father. When we reached the part of the cemetery where Rosa believed his grave was located, it became obvious that we would not be able to penetrate it on that day. We thought we might come back the next day, perhaps with some tools, to try to hack our way through the impenetrable brush and weeds. The man whose grave we were seeking had died almost sixty years ago, but three of his children were still alive in 1998, scattered throughout the world. Finding his grave, placing a stone on it, would enable us to honor the memory of an ordinary person, forgotten by history and remembered only vaguely by his immediate family. But nature and human neglect had conspired against our intent.

Markus was inducted into the army in July 1914, during the first, partial mobilization—and he no doubt went off like thousands of other young and loyal Czernowitz Jews, to the hurrahs and shouts of residents lining the Hauptstrasse and the Ringplatz, ready to fight for his emperor, sure of victory, singing martial songs. "Triumphant, we shall beat the Russians and the Serbs—and show them we are Austrians" was the hymn of the day.[40] Patriotism and love of the old Franz Joseph were powerful incentives to join the fray.

But the war did not proceed as optimists had anticipated. In its early days, Czernowitz's inhabitants celebrated small victories by Austrian units in the border clashes near the city. Before long, however, Czernowitzers began to receive news about Russian military successes in neighboring Galicia. Rumors about Cossack excesses soon followed: there was word of murder, plunder, rape, fire—Jews and local peasants were fleeing westward in huge numbers. By the end of August 1914, the rail connection between Czernowitz and Vienna through Galicia was interrupted; flight from the city to the imperial capital was now only possible by means of a much longer southwestern exit route, through Dorna-Watra in southern Bukowina (now part of Romania).

Many wealthier members of the Jewish bourgeoisie set off on this route immediately. Among them were Adolf and Lottie Rubel, Lotte Hirsch's maternal grandparents, as well as her parents Cäcilie Rubel Gottfried and Max Gottfried and her older sister, Fritzi. Then, as the czar's army advanced and was about to take the city—and only hours before retreating Austrian troops blew up the bridges across the River Pruth—thousands of additional Czernowitz citizens, in largest part Jews, fled toward Vienna and the Austrian heartland. Most of the younger Wurmbrands, including Markus Hirsch's wife, Emma, and their two young children, Lilly and Carl, left with this group.

Vienna became both a haven and an oasis for many of these refugees. For the better-off members of the Czernowitz middle class who had some of their money deposited in Austrian banks or for those like Max Gottfried, a lawyer in the employ of the Imperial Ministry of Finance, who were able to retain or attain a professional position, the capital provided a comfortable abode. Max's father-in-law, Adolf Rubel, of the same generation as Yohanan Wurmbrand but much more assimilated and well-to-do—a man who had risen socially during Franz Joseph's reign from carpenter to furniture factory owner—became ill and died soon after arriving in Vienna. His wife Lottie, after whom Lotte Hirsch was named, was a victim of the 1918 influenza epidemic and was buried in Moravia, where a part of the family resided. But despite these losses, for the others in this family the capital city provided an energizing cultural treat. "My parents really enjoyed Vienna, even though it was wartime," Lotte told us. "They used to tell me about going to the theater, to concerts, to lectures. They had many of their relatives with them. My father continued to work for the ministry and to receive his salary. 'We weren't at home but we were, after all, still in Austria,' he used to say. My sister Fritzi attended Gymnasium. Her love for Vienna and everything about it—literature, culture—became so strong then. But it happened to all of them." Carl and Lilly Hirsch, less affluent and much younger, were also shaped during these refugee years in the capital. Their stories of life on Heumühlgasse 4, where their brother Kubi was born, are still vivid in recollection.

"When Emperor Franz Josef died, my mother was intent on attending the funeral," Carl was fond of recalling with a laugh. "She left me and Lilly, at

Figure 11. The former Dreifaltigkeitsgasse 41, where Lotte Hirsch spent her childhood and youth, as it appeared in 1998 and 2000 (Photograph by David Kessler)

four and five, in charge of two-month-old Kubi and walked to the center of the city by herself. She just had to be there."

"Being in Vienna reinforced their Austrianness," Lotte emphasized as we left the Jewish cemetery and walked toward the apartment in the center of Czernowitz to which her parents returned from Vienna after the war ended and in which she grew up.

Marianne and I were eager to see the home of Lotte's childhood and youth, hoping to be able to go inside and to help her relive some of her early memories. We stopped in front of an imposing three-story turn-of-the-century Viennese-style bourgeois apartment house on the former Dreifaltigkeitsgasse, now number 63, Bogdana Khmelnitskogo. The stucco walls, like the wooden window frames and the elegant entrance door, were peeling badly, but their beauty, however faded, was still evident. "This is where I lived for the first twenty-seven years of my life, Dreifaltigkeitsgasse 41," Lotte pointed and repeated the address, ignoring the number change.

"Up there are our windows. We had half of the second floor. After the First World War ended, my parents and my sister Fritzi were eager to return home to Czernowitz and to their apartment as soon as they could. You see, my mother was already in her forties and had a sixteen-year old daughter, but to her horror, she found out that she was pregnant, with me. She wanted to deliver at home. When they left Vienna, she was already very big, and she had to be lifted through the window of an overcrowded train in which my relatives barely managed to find a spot. They found their apartment plundered and many of their belongings gone. When it was time to have the baby, my mother was forced to go to a clinic. It was embarrassing for someone of her class background."

Indeed, the city into which Lotte was born in May 1918 was radically different from the one her parents had left a mere four years earlier. Within months, the Habsburg Empire would be no more and the Bukowina would come under Romanian rule. Czernowitz would be renamed Cernăuţi, and within two years the official language would be Romanian. Still, Lotte would be raised to speak German and acculturated to a way of life that was increasingly being threatened and assaulted. Her generation, despite its mandated schooling in Romanian, would continue to nurture the German-Jewish lifeways of their parents and would even produce an important German literary culture. As the Czernowitz poet Rose Ausländer later observed, "in spirit, we remained Austrians; our capital was Vienna and not Bucharest."[41]

But what was left of that world now, in 1998? What might Lotte and Carl find upon entering the apartment, now occupied by Ukrainians with little knowledge of the city's Jewish past? We observed Lotte's eagerness and her trepidation. Rosa and Felix were there to mediate: we decided to go upstairs and to knock, hoping to find in her old apartment some remaining traces of the long years—the good times and the bad—that she and her sister and parents had spent there.

It would not be until much later, however—after several years and subsequent trips to this city—that we would be able to sort out the contradictory emotions that her powerful return visit to her family home elicited in each of us.

# THREE

# Strolling the Herrengasse

It is striking . . . that the places people live in are like the
presences of diverse absences. What can be seen designates
what is no longer there: "you *see*, here there used to be . . . ,"
but it can no longer be seen.

MICHEL DE CERTEAU
*The Practice of Everyday Life*

SEPTEMBER 1998: ON THE KOBYLYANSKA

On our third day in Chernivtsi, Lotte suggested that we return to the
Herrengasse and stroll along its sidewalks as she had so often done in her
youth. We agreed, of course, looking forward both to the walk and to her
further recollections of the past. There are many photos of the young Lotte
on the Herrengasse in our family albums and photo boxes—photos in which
she is always fashionably dressed, usually with one or more companions, and
in which she appears glad and unhurried, smiling at the camera, happy to
be seen. When we planned our trip to Chernivtsi, the Herrengasse was a
must-see highlight on our agenda. Because of the rich visual archive and the
many stories and anecdotes connected to the Herrengasse, this walk, more
than any other, promised to put the contrast between the remembered city
and the present urban landscape into especially sharp relief.

The Herrengasse, now called Olga Kobylyanska in Ukrainian, had most
tangibly reflected Czernowitz's efforts to establish an urban space that emu-
lated the Kärtnerstrasse or the Graben, two of the most elegant residential,
shopping, and promenading streets in Vienna. It was carved out near the
top of Czernowitz's terraced setting—below it lay the Turkish fountain
and the old Judengasse, central sites of the area which in the eighteenth and
nineteenth centuries was known as the Jewish ghetto, where the hilly city

Figure 12. Herrengasse, ca. 1911 (Hirsch-Spitzer archive)

descends toward the train station and the River Pruth. Like its Viennese inspirations, the Herrengasse had quartered members of the city's upper bourgeoisie in apartments and professional offices located above ground-level shops and cafés. Its impressive buildings had been constructed during Emperor Franz Joseph's reign—the majority during the "good years" of economic prosperity in the Bukowina, from the mid-1870s through to the beginning of the twentieth century. Largely because of the yellow and ochre colors in which they had all been painted and the evenness of their sill levels and window and terrace sizes, the Herrengasse's buildings projected a sense of aesthetic homogeneity and uniformity. And yet they were also individu-ated through differences in detail, ornamentation, and façade. As an urban ensemble, they provided the pleasing physical environment that had sup-ported one of this street's most popular public functions until the end of the 1930s: its service to the city's middle class as the choice location for shopping, pleasurable ambling, and leisurely interaction.

Starting our walk on the Ringplatz (now Pl. Zentraina), from which the Herrengasse angles off, we proceeded along its approximately half-mile length to the street's endpoint—its intersection with the large Neuweltgasse (now Shevchenka), which had been one of the roads marking the bound-ary of the Jewish ghetto set up by the Romanian authorities in 1941. As on previous days, we brought along our pre-1918 German-language map of the city to help orient Carl and Lotte in relation to present-day Ukrainian street names. We also carried a small folder containing photos taken on the Herrengasse in the 1920s and 1930s and reproductions of some of the picture postcards showing Herrengasse street life, storefronts, restaurants, and cafés in the Habsburg decades before the start of the First World War and in the interwar years. We hoped to use these as mnemonic devices of sorts, to help Lotte and Carl recall and identify buildings and sites that had been familiar to them in their youth, but also to compare the Herrengasse as it had been photographed then with what it had become now. And, as we had always done, we referred to this street and its identifiable sights and surroundings by their old German names.

Two things struck us immediately. Externally, at least, the buildings on the present-day Olga Kobylyanska and the stone-paved street from which vehicular traffic was largely absent still resembled pre–Second World War depictions of the Herrengasse on cards and photos. No structures appeared to have been visibly damaged during the war, none seemed to have been torn down, no Soviet-style buildings had replaced Habsburg-era originals.

But as was true in other places in the city that we had already visited, Herrengasse buildings and storefronts had also been neglected during the decades of Soviet rule. The lengthy inattention had now left most of them dirt-encrusted, with cracked and dented walls and broken-down entrance-ways and with windows soiled by a dulling brownish patina of dust and grime. While mending and patching was certainly evident on a few of them, almost all of the structures required some façade, window, and door repairs, and virtually all needed external and interior paintwork. Untended ivy vines, moreover, clung to walls and terraces of a number of the buildings, occasionally fastening to power lines and stretching, like torn curtain tops from one side of the street to the other. "Look how they've neglected the Herrengasse," Lotte observed soon after we began our stroll. "It used to be so fashionable."

A score of small commercial stalls, many of them operated by Ukrainians in their twenties and thirties, lined the sidewalks, clustering at the intersection of side streets. Often consisting only of a portable glass-topped case, supported by folding wooden or metal legs, they offered cigarettes (individually or in packs), batteries, plastic carrying bags, combs, small mirrors, and a variety of other low-cost items for sale. The prevalence here of this informal commercial sector in cheap goods—as well as in those other parts of Chernivtsi that we had passed through since our arrival—reflected the generally difficult economic transition that Ukraine was undergoing at this time, seven years after its independence from the Soviet Union. The street stalls, we learned from Felix Zuckermann, were part of an underground economy that operated free of taxes and free of currency exchange rates set by the government. Arrears in the payment of pensions and salaries to public sector employees (as Felix, who had not received his high-school teacher wages in three months, informed us) were normal. Barter was widely practiced. Except for a relatively small minority, most people had little cash, and many were strapped if not impoverished. When we looked at the Olga Kobylyanska and the people inhabiting it that morning, we certainly noticed that the cosmopolitanism that was reflected in our prewar postcards and photos of this urban setting—its ethnic and class heterogeneity—appeared to have vanished. Wartime displacement, emigration, "classless" Soviet communism, and a post-independence Ukrainian economic transformation that had as yet benefited only a small segment of the population had clearly taken their toll.

When we set off on our exploration of the street, Lotte and Carl were most interested in showing us where old commercial establishments had been located. "Here," Lotte indicated almost immediately, at the intersection of the Herrengasse with the Ringplatz, pointing to a still-beautiful building (now a bank) highlighted by a tall, graceful tower, ornate friezes, and sculpted ornaments. "This was the Café Habsburg. The building was called the Drei Kronen-Haus. This café was one of the two favorite and best coffeehouses in Czernowitz. The other one, on the corner of the next block, was the Café de l'Europe." Indeed, the Café Habsburg, which, like its famous counterparts, the Café Demel and the Café Central in Vienna, had served its Herrengasse clientele rich pastries and Viennese coffee topped with whipped cream, had advertised itself as "The Most Elegant Establishment in the City." Not to be outdone, its competitor, the Café de l'Europe (or the Europa, as it was known to the locals) had promoted itself in the local German-language press and in the 1907–8 *Illustrierter Führer durch die Bukowina* (Illustrated Guide through the Bukowina) as "The Rendezvous Place for the Best in Society."[1] It touted its excellent billiard tables and the availability of the most popular local and international newspapers, magazines, and humor reviews as noteworthy attractions. "And this was the Europa," Lotte said, pointing out the building that gracefully rounded the next corner, some two dozen steps from the former Habsburg. "They had music and a little dance floor in this place. My sister Fritzi and I used to come here to dance." We peered in through dust-encrusted windows; the storefront seemed empty, closed up.

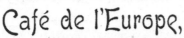

Figure 13. "For the best in society": advertisements for cafés and other fine establishments in Czernowitz (Hermann Mittelman, ed., *Illustierter Führer durch die Bukowina, 1907* [Czernowitz: Verlag der Buchhandlung Schally, 1907–8]; republished by Helmut Kusdat [Vienna: Mandelbaum Verlag, 2001])

As we proceeded further, Lotte's eagerness to find the sites where various stores and business places had existed and her frustration with the grime of the buildings that disguised their former location were especially apparent in her look of disappointment and in her observation (which she repeated a number of times that morning) that "the Herrengasse has changed a lot." She, after all, daughter of a lawyer, the sister of one of the first women to receive a Ph.D. in the Bukowina, and a student in the private Hoffmann Lyzeum, had belonged to that middle-class stratum of Czernowitz/Cernăuți Jews that Herrengasse merchants had wished to attract. Carl's class origins were much humbler, and he had spent less time shopping on this street. Lotte recalled the establishments that had existed here: the Bukowiner Teppichhaus Leon Wittner, exhibiting high-quality Persian and Turkish carpets for sale in its display window—the store where her parents had bought the large blue-patterned Smyrna rug that had decorated their dining room and which had to be sold for a pittance in the early war years after the dissolution of the Jewish ghetto. She also remembered Max Falikmann, a store near Wittner's that sold drapes, curtains, and other housewares, and an attractive millinery atelier, Zur Französin, specializing in the latest Paris-inspired and imported ladies' hats. "Schneider Katz, a ladies tailor, was also on this street, some-where just around here," Lotte added. "He sewed my first all-new outfit from a stunning fabric—a dark blue suit with thin white stripes and a pleat in the back. Before that I wore Fritzi's hand-me-down clothing. Sometimes the garments were turned inside out and resown. Katz was very pleased to have a young customer like me because he thought that I would be coming back there many times over the years. And he was right. At least for a few years. I had things altered, remade, and, once in a while, I was able to have something new made just for me, like that striped suit."

"And there was also a photographer somewhere here on the next block," Carl inserted, pointing toward store windows near the corner of what had been the Armeniergasse (now Virmenska). "Foto Splendid it was called—an atelier, but it also had a street photographer who photographed people walking by. Before we were married, I saw Lotte's photo in a frame in the store window. The store photographer had snapped her picture but, for some reason, she didn't purchase it. It was a good one, however, so they decided to display it in a frame as an advertisement. I went in, bought it, and gave it to her as a gift. I think she was impressed."

Halfway up the length of the street, we passed two official-looking build-ings, the Bridal Registry on the left and, across the street, the municipal Fed'kovych Museum of Chernivtsi, originally the administrative seat of the Greek Orthodox church. Dating from the 1870s, both buildings testify to the centrality of the Herrengasse in the public lives of the city's diverse population groups. We did not visit the museum, however: Carl and Lotte were more interested in private and familial forms of remembrance than official ones. A bit further up, we approached the stately pink-and-white

Greek Orthodox cathedral on the right-hand side of the street. Set into a well-kept little park with benches and flower wells, and located between the old Bischof Hakmanngasse (now Gakmana) and the Kathedralgasse (now Katedraina), this strikingly handsome structure had been designed by a Viennese architect on the model of the magnificent St. Isaacs Cathedral in St. Petersburg and constructed over a twenty-year period beginning in the mid-1840s. During the early Soviet era after the Second World War, when public religious worship was banned, the cathedral building was transformed into a crafts museum and art gallery by the communist authorities, but it was later reconsecrated and reestablished as the city's principal Greek Orthodox place of worship. A mass, with music and song audible in the street, was being celebrated as we were walking by, and we made a brief detour into the cathedral's park grounds to listen, sit on a bench, and rest. For the first time since our arrival in Chernivtsi, beggars approached us.

Much of the rest of our Herrengasse stroll—the two blocks between the old Armeniergasse, Maria Theresiengasse (now Tscheluskintsiv), and the Neuweltgasse—contained residential buildings in which many doctors' and lawyers' offices had once been located. But on the right side of Kobylyanska, a large pink building, a music academy, was identified by Carl and Lotte as the former Polish National House, built by the Polish minority as a cultural center, and on the left side of the final block, beyond the Maria Theresiengasse, we came to Das Deutsche Haus (The German House). This imposing building, blending neo-gothic and Jugendstil architectural styles (and, as such, out of character with other buildings on the street) had been inaugurated in 1910, two years after the opening of Das Jüdische Haus on the Theaterplatz (also called Elisabethplatz, now Pl. Teatraina). The German House, the largest of the "national" houses that were built in the city during the Habsburg era, had, according to Carl, been constructed at the initiative of the Organization of Christian Germans in the Bukowina—a group of local German-speaking residents who wished to set themselves apart as a national group from the numerous German-speaking Jewish inhabitants who had become so prominent and influential in the city. It had contained a restaurant, café, and wine cellar, a large hall and an auditorium for performances, dances, and films, and had housed the editorial offices of the *Czernowitzer Deutsche Tagespost*, a German-language newspaper. It had also been the headquarters of various German clubs and organizations that were, in practice, unwelcoming to Jews. Still, Lotte recalled attending a few musical and German literary events there, and especially remembered the occasion in the 1930s when the German House had hosted a performance by the Vilna Yiddish Theater group in its attractive auditorium. That event, Rosa Roth Zuckermann later told us, was quickly sold out, attended by large numbers of Czernowitz Jews who had never before stepped foot into the interior of this building.[2]

As we neared the end of our Herrengasse walk, the two of us who had never been in this city before found ourselves thinking that things looked much as we had expected. The stories we had heard and, especially, the depictions of the Herrengasse in photos and cards had prepared us for the general look of the street and its buildings; the Habsburg era imprints were everywhere. But both of us also realized that something vital at the core of our expectations was missing. The small street photographs in Lotte and Carl's albums and photo boxes had almost always shown the street busy with people in motion—natives to the city, generally well-dressed Jews and non-Jews, as well as people in the background who looked less well-off, blue-collar, working class. They had also shown store signs, posters, and event-placards—in Romanian language for the most part, but also displaying German, Polish, and Ukrainian names and phrases, attesting to the diverse, multiethnic fabric of the urban space and surrounding landscape. Snapped by street photographers who had made a livelihood from the sale of such souvenirs, these pictures had provided us with a small but fascinating window into the city's cosmopolitanism and into moments of the lives of Carl and Lotte's generation and that of their parents before the outbreak of the war. The present aspect of the street did not, however, mirror the street life depicted in the images.

Even with our visual aids and map, Carl and Lotte could now only guess where exactly the businesses they remembered might have been located. On the modern street, few stores were occupied, and fewer still contained items that would be considered enticing by Western middle-class consumer standards. One store sold hand-produced Ukrainian products—sweaters, shawls, hats, pillowcases, and table settings, displaying the artistic skills characteristic of this part of Europe. But, for the most part, the clothing and shoes in the few active window displays looked unfashionable to us, if not somewhat drab, and the household electronic goods (other than the imported ones) were either secondhand or dated and qualitatively inferior to the ones with which we were familiar. And, no doubt reflecting the depressed economy and the early hour of the day, the stores appeared to be quite empty of customers. Only a handful of people were shopping in the Olga Kobylyanska shops and street-stalls that morning. Business was bad. The material and aesthetic lushness of the Herrengasse of the past was hard for us to imagine.

Writing about Chernivtsi in 2004, a group of Berlin architects would reflect our own impressions in 1998: "We experienced cities that at first appearance seemed familiar. European metropolises: boulevards, broad avenues, market squares, eclectic and Art Deco buildings that exuded the glamour of a long-gone golden age. Still something was different: the articles in the window displays did not reflect the buildings. . . . The present urban society has different origins and speaks a different language. The meaning and function of the buildings and urban spaces has changed over the course of history. In Chernivtsi we felt most strongly the contradiction between the original function of the buildings and their current use. . . . The former Hotel Bristol . . . is inhabited as a student dormitory. The former Jewish Temple is a movie theater, and the former Hotel Bellevue is the seat of the municipal newspaper."[3] Ambling back to sit on a bench by the cathedral, we took some moments to contemplate these changes.

## SUMMER 1998: THE PHOTO DONATION

If the street photos from the Herrengasse had become such a point of focus on our walks through the city, it was because of their role they had played in our preliminary research, three months before our trip to Ukraine.[4] In July of 1998, Carl and Lotte had made arrangements to visit the photo archive of the United States Holocaust Memorial Museum, where our son Oliver was working as an intern, to donate family pictures from Czernowitz/Cernăuți and the Bukowina. The photos were intended to enhance the museum's small archival collection of images from that city and surrounding region. Selected pictures would be catalogued by date, place, and type and labeled with additional information provided by the donors. Some of the photos, Lotte and Carl were told, might be displayed on the museum's website.

At the time, it had been a goal of the museum's photo curator to document Jewish life in Europe broadly, before, during, and after the Holocaust, and, over the course of years, the museum archive acquired many such photographs through private donations and from images scanned from books and other collected holdings. In Washington, we observed Carl and Lotte's donation, and the oral history interview that accompanied it, with close interest because, as scholars, we wished to gain some sense of how such a photographic archive is constructed and of the assumptions and presuppositions that shape its development. Since both of us viewed the Holocaust Museum as a site where an "official story" of the Holocaust (and of the Jewish life that was destroyed by it) was displayed for popular consumption, we wanted to learn more about how that story takes form, and the role that visual images play in shaping it. According to what questions and suppositions were images selected for the archive—both by individual donors and by the archivists who receive, catalogue, and display them?

Lotte and Carl had approached the donation with divergent interests and investments. Carl, perhaps because of his training as an engineer, was systematic. He had researched the archive and its mission and carefully read the instructions sent to potential donors. At home, he had searched through his albums and photo boxes and chosen images that he believed would be of interest to the museum—a very small number. He picked out the only remaining portrait of his parents, somewhat torn and faded (their wedding photo ca. 1910); an old picture of his mother and her sisters dating from the 1930s; some school photographs from the elementary and high schools he had attended; and several pictures from the late 1920s of his Labor Zionist Hashomer Hatzair group—portraits of members and informal snapshots of summer outings and trips. He also included a photo of himself as a young man with his mother, taken in the Cernăuți main square (the Ringplatz) in the 1930s. He selected no pictures of his brother Kubi and sisters Lilly and Rosa, or of other family members, and no informal snapshots of himself. He did, however, bring some twenty additional images to the museum, all of them connected to his institutional affiliations, schools, and workplaces before the war. He labeled each image with a brief description, dating it carefully, and identified all the depicted persons he could remember.

Lotte was much more hesitant, almost resistant. Why would a museum be interested in some poor-quality snapshots of her friends and relatives? Or in school pictures of her class in the Hoffmann Lyzeum? Who would ever care to look at what after all were private images, meaningful only to her and her family and friends? She went back and forth examining the albums and boxes, choosing, discarding, but also considering backing out of the donation altogether. She did have just one photo she believed to be significant: a portrait, taken in the 1920s, of her father's Freemason lodge—of a group of affluent, well-dressed, rather plump men and some of their wives (no doubt invited for a special occasion), looking quite cheerful and self-satisfied. In the end she decided to bring this photo to the museum and two additional envelopes of images as well, as though just in case. In the envelopes, she inserted a few photographs that had belonged to her older sister, Fritzi (of participants at a piano recital; of her brother-in-law and his mother; of Fritzi herself), and about a dozen from her own collection: school photos of students and teachers; of outings at the local riverfront; of fun times with other young people. Lastly, she added some of herself with relatives and friends taken by street photographers on the Herrengasse. These were among her favorites, she said.

The photo donation was accompanied by an interview in which the archivist asked Carl and then Lotte to contextualize the images and to place each, briefly, into their life narratives. She asked questions about Czernowitz during the war years, about the ghetto and the deportations, the role of the Jewish councils, about Jewish resistance and everyday life in extreme circumstances. The photos visibly affected Lotte and Carl emotionally, and Marianne and I were in turn moved to be witnesses to the memories they so evidently evoked. We wondered how the images and the stories to which they gave rise would become part of the museum's archive.

The archivist selected some of Lotte and Carl's pictures and discarded others with confident gestures. "What determined the choices?" Marianne asked her. An important material consideration, she responded, was the quality of a print. But more importantly: she was not interested in photographs that could have been taken anywhere (she rejected Carl's precious portrait of his parents). She preferred images of public and institutional rather than personal, familial, life. She selected every one of the pictures taken on the Herrengasse. From every European city or town, she said, she wanted to have at least one pre-Holocaust photo showing Jews in normal circumstances, walking comfortably and confidently down its main street.

It was astonishing, Marianne observed later, how assuredly and rapidly the archivist chose among the photos offered by Carl and Lotte, and how, in her selections, the public and institutional pictures trumped the private and familial. What struck me as most notable, I responded, was the archivist's desire to acquire street photos for the museum of Eastern and Central European Jews in circumstances of pre-Holocaust "normality"—of Jews walking down main urban avenues as part of their everyday routine. These images, it appeared, were being collected as part of a larger organizing principle undergirding the museum's holdings—the narrative of "before, during, and after" the Holocaust. But what, I wondered, could such street photographs in themselves reveal to historians, in Cernăuţi or, for that matter, in any other city: about the place, about Jewish life before and during the war, and about the role of family pictures in personal, familial, and cultural memory? What did they withhold? Our stroll down the Olga Kobylyanska in Chernivtsi a few months later made us return to these questions on site.

## LOOKING AT STREET PHOTOS

As in so many other European and American cities in the decades between the First and Second World Wars, street photographers on Cernăuţi's main pedestrian shopping and coffeehouse streets photographed passers-by—earning money by selling small prints of the images taken. The photographs were made with portable, compact tripod-mounted box cameras using foldable optical viewfinders and single speed shutters tripped by a nonremovable cable. The image was exposed on 2.5-by-3.5-inch direct-positive paper (sometimes on postcard stock with an imprint of a photographic studio) that was developed on-the-spot in a tank attached to the camera. This relatively quick procedure—a predecessor of the "instant" Polaroid technology—permitted photographers to offer the public inexpensive finished souvenir pictures to take home or, in cases where the photographers were sponsored by a studio, the opportunity to order enlargements or more formal posed portraits.[5]

Certainly, when one looks at the photos of passers-by taken by street photographers on the Herrengasse and on Cernăuți's other pedestrian shopping and coffeehouse streets in the decades between the First and Second World Wars, the persons centrally depicted within them seem to project a sense of confidence and comfort. In all of Lotte's street photos, as well as in the many others from the late 1920s and 1930s that Marianne and I acquired from emigrants and their present-day family relations, that characteristic seems as consistent as the fact that the people pictured are usually walking, on the move—subjects of a snapped photo, not a posed one.

The street photos are telling objects, conveying how individuals perform their identities *in public:* how they inhabit public spaces and situate themselves in relation to class, cultural, and gender norms. Indeed, the desire to recall and display such a performance may be the salient factor explaining why persons bought and kept the original photos (or their enlargements) and why they exhibited them in family albums. When they are then transferred from a personal holding to the public archive—as in Lotte and Carl's museum donation—these images, at the juncture of private and public, of domestic and urban space, bridge a gap between memory and history.

Conveyed within all of them is the essence of photography: the "capture" of an image at a particular moment in time—the fact that a photo (in the pre-digital era, at least) is assumed to "adhere to" its referent, and as such, as Roland Barthes observed in *Camera Lucida,* "in Photography [we] can never deny that *the thing has been there*," that the image depicts something "'that-has-been'... absolutely, irrefutably present."[6] Hence their documentary value to an institution like the Holocaust Museum that aims to construct an authoritative historical archive while also hoping to reactivate and reembody it as memory. Additionally, each of the street photographs also reflects place and space—an urban street location depicting buildings (in often recognizable architectural style) as well as storefronts, display windows, and commercial signs. These are background to the street strollers, to be sure, but they also carry information about the larger social and historical context in which life took place. That information, which Barthes called the *studium*, is of historical value, just as the connection between the viewer and the individuals depicted in the images—whether these viewers are contemporaries, familial descendants, or more distant observers—provokes the work of memory and postmemory. In fact, like all photographs, these street photos also reflect something "already deferred" (to quote Barthes again), not only the instant of time when they were taken but the *change-over-time* central to their historicity—change between photos of the same subject as well as of different subjects taken at different moments in time; and change between the time when these photos were actually snapped and the present time when we, as viewers, look at them.

Those who view these photos, whether in private collections or in public museum holdings, do of course bring knowledge to them that neither their subjects nor photographers would have possessed. Not only may these viewers be able to contextualize the images historically, inserting them within a broader tapestry of cultural-collective or personal-familial memory, but they inevitably also bring to them an awareness of future history—of events yet to come that could not have been known at the time when the photos were taken. This is at the heart of the Holocaust Museum archivist's desire for them: in her eyes, they reveal a normality in Jewish life and a social integration that was violently disrupted and destroyed with the beginnings of persecution, ghettoization, and deportation. Familial descendants might recognize in them some of the fabric of family life that had been passed down through stories and behaviors, while extrafamilial viewers of subsequent generations might connect to them in a different way: through their repeated long-term exposure to a shared transgenerational archive of street images that provide visual glimpses into urban life of the past. The very conventional nature of the street photographs invites an affiliative look on the part of viewers who are able to project familiar faces and scenes onto them and thereby, through them, to reembody memory.

When seen as nothing more than as historical documents, the street photos from Czernowitz/Cernăuţi are quite limited. On first glance, we might in fact see them as the archivist had hoped—as images of urban Jews in apparent comfort strolling down a busy main street of an Eastern European city in the years before the outbreak of the Second World War, seemingly belonging to the place, indistinguishable from other persons who share their

Figure 14. (Here and facing page) Strolling the Herrengasse (Courtesy of David Glynn, Nicole Madfes de Petcho, Miriam Taylor, David Kessler, Irene Fishler Collection, and the Hirsch-Spitzer archive)

economic background. In Lotte's photos and in all others we have looked at or collected, the clothing worn by the strollers, generally fashionable and frequently elegant if not ostentatious, suggests their class situation and affluence—their membership in the city's bourgeoisie and their public assertion of this fact. Indeed, in their seemingly casual walk down the city's main avenues and their apparent willingness to let themselves be photographed and to purchase the prints, they seem to be publicly displaying their freedom to inhabit and to claim public spaces and to move through them, *flaneur*-like, at ease and in leisure within the urban landscape, proclaiming their unmarked presence there, glancing about but also ready to be looked at and to be seen.

And yet what remains invisible in these photos, or hardly perceptible behind the palpable display of Jewish bourgeois comfort, is the assimilationist trajectory that this class identification manifests and represents. Only through a comparison and contrast with Jews residing in nearby smaller villages of the Bukowina or Bessarabia, or in larger nearby towns like the Hasidic center of Sadagora, or with less affluent working-class Jews living in the lower-city area around the Judengasse, or with impoverished non-Jews relegated to the background of these images, can one begin to gain a concrete visual sense of the class mobility and differentiation that Habsburg-era Jewish emancipation had engendered and enabled. These are the historical layers that the snapshot of *one* moment in time cannot possibly reveal.

But perhaps even less apparent in the street photographs than this is the fact that the city through which the strollers move in photos from the 1920s and 1930s is no longer Czernowitz, the "Vienna of the East," the liberal, predominantly German-speaking Austro-Hungarian provincial capital with which the large Jewish bourgeoisie there so strongly identified. It is the Romanian city of Cernăuți. Physical evidence of the transformation can be detected in some of the images: street names have been changed, and they as well as the store signs and placards are written in Romanian, not German. The ideological environment accompanying the Romanian takeover, however, is hardly evident beyond these Romanian street and shop names and advertising displays: the reality that not long after the postwar political transfer of the Bukowina and its absorption into Greater Romania, the region's new rulers instituted a strict policy of Romanianization. Under this rubric, the Romanian language became the language of transaction in business and governmental affairs and the primary language of instruction in state schools. Romanian-born nationals were also privileged in professional and public appointments and promotions, and Romanian cultural institutions and nationalist values were fore-

Figure 15. "In the background . . .": a street photograph captures class differences in Czernowitz (Photograph courtesy of David Glynn)

grounded to the detriment of others. Transfer of political sovereignty from Habsburg Austria to Romania, moreover, had immediate dire consequences for Czernowitz Jews. They were relegated to the status of Romanian "subjects" not "citizens," and many of the emancipatory civil and political rights that they had acquired by 1867 in Habsburg lands were taken away from them (these would be only partially reinstated in the mid-1920s).[7]

Most ominously, the Cernăuţi street photos do not even hint at the existence and rapid growth of Romanian anti-Semitism and fascism in the decades of the 1920s and 1930s—the increasing restrictions, quotas, discriminatory exclusions, harassment, and violence that Jews came to face and endure under Romanian rule. It was, for example, outside of the Café l'Europe on the Strada Iancu Flondor (as the Romanians had renamed the Herrengasse)—almost directly across the street from where photographers snapped pictures of strolling passers-by—that an incident occurred in the fall of 1926 that fed right-wing Romanian anti-Semitic hatred and resulted in the assassination of David Fallik, a Jewish student. A teacher of Romanian history named Diaconescu, who had been a government-appointed external examiner for the qualifying baccalaureate examination for admission to university studies, was accosted and manhandled on leaving the café by an angry crowd.[8] The assailants, mainly Jewish high school students and a few Jewish adults, were enraged by the fact that Diaconescu had failed ninety-two out of ninety-four Jews who had taken the test at the Aron Pumnul Lycée—a deliberate strategy, they maintained, to introduce an illegal *numerus clausus* ("limited number" or quota) policy and deny Jews university admission.[9] Earlier in the day, Diaconescu had been confronted publicly on the same matter by David Fallik, one of the failed students, who questioned his motives and who, frustrated by the response, had then shouted "Down with Diaconescu!" Fallik and others from the Herrengasse incident—twenty-four altogether—were arrested, charged with "assault of a public official in the performance of his duty," and put on trial. The local Romanian press fueled an anti-Semitic backlash by charging that Fallik and the other accused Jews had not just acted spontaneously from anger or simply insulted Romanian authority. Their aggression, it was alleged, was in fact at the vanguard of a long-planned attack by Jews on the "genuine citizens" of the Romanian nation. A few weeks later, while the defendants were leaving the court during a recess in their trial, a Romanian student and fascist sympathizer from the University of Iaşi, Neculai Totu, shot David Fallik twice in the abdomen.[10] Fallik died two days later. His killer confessed to premeditated murder but justified his actions because "the Jew Fallik . . . had struck a teacher, and in striking a teacher . . . had struck the State itself." Judged "not guilty" after a ten-minute jury deliberation in a trial in the Southern Bukowina city of Cîmpulung, Totu was touted as a hero. His lawyer, one of hundreds who had volunteered for the honor of defending him, celebrated his client's release with a portentous threat to Jews. Like Fallik, the lawyer announced, "so will die all the country's enemies, by innumerable bullets . . . fired against the filthy beasts."[11]

Without the benefit of historical contextualization, therefore, the pre-Shoah "normality," "comfort," and the documentation of Jewish "belonging" that the Holocaust Museum archivist wished the street photographs to display is, in fact, significantly compromised. And even when read contextually and comparatively, employing cultural and historical knowledge from our present-day perspectives, the photos still cannot reveal to us the contradictions at the heart of these city strolls: that the middle-class Jews depicted within them continued in large measure to live, and to walk through the streets, as though they were really still in Habsburg Czernowitz and not in Romanian Cernăuţi. In all likelihood, the conversations they had with each other on the street, in the stores, at the cafés, and at home were in German, not in the mandated Romanian. "I remember it as an Austrian way of life," writes Pearl Fichmann. "Those traditions were nurtured in the home as if Romania was only an incidental whim of history."[12]

Whatever their significance, the dynamic street scenes depicted in the photos were, of course, gone, in the past, evocable on the Olga Kobylyanska in 1998 only in Carl and Lotte's nostalgic memory. As we talked on the park bench, and as we looked at the photos together, their stories filled in the images, deepened their meaning, provided a fuller and also a more contradictory picture of the city's layered past. When we looked up, however, we were once again struck by the appearances of a very different present.

And yet, despite the apparent economic difficulties that Ukraine was undergoing at the time of our visit, we realized that this street and the Ukrainian Chernivtsi through which we were strolling was anything but a museum display contrasting a bygone, culturally "richer," past era with a seemingly less attractive present. The contemporary city and street were very much alive, despite their relative poverty, animated by a new energy and activity—different from what they had once been, to be sure, but inhabited by a large youthful population for whom Chernivtsi, not Czernowitz, was home, and for whom the present and future, not the past, were the focus of engagement. In contrast to the prewar era, the number of Jews in the city was now small, most of them ex-Russians or Bessarabians who did not at all identify with German culture. We four—Carl and Lotte who had once lived here, and the two of us for whom this place had existed only through the images and stories on which postmemory feeds—were here only as sojourners. With our camcorder and still cameras, shooting videos and photos of ourselves and of our surroundings, we created new images and stories that blended points of memory into present-day settings. Things had certainly changed. But life continued.

# FOUR

# The Idea of Czernowitz

At home, we spoke German—my mother sang us German lullabies
and ballads. But we couldn't stay with the German language. At five,
we had to go to the Romanian kindergarten and then to Romanian
school, where we only had a few hours of German. I had a lot of
difficulty with the transition. I missed the close connection to a
language, with words that lived in me and in which I lived. I never
learned German systematically, but I always spoke and read it. But
my German remained stuck in the "then"—archaic—but still, it is
my language, and I always return to it.

ILANA SHMUELI
"Über mein Czernowitz erzählen"

"I knew that Romanian students were beating up Jews, but I went to school
with many young Romanian men, and I could never associate them with
such acts," Lotte explained as we came into sight of the building that had
housed the Cernăuți University, and where some departments of the Jurii
Fed'kovych University are still located. We had asked Lotte and Carl if,
after our Herrengase stroll, they would take us to see their former schools
and the site of the private girls' school that Lotte's sister Fritzi had started
in the 1930s and where she met her future husband, Eduard Bong, a fellow
teacher. As Jewish teachers, neither could find work in state schools by that
time. Carl had shown us the junior and senior high school he had attended,
the predominantly Jewish Liceul L-3, on the Kuczurmarerstrasse (now
Tchervonoarmiyska), near the Austria-Platz. It was an imposing building
with a large circular staircase, presently still in use as a high school. Carl
had good memories of his school days: he had excelled in mathematics and
sciences but had also learned Latin and some Greek, and he was proud of

still being able to recite French and German poems that he had been made to memorize.

"When I started school here in 1922," Carl had explained, "the language of instruction had just been changed to Romanian, but most of our teachers did not know it. It was pretty funny." The private Hoffmann Lyzeum (in Romanian, Școala particulară de fete Hoffman) that Lotte had attended in the early 1930s was located nearby on the Altgasse (now Lesi Ukrainki), in the Morgenroit building that had once served as a Yiddish cultural center, next to the Scala movie theater, formerly the venue of the Yiddish theater. "I was lucky that my parents sent me to a public Romanian elementary school," Lotte had told us when we looked at the building that had housed her high school. "I learned excellent Romanian there, and that would stand me in good stead in the Hoffmann Lyzeum. You see, even in the private schools, they were required to teach us Romanian language and literature, and to use Romanian as the language of instruction, because we had to be prepared to take the national baccalaureate exams. We had to compete with students whose native language was Romanian. I was amazed that I passed the baccalaureate on the first round; I didn't think I would. But it did not do me much good, did it? I still could not study medicine and fulfill my lifelong dream to become a doctor. By 1936, you see, Jews were no longer admitted to medicine. And my parents would not let me go study in France. I cried for the entire summer after my baccalaureate. My father insisted I study law and I did for a year, though it was already hard for Jews to be admitted to that faculty. I hated law, so I enrolled in languages, which I liked and was always good at, but that was never my first choice. It was just one of the few faculties that still accepted Jews. It was during that latter time that I walked to class, and saw them."

"Whom did you see?" we asked in unison.

"I wasn't that close, so I could not be absolutely sure, but I saw a large group of boys I knew from my classes standing with clubs in front of the university. Something told me that they were waiting for Jews to beat up. I turned on my heels and went back home. To this day, I still cannot believe that the boys I knew, the boys I had flirted with and went to school with, would do such a thing."

"I had left Czernowitz long before that time," Carl added," but I experienced at least one such beating when I was finishing my studies at the Bucharest Polytechnic Institute. My brother and I went to have a free lunch every day at a cafeteria for war orphans, but unfortunately that cafeteria was right near the medical school, a notorious hotbed of anti-Semitic thugs. After

I got a severe beating, I convinced the authorities to serve those free meals to us in the dormitory where we were staying."

## ROMANIANIZATION

Throughout the 1920s, ideologues of Romanianization employed the educational system as the main institutional medium to transform the predominantly multiethnic Northern Bukowina into an overwhelmingly Romanian province. Their most persistent and intense attack was on the urban state-supported secondary schools—the lycées and gymnasia—and on the university in Cernăuţi. In these institutions, German and, overwhelmingly, German-speaking Jewish students predominated in enrollment—a reflection of their status as an urban elite during the Habsburg era. The measures implemented by the Romanian authorities did not spare the Ukrainian or Polish lycées, but, by far, their main thrust was directed at the German-Jewish Liceul de Stat No. 3 in Cernăuţi and the German Liceul Real No. 2, where the vast majority of registered students were also Jews.

As Irina Livezeanu has indicated in her discussion of the nationalization of the secondary schools in the Bukowina, "to many Romanians ... Jewish preponderance in urban secondary schools, and especially in the provincial capital's lycées, flew in the face of national pride and nationalist goals."[1] Even though Romanian, as the main language of instruction, and classes in the "history and geography of the Fatherland" were mandated in the curriculum, the more extreme Romanian nationalists increasingly also pushed for the drastic reduction in enrollment, if not exclusion, of Jewish youths from state-run academic institutions, especially from the university. Romanian youths, enrolled in larger numbers, would then gain the training to dominate all sectors of the economic and cultural scene.

It may seem surprising, but initially the policy of Romanianization instituted in the Bukowina was, in fact, predominantly aimed at Ukrainians in the province. They not only made up the majority population in the Northern Bukowina but had also established an energetic Ukrainian National Committee for the Paris Peace Conference that opposed Romanian ambitions and actively claimed the province as part of a West Ukrainian state. Although the Ukrainians failed to gain diplomatic support for their claim—largely because, unlike the Romanians, they had neither the backing of a victorious Allied power nor a convincing legal argument to support ethnic or national association with a prewar state—the dispute continued, escalating into a brief military conflict in the Northern Bukowina in 1919. Romanian forces prevailed after some initial setbacks, effectively sealing Peace Conference approval for the annexation of the province into Greater Romania.[2] But the confrontation fed Romanian nationalist insecurities, especially in nascent right wing groups, reinforcing their distrust and hostility toward potential challengers or competitors from other ethnic communities. The Ukrainians in the Northern Bukowina and Hungarians in Transylvania were perceived as threats. But very quickly, so were Germans and, especially, Jews—groups that had strongly identified with and benefited from a dominant German-language culture and from Habsburg imperial rule.

In order to quell occasional outbreaks of unrest on the part of Ukrainian nationalists in the Northern Bukowina in the early 1920s, Romanian authorities imposed a range of temporary restrictive measures in the province, including martial law, censorship, confinement, and limitations on group assembly—actions intended to eliminate Ukrainian organizations that were considered breeding sites for irredentist "troublemakers."[3] The main regional effort of Romanian authorities throughout the 1920s, however, was focused on gaining Romanian economic and cultural dominance in the Bukowina through the curtailment of Habsburg-era pluralism and the institutions sustaining and benefiting non-Romanian groups. The central element in this process was the Romanian language—the requirement that Romanian be used in legal, administrative, and commercial transactions. In its most visible and, perhaps, least alarming public dimension, this required the replacing of "old era" German public signposts with Romanian ones and the confiscating by the police of so-called "Austrian icons" from public establishments: from inns, coffeehouses, and restaurants.[4]

The language requirement affected many Habsburg-era civil servants who could not maintain jobs without passing a proficiency exam in Romanian. Max Gottfried, Lotte's father, who had worked as a lawyer for the Austrian Ministry of Finance and who was largely monolingual in German, had to seek employment in the private sector in the 1920s. He never learned enough Romanian to go to court and had to leave that task to his Romanian-speaking colleagues. Teachers who taught in Ukrainian or in German—the latter consisting primarily of Jews—were either fired or demoted from state-supported educational facilities.

There is, in fact, little doubt that, despite its broad impact on all non-Romanian populations in the territories acquired after 1918, it was the Jewish population that was most profoundly affected by the policy of Romanianization in the northern Bukowina. In Cernăuți, middle-class and wealthier Jews with the financial means to do so responded to the increasing exclusion of

Figure 16. Postcard of Str. Regele Ferdinand, Cernăuți, the former Enzensberg-Hauptstrasse, featuring the famous Schiffhaus. The writing on the front of the card illustrates the stubborn persistence of German even as Romanianization was being imposed. (Hirsch-Spitzer archive)

their children from the public schools by enrolling them in private schools—many of which were established during this period. Yet the reintroduction of the baccalaureate examination in Greater Romania in 1925 to screen secondary school students for university admission and the increasingly restrictive enrollment practices in the various university faculties were much more insurmountable barriers. Jewish students, who had regularly made up at least one-third of the total university enrollment, were specifically targeted in the undeclared *numerus clausus* policy that was not only intended to block their university admission but also their eventual entry into the postgraduate professions and the leadership stratum of society. The Fallik killing in 1926—an extreme, well-publicized, but by no means isolated incident of right-wing violence directed against Jews during these years—illuminated the increasingly open anti-Semitism of these times. Indeed, throughout the 1920s, militant right-wing Romanian students, lending numerical support to extremist nationalist and openly anti-Semitic political groups like Alexandru C. Cuza's League of National Christian Defense (LANC or Liga Apărării Național Creştine) grew more numerous. Cuza, a professor of law at Iași

University, had defended his own and his league's anti-Semitic agitation because the *jidani* (equivalent of *kikes*) in Romania, "enemies of Christianity, had gained economic control of the cities and destroyed the middle class." The "first objective" of the LANC, therefore, was "*the elimination of the kikes* from all branches of activity, especially the universities."[5]

The agitation against Jewish rights and for the implementation of the *numerus clausus* escalated greatly in 1923—precisely during months of debate in the parliament about the new Romanian constitution. The Treaty of Saint-Germain, signed between the newly created Austria and the Allies at the end of Paris Peace Conference, had not only transferred the Bukowina to Romania but had also imposed articles to be incorporated into the Romanian constitution that recognized Jewish emancipation and granted Jews citizenship rights which included various minority protection clauses.[6]

Mentored by Cuza and led by the firebrand student activist Corneliu Zelea Codreanu, incidents of violence and intimidation of Jews and the lockout of Jewish students from universities intensified with the passage of the new constitution in 1924. The growing and ever more virulent anti-Semitism, moreover, was openly justified as necessary to protect "true Romanians" against the "threat of Bolshevism" and "alien domination." Right-wing agitators used anti-Semitic rhetoric to stir up students nationally against the moderate democratic and socialist groups that emerged on the Romanian political and cultural scene after the war. Not surprisingly, but also most portentously, in 1927 anti-Semitism became the central hate measure to attract supporters for the newly founded League of the Archangel Michael—the fascist "Iron Guard," as it came to be popularly known, that Corneliu Codreanu established as a potential mass movement promising Romanians "resurrection and salvation" and the end of "their slavery to kikes."[7]

With the Iron Guard, Codreanu attempted to organize on a basis that went beyond his original supporters among students and younger Romanians, hoping to attract a larger and potentially much more significant group—the peasantry. It was, however, not until the economic effects of the worldwide depression began to have an impact on Romania in the early 1930s that the suitable conditions to implement his plan arose. The sharp fall in prices for agricultural products had dire consequences in the countryside, where desperate peasants, surviving largely on credit through high-interest loans that right-wing agitators propagandized as deriving from Jewish moneylenders, became receptive to his radical anti-Semitic message. In the political realm, as well, peasants and young urban ethnic Romanians were disillusioned by the failure of the National Peasant Party to deliver on many of the reform promises that its leaders had made when they gained power from the long-ruling National Liberal Party in an electoral landslide in 1928. Anti-Semitic disruptions, which in the 1920s generally occurred in or close to academic centers, now broke out in rural market towns and villages. They involved thousands of persons, incited to rage against Jews by Iron Guard or Cuza-inspired LANC agitators, and projected the impending threat of pogroms.[8]

In the Bukowina, right-wing ideas driven by anti-Semitism also took hold among the non-Jewish Volksdeutsche (ethnic German) minority, many of whose members became supporters of National Socialist ideology emanating from Germany, especially after Hitler's accession to power in 1933. Extremism also intensified within the ethnic Ukrainian majority which, under a new generation of young leaders, established a radical nationalist and anti-Semitic Legion of Ukrainian Revolutionaries—an organization that advocated not only for an independent Ukrainian state, but also for one in which neither Jews nor other ethnic minorities would be permitted.[9]

When the Liberal Party returned to power in the Romanian national election of 1933, moreover, it concentrated its efforts for economic recovery on the build-up of the industrial rather than the agricultural sector, which led to the further impoverishment of the rural areas and to an overall fall in the standard of living. Instead of being able to stem support for radical groups like LANC or the Iron Guard, the Liberals were chagrined to realize that the unstable and difficult economic situation fueled their growth. In order to maintain themselves in power, therefore, the Liberal authorities briefly resorted to the use of raw force against Iron Guard radical national-ists. The government banned the group for some years, after a number of Iron Guard members were implicated in and convicted for their role in the assassination of the Liberal Prime Minister I. G. Duca in 1933. For the most part, however, until their electoral defeat in 1937, the Liberals attempted to undercut the more extreme right-wing nationalists by appropriating and implementing measures, or at least taking up rhetorical positions, that the extremists had promoted in their appeal to the ethnic Romanian public.[10] In 1934, they appointed the Bukowina-born historian of Romania Ion Nistor as minister of labor. He initiated their new Anti-Crisis Program with a speech in which he stated that Romanians needed to "proceed in a careful but determined manner in order gradually to wrench the bread out of the mouths of the Jews."[11] In 1936, the Liberal-dominated legislature passed a Protection of National Work law mandating that 80 percent of the employees/workers in any enterprise and at least 50 percent of management had to be Romanian.[12]

In Cernăuţi, radical anti-Semitic groups continued their agitation during the mid-1930s. Codreanu supporters, students, and other toughs, as Lotte confirmed in her recollection about this time, regularly blocked Jews from entering the university and from passing through the gates of the city's main park, the Grădina Publică, the much-beloved Volksgarten of the Habsburg era. Scuffles and fights broke out when Jews resisted such intimidation.

One incident in 1936 in Cernăuţi brought back memories of the Fallik slaying ten years earlier and of the anti-Semitic passions it had unleashed. A clash in the city park in the summer between radical rightist Romanian youths and young Jews belonging to a Bund-spawned socialist group, determined to resist bullying and anti-Semitic excesses, led to the knifing and death of one of the leaders of the Romanian gang. The police arrested thirty members of the Jewish Jugendbund who had been involved in the fray and, in the course of beating the group's leaders, apparently pushed one of them, the 26-year-old optometrist Edi Wagner, out of a second story window—a fall that led to his death.

Wagner, a talented musician, passionate about folk music and especially the balalaika, had also been the organizer of a young people's orchestra. News of his death caused great consternation among Jews in the city and added greatly to the general unease within the community. But the Grădina Publică confrontation also stirred up non-Jews. Some twenty thousand people—Romanians, but also many Ukrainians and Volksdeutsche—converged on the Piaţa Unirii by the city hall to mourn the Romanian youth killed in the park, while ignoring Wagner's death altogether. They assembled under a large banner held up by blue-shirted paramilitary members of Alexandru Cuza's LANC that read: "Christians United against the Jews."[13]

When, in the election of 1937, no single contending party was able to muster the necessary 40 percent of the vote to form a government, King Carol II of Romania, who had returned to the throne from exile in 1930, appointed a minority group to power—the National Christian Party (PNC), headed by the Transylavanian poet Octavian Goga and Alexandru Cuza.

In foreign policy, as Paul Shapiro has argued, this "Germanophile government . . . burned [Romania's] bridges to the Western Powers and turned it toward [Nazi] Germany."[14] In domestic affairs, Prime Minister Goga immediately promulgated a series of administrative measures that would insure "Romania for the Romanians" by attacking the economic, cultural, and citizenship status of the country's Jewish minority. Most far-reaching of all, Goga's so-called Revision of Citizenship decree of January 1938 invalidated all citizenship papers granted to Jews after the First World War—quickly rendering some 225,000 Jews (over 33 percent of the total Jewish population of the country) stateless, regardless of nativity. A large percentage of those persons lived in the Bukowina, and especially in Cernăuţi.[15]

Loss of Romanian citizenship left Jews without elementary rights in the state. Some professional associations viewed the decree's promulgation as license to oust Jewish practitioners among them. The Bucharest bar association expelled all of its Jewish members. Jewish physicians and pharmacists holding foreign diplomas were required to prove their right to continue to practice—and any of them who had been stricken from the citizenship rolls due to the decree immediately lost their licenses. Press privileges were withdrawn from Jewish journalists, and newspapers and periodicals owned by reclassified Jews—fourteen in Cernăuţi alone—were shut down. Jewish petty merchants, stripped of citizenship, were forbidden to sell alcohol or tobacco in the cities and to carry out any commercial transactions in the rural villages—interdictions that meant ruin for many of them.[16]

At the same time, PNC Supreme Chief Cuza also launched an all-out anti-Semitic terror campaign that foreshadowed the Nazi Storm Trooper rampages against Jews that would take place in Vienna and throughout Austria in the aftermath of the Austrian Anschluss with Germany in March 1938. He unleashed his paramilitary supporters, the Lancieri, against Jews, allowing them to intimidate and plunder almost at will—profitable undertakings that swelled membership in the group from thousands to tens of thousands within weeks. Only Goga and the king, unwilling at this time to further alienate non-Fascist countries to whom Jewish leaders appealed, managed to persuade him to curb the violence.[17]

In his memoir, the Czernowitz-born journalist and poet Alfred Kittner recalls the immediate effects of the Goga-Cuza regime. Referring to the interdictions against Jews as officials even in private educational institutions, he relates how the elderly Professor Hoffmann, the director of the well-regarded Hoffmann Lyzeum where Lotte had been a student, had to give up his position to a gentile Romanian. "The Gymnasium was also not permitted to keep its old name in 1937," Kittner indicated, and "was renamed Liceul de fete Julia Haşdeu." And regarding his own fate as a journalist, and that of the German-language Jewish newspaper *Der Tag* (The Day), where he was working at the time, Kittner writes:

> After working at the paper for several years, first as local reporter, then as secretary of the editorial department and finally as editor of the editorial pages, I was again jobless when the paper was shut down by the fascist

Goga-Cuza regime.... First they decreed that the first page, a news page, appear in Romanian, though the lead article could still appear in German. That lasted only a few months. Then the entire paper was decreed a democratic Jewish rag and was closed down. The reporters lost their discounts on public transportation, and we had to resign from the journalists' union, or rather, we were kicked out.[18]

To be sure, the overall financial position of Jews in Romania in the late 1930s was still strong enough so that a boycott declared in reaction to Goga's decrees had a profound effect. Coming on the heels of a general international recession in 1937 in which the Western market for Romania's agricultural products dried up, the withdrawal of bank deposits by Jews, their sale of stocks, and their refusal to make tariff and tax payments managed to paralyze the country's economic life and to ruin its credit status abroad. But while economic factors, together with the increasing instability, did undoubtedly affect the king's decision to terminate the right-wing government he had empowered, few of the measures against the Jewish population that had been implemented were withdrawn.[19]

As the 1930s neared their end, the prognosis for Jews in Greater Romania was indeed a bleak one. And yet unlike in Germany or Austria, where Nazi *Entjudung* (removal of Jews) policies at this time were directed at forcing Jews to abandon German lands through emigration, the topic of emigration—how to get out and where to go—did not seem to have been at the forefront of contemporary discussions among Romanian Jews. Dedicated Zionists certainly continued to contemplate a move to Palestine, and others made inquiries as well. Carl Hirsch writes in his memoir: "While I was out of work [in] early 1938, I wrote a number of job applications to different foreign countries (their respective departments of public works) and I got a few replies, one from Ecuador and one from Turkey. But in the meantime I was [again] employed, and didn't follow up on these offers."[20] Generally speaking, while emigration was certainly being considered—and undertaken by a small minority when possible—there seemed to be no sense of panic among Jews in Romania about "getting out" such as erupted among their coreligionists in Germany and Austria during these years.

"Many of us thought, Romania is not Germany," Carl told us. We had interrupted our walk through the city in order to have coffee and a pastry, but continued to videotape Carl and Lotte as we carried on with our conversation. "We were hoping that war could be avoided. The Hitler-Stalin pact and Chamberlain's appeasement of Hitler made some of us think that it could be, but, of course, we were naïve. We saw what was happening as a moment of madness that would blow over."

"By that time, we were no longer allowed to speak German on the street or in any public places," Lotte observed. "I can still hear them yelling at us everywhere: 'Vorbiți numai românește!' [Romanian only!] Signs were posted in all the schools. This was aimed at Jews. Many people did not know Romanian very well, and they had to make up words if a policeman walked into a shop. Or they would translate literally from German. We had a lot of laughs at the creative solutions they came up with."

I asked Carl and Lotte about Aharon Appelfeld's first novel, *Badenheim 1939:* "I always thought *Badenheim* was an allegory about Austrian and German Jews, going to coffeehouses, taking the waters, listening to concerts, refusing to see that the world was closing in around them. Do you think he could have been describing Romanian Jews and, particularly, the Jews in Czernowitz, during the late 1930s?"

"Appelfeld was a child in Czernowitz then," Carl replied. "We were not as carefree as all that, we were worried, but not enough to flee. In fact, those who had gone to Western Europe to study—Hedy Brenner, Paul Celan, many others—came back, one by one, after Kristallnacht and the Anschluss. The war, as you know, came to Czernowitz much later."

RESISTANCES

Jewish resistance to Romanianization and Romanian anti-Semitism was, of course, a topic that repeatedly emerged during this trip. Carl took a packet of old photos he had brought along on the trip out of his briefcase, and after we ordered some more drinks, he and Lotte settled in to talk to us about this subject. "Look," Carl said,

> I wouldn't exactly call it "resistance," but even when I was still very young and in elementary school, my mother sent me to another school in the afternoon where we learned modern Hebrew, reading, writing, and conversation. It was called the Safa Ivria, and I went there every day throughout my early school years, and I learned Hebrew pretty well. Like many other Czernowitz Jews, my mother believed that the recent Balfour Declaration and the establishment of a British mandate over Palestine were steps towards a Jewish homeland. In that sense she and the others hedged their bets about the future of Jews in the diaspora by flirting with Zionism. And learning modern Hebrew was a way to give us a secular Jewish foundation and to supplement our public education. In the summer of 1921,

after my father died, I was also sent by a charity organization to a vacation Hebrew-language summer camp in the Carpathian mountains. It was run by the people from Safa Ivria, my Hebrew School.

But there was also Yiddish—the Yiddish supporters were in competition with Zionists pushing Hebrew. A year after the Hebrew camp, my mother sent my sister Lilly and me to a summer camp near the Polish border that was run by the Yiddisher Shulferain. As war orphans we went there for free, we did not have to pay a fee. We were encouraged to learn to speak Yiddish there and taught to read Yiddish stories and poems. Eliezer Shteynbarg, the famous Yiddish poet who lived in Czernowitz, visited the camp, and we read many of his poems, mainly fables from everyday life. Politically, these Yiddish-speakers were socialists—Bundists and cultural nationalists. They wanted socialism to transform European society so that Jews could be accepted as a national minority in the countries where they lived. They viewed socialism as the antidote to fascism and anti-Semitism (which they blamed on capitalism). They did not want *aliyah* [emigration] to Palestine, and so they fostered Yiddish and not Hebrew. [21]

Having heard Carl talk on many occasions about Hashomer Hatzair, the youth group that had meant so much to him, I asked him to tell us about the role of labor Zionism in relation to the situation at the time and about his choice to join this youth group.

"I joined Hashomer Hatzair when I was in the eighth grade, between my thirteenth and fourteenth birthday," Carl answered. "Probably Jascha Flexor, my close friend, convinced me to join. The few years with Hashomer were very important for shaping my Weltanschauung. Part of it was the critique of the bourgeois world to which our other classmates aspired to belong; part of it was the opposition to the world of our fathers."

In his memoir, Carl expands on these points:

But I abandoned my allegiance to Zionism itself after a few years. I realized that the land of Palestine was not an empty land ready to receive Jews. The determined *chalutzim* [early Jewish immigrants to Palestine] hoped to overcome these difficulties or did not want to think about them, but I explained to my group, sometime around 1931, that I am abandoning the Zionist goal but not the ideals and moral values we learned in the movement and not my belief in socialism. I told them that I hoped the coming proletarian revolution would solve not only the plight of the proletariat but also the Jewish problem, which we considered caused by economic problems of capitalism—quite naïve I could say retrospectively. But, when I meet some of my old friends from Hashomer in Israel now, after sixty years, we still feel close. This was probably the most formative influence on my character.[22]

The Zionist youth movement Hashomer Hatzair had been brought to Cernăuți from Vienna by a group of young men and women who had spent the First World War as refugees in the imperial capital. In Vienna, while their fathers or older brothers were off fighting in the trenches and battle-fields of the war, many young Bukowinians had become members of a Jewish youth organization—the Shomrim (Hebrew for *watchmen* or the *guardians*, the plural of *hashomer*, or *guard*), named in honor of young Jews who had established sentry units to safeguard Jewish settlements in Palestine during the Second Aliyah.[23] The Shomrim had originated in Galicia in 1913, but the organization evolved and grew in membership in Vienna during the war and refugee years, where it merged with Ze'irei Zion (the Youth of Zion), a youth movement stressing Zionism, Jewish history, and socialist thought, and became known by its new, combined name, Hashomer Hatzair (The Young Guard).[24]

"Look, have you seen these photos before?" Carl asked, searching through his packet to extract a few. "Here is one that you definitely know. There is another copy of it that was published in Gold's *Geschichte der Juden in der Bukowina*." He pointed to a portrait of his own Hashomer Hatzair group. We estimated that it must have been taken in the early months of 1928, when Carl was sixteen years old, some ten years after the youth movement had been established in Cernăuți. In the photo, Carl is standing near the middle of the second row, one of eleven extremely serious-looking young men belonging to the Kwuzah Ophek—his Hashomer core unit. Seated in the center of the front row is the group leader (the Rosh Kwuzah), Israel (Lulziu) Chalfen, who was about four or five years older than Carl and a future medical doctor who would emigrate to a kibbutz in Palestine and write a biography of Paul Celan's youth. Jascha Flexor, Carl's best friend, stands first left in the back row, and Jano Melzer, Kwuzah Ophek's previous leader, is next to Carl, behind Chalfen. The pose is formal, taken in a studio with background props, and Carl and the others are all wearing buttoned-up jackets, dress trousers, and well-shined street shoes or boots. Only their broad shirt collars, worn open and folded over on the outside of their jackets, hint of some shared organizational outfit.

"The funny thing about the Hashomer," Carl said amusedly, "was that, despite its Hebrew language and aliyah ideology, it came to us through Vienna, in German. It was quite similar to the *Wandervogel* and other early twentieth-

Figure 17. Carl Hirsch's Hashomer Hatzair group in Cernăuţi, 1928. Top row, from left, Jascha Flexor, Moses Brachfeld, Jano Melzer, Carl Hirsch, Grischa Levant, Menachem Bickel; bottom row, [?] Schlomiuk, [?] Singer, Israel Chalfen, [?] Gredinger, Max Chalfen. (Hirsch-Spitzer archive; this photograph also appears in Hugo Gold, ed., *Geschichte der Juden in der Bukowina,* vol. 1 [Tel Aviv: Olamenu, 1962], facing 149)

century German youth movements. Their outdoor and athletic activities appealed to us greatly, and we loved the summer camps and excursions into the mountains of southern Bukowina, the rafting trips on the Bistriţ River. And, in spite of learning a little Hebrew and singing Hebrew songs, we spoke German at our meetings."

"Paradoxically," I observed, "the Hashomer seemed to consolidate your allegiance to German language and culture." Carl did not disagree.

Certainly, by the time Carl's photo was taken, the popularity of Hashomer Hatzair was at its height. Carl and the others in his core unit belonged to the most influential Jewish youth movement in this region of Eastern Europe—one that had successfully reached across class lines to attract students as well as young workers. And the appeal of their movement in Cernăuţi, as in Vienna, derived from its successful combination of features from three contemporaneous sources: the character-building principles associated with Boy Scouting; the close-to-nature ethos of hiking and physical fitness popular in

Austrian and German *Wandervogel* youth movements from which Jews had been excluded; and a socialist-Zionist ideology stressing educational growth, a collective, communal lifestyle, and ultimate fulfillment through aliyah—emigration and pioneering settlement in Palestine in a kibbutz.[25] Indeed, in its goal of fostering a Zionist national consciousness among Jewish youth—by building Jewish self-awareness and advocating a Jewish national revival in a homeland of their own—the movement did, as Carl indicated, turn away from "the world of our fathers." Its principles, like that of other Zionist organizations, rejected the emancipatory/assimilationist ideology that had characterized the integration of Jews into the dominant European cultural and political mainstream since the end of the eighteenth century.

In Romania and throughout Eastern and Central Europe in the 1920s and 1930s, moreover, the physicality of Hashomer—its stress on its adherents' athleticism, strength, endurance, and on the repudiation of promiscuity and "vices" like alcohol and smoking—was also intended to project the image of the virile "New Jew" and counter anti-Semitic stereotypes of the "effeminate Yid."

In this regard Hashomer members during these decades shared a goal with younger associates and supporters of other Zionist organizations—the largely "national-revival" oriented Blau-Weiss, which Rosa Roth Zuckermann had joined, the Marxist-oriented Poale Zion, to which Carl's Aunt Shulamith (Fritzi) Wurmbrand belonged, and the revisionist, militant Betar. They also complemented non-Zionist, Marxist-socialist, Jewish organizations such as the Jugendbund affiliated with the Bund, to which the ill-fated Edi Wagner and his group of young men had belonged.[26] The "New Jew" was not only meant to be physically fit but also, through an emphasis on manual and agricultural training, able to dispel or undermine the hoary cliché that only associated Jews with commerce, finance, and bent-over bookishness.

Hashomer Hatzair, moreover, as indicated by its name, was also meant to serve as an organization of sentries or guardians willing to stand collectively in protection of Jews against external attack. As such, the "new" Jewish young men and women in this group again shared a purpose with other Jewish youth movements throughout Europe during these decades. Resistance—self-defense—was an element in the ethos of all of them. Despite this fact, however, Hashomer members seem not to have grouped together to oppose anti-Semitic hooligans with force in Cernăuți in the 1920s and early 1930s, the way members of the Jugendbund did in the Grădina Publică in 1936—and neither Carl nor Lotte could recall any incident of militant resistance by Shomrim during these times. Hashomer responses, and those of other

Figure 18. Hashomer Hatzair outing in the Romanian Southern Bukowina resort town of Dorna Vatra, on the Bistriţ River, 1930 (Hirsch-Spitzer Archive)

moderate organizations in Greater Romania in these decades, thus differed from those that would be manifested by its leaders and members who still remained in Europe during the Second World War and the Holocaust, when many of them were involved in orchestrating resistance in ghettoes and camps. And, of course, they differed significantly, both ideologically and in militancy from Ze'ev (Vladimir) Jabotinsky's Betar, which had relatively few adherents in the Bukowina and throughout Romania. That activist organization, Zionist without a socialist component, called for systematic training for young Jews in the Diaspora countries and especially in Palestine, where self-defense, boxing, street fighting, small arms use, and paramilitary tactics were taught to its members. Betar promoted aliyah to Palestine by any means possible, whether legal or illegal, and the creation of a Jewish state on both sides of the Jordan river.[27]

"Zionism had strong appeal. But when you think about Jewish resistance to advancing Fascism, don't forget communism and the Soviet Union," Carl pointed out. "While I leaned to the left, I was never actually a communist," he elaborated. "I was a sympathizer. My main interest was to finish school and not risk prison. The Communist Party was illegal in the 1930s, and any leftist activity was forbidden and punishable by long prison terms, beatings, and so forth. Initially, when I was an engineering student, I did participate in discussion groups, and once, in August 1933, they asked me to take part in an antiwar demonstration to commemorate the outbreak of World War I. Because police were all around, the demonstration never took place. But I and a few others were arrested and spent the day in jail. There I was made to witness some heavy beatings by the police, probably as a warning to us. And, I must say, they were successful. I was healed from any further involvement in illegal activities. But when the Red Army marched into Czernowitz in June 1940, I rushed back from Bucharest to hail them."

Certainly, despite the dangers involved in open advocacy and activism, many Cernăuţi and Greater Romania Jews, especially intellectuals, workers, and the less affluent, were drawn to communism and socialism. Among these were Carl's younger brother, Kubi, and Mischa Flexor, the brother of his best friend Jascha, as well as close friends he made during his student engineering days in Bucharest, Lionia Oigenstein, Ernst Neulaender, and Carol Neuman. Neulaender (under his nom-de-guerre, Walter Roman) and Neuman both left Romania in 1937 to fight in the International Brigades against Franco in the Spanish civil war. Neulaender would also later become a member of the French Resistance.[28] They and others admired the egalitarian promises of the Russian Revolution and viewed the Soviet experiment and transformative Marxist ideologies as essential bulwarks against the ever-growing threat of fascism. Indeed, it was perhaps precisely because communism and socialism seemed progressive and forward- and outward-looking—like Zionism, connected to an internationalism that contrasted profoundly with the narrow, restrictive, and exclusionary volkish anti-Semitic nationalism that dominated the Romanian state and politics—that they appealed to so many Romanian Jews.

## THE IDEA OF CZERNOWITZ

"It has always been fascinating to me," I observed, "that throughout these decades of Romanianization and the growing anti-Semitism in Cernăuţi, no matter what your political leanings or affiliations, your bond to German culture and to the German language remained strong. Do you think that we could also think of that as 'resistance'?"

Lotte agreed: "Maintaining the German language and our identification with German culture was very important to us when I was growing up. My sister was sixteen yeas older and a teacher. She took a very active role in my education, and she insisted I learn to speak correct Hochdeutsch [standard German]. We did not really consider ourselves Romanian."

This adherence to German was a core ingredient of what we had begun to think of as "the idea of Czernowitz." That idea, which was both a mental construct and an ideological response, found form in a dual identification for many middle-class and working-class Jews of the interwar generation and their somewhat older siblings: both with a Habsburg world of yester-day that these Jews referenced nostalgically (even though the vast major-ity of them had never personally experienced it) and with a contemporary Austro-German Kulturkreis—a "Deutschtum," to use Karl Emil Franzos's term—from which they were, in fact, geographically and politically removed. Serving as bridge and connection to both of these, the German language gave them access to a rich literary and cultural realm that enabled them to view themselves as still within the circle of Western European cultivation, cosmopolitanism, and urbanity that their parents and grandparents had so esteemed. And it provided them with the hope of an ongoing continuity with that realm, no longer legal and political to be sure, but cultural, through projection and identification. It is important to emphasize, however, that that "German" Czernowitz, for them, quite naturally included the multi-cultural and multilingual flavor that had always animated the city's public life: the mixture of languages (German, Yiddish, Romanian, Ruthenian, Russian) that resulted in a characteristic local jargon; the intersection of West and East, urban and rural, modern and traditional. Rose Ausländer evokes the particularities of Bukowina's German that emerged from all this: "The different linguistic influences naturally colored the Bukowina German—unfavorably, from the perspective of the linguistic purists and the insecure. But the language was also enriched through new words and expressions. It had a special physiognomy, its own palette. Under the surface of the speak-able, there were deep, far-reaching roots to the area's many cultures—roots that intersected in multiple ways, and that endowed the sound of words with resonance and imagery, spice, and power."[29]

Czernowitzers still like to debate about whether they spoke Hochdeutsch or "Czernowitzer Deutsch." Zvi Yavetz argues that spoken Czernowitzer Deutsch had its own unique syntactic and grammatical rules: "There was no imperfect. In Czernowitz no one said 'ich lebte, ich hatte, ich sagte [I lived, I had, I said].' People used the perfect. 'Ich habe gelebt, ich habe gehabt, ich habe gesagt, etc.' In classical German, the sentences are long and the verb appears at the end of the sentence, almost always following several complicated subordinated clauses.... In Czernowitzer Deutsch, sentences are short, and the verb appears right after the subject."[30]

Even those who spoke the most correct Hochdeutsch, however, acquired and incorporated the city's linguistic mixture into their daily speech. In Czernowitz, German was spiced with Yiddish and various other regional expressions. *Schmetten* was routinely used instead of *sauer Rahm* for sour cream, from the Slavic equivalent *smetana*, for example; *vinete*, from the Romanian, for eggplant; or *mamaliga* for the Romanian cornmeal dish. *Vişniac* was the fermented sour cherry brandy, from the Romanian *vişine*, instead of the German *Weichseln*, for sour cherries. *Trask*, from Ukrainian, was used to describe a big party, and *puretz*—the Ukrainian term for rich person—was used to mock someone who was putting on airs. Other standard Ukrainian-based expressions were so common that many did not even know they were not German words: *piste* for boring from the Ukrainian *pusto* (empty) and *dillen* for make endless, meaningless talk. These words were Germanized and incorporated into grammatical German sentences that remained incomprehensible outside the region: "Dill mich bitte nicht mit diesem pisten Gerede" ("Please don't keep bugging me with your boring talk"). Many of the Yiddish expressions used routinely also had Slavic origins, among them *Babe* (grandmother), *Tateh* (father). Czernowitzers of all ethnicities shifted into Yiddish to spice up their German, their Romanian, or Ukrainian. You did not have to be Jewish to speak some Yiddish words and understand them. Anyone would know *meshugge* (crazy), *metziyeh* (bargain), *tsures* (worries), or *meshpuche* (family); or that a *groisse toive* was a big favor, or that if you admonished someone to "hakh mich nicht im czainik," you meant for them to stop annoying you with their banter (literally: to stop knocking on the kettle). Anyone would be able to sing "Oyfn pripetchik brent a faierl" (in the fireplace burns a little fire) Some expressions were utterly unique to Czernowitz, such as the incredibly common exclamation "Ahi!" or "Ahi—auf dein Kopf." It occurred so often that a statistician was moved to do a survey about its frequency in the late 1930s. Its source is unknown, but some have speculated there was a feared Ukrainian executioner named Ahi and that the expression originated as a warning about his presence in the vicinity.[31] In one of his characteristically apt comments on the Czernowitz-L listserv, Cernăuţi native Hardy Breier sums up the linguistic mixture well, "We read Rumanian, Yiddish and of course German. We cursed in Russian, Ukrainian and Yiddish. But never in German! Never heard German insults."[32]

For Cernăuţi Jews, the city's Austrian identity disappeared gradually, almost imperceptibly. Vera Hacken describes the atmosphere of her youth in the 1920s in lyrical terms: "Separated from the cultural, social, and religious Jewish life [in the rest of Europe], we nevertheless blossomed and were able to live in the comfort of a few, yes, idyllic years in which we could still breathe freely. The Great War was over. The general Romanianization had not yet shown its teeth, the Romanian anti-Semitism had not yet found the time to become militant, Hitler's hoarse warnings had not penetrated our world. Czernowitz still breathed the unchanged air of the old Austrian spirit of the bourgeois idyll for which the Bukowinians spread throughout the world still yearn today."[33]

The fact that Lotte's and Carl's parents and many of their contemporaries, who were only in their forties at the end of the First World War, never actually learned more than a few words of market Romanian shows how much they resisted the policy of Romanianization. Although their children were schooled in Romanian, the parents insisted that they be taught correct German, as well as French and, in many cases, English. As Aharon Appelfeld's reminiscences of his grandparents indicate, moreover, Yiddish also continued to be spoken in the villages around Cernăuţi, especially by the older generations and by rural Jews who, like their urban counterparts, resisted the imposition of Romanian. But, importantly, Yiddish continued to be practiced as a literary language among urban Yiddishist intellectuals and was reinforced by visits of Yiddish writers and theatrical performance groups. They fostered language instruction in Yiddish schools and thereby strengthened the connection to international Jewish movements advocating Yiddish as the national diaspora language of the Jews.

And yet, the imposition of cultural Romanianization was often violent. The last German production in the beautiful Cernăuţi Municipal Theater took place as early as January 22, 1922. It was Schiller's *The Robbers,* appropriate for a theater at whose entrance a larger than life statue of the great dramatist had stood since the theater's construction, almost two decades earlier. On that January evening, Romanian students stormed the theater, stopping the performance under the pretext that the length of the play would delay a Romanian performance scheduled to take place later during the evening.[34] The interrupted Schiller performance resumed the next night in the German House. The statue of Schiller was also moved there and the Municipal Theater, now graced by a new statue of the Romanian poet Mihai Eminescu, devoted itself to presenting Romanian classics, performed by traveling as well as local companies. Nevertheless, German and Yiddish theater did continue to be staged in the 1920s and 1930s in German and Jewish cultural centers and in the philharmonic hall, with memorable guest performances by troupes from the Vienna Burgtheater, the Operetta Theater, the Reinhardt Bühne, and the Vilna troupe.

"My sister took me to the Deutsches Haus to hear fairy tales performed in German, and later to concerts in the Musikvereinssaal," Lotte recalled. "I heard Rubinstein and Furchtwängler, for example. My parents spoke some Yiddish, so they took me along to the Yiddish plays, and to German ones, but they never attended the Romanian productions of the National Theater. I did see some great Romanian classics there, and it was a place I could go to with my Romanian and also with my Jewish friends. But our cultural life, our literary conversations and discussions were in German."

Describing Jewish Cernăuţi's social and intellectual life during the interwar years, Zvi Yavetz writes that "one could say that Czernowitz Jews tended to consume rather than to produce culture." He emphasizes the enthusiasm with which primarily the wealthier bourgeoisie attended concerts in the Musikvereinssaal and the Toynbeehalle or welcomed the Bucharest opera and the Vilna Yiddish theater, and enumerates the many international films playing in the city's six movie theaters. But there were few visual artists and few, if excellent, musicians, he maintains, warning, "Paul Celan stated that Czernowitz was a city in which people and books used to live. One should not succumb to nostalgia. Only for a few was literature a point of reference. One loved poetry, but there's no doubt that the large majority preferred the songs of Josef Schmidt to the poems of Alfred Margul-Sperber or Rose Ausländer that appeared in the daily newspapers."[35] Despite his skepticism, however, Yavetz describes a vibrant intellectual scene in which literary and philosophical discussion flourished among young people whose formal studies suffered greatly under anti-Semitic restrictions but who furthered their education in more informal circles. And some of the poets Yavetz sees as underappreciated did manage to forge a remarkable body of literary work. In a recent documentary, the contemporary Yiddish-language Chernivtsi writer Josef Burg remarked on the paradox of the evolution of the Bukowina's remarkable German-Jewish literature: "When Bukowina was part of Austria for two hundred fifty years, there was no major writer with the exception of Karl Emil Franzos. In contrast, between 1918 and 1945, we witnessed a flowering of a generation of wonderful writers. I have trouble understanding this phenomenon. Maybe it was a natural reaction, a way to protest against a world that had disappeared."[36] Or maybe, as Andrei Corbea-Hoisie has suggested, Cernăuţi Jews threw themselves into cultural production as the possibilities of any political influence vanished.[37] But what, ultimately, could the influence of a German-language literature so far removed from the centers of German culture possibly be?

Throughout the 1930s, a group of Bukowina writers, among them Alfred Margul-Sperber, Rose Ausländer, Alfred Kittner, and Siegfried Laufer, sought to answer this question by collecting and selecting the poetry of a number of Jewish German-language writers from the Bukowina with the aim of publishing with a major German or Austrian press a definitive and representative contemporary anthology. Some of these writers had worked together in the 1920s on the local cultural magazine *Der Nerv,* modeled on Karl Kraus's satirical Viennese *Die Fackel* (The Torch) and on other modernist experimental European literary ventures.[38] The planned anthology soon acquired its name, "Die Buche" (the beech tree), a title synonymous with the regional name Bukowina and the culture of the so-called Buchenland, punning also, of course, on *Buch*, or book.

The story of "Die Buche" is in many ways emblematic of the vicissitudes of Bukowina's German-Jewish culture in the interwar period. With it, its editors sought more than recognition of their own place in German-language writing. They sought to monumentalize the persistence of German and of "the idea of Czernowitz" within and despite the city's transformation into Romanian Cernăuți.[39]

In a speech given in Cernăuți some time in the early 1930s, during the rapid rise of National Socialism in Germany and of the Iron Guard in Romania, Alfred Margul-Sperber, poet and editor, poignantly articulated the idea behind the anthology project. Margul-Sperber challenged his audience to consider with him whether more than a decade after the adoption of Romanian as the official language, such a thing as a German-Jewish poetry of the Bukowina did indeed still exist. In an attempt to answer this question, Margul-Sperber moved from textual to contextual concerns, insisting that the production of Bukowina's Jewish German-language poets was marked by a four-part "tragedy." First, these writers were mostly poets at a moment when lyric poetry was losing its readership. Second, these poets were Jews, and thus the non-Jewish readership wanted nothing to do with them, while Jewish readers were no doubt plagued by worries other than poetry at the moment. Third, these Jewish poets wrote in German, a special tragedy at a time when even Jewish writers living in Germany itself were in the process of being exiled from their mother tongue. And last, Margul-Sperber concluded, these poets lived in the Bukowina where they had "neither echo nor audience," where there were no German-language journals or presses, only daily newspapers with minimal cultural content. "Die Buche" was to provide a

Figure 19. Poets on the Herrengasse: Selma Meerbaum-Eisinger (right) with her friend Else Schächter, May 1940; Paul Celan (looking back toward camera), 1930s; Alfred Margul-Sperber (with hat) and Moses Rosenkranz (center), 1930s (Meerbaum-Eisinger, privately owned, printed by permission of Hoffman und Campe Verlag, Hamburg; Paul Celan, courtesy of Pearl Fichman; Margul-Sperber, courtesy of Literaturhaus Berlin)

forum for, and a monument to, a literature that, according to him, managed to remain youthful and energetic despite these inimical circumstances.[40]

From its inception, the anthology project was plagued by fundamental difficulties. Who should be included? The selection was ruled by the poets' place and culture of *birth,* but some of the most important poets who were approached declined precisely on this very basis. Thus Bukowina-born Victor Wittner, a poet living in Vienna since the First World War, responded: "Unfortunately I cannot contribute to your collection out of principle. Writing, I feel myself as a *German* poet and not as a Romanian, or Jewish poet, nor as a Romanian Jew." Joseph Kalmer declined because, as someone supporting himself with his writing, he could not publicly declare himself a Jew.[41] Each of these letters sent to Alfred Margul-Sperber reflects the tremendous ambivalence of writers who were working through their cultural affiliation with their native Bukowina, which fed their writing even as they tried, repeatedly, to sever themselves from it.

More vexing than the question of inclusion was the issue of publication. In 1936, satisfied with a working draft of the collection, Margul-Sperber sent it to the Schocken Verlag in Berlin. The editor, Moritz Spitzer, responded promptly that "it is difficult to justify 'here' the publication of an anthology of German writings by Jews whose only commonality lies in their belonging to a distant, non-German land." Spitzer sent another letter a few months

later, expressing both his appreciation of some of the poems and his continued ambivalence about publishing the book. But in December 1938 the decision was made for him by Hans Hinkel, the cultural director of the German
Reich, who shut down the Schocken publishing company and forced the
return of all outstanding manuscripts.[42]

It is ironic that even as Germany was expelling its own Jewish writers, the
German language should be seen as a vehicle of resistance and of cosmopolitan freedom in this former Austrian province. Writing in 1937 about the relationship between Germans and Jews living in the Bukowina, Margul-Sperber
begins with "words of thanks . . . that Bukowina Jews owe to the German
people and to their culture." Before Jews encountered German civilization,
Margul-Sperber continues, they found themselves in a cultural condition
that was "unworthy of human existence. . . . Emancipated from the ghetto,
Jewish youth sat at the feet of German teachers from the West and eagerly
absorbed everything new, great, and beautiful that Western culture and
civilization could procure for them."[43] Margul-Sperber's exaggerated and, by
1937 anachronistic rhetoric reveals the long-standing insecurity Bukowina's
Jews suffered in relation to German culture and language. Despite their reading exposure to German literature and especially to its classical literary icons,
those continuing to speak and write German became more and more linguistically isolated. Many of the poets in the "Buche" anthology, for example,
had had Romanian as their primary language of instruction; they also heard
Yiddish, Russian, and Ukrainian on a daily basis. Many also studied French,
and some studied Hebrew. In his poem "Topography," Alfred Gong sarcasti-
cally mimics the linguistic mixture spoken in Cernăuţi:

und die Steuerbeamten nahmen Bakschisch
und sprachen rumänisch. Alles andere sprach
jiddisch, ruthenisch, polnisch und ein Deutsch
wie z.B. "Ich gehe fahren mich baden zum Pruth."

*the income tax agents took bribes*
*and spoke Romanian. All others spoke*
*Yiddish, Ruthenian, Polish and a German*
*like, for example, "I am going to drive to swimming in the Pruth."*[44]

But the region's linguistic mixture was also celebrated as a healthy influence on Bukowina German. In her retrospective writings, Rose Ausländer
articulately comes down on both sides of this divide: "German remained the

mother tongue and language of culture until the end of the Second World War, though it suffered severe ruptures and distortions. Through the influence of so many languages, and especially Yiddish (over one third of the population was Jewish), an idiom emerged from which the culturally and linguistically fastidious—taking their cue from Vienna—distanced themselves.... Oh how the Viennese scorned that 'Buko-Viennese' German! We suffered from a sense of inferiority due to our language."[45] Ausländer's Bukowina poems emphasize not just the *German,* but the *multicultural and multilingual* character of the city; she insists, always, on the city's *four* languages, as in her poem "Bukowina II" (1976): "Viersprachig verbrüderte / Lieder / in entzweiter Zeit" (quadrilingual fraternizing / songs / in a time asunder).[46]

Living, as is repeatedly emphasized, in the easternmost outskirts of the former empire, the writers of the Bukowina had to assert their linguistic and cultural Germanness with every means available. Could their marginality and deterritorialization explain what has virtually become a critical commonplace among students of this literature, that Bukowina's interwar poets were not linguistic or aesthetic innovators, but wrote in rigorously classical German and traditional poetic form that ignored the modernist turn poetry had taken in Western Europe?[47]

The distinctiveness of Bukowina's German poetry may well lie precisely in the constitutive and determining tensions and contradictions amidst which it took shape: the celebration of German as transhistorical, pure, and redemptive, on the one hand, and the consciousness of German as the language of increasing prejudice, irredeemably sullied, on the other. Thus one can read its sentimental neo-Romantic themes as either a form of political evasion and denial or as an ironic commentary on impending historical tragedy. Its classical form could be a refuge from historical danger and fear or a poignant counterpoint to what was to become an increasingly crushing and despairing content. The postwar German poetry of Paul Celan and his generation emerged out of these contradictions. As the "language of the murderers," however, German had to be broken, rejected, and reclaimed in different terms by this new generation of postwar Czernowitz writers, forging a trenchantly contemporary modern and postmodern aesthetic and a break with the German of the interwar years.

Among the group of Jewish Cernăuţi writers and intellectuals of the 1920s and 1930s who perpetuated German and the "idea of Czernowitz," there were several dissenting voices: writers who chose Yiddish as their literary language and who repudiated the assimilationist trajectory of their compatriots. While Margul-Sperber was celebrating the rich influence of German culture,

Eliezer Shteynbarg and Itzik Manger worked to reclaim a different historical tradition. In 1939, the Czernowitz-born Manger declared: "Modern anti-semitism, precisely because it achieved such a brutal form in the classic land of the Jewish Enlightenment Movement, has liquidated—and, one would think, forever—the notion of assimilation as a solution to the Jewish prob-lem." The "German Jew," Manger writes, "in himself, and with himself, . . . carried a bastard: a foreign language; a foreign melody. And so long as he does not abort the foreign element he will not be able to discern the way to Jewishness."[48] Shteynbarg and Manger "abort[ed] the foreign element" by writing in Yiddish and by actively building Yiddish cultural and educa-tional institutions. Shteynbarg, born in the small town of Lipcani in 1880, did not move to Cernăuți until after the First World War. His traditional rural Jewish education and native Yiddish prepared him well to become what Ruth Wisse calls a "neo-folk poet," writing fables emerging from Yiddish folk stories, the Zohar, the Talmud, as well as modern Yiddish and Hebrew literature. It also led him to promote secular Yiddish education by forming the influential Yiddisher Shulferain, a Yiddish children's theater, and the Yiddish summer camps in nearby Wizenka, one of which Carl attended.[49]

In contrast, Manger, born Isidore Helfer in Czernowitz in 1901 and edu-cated in German, had literally to "abort the foreign element" when his family moved to Iași during the First World War. His immersion in the Yiddish folk culture of Bessarabia enabled his transformation into a folk bard and Yiddish troubadour. Manger returned to Cernăuți after the war and became active in the Yiddish-German circles of Shteynbarg, Kittner, and Margul-Sperber, but he soon moved on to Warsaw, realizing that, as David Roskies writes, "for the Jews (as for the entire bourgeoisie) of Czernowitz, real culture was German high culture."[50] But Manger's choice of the ballad as his primary genre—according to Roskies that "least Yiddish of folk genres"—connects him to the German poetry of Goethe, Schiller and Hoffmannsthal as much as it does to the Yiddish folk traditions he celebrated.

In interwar Cernăuți, Shteynbarg and Manger enjoyed tremendous popu-larity and an avid readership. Many Czernowitz survivors recall hearing Shteynbarg read from his fables or seeing his children's plays. Alfred Kittner also recalls sold-out lectures and readings by Manger in large lecture rooms in the late 1920s.[51] Kittner, Margul-Sperber, and Manger would often drink the night away in the bars of Cernăuți, discussing, among other things, Margul-Sperber's translations of Manger's ballads into German. In his secularism, his sought-after marginal and exilic status, his repudiation of (Yiddish) high modernism, and his bitterness about being underrecognized by the (Yiddish) literary establishment, Manger shows more than a few commonalities with his compatriots writing in German.

Still, few others followed their example. Vera Hacken recalls Shteynbarg as "the great master, my model, my teacher, my friend. . . . But I disappointed him. As soon as the German language and its literature became familiar to me, I fell head over heels in love with it, and wrote only in German. His 'Verotchka, write Yiddish!' remained without response. . . . My love of German never waned. . . . Late, very late in my life, I redeemed my promise and wrote a play, in Yiddish. Six million Jews had to die, as martyrs, in His [God's] name, until this soul heard the divine voice, that loving voice that spoke to my conscience, and I began to write in Yiddish. It was too late."[52]

### DEPARTURES

Our walk had taken us to the Elisabethplatz (Theaterplatz) and the statue of the Ukrainian national poet Olga Kobylyanska. The theater whose entrance she graced now exclusively presents works in Ukrainian.

"We were shocked to hear in late June 1940 that the Soviets would be occupying Czernowitz in the next days," Lotte recalled as we contemplated the theater and the stately Jüdisches Haus nearby. "There was an announcement, and preparations started immediately. My sister and I walked through the streets. In front of every official building there were enormous crates where all documents and archives would be stored. Fritzi, my sister, was suppressing tears. 'You see,' she said, 'the world that is being packed away in these crates will never return.' She seemed overcome by despair. I was puzzled, perhaps sad, but not in despair. A little curious too, ready for something new: who are these Russians, what's ahead? You see, there were sixteen years between us. Fritzi was born in the Austrian Czernowitz; she had spent the first war in Vienna with her parents. Until the age of sixteen, she knew nothing but Austria. The sudden transformation of Czernowitz into a Romanian city had been unbelievable to her. And now, more change ahead."

As we returned to the Cheremosh Hotel, we puzzled over the many contradictions of that crucial moment in Cernăuți. How was it that, for Fritzi, it was the *Romanians* who seemed to be taking the old world away with them in enormous crates? That statement underscored the stubborn resistance with which Cernăuți Jews had perpetuated the idea of Czernowitz until June of 1940.

# FIVE

# "Are we really in the Soviet Union?"

Our dilemma can best be exemplified by a joke circulating at that time: "Two trains meet on June 28 in a station between Bucharest and Czernowitz, one going South with refugees from Czernowitz, the other going North with returnees to Czernowitz. Looking out of the windows, across the tracks, two brothers recognize each other. One is on the train going North toward the newly Soviet Northern Bukowina, the other joined ethnic Romanians fleeing South from territories that had been annexed by the Soviets. As the trains pull out of the station in opposite directions, the two brothers simultaneously yell to one other, gesticulating wildly: "Meshugenner! [You fool!] *Where* are you *going?*"

CARL HIRSCH
"A Life in the Twentieth Century"

THE "RED SQUARE," 1998

"I was right here in this very spot on the Ringplatz when the Red Army marched into Czernowitz in the summer of 1940," Lotte told us on our fourth day in the city. As on previous days, the taxi from the hotel had left us off on the city's main square. By now we were familiar with the central area of the city and knew how to find our way to some of the sites of my parents' childhood and adolescent years, to their schools and the homes of their friends and relatives. We had spent the previous days walking, taking pictures, and encouraging Lotte and Carl, as well as Rosa Zuckermann and

Matthias Zwilling, our faithful guides, to share their recollections as we videotaped them in front of landmarks of their past.

"I was with my sister and some other friends," Lotte continued. "There was great excitement in the air. I wasn't as 'red' as some of them. I was more contemplative, less political. But it was impressive to see these young soldiers march into the city." The day she referred to was June 28, 1940. Soon the Ringplatz, then called Piaţa Unirii (Union Square), was renamed the Red Square, and a Soviet flag was raised above the city hall. Chernovtsy, the new Russian name for Cernăuţi, would become the capital of a province in the Ukrainian Soviet Socialist Republic, one of the fifteen republics of the Soviet Union. The on-the-surface symbolic transformation of the city was rapid and efficient.

For us, standing in the center of Ukrainian Chernivtsi in 1998 after forty-five years of Soviet and nearly ten years of Ukrainian rule, the transformation was easy to visualize. Not only were all signs still in Cyrillic lettering, but the former Ringplatz itself was flanked by an enormous Soviet-era concrete wall that violated the square's turn-of-the-twentieth-century architectural harmony. Now, in 1998, we were in a Ukrainian city whose core of Mitteleuropa architecture, a vestige of a vanished past, could just barely keep the discordant Soviet-era suburbs at bay. But as we stood on the former Ringplatz facing the beautiful city hall or on the square facing a smaller version of the Vienna Burgtheater, we could begin to imagine how unprepared the city's multiethnic population of 1940, and in particular the German-speaking Jewish residents who had lived under Romanian rule for over twenty years, must have been for the nearly instantaneous transformations this border city underwent during what would turn out to be its first annexation by the Soviet Union. Dorothea Sella's questions in her fictionalized memoir, *Der Ring des Prometheus,* express this shock:

> Was the square on which we were standing indeed our "Ringplatz"? Were we still in Czernowitz? Were these streets, through which what seemed like the entire Soviet army was marching from the north, through the center of the city to the south, really our Bahnhofsstrasse, our Hauptstrasse, our Rathausstrasse, our Siebenbürgerstrasse? . . . A remarkable spectacle! The onlookers reacted in different ways. Some looked fearful, others confused, and others still—actually only young people—were visibly delighted and reached toward the soldiers with their hands and with bunches of flowers. You could see from the expression on the soldiers' faces that they were not accustomed to such a positive reception, which stunned them.[1]

Figure 20. The Red Army welcomed in Cernăuţi, June 1940 (Vydavnychyi dim "Al'ternatyvym," vol. 1, reproduced in P. R. Magocsi, *Ukraine: An Illustrated History* [Seattle: University of Washington Press, 2007], 273)

## THE HITLER-STALIN PACT AND ITS AFTERMATH, 1939–1940

By the late 1930s, Carl and many of his Czernowitz friends had settled, at least temporarily, in the Regat, the core region of the Romanian kingdom south of the Bukowina. Most of them had recently completed (or had had to interrupt) their university studies in Cernăuţi or in Bucharest, Prague, Brno, or even Paris, and had to think about finding employment in their fields. Their opportunities were severely limited by the growing anti-Semitism in Romania and the rest of Europe. Carl, for example, studied mathematics but went into engineering because, in late-1930s Romania, the prospects were slightly better for engineers: teaching jobs in state schools and universities were already closed to Jews. Lotte and her classmates, six years younger, had fewer opportunities still. We knew Lotte had intended to study medicine, but the only European medical schools in which Jews could still enroll were in France and further west, and her parents would not permit her to go so far away. Had she gone, her studies would have been interrupted by the start of the war, as were those of Paul Antschel (Celan), two years her junior, who enrolled in the Romance Language faculty of Cernăuți when he could not return to his medical studies in France in the fall of 1939. Lotte's best friend, Hedwig Brenner, began her art history studies in Vienna and was lucky to return home just days before the Anschluss in 1938.[2] Cernăuți Jews of this generation, like their contemporaries in other parts of Europe, had to adjust to such anti-Semitic restrictions and to settle for those available jobs that would provide them with the best training and salaries.

In his memoir, Carl describes the rapid political changes that were to have such a direct and significant impact on his life: "On August 23 [1939] I went with my supervisor to inspect some highway construction work, and we ended up in Bucharest to give our report to the central Highway Department. As we arrived in Bucharest, the newspapers announced in a special edition the conclusion of a non-aggression pact between Hitler and Stalin. War was in the air. I said in jest to my friends that the Soviet Union has joined the Anti-Comintern Pact [concluded earlier between Germany, Italy, and Japan against Communism]."[3]

Although he was certainly aware of the ironies surrounding the agreement between Germany and the Soviet Union, generally referred to as the Hitler-Stalin Pact or the Ribbentrop-Molotov Nonaggression Pact, Carl could not foresee its profoundly devastating effects on the inhabitants of Cernăuți and the Northern Bukowina. It was this agreement that opened the way at the end of June 1940 for the Soviets to take over from Romania Cernăuți and the region in which it was located. The ensuing twelve-month period of Soviet rule, entailing radical political, social, and economic transformations, was capped in its concluding weeks by the deportation to Siberia of thousands who, for social or security reasons, were deemed suspect by the communist authorities. The majority of these deportees were Jews. Soviet rule was then abruptly interrupted by the German-Romanian invasion of this part of the Soviet Union, the reimposition of Romanian authority in the Bukowina in late June 1941, and by intense reprisals and a series of massive Romanian deportations of Jews and other "undesirables" to the area between the Dniester and Bug rivers that came to be known as Transnistria. Although certainly not as clear at the time as it has become in hindsight, the Hitler-Stalin Pact also marked the moment when all hopes of "belonging," "citizenship," "permanence" and "home" that Cernăuți/Czernowitz Jews might still have had were essentially shattered. Within months of its announcement, Jews here realized that they would be marginalized, excluded, displaced, and persecuted on either side of this new, and ultimately unstable, political divide. They truly belonged nowhere.

Much, of course, has been written about the nonaggression pact and about the events surrounding it that led to the outbreak of the Second World War. But its specific implications for the population of Cernăuţi and the Northern Bukowina were not immediately apparent—even, it now seems clear, to its German cosigners. The pact, negotiated and signed in Moscow by Hitler's foreign minister, Joachim von Ribbentrop, and his Soviet counterpart, V. M. Molotov, was, as George Kennan so aptly observed, "relatively innocuous in itself, although highly sensational as a political gesture."[4] It declared the mutual renunciation of aggression against the other by both the USSR and Germany and affirmed that each would remain neutral in a conflict where the other was attacked by a third party. Shocking as this was at the time in political terms for Great Britain, France, and for liberal and left-leaning persons throughout the world who had hoped to enlist the Soviet Union as a military counterweight to Nazi territorial expansionism during the late 1930s, it was the secret protocol that was attached to the pact—and the implementation of this protocol—that had the most dire international consequences. In effect, this protocol divided Eastern Europe between Germany and the Soviet Union into "spheres of influence" and defined zones in which each would take exclusive responsibility "in the event of a territorial and political rearrangement."[5] The Soviet sphere of influence under this agreement was to include Finland, the two Baltic states of Latvia and Estonia, roughly the eastern two-fifths of Poland, and the Romanian province of Bessarabia.[6] The remainder of Eastern Europe, to the west of the Soviet sphere, was to be Germany's.

If Jews living in Cernăuţi and the Northern Bukowina did not immediately perceive the ominous future that the Hitler-Stalin Pact heralded for them, it was because this Romanian-ruled region had not been mentioned at all in the original spheres of influence of the secret protocol. Even after Germany's attack on Poland a week after the pact was signed—which immediately led to the outbreak of the Second World War and to the "territorial and political rearrangement" that "permitted" German and Soviet moves into their respective spheres of influence—the Bukowina seemed peripheral to the main territorial interests of the leading powers. The neighboring province of Bessarabia, on the other hand, had long been an issue between the Soviet Union and Romania, and it was as an appendage to the resolution of its political status that the Northern Bukowina and Cernăuţi were drawn into the fray.

Bessarabia had been part of the Russian Empire for more than a century, from 1812 until 1918, but was annexed by and made a province of the Kingdom of Romania in the aftermath of the Bolshevik seizure of power and the Paris Peace Conference boundary rearrangements that had ended the First World War. Soviet Russia, however, never recognized Romania's right to Bessarabia, and although initially too weak to contest this award effectively, kept alive the "ownership" of Bessarabia as a key issue of contention between the two countries for more than two decades. Then, at the end of June 1940, while Germany was involved in its Blitzkrieg through the Low Countries and in France, the Soviet Union sent an ultimatum to Romania, demanding the immediate restoration of Bessarabia to its control, as well as Romania's abandonment of the Bukowina—a province which had never before belonged to Russia. Soviet Foreign Minister Molotov justified the latter, insisting that "Bukowina is the last missing part of a 'unified Ukraine' and that for this reason the Soviet government must attach importance to solving this question simultaneously with the Bessarabian question."[7] While some German pressure on Romania's behalf did result in a follow-up Soviet concession to limit its demands only to Bessarabia and *northern* Bukovina, Molotov further justified the takeover, declaring: "The transfer of Northern Bukovina to the Soviet Union could constitute in only an insignificant degree . . . a means of compensation for the tremendous damage inflicted on the Soviet Union and the population of Bessarabia by 22 years of Romanian domination in Bessarabia."[8]

The Soviets demanded that Romania evacuate its military and civilian governmental authorities from these areas within a period of four days, beginning on June 28, 1940, and that the principal Bessarabian and Bukowinian cities of Chişinău (Kishinev), Cernăuţi, and Akkerman be totally free of Romanian forces by the end of the first day. They also requested a Romanian guarantee that, in the process of troop and civilian withdrawal, the railroads, airports, telegraph installations, parks, and other potentially important strategic and industrial installations would not be damaged.

In seeking a response to the Soviet ultimatum, the Romanians turned to Berlin for help. The Nazi government, however, perhaps already anticipating Germany's own future invasion and defeat of the Soviet Union and the nullification of all Soviet territorial gains, advised the Romanian government not to resist the Soviet demands and to bow to Molotov's ultimatum.[9] The Romanian Crown Council then reluctantly agreed to withdraw and began to pull out its military and civilian authorities. By two in the afternoon of June 28, Soviet troops were crossing the Romanian border into Bessarabia and the Northern Bukowina.

The Soviet arrival in the Romanian-ruled territories immediately set in motion a massive two-directional shift of population, reflected in the joke that Carl remembered so well—into the Romanian core of the Regat, and outward from the Regat, to regions taken over by the Soviets. Within a week after June 28, some two hundred thousand Romanian refugees from Bessarabia and the Northern Bukowina crossed the borders into Romania. Alternatively, masses of Romanian citizens—perhaps more than one hundred thousand, including many Jews, Communist sympathizers and officials, and persons with family links to Bessarabia or the Northern Bukowina—moved to the Soviet-occupied territories. In addition, some eighty thousand ethnic Germans—mainly long-term rural settlers—were evacuated from Bessarabia and repatriated to Germany, and some thirty thousand from the Northern Bukowina.[10]

In their hasty retreat from the Bukowina and Bessarabia into the Regat, Romanian military forces took back as much equipment and moveable property as possible. But some troops and officers, feeling angered and embittered by what agitators portrayed as a great national humiliation, sought vengeance by violently attacking the civilian population—especially Jews—in towns and villages through which they were retreating. Looking for scapegoats and stirred up by anti-Semitic hate-mongers who accused local Jews of assaulting retreating Romanians and of facilitating and supporting the Soviets in their takeover, soldiers, aided by local peasants, plundered homes and property and beat, raped, and killed Jewish inhabitants.

More than at any previous moment in the past, Jews in the Northern Bukowina found themselves in a particularly precarious position as a consequence of all these events. Even though the Jewish population had suffered from Romanian anti-Semitism and saw the Soviet takeover as a possible salvation, and even though the underground communist movements counted many Jews among their members, thousands of Jews would be stripped of their material possessions and persecuted by Soviet authorities as "capitalist enemies of the State" in the course of the ensuing "Russian Year." Yet, at the same time, within a segment of Romanian public opinion—particularly among Romanians who had been directly or indirectly connected as soldiers or civilians with the Bukowina, Bessarabia, and their urban capitals—Jews living in Romania were also viewed as potential, if not active, "communist enemies of the State," to be blamed for facilitating and sustaining a regime that had so ignominiously stripped Romania of its territory and national glory.

In June of 1940, Jews from Cernăuți who, like Carl, were living and working in the Regat followed closely and with increasing alarm the distressing news of the war in Western Europe and the expanding power of right-wing Romanian movements. Jews were still serving in the military, though in ever more restricted capacities, and thus men were occasionally called up to the Romanian Army as reservists. At the time, Carl had a job on the Black Sea coast, his brother, Kubi, and friends Mischa Flexor and Sidy Lebcovic were in Bucharest; Bubi and Hedy Brenner had moved to Romania's oil capital, Ploeşti. They all returned frequently to visit their families in Cernăuți, concerned that the Northern Bukowina would be occupied by the Soviet Union following the Soviet ultimatum and that they might be cut off from one another. "In early June, I took all my money out of the bank in Bucharest and brought it to my mother in Czernowitz," Carl writes in his memoir. "It is striking for me now that, at a time when the German armies were overrunning France, the atmosphere in my home town was totally normal. It was the calm before the storm."[11]

The events of June 28, 1940, required a split-second decision, the choice between two "spheres of influence," fascism or communism, Antonescu and Hitler or Stalin. For some, the choice was obvious: they were leftists, communist sympathizers, ready to try living under the new order. For others, it was more difficult to make a decision in the split second available, and the decision that was made became more difficult to understand and to explain in retrospect. "It will always be a mystery to me why I preferred to stay in Cernăuți instead of fleeing to Bucharest," writes Manfred Reifer, a Jewish politician who, as a member of several Zionist organizations and as a Jewish deputy in the Romanian parliament, knew he would be targeted by the Soviet authorities. "Was it the law of lethargy, or the hope that one would be able to choose later, or the fear of the Iron Guard's rule in Romania? Maybe it was the curiosity to experience a socialist state that led me to remain in my native city? I understand it as little today as I did then."[12]

For Carl these days in June 1940 were among the most significant in his youth:

> I was in a kind of confusion. I had left all my things behind in Silistra [on the Black Sea coast] except my documents (which I had taken along in a briefcase), I had lost contact with my brother, but I went to the Bucharest Railway Station and took the train to Czernowitz. . . . In all stations we

met trains going the other way full of refugees from Bessarabia and Northern Bukowina, mostly ethnic Romanians. Around noon the next day, we arrived at Adancata, around 25 km. south of Czernowitz, and were informed that there was no continuation to Czernowitz by train. With a number of other similar adventurers, I started on foot. . . . After staying overnight in a small town, we continued our walk the next morning. We didn't meet any remnants of the Romanian army, they had left on the 28th, and on this morning of the 30th, we met the first Soviet troops just south of Czernowitz. They probably were elite troops, blond youngsters on fine horses; we greeted them enthusiastically.

In our attitude, and that of most Jews from Czernowitz, there were two positive aspects to the upcoming Soviet rule of the Bukowina: one was our sympathy toward the Soviet experiment shared by most of the liberal community throughout the world, and the other was the fact that this was our salvation from the coming German rule of Europe. Even wealthy Jews who at the time did not suspect that Siberia might be their next home were carried along by fear of German rule.[13]

Of course, neither Carl nor his friends knew at the time that their "sympathy toward the Soviet experiment" would be short-lived and that a mere five years later, two of which were spent in Soviet Chernovtsy, he would cross the same border in the other direction, exclaiming, "Der Schlag soll sie treffen!" (May they be hit by lightning!) In his memoir, Carl does foreshadow some of this profound disillusionment, considering in turn what they knew about the Soviet regime before 1940, what they allowed themselves to know, and what they were to learn firsthand in due time: "The pact between Hitler and Stalin should have made us think. . . . We read about the trials in Moscow in the late thirties. . . . I knew there was something fundamentally wrong in it, but . . ." This mix of foresight and hindsight in his and other narratives is interspersed with descriptions of the first days of Soviet rule and the sense of relief and hopefulness that the takeover had brought.

The written and the oral accounts about this period are severely strained and disrupted by the struggle to disentangle conflicting memories and allegiances as perceived at different moments in time and to disentangle, as well, their contradictory emotions about this difficult year. Florence Heymann echoes the surprise I have always felt at the centrality that this year, 1940–41, occupies in the memories of the Czernowitz Jews we have interviewed and read, and at the vehemence of the disappointment and disdain for the Soviet regime that they frequently present. She writes: "It seemed that the Soviet year had at times marked them even more than the following years when

Romanians and Germans invaded the city and dragged the Jewish population into the maelstrom of the Shoah."[14]

In Carl's memoir, for example, the chapter on this 1940–41 year elicits a telling chronological break within his account, resulting in a distinctive form of stocktaking and self-reflection. It is only when writing about himself at 28 that he feels he has to explain to his readers who "the person who went through these events" was.[15] He uses this particular chapter as the place in which he carefully traces the formative influences of his youth: the Hashomer Hatzair labor-Zionist movement to which he had belonged, his assimilated Jewishness, his attachment to the German language and culture, his left-leaning politics, his attitudes toward work and play. We might speculate that, unconsciously at least, he felt the need for the more probing and intense self-questioning he provides in this chapter of his memoir because it reflects the political and ideological biographical accounts that the Soviet regime routinely demanded of its citizens. Other witnesses' descriptions of this moment are also riddled with various forms of self-justification: "As a Deputy I had always vehemently opposed the persecution of Communists," Manfred Reifer said. And Pearl Fichman stated, "My world views were in accordance with a socialist world order."[16]

The radical ideological shifts these new Soviet subjects underwent at the time and the high stakes that were attached to being on the "correct" side, as well as the arbitrariness of that determination, color their accounts even decades later. As Manfred Reifer elaborates: "Everyone rushed to break with the past, to abandon tradition, and to accommodate to the spirit of the new order."[17] But even more is at stake in retrospect. These witnesses are relating their recollections of that period after the fall of the Soviet Union to younger readers and listeners who might have difficulty imagining their enthusiasm, however short-lived, for the Soviet annexation. In their narratives they therefore try to evoke the emotions of the time, while, at the same time, also maintaining the rightful skepticism about the Soviet Union that they project onto, and thus also share with, their listeners. Note, for example, Carl's telling formulation when he asserts that his "sympathy for the Soviet experiment" was "shared by most of the liberal community throughout the world." They have to convey the promise of the communist revolutionary ideals and their international appeal, as well as the empowerment they felt at being part of a movement that promised vast social changes, especially at a moment when fascism was closing in around them. At the same time, their accounts have to allow the plot of disillusionment to unfold in its own rhythm. They have to represent the positive changes that were introduced by the Soviets, as well as the growing fear, suspicion, and persecution many were to suffer. And, in retrospect, they have to be careful not to equate or relativize Soviet with Nazi forms of persecution. All this requires no small amount of narrative skill, combining suspense with modulation, irony, and self-questioning.

Standing on the former Red Square, Carl recalled for us his brother Kubi's response: "Kubi was very enthusiastic when he arrived in Czernowitz in late June of 1940. He exclaimed in bright-eyed disbelief: 'Carl, are we really in the Soviet Union?' This is to show how blind most of us were about the reality of this so-called workers' paradise. Just to show you our mentality: at our 1941 New Year's celebration, we raised our glasses to meeting next year in Communist Bucharest. How little we knew."

"Well, I was certainly caught up in it too," Lotte added, smiling at her former self. "My parents got so worried when I stayed out until midnight to see the performances the Soviets brought to seduce and impress us. My sister and I attended every one of them." Pearl Fichman also describes these days in her memoir: "In the first week or so they brought Moysseiev dancers, who performed in the central square of town. . . . Soon after came a group of outstanding Jewish writers, who delighted us with readings of their poetry and also sang some rousing Jewish revolutionary songs. Within the next few years all these writers were put to death."[18]

THE RUSSIAN YEAR, 1940–1941

Disillusionment unfolded at a rapid pace indeed, although always modulated by the disturbing news of Hitler's war, which served as an unsettling counterpoint. More and more, Czernowitz Jews came to see that, like other European Jews, they were trapped between two deadly regimes in which they were undesirable others—objects of persecution, deportation, and eventually annihilation in one regime; of repression and suspicion in the other. They had to face radical changes in the fabric of their daily lives, in their sense of personal, professional, and group identity, and they had to do so in the context of their growing fear of a rapidly expanding war. The enormous psychological effects of these changes are difficult for us to imagine today.

Thinking about these changes in Ukrainian Chernivtsi, in the shadow of bygone Austrian and Romanian times, brought this layered history home to me with great force. Surely, I thought, these changes affected people differently depending on their age, gender, or class status. Lotte and Carl, and their friends, for example, had always conveyed a sense of youthful excitement when they discussed this shaping moment in their lives. For Lotte and Carl, in particular, the Soviet annexation of the Bukowina coincided with their meeting, their courtship, the complicated matter of Lotte's involvement with two other young suitors, and their eventual decision to marry: this private drama too has to find a place among their narratives of the history they shared with their compatriots—and it has to do so without overshadowing that history or being overshadowed by it. "We were young," they would often repeat, and that phrase is meant to explain a great deal.

"Do you know what happened right here?" Carl had walked us to what we had already come to know as the Rudolfsplatz and stopped in front of the imposing century-old brown building with its three arches, the Philharmonic Hall, the old Musikvereinssaal. Broad steps led up to its still elegant glass doors.

"Here, in that fall of 1940, I ran into an old friend, Etzia Weitzmann, who was walking down the street with a very attractive blond lady. I had been away from Czernowitz for several years and was glad to meet old friends and make new ones. I was getting settled: I had to find work, buy clothes and books from fleeing Romanians, since I had left everything on the Black Sea coast when I rushed up here in June. Etzia introduced me to Lotte Gottfried, and I remember saying I hoped we would run into each other again."

"We did," Lotte said. "Although our families lived on the same street, we did not know each other. Carl was older, he had gone away for his studies, and we moved in different circles anyway. If the Soviets had not invaded Czernowitz, we probably never would have met. In that fall of 1940, I started working as a secretary in a textile plant. And one day the young man I had met through Etzia Weitzmann came there on official business: he worked as an engineer in the Textile Trust. Well, he kept coming there frequently, seemed to have more and more official business there, and that's how it all began."

The military regime that had initially taken over the city was quickly replaced by a civilian one, which worked hard to institute a policy of "Soviet Ukrainianization." The top jobs throughout the city were given to officials brought in from Moscow and Kiev, but local Ukrainians came to hold secondary offices. Some Jews who had lost their positions due to Romanian anti-Semitic laws were reinstated by the Soviets, but the policy of Ukrainianization generally barred Jews from most high-level positions. Within the Jewish population the only people who were rewarded with important public and party positions were those who had been activist members of the previously underground Communist Party. In turn, a number of these "influentials" were then able to help their friends find the best employment and to protect them from ever-increasing persecutions.[19]

Younger people looking for employment or trying to continue their schooling to university level first had to learn Russian or Ukrainian. Work was mandatory for anyone over eighteen, but many found it difficult if not impossible to find jobs and had to survive by selling their household goods. Employment became the measure of "proletarianization," which was reinforced by a new dress code that abandoned expensive-looking clothes, ties, and jewelry—all symbols of a bourgeois life that had become dangerous. Some, like Manfred Reifer, could only secure the necessary employment in exchange for bribes: "I was denounced and thus could not be considered for teaching positions in primary or secondary schools. . . . But through a Ukrainian I knew I came into contact with a school inspector . . . and arranged with him the exchange of a teaching position for a winter coat, a pair of shoes, and a hat. The deal worked out, I delivered the goods and he the job." Soviet currency was introduced in September, and since individuals were allowed to exchange no more than 1,000 Romanian lei, at a fixed rate of 40 lei to the ruble, most middle-class families lost their savings overnight. (In 1941, one U.S. dollar was worth about 150 lei; Carl's salary as an engineer in Romania in 1940 had been about 5,000 lei per month.)[20]

Initially, the Soviet annexation was perhaps most difficult for older people: Lotte asserted that 1940–41 was "devastating" for her parents. Her father, my grandfather, almost sixty, had lost any possibility of employment as a lawyer and no longer received the pension he had been collecting during the Romanian period for his work as an Austrian government employee. Pearl Fichman describes her parents as equally apprehensive and dismayed, although fortunately for them, Fichman's father had already sold his small store before the communist takeover, so that the Soviet overseer who had been assigned to their house registered him as a clerk rather than an owner. Property owners, along with bankers, business people, merchants, and known activist Zionists and Bundists, were issued identity cards inscribed with "clause 39," an identification that (unbeknownst to its holders at first) marked them as social or security suspects and as likely candidates for deportation. On the other hand, professionals, such as engineers, teachers, lawyers and workers were issued an identity card marked "40" and were thus classified as "useful to the state."[21]

Interestingly, women from bourgeois Jewish families tended to fare better in the new order because many had long dealt with local Ukrainians, either as household help or in the marketplace, and could communicate in rudimentary Ukrainian. Even so, many homemakers were unable to manage the ordeals of shopping by themselves; they had to engage their children and elderly parents to stand on the innumerable queues that soon became standard at food stores and markets. Food, even bread, became more and more scarce; some items, like sugar and butter, were hardly ever available. The lively black market was illegal and risky, for Soviet police tried to halt it through numerous arrests.[22]

Bukowina university students, like their counterparts elsewhere in the Soviet Union, were paid a salary that corresponded to that of a regular worker,[23] but Lotte had almost completed her four years of study and all the coursework for her "licența în litere." Short only the final qualifying examinations that had been cancelled due to the Soviet invasion in June, she now had to find work. With her gift for languages, she took private lessons in Russian and found the secretarial job in the textile factory—"perhaps more for my looks than for my training," she admitted to us with a smile. The salary was minimal, but her sister was able to obtain a teaching job in a Ukrainian secondary school, and, together, they were able to support their parents.

With the massive nationalizations of all property and production, new offices were being created, and thus new kinds of administrative jobs became available. Carl first worked as a civil engineer for the highway department, then the housing authority, and then, through his friend Mischa Flexor, he secured a job at the Textile Trust, which oversaw the work of six textile factories. In both these latter positions, he was supposed to manage projects of reconstruction and rehabilitation, but little was actually being rebuilt. His brother, Kubi, worked for the city government as an engineer even though he had not yet passed his final examinations. Their sister Lilly was able to continue her work as an accountant in a factory in which she had worked since 1926. Conditions did not improve under the Soviets, as she had hoped; she continued to work extremely long hours for minimal pay. Their younger sister Rosa worked as a seamstress in a cooperative, a profession for which she had apprenticed in the previous years. In her recollections, Lilly also expressed her initial enthusiasm for the regime change and her subsequent shock at the worsening economic conditions, the lack of food, and the incidents of state repression: "A woman I worked with was arrested for stealing a piece of bread for her children! Many were arrested and deported, not just rich people, people like us, Social Democrats and others," she recalled.[24]

And yet, Jewish, especially Yiddish, culture was allowed to develop, albeit within restrictive parameters set by the Soviet authorities. Yiddish theater groups from Kiev, under the direction of Moshe Goldblat, and from Kishinev, directed by Jacob Shternberg, gave guest performances of works by approved writers—a group that included Sholem Aleichem. Yiddish newspapers were limited to *Der Arbeter,* which appeared irregularly, and the Kiev *Shtern,* which reported on the Bukowina. Writers were expected to publish socialist realist works, and the holdings of public and private libraries were subjected to examination and the removal of "unsuitable" books.[25] The new government's policies about Jewish elementary and secondary education, however, were initially quite supportive of the long-standing Yiddishist position, claiming Yiddish to be *the* ethno-national language of the Jewish people. In conformity with Stalin's national policy, Jews were considered one of the national groups that formed the Soviet Union, with Yiddish as their language.[26] While Hebrew (which was associated with Zionism and settlement in Palestine) was actively disallowed in both its spoken and literary forms, Yiddish, as a potential agent for proletarian literature and arts within the USSR, was encouraged and bolstered. In the Bukowina, a number of Jewish educational establishments were founded, including the large No. 26 high school in Chernovtsy (for fifteen hundred students), with Yiddish as their principal language of instruction. With education now freed of cost (unlike under the Romanians), compulsory school uniforms abolished, corporal punishment forbidden, and new cultural and athletic extracurricular activities introduced, this new system was initially welcomed. "The teachers we had were almost uniformly excellent, including the few imports from [Soviet Russia]," recalls Hardy Mayer. "Czernowitz (and our school) were visited by famous Yiddish writers and actors, such as Dovid Hofshteyn, Itzik Fefer, Leyb Kvitko, Samuel Mikhoels. . . . There were lots of extracurricular activities (mostly within the framework of the Young Pioneer organization) . . . but there was also subtle and not-so-subtle indoctrination with Marxist-Leninist ideology."[27]

But, as Dov Levin indicates, Yiddish-language instruction and cultural dissemination was also greatly impeded by the fact that "only a few pupils could speak it, and even fewer were able to read and write it or understand its grammar. . . . At the end of the year there was criticism that the average pupils . . . 'still had a poor command of the language, a poor vocabulary, and a weak sense of sentence structure, and that many of their expressions still derived from German.'"[28]

University students were immersed in courses, for the most part taught in Russian, by professors who were brought in from Soviet Russia for the purpose of transforming the university. As Pearl Fichman writes: "The teacher was faced with an unusual task, namely, teaching a class at a university where practically nobody understood him or the textbook. After every few sentences he stopped to ask: 'Sie verstehen, Genossen?' (Do you understand, comrades?)

This was the extent of his German."[29] But the university students were more intimidated by the rigid Stalinist political education to which they were subjected than by their linguistic difficulties. As the atmosphere at the university began to erode in response to the first arrests and deportations, all teachers and classmates became potential informants. "We feared each other," writes Fichman. Conversations became more codified, suspicions grew. One particular teacher appears in several narratives as especially charismatic and therefore also as suspicious: "He played the piano and recited poetry, to our delight. He dared recite Yessenin, a symbolist poet, a poet not accepted by the official line. Officially we were supposed to admire Mayakowski, who glorified the Soviet Union. . . . Whether this Russian teacher was truly critical of the party line or whether he was trying to play a game initiated by the NKVD, will forever remain a question in my mind."[30]

Most distressing, according to Zvi Yavetz, was that schoolchildren were taught not just to praise Stalin and the revolution, but also (at least in the initial months after the Soviet takeover) to defend Hitler and "his just war," so as to conform to the spirit of the Hitler-Stalin Pact.[31] Dorothea Sella mentions a shocking detail in this respect: "On November 7, 1940, we celebrated the anniversary of the October Revolution for the first time, by participating in the required demonstration. . . . We were lined up, and waved energetically as we passed the main platform, when I noticed, next to Soviet generals and honorees, a group of Wehrmacht officers. The smiles that they exhibited struck me as unpleasant and oppressive, because of the irony that they just barely concealed." Still, Sella's communist friend Andi, also a Jew viewing the same scene, refused to judge the wisdom of the pact, assuring her that "Stalin knows what he is doing."[32]

Except for the most die-hard Communists, it was not a question of whether one became disillusioned with the Soviet regime, but how soon one became aware of (or victimized by) its corruption, oppression, and deceptiveness. Class and age were factors in the speed of that disillusionment. Zvi Yavetz writes that "I have to say that none of my classmates was distressed that the Russians nationalized all our goods. On June 28, 1940, I was the son of a millionaire. On the 29th, that of a pauper because he had nothing left."[33] Carl writes that initially "we didn't feel the invisible hand of the KGB [sic]. Sure, there were a lot of victims, like the owners of expropriated factories, shops, and apartment houses, but this didn't touch us directly; we saw it as social justice that these shops and industrial plants now belonged to the people as we were told."[34] It is possible that the expansion of the war throughout Europe influenced their viewpoint: the Soviet regime, no matter how flawed, still seemed to represent their potential salvation from Hitler and the Nazis.

The local press, however, including the leading Russian-and-Ukrainian-language newspaper, *Radianska Bukowina* (Red Bukowina), published little news about war-related events. "Due to the Hitler-Stalin pact, the Soviet press did not publish a single article about the persecution of Jews in the territories occupied by German troops," writes Mariana Hausleitner.[35] Lotte and Carl do recall the BBC German-language broadcasts on the small Grundig short-wave radio Carl's cousin, Rosa Roth's brother Paul, had brought back to him from Bucharest shortly after the Soviet annexation in 1940. Listening to foreign radio stations was quickly outlawed under the new regime. But Carl, always a chance-taker, did not relinquish his radio as mandated and continued to tune in to broadcasts in extreme secrecy. For the most part, however, the access of most Chernovtsy residents to news during this year of relative calm before the German-led invasion of the Soviet Union was severely restricted.

Indeed, as the year moved along, more and more personal freedoms were curtailed. Non-communist Jewish organizations had to be disbanded. Even though synagogues continued to hold services, Jews were required to work or attend school on the Sabbath and on holidays—a reflection and consequence of official Soviet disapproval of religion. In defiant response to this, Pearl Fichman fasted for the first time in her life on Yom Kippur, 1940. She recalls: "Suddenly I became aware that the citizen was a kind of prisoner."[36] Official identity cards featuring the inscription "Jew" were issued to the area's Jewish inhabitants—a seemingly worrisome discriminatory action were it not for the fact that, in keeping with the Soviet nationalities policy, residents belonging to other "national" groups—Ukrainian, Russian, Romanian, Polish, Tartar, and others—were also identified on the cards. The identity documents, in other words, reinforced the notion that Jews were also an ethno-national group, like any other in the USSR. But the identity cards, with their appended clauses (including numbers 39 and 40), also served as an efficient means of sorting and finding people for purposes of arrest or deportation. And, as the weeks and months passed, the shadow of the authorities grew larger and increasingly more ubiquitous. Even the shortest trips required travel permits; participation in state-sponsored public holidays and meetings became mandatory; interrogations, arrests, and the real or perceived invasion of privacy made people feel exposed and insecure. Still, Carl writes, "In retrospect it was a fairly quiet time until the spring of 1941 when the invasion of Yugoslavia started a new period of war activity abroad. We felt secure with the shield of the strong Soviet army. We were not very happy with the way communism was carried out in the Soviet Union, but still believed it just needed to be done better."[37]

DEPORTATIONS, 1941

Our walk now took us to the Chernivtsi train station, a grand and ornate neo-Baroque building, in the Viennese style of Otto Wagner, standing on a large, virtually empty square. Clearly it had been built at a time when the city was a more popular destination: like so many of the city's buildings, it served as a faded reminder of a grander bygone era. But this station was also a witness of the voluntary and involuntary departures of residents of Czerno-witz/Cernăuţi/Chernovtsy, departures that during the early 1940s became more frequent and more desperate.

"It took just one day to shatter the last vestiges of faith in the Communist ideals," Carl told us as we stood by the station's entrance. He and Lotte began to evoke for us the fatal day of June 13, 1941, less than three weeks before the Soviet retreat from the region. War between the Soviet Union and Germany was imminent. NKVD units entered thousands of households, gave the inhabitants an hour to pack, herded them into open trucks, and transported them to this very railway station. The next morning some children and young people were picked up at school or university so that they could be deported along with their parents.[38]

Who was deported? Of the nearly four thousand people who were arrested in Chernovtsy and its neighboring villages on June 13 and subsequent days, 80 percent were Jewish. They included those considered enemies of the regime: holders of the "clause 39" identity cards, land and property owners, industrial-ists, rich farmers—exploitative capitalists, in the minds of Soviet ideologues— as well as public figures and activist members of outlawed political parties and youth movements. But, as Dov Levin writes, they also consisted of "thou-sands of rank-and-file members of Zionist parties and Bundists, irrespective of whether they had previously undergone interrogation or . . . [been] over-looked by the security forces." Indeed, "the mass deportation . . . was not the first of its kind during that year in northern Bukovina, except perhaps in its dimensions; previous deportations had also included a large number of Jews, mainly those who had served in the Romanian government apparatus."[39]

"In our apartment house they deported a couple with a ten-year-old daughter," Pearl Fichman writes. "The man had owned a small furniture store which had been nationalized by the government. Across the street from us they deported a family whose son and daughter had been known as Communists. The father, Mr. Ippen, was a Socialist, the son had volunteered to fight on the Republican Side in the Spanish Civil War and was killed in Spain. It became known that the entire family was non-grata because the son was supposedly a Trotzkyite. The daughter and son-in-law were Communists, but since they lived in her parents' apartment, everybody in the house was taken away. They then sealed the place and a commissar or an officer moved in and inherited the entire household. . . . Many Russians considered it a fact of life that people would disappear by the favor of their government."[40]

During the same days, Manfred Reifer heard a radio news report about the "mass attempts to resettle from Czernowitz. 'Of the thousands who wanted to relocate, only some could be accommodated,' the announcer said. I now understood the mendacity of the Soviet propaganda machine."[41]

There was, however, little time to assess the impact of these "resettlements." By Sunday, June 22, the Soviet Union was at war with Germany, and Chernovtsy was again on the front line. For the Jewish population, there were more—and even deadlier—dangers ahead. Nevertheless, in retrospect, many Czernowitz Jews would consider the deportations of June 13, 1941, in Dov Levin's terms, as "the epitome of everything that occurred under the Soviets in 1940–41, and . . . the symbol of that eventful year."[42]

"I was deeply outraged when I passed the station on my way to a textile plant and saw all these people in cattle cars waiting to be shipped to Siberia," Carl told us by the station. "I said to myself that I would never forget and forgive this lack of humanity. But, you know, it's strange. As soon as the Nazi deportations began in October—and they also left from this spot—I did forget. Remember, by late June the Soviets had already left the city."

"And, once again, we were faced with an impossible choice—to flee with them or to stay here, waiting for the Germans to come," Lotte said. Even in retrospect, she was awed by the magnitude of this decision and the lack of information that made it so difficult. "It was truly confusing."

TWELVE DAYS, SIX VOICES, 1941

How do people make choices in extreme circumstances, with virtually no independent political information, in the midst of individual, familial, and communal constraints and responsibilities, with little knowledge of the consequences their decisions might have for them personally or for their families? What factors determine their choices? With the interregnum days of June 1941, we reach another dramatic turning point in our story, another point in which spur-of-the-moment decision making was required. Here, again, the women in our story tend to remain behind to take care of aging parents and incapacitated family members. Here, again, youth enables risk and experiment, and friends and family are separated by shifting borders and confusing times. Here, again, the course of history could in no way have been foreseen. In order to understand and to convey how individuals live such moments of choice, we quote or paraphrase oral and written accounts by Lilly Hirsch, Lotte Hirsch, Dorothea Sella, Pearl Fichman, Mischa Flexor, and Carl Hirsch.

It's a Sunday, my only day off from work. It is late June, and the weather is finally warmer, so it seems like the perfect day to climb Mount Cecina with my friends. All winter long, I've been looking forward to our Sunday excursions. I'm in the process of packing a few things for a picnic and getting my rucksack together. My mother is returning from the market with some eggs, some farmer's cheese, some fresh peppers and cucumbers, a loaf of bread. She may have brought something I can take along. But she opens the door and yells: "Hitler just attacked the Soviet Union. I heard that there is fighting right outside the city and that the planes at the airport have been destroyed." "It's not true! You're just saying that because you don't want me to go on my outing!" My brothers quickly turn on the radio: it's a good thing we've managed to hold on to that short-wave radio, but now it has the awful sound of Hitler's voice saying, "One hundred fifty Russian divisions are on our border and we have to defend ourselves." My brother Kubi recalls a political meeting he'd had to attend a few days earlier. Now it makes sense that the commissar talked of war and of the victory that would be ours. Kubi had not understood what he was talking about at the time. What will happen to us? My brother Carl, ever the student of history, checks the encyclopedia: "Napoleon began his invasion in early June of 1812," he finds, "by October he was in Moscow." We're sure it will take Hitler less time.

*Lilly Hirsch*[43]

Something major must be going on because the manager of the textile plant is keeping all of us here overnight. I know my parents will worry; I wonder how I can get a message to them that I am alright. I feel even more anxious and cut off from them when I hear that we're at war. The Russian colleagues immediately start making plans to leave, to go home. They ask some of us

Romanians whether we want to come along. I'm more worried about my parents, my sister. I wonder whether they are stocking up on bread, getting water, preparing for what is ahead. They release us in the morning; I guess they have better things to worry about. When I walk home, I run into Carl. "Your sister asked me for help last night, and I went to the factory to try to get you released. Your manager thought I was there as a representative of the Textile Trust. He got very defensive, telling me that the Trust is not to interfere with him and his office! But I was only there in my private capacity!" We both laugh.

He's off to work. I watch him walk away: he's handsome, self-assured even at such a time. He's been at my house a lot these last few months. More and more. At first, he was very shy, discouraged by the fact that I was dating two other young men or maybe by how different we are. I like to go dancing, ice skating. He is so serious, involved with his friends from Hashomer Hatzair, a group I've never joined. My parents have been rooting for him, so has my sister, and my cousins. "He's the one," they keep saying to me. "He's so dependable, so earnest, this is someone you want to spend your life with." But is this a time to make such a decision? And yet, we've gotten close. He even took me to a David Oistrakh concert a few weeks ago; that was a great evening. But then there's also Jascha. What should I do? I've never been in a hurry to get married. In this sense I'm very different from my friends. I wanted to study, to travel, to be independent, but of course the times we're in create a different kind of urgency.

*Lotte Gottfried Hirsch*[44]

Hearing the nearby shooting and watching the retreat of the Soviet tanks from the Southern front, my mother sighs: "I wish we could just hang on to one of those tanks and go along with them; here we are lost." She is of the generation who fled westward from the Russians toward the Germans and Austrians when the First World War started. Now she sees salvation in the East, though fleeing from the Romanians and Germans to the Russians seems impossible.

Andi and I see no way out and are in despair. But there is something we must do immediately: we must burn all the Marxist literature we've accumulated during our year at the Soviet university. What a scene in our kitchen. The broad Russian stove has never burned so well as today, fed by the writings of Marx and Engels, Lenin and Stalin, the Russian edition of *Capital* that Andi just bought for so much money, the history of the Soviet Communist Party in Russian, Ukrainian, and German, our lecture notes and term papers, all influenced by Marxist-Leninist teachings. All that was swallowed by eager flames. Once in a while we take a break so the smoke coming out of the chimney would not be suspicious. When there is nothing left to burn, we turn to each other as helplessly as before. And then we hear that teachers and students from the university might be evacuated together.

*Dorothea Sella*[45]

My knapsack is packed; I'm ready. Our professors and fellow students suggested that we can be evacuated with them when they go. It looks like the Soviet army is offering no resistance so they will soon be gone and I may join them. How will we even find out what is happening? The day after the war began, our radios were confiscated. We had to bring them to the former stock exchange for collection. We took ours right away: I'm sure no one wanted to risk being found with a radio. It's been frightening, the last days to watch the panic among the Russians. And to see what's happening to our young men. Some were just taken off the street to the Soviet army; no questions asked, no good byes. Yuda comes to tell me that his brother was taken in this way. Friends have been coming by to discuss our alternatives. The hospital staff is leaving today and my friend who is a doctor stopped to ask whether I would take care of his parents, his sister and her child while he was gone. The university students are going now. My friend Martha is at the door, asking me to come along. I look at my crying mother and my destitute father and I know that they will be lost without me. The die is cast. Martha leaves, I stay here with my parents.

*Pearl Fichman*[46]

The Russians are all getting evacuation orders from the managers of the Textile Trust. What about us Jews? We've been talking day and night, shall we try to go with them? What will it mean for us? They can't give us any official papers but they encourage us to come along anyway. Romania has joined the war on the side of Germany; no doubt, we're better off with Stalin than with Antonescu. Many of my friends agree that this is the course to take. When I leave work, I still have not decided what to do; Sidy and I stay up late into the night talking. Friends drop by to tell us they are leaving. Sidy is sorry to leave in this beautiful spring season; we have new potatoes and cherries in the pantry. I reassure her that we'll be back in three days; surely the Soviet army will prevail. When we get up it's still dark out. Sidy lays out some bread and cheese for breakfast, she's boiling water for tea. "Sidika, let's go. We can't risk waiting. They say there's shooting at the edge of town, let's leave while it's still dark out." The breakfast stays on the table when we walk out the door, carrying just our pyjamas and half a loaf of bread in our rucksacks.

*Mischa Flexor*[47]

When I come home from work, my mother, brother, and sisters have their rucksacks packed. They are ready to go. My mother remembers the last war when she fled to Vienna with two toddlers; now she is ready to flee in the opposite direction. I rush to Lotte's: I am not going anywhere without her. We've talked every day, considering all the pros and cons. For her, the concern for her parents comes first. Her father and her sister have heart conditions, they cannot undertake such a flight. She's decided to stay here. I worry about leaving without papers: what if we're turned back and get caught in some kind of crossfire? I go home and say to my family: "Unpack, we're staying." I wonder what Mischa and my other friends will do.

The next morning, I find out that he's left with Sidy, and so has Fred Bernard, and others. Did we make the right decision? Only time will tell, I guess. I spend the following days with Lotte. We watch the fires burning below. The Soviets have set fire to buildings, disabling the power station, the water works. By gas light, Lotte and I spend three days reading *The Magic Mountain* together. What can keep one's gloomy thoughts about the German–Romanian invasion at bay if not this masterpiece of German literature?

*Carl Hirsch*[48]

# SIX

## *The Crossroads*

Niemand
zeugt für den
Zeugen.

*No one
bears witness for the
witness.*

PAUL CELAN
*"Aschenglorie"*

These three lines resist even the best translation.

JACQUES DERRIDA
*Sovereignties in Question*

### THE CERNĂUŢI GHETTO, 1998, 1941–1942

If there is one story from Carl and Lotte's wartime experiences that needed to be visualized in a specific place, it is the fateful moment on October 15, 1941, in which they evaded deportation to Transnistria, the region where two-thirds of the Jews of Cernăuţi were forcibly relocated and where more than half of those met their death.[1] We had both heard that story repeatedly, and we knew it well: it is a story they liked to tell. In fact, I had always envisioned that place—where they turned right instead of left—as the life source from which I sprang: it led directly to my parents' marriage in the Cernăuţi ghetto, to their survival during the years of war, and eventually to their escape from Soviet Chernovtsy to Romania, where I was born. They had always described it as located at a corner, a corner where they turned back, into the ghetto, instead of following the other deportees toward the train station. As soon as our trip to Czernowitz was in the plans, we knew we had to see that corner.

"I know stories, but they are not exactly attached to places or to sites," I wrote in my journal on August 27, 1998, one week before our trip. "I even know some of the addresses, street names, house numbers connected to my parents' childhood homes and the homes of family friends. But where was the place they turned around and decided not to go to the train station? And in which Konditorei [pastry shop] did they stop to celebrate their wedding? Are there Konditoreien now?"

We started our walk in front of Lotte's family apartment on what used to be Dreifaltigkeitsgasse (in Romanian, St. Sf. Treimi)—only one block from where my father had lived with his mother, brother, and sisters. We had visited Lotte's former apartment two days before, but now we were back to relive the first days of their internment in the Cernăuți ghetto, beginning on the 11th of October 1941, the day the ghetto was formed.

We had now been in Chernivtsi for a few days and were having a good time together, an adventure, with our routine of walking, visiting, and videotaping Lotte and Carl's narratives and explanations. Lotte and Carl were becoming ever better narrators of their life histories, telling them together, negotiating on some fine points, arguing about others. I was getting to know other sides of them—or, more precisely, qualities that had been dormant, submerged beneath the daily custom of our lives in Romania, Austria, the United States, were coming to the fore. Our walks through the city together and the scenes they evoked in narration, at the places where they had occurred, enabled disparate fragments, frozen in memory, to come together into something more akin to a life story with depth, continuity, causality, and motivation. So far, it had been the story of the *before:* even the difficult Soviet year of 1940–41, with its sense of impending doom and critical decisions, had moments of hopefulness and illusion.

Standing in front of Lotte's apartment and preparing myself to hear about October 11, a day I had visualized so vividly in daydreams and nightmares throughout my childhood, somehow filled me with dread. Although it was a sunny September day, with only a light autumn wind blowing, I was shivering.

We were again walking with my cousin Felix Zuckermann and Rosa's friend Matthias Zwilling, and with our friend Othmar Andrée. "In those days I worked at the railroad administration office from eight to one and from four to seven," Carl began:

In August, I had gone to the Railway Engineering Service in search of a job. I had done practice work there as a student in 1935. They hired me as an engineer under a program in which Jews could do work service as a substitute for the military service from which Jews were now excluded.

Before work, on that Saturday, the 11th of October, I stopped at Lotte's house to say hello like I often did since we began going out together. As I was walking along, a neighbor stopped me and said, "Read this," and showed me an ordinance that was posted on a nearby building. It said: "Anyone who harbors Jews or other undesirables, anyone who owns fire-arms, etc., will immediately be put to death." I told her I didn't think that that concerned us, and I went to work. What was I supposed to do? At 1:00 P.M., when I come home for a meal, I see that everyone is carrying knapsacks and bundles. What's that, I thought? When I came home to my mother's, they were all packed to go. Lotte's family had arranged for us all to go to their cousin Blanka Engler's apartment in the Steingasse within the newly established ghetto. We were eleven, my mother, two sisters, my brother, Lotte and I, her father and mother, her sister, her sister's fiancé, and his mother.

I had heard about this generous offer of Lotte's older first cousin Blanka Morgenstern, who was married to Julius Engler.

We were still standing in front of the house on Dreifaltigkeitsgasse. Lotte gestured, "The ghetto was formed, and our part of the street was outside of it, and we had to be inside the area that would be closed off as the ghetto by six in the afternoon. Since Blanka's place was already terribly overcrowded, Carl's sisters arranged to go with their mother and their brother Kubi to their friend Mania Haller's, who also lived nearby, right where the ghetto began at the bottom of Dreifaltigkeitsgasse. But when it was time for us to be deported a few days later, we all eleven of us left together."

As I was standing there, remembering other narrations of this story and trying to imagine and to visualize it more clearly, I realized both how much I already knew about the events of the day and, ironically, how unimaginable they had remained for me. Leo was videotaping, the others were listening, a few passers-by stared. Some trucks drove by, and I worried about the noise on the tape. "How did you know to go—was there any order in writing, any ordinance?" Othmar Andrée asked my parents.

"The members of the Jewish Council went from house to house and said, by 6:00 P.M. you have to be within this perimeter—between the Str. O. Iosif, which was the former Steingasse [now Pereyaslavska], and the St. Mărășești, the Neueweltgasse [now Shevchenka], extending north and east and includ-ing the Judengasse [in Romanian, Evreiască; now Shalom Alejhema] and the poorer Jewish neighborhood nearer to the train station," Carl responded.

"They said we should bring warm coats, other clothing, food for a few days, as much as we could carry. Nothing was posted. They told us to place the apartment keys in an envelope with our names on it and that we would have to hand those envelopes to the authorities when we arrived in the ghetto. I said, 'We're leaving—we must set the house on fire.' Do you remember, Lotte?"

Lotte nodded. "My father said, 'This cannot be possible!'" She had quoted this exclamation of my grandfather's on many occasions, always with a smile that indicated pleasurable memories of her father's incongruous sense of justice. "'This violates the Declaration of the Rights of Man.' He was a lawyer."

We had been walking a few blocks now, slowly, talking and videotaping. I studied my parents' faces and gestures as they moved through the same space one more time. I looked at the rutted and irregular cobblestones and wondered if, even then, they had stuck out in the same places. "Marianne, Leo, come here, look," Carl called to us, pointing. "*Here* they made a fence and soldiers stood here. *Here* was the edge of the ghetto. And *here,* now we are inside the ghetto." He stepped inside the boundary he had drawn for us in the air. "And *here* we moved into Blanka's apartment, *there* on the second floor." The three-story building looked very much like the one my mother had grown up in. The tree-lined street was quiet in the September mid-morning—surely quite different from that fateful cold late afternoon in October so many years ago. "The next morning we went out to talk to everyone," Carl continued:

> We could move around freely inside the ghetto; everyone was dressed casu-
> ally, in sweaters, for the trip—to the ghetto and beyond. Word is out that
> the ghetto is only temporary and that we would be taken eastwards, some-
> where across the Dniestr. We knew that, for us, now start the *Forty Days of
> Musa Dagh* (you know, that novel by Franz Werfel about the Armenians
> chased out of their homes and into the desert by the Turks in World War I).
>
> We're on a Sunday. We're here Monday, Tuesday. On Wednesday
> [October 15] everyone living on the Steingasse (where we were staying) and
> surrounding streets was supposed to go to the train station for deportation.
> We had known that this was coming and, of course, we were packed to go.
> It's how we had come there to Blanka's; we never unpacked. We met up
> with my mother, brother and sisters, and we all went outside and saw a lot
> of peasants with horse-drawn carts waiting for customers to transport to
> the train station, and Lotte's father said, 'It's a sunny day, a good day for
> traveling.' So we loaded all our things, for eleven people, onto one of these
> carts and waited our turn to go.

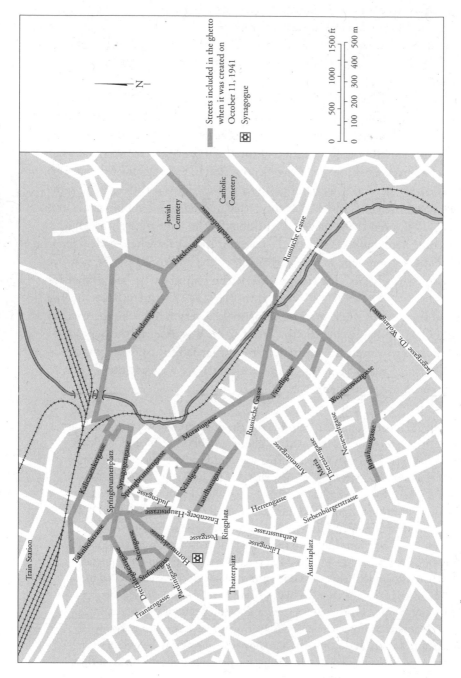

Map 3. Czernowitz, showing the streets included in the ghetto in its first configuration in 1941, based on official Romanian information published in Cernăuți in the Romanian-language newspaper *Bucovina* on the day the ghetto was established.

STREET-NAME EQUIVALENTS IN GERMAN, ROMANIAN, AND UKRAINIAN

| German | Romanian | Ukrainian |
|---|---|---|
| Armeniergasse | Dmitri Petrino | Virmenska |
| Austriaplatz | Ghica Vodă Piaţa | Soborna Ploshcha |
| Bahnhofstrasse | I. C. Bratianu | Gagarina |
| Bräuhausgasse | Războieni | Lukjana Kobylyci, Lukiana Kobylitsi |
| Dreifaltigkeitsgasse | Sfânta Treimi | Chmelnys'koho, Bogdana Khmelnitskogo |
| Enzenberg-Hauptstrasse | Regele Ferdinand | Golovna |
| Franzengasse | 11 Noembrie | 28 Tchervnia, Tchernishevskogo |
| Friedensgasse | Stefan Tomsa | Lubens'ka |
| Friedhofstrasse | Cimitirului | Zelena |
| Herrengasse | Iancu Flondor | Kobylyanska |
| Hormuzakigasse | Hormuzachi | Zan'kovec'koji, Zankovetskoy |
| Jaegergasse (Dr. Wolangasse) | Petru Rareş | Bukovyns'ka, Bukovinska |
| Judengasse | Evreiască | Shalom Alejhema |
| Kaliczaenkergasse | Caliceanca | Odeska |
| Kaliczaenker Hauptstrasse | | Bilorus'ka |
| Landhausgasse | General Mircescu | Septyc'koho, Sheptiskogo |
| Liliengasse | Constantin Brâncoveanu | Ivana Franka |
| Maria Theresiengasse | Mirin Costin | Tscheluskiutsiv |
| Morariugasse | General Averescu | Petra Sagaydachnogo |
| Neuweltgasse | Mărăşeşti | Sevcenka, Shevchenka |
| Pardinigasse | Dionisie Bejan | Klari Tsetkin |
| Pitzelligasse | General Foch | Yaremchuka |
| Postgasse | Bucureştilor | Khudiakova |
| Rathausstrasse | Regina Maria | Golovna |
| Ringplatz | Piaţa Unirii | Zentraina Ploshcha |
| Russische Gasse | Romană | Rus'ka, Russka |
| Schulgasse | General Prezan | Skilna (Shkilna) |
| Siebenbürgerstrasse | Ştefan cel Mare | Golovna |
| Springbrunnengasse | Ion Creangă | Sahajdacnoho, Sagaydachnogo |
| Springbrunnenplatz | Fântânei Piaţa | Golovna, B. Khmelnitskogo, Gagarina cr. |
| Stefaniegasse | Eminescu | Gorkogo (Hor'koho) |
| Steingasse | O. Josif | Pereyaslavska |
| Synagogengasse | Wilson | Barbjussa |
| Theaterplatz | Viktoriei Piaţa | Pl. Teatraina |
| Wojnarowiczgasse | Olteniei | Fuchika |

My mother had been gesturing. "May I add something here? This is something, Carl, which you don't totally admit. They said, now the Steingasse is on, and we put everything on that wagon. Everything. We had pillows, bedding, pots, all our elderly sick relatives on foot, everyone carrying something. What you won't admit is that a Romanian soldier came to our door and said, 'Ok, now you have to go.'"

Carl was impatient, "There's no point. Everyone was already outside, we all knew. We have to tell the same story. The soldier is beside the point. The Jewish Council said, get ready."

"Yes, the Jewish Council worked with them, they hoped perhaps to save at least a few people." She was ready to agree, "Yes, we knew we had to leave."

"Actually, remember, we had found a cart, and the husband of your other cousin, Hermann, rushed to take it away from us, so everything got delayed. We had to find another driver who was available! It was chaos that day."

We were on what used to be the Steingasse, standing on the street where they stood with hundreds of others, with carts and belongings. Did a soldier come to the door to summon them to get out, or were they already prepared to do so anyway? Did it really matter? These were things we would have to sort out later, I knew. I had heard some stories, from several sources, that said that some rushed to leave in the first days, convinced that they would get better lodging in Transnistria that way. Max Gottfried's comment that it was a sunny day, a good day for traveling, certainly indicated a certain resignation, at least on his part, if not an actual willingness to go along with what the authorities had mandated.

I barely had time for some of these thoughts, while Carl continued his narrative:

While we were standing there on the street, a neighbor came by and pulled me aside. "I hear that some professionals will be allowed to stay in Czernowitz," she said. "Some waivers will be granted." I asked around. My sister Lilly had heard the same thing from another source but had not dared to believe it. About a half hour later—we were still on that street, there were lots of carts ahead of us and everything was moving really slowly—a Romanian major walked by, and I said to him, "*Domnule maior,* I hear that professionals will be allowed to stay. I am an engineer." He looked at me quickly and said, "Stay." That's all.

Imagine, I was on my way to the station with eleven people: my old mother, Lotte's old parents, her sick sister, the old mother of my brother-in-law. All were scared. Lotte and I had to act. So we took the carriage and . . .

Figure 21. Cernăuţi ghetto commemorative plaques; the streets of the ghetto are marked on the older plaque, above; see also map 3 (Photographs by Leo Spitzer)

Othmar Andrée, deeply engaged in a narrative he was hearing for the first time, interrupted: "But wait, you had nothing in writing, and that Romanian major was gone. How could you . . . ?"

"He had said only three words," Lotte pointed to the ground. "'*Rămăi pe loc.*' Stay right here!"

We now came to a small rectangular marble memorial plaque mounted about six inches above a tall doorway on a building on the Steingasse. "This," Matthias Zwilling indicated, "commemorates the Czernowitz ghetto." The plaque, at that distance, was utterly illegible. Only a *menorah* and a map of the tangled ghetto streets carved into the marble could be made out with any clarity. But across the street a new, more legible commemorative plaque had also recently been installed. Together we deciphered the Ukrainian and Yiddish inscriptions: "Here, in this place in 1941, was the location of the Czernowitz ghetto where 50,000 Jews were incarcerated." That plaque was on the wall of a building on a busy crossing of five streets, two leading down a steep hill toward the railroad station, one toward the northwestern section of the city, and two others toward the old Jewish quarter.

Here was "the corner" we had heard so much about. But it was not at all a corner; it was a major intersection, a large traffic-filled square that used to be called the Springbrunnenplatz, the Fountain Square (Romanian, Piaţa Fântânei). It was noisy, but we stopped there anyway, and my father's narrative continued. Passing pedestrians looked puzzled or amused as my parents, as though in a trance of memory, gestured in different directions, drawing the scene for us with their arms and their bodies.

"*Here* were the carriages in a row on their way to the train. *Here* there was a chain of soldiers, and here, on this side, was only a single soldier. So I brought the carriage over here to the single soldier, and I gave him 100 lei. I said nothing."

Although I had heard all this before, it seemed more difficult to believe now on this wide, expansive cobble-stoned square.

"You went this way while everyone else was going that way, and he let you through?" Othmar asked in disbelief.

Carl nodded, "Yes. On the Schulgasse [Romanian, General Prezan; now Shkilna], only two blocks from here, there was the Lehr family, distant cousins, and we knew that their street had not yet been evacuated."

Leo handed me the camera and started gesturing himself. "That way is to the train station?"

"Yes, and this way was back inside the ghetto. We thought, where to go? Maybe the Lehrs will take us in?"

"You *paid* to get back inside the ghetto?"

"Baksheesh," Carl said, shrugging his shoulders matter-of-factly. "We went on to the Lehrs. There were already about thirty to thirty-five people there, but they took us in, eleven more. My siblings slept in the laundry room behind the house, and for the rest of us they found some floor space some-

Figure 22. Deported Jews on the banks of the Dniester, 1941 (Courtesy of Yad Vashem)

where. This was on a Wednesday. On that evening, in the Jewish Hospital, which was the seat of the Jewish Council at the time, the Romanian mayor came and said . . ."

My mother added an explanation, "The mayor was Traian Popovici, and he was very friendly to the Jews."

"He spoke in a mixture of German and Yiddish," Carl specified. "He said, *'Ich hob fir euch eine gute Bashere,'* I have good news for you. You are staying here.' You see, he had to arrange for professionals with technical skills to stay. He couldn't run the city otherwise. Only later, he changed it to say that only *part* of the Jewish population will be able to stay. So Sigmund Lehr, the cousin we were staying with said, '*Mazel Tov,*' and he went to the basement and got out some champagne, and we all drank champagne and celebrated."

These details had been recalled before, but now we had turned into the street that was the Schulgasse, and we were looking at the house that had belonged to the Lehrs, a villa behind a wrought-iron fence, both badly in need of a paint job. We were visualizing forty people crowding around a room, drinking champagne together, and allowing themselves to have hope.

I turned to Felix: "Your mother and her family had already been deported by that time?"

"Yes, they went on the very first day. Bad luck, I suppose. Only a little more than a month later, she lost her husband, her child, and her parents to typhus in Bershad. She survived there all alone."

"And you, Matthias?"

Matthias Zwilling shrugged. Clearly he had not wanted to interrupt Carl and Lotte's narrative with his own. "My mother and I were really lucky," he told me quietly. "My mother was a doctor working in a hospital, and there she had gotten to know the daughter of the rabbi of the synagogue on Kobylicistrasse, who was working as a nurse. We were able to find shelter at the rabbi's house." Through his mother's profession as a doctor, they managed to join the twenty thousand Jews who evaded deportation to Transnistria and survived the war in Cernăuți.[2]

When we returned to the United States some weeks later, we sought out the testimony of Traian Popovici, the mayor of Cernăuți, who sometime between the end of the war and his death in 1946 described the dramatic events of the same days from his own, quite different, vantage point.

On that 10 October, I was summoned to the governor's office. General Calotescu instructed me to see that the bakeries baked more bread than usual to supply the Jewish population that was going into the ghetto and hand them out four loaves per head as they embarked on the trains.

It is in the governor's office that I found out the deportation of the Jews from Cernăuți had been decided. At the same time, I learned about the other measures concerning their internment in the ghetto—the goods they left behind at home were to be collected and handed over to the state for safekeeping. . . .

I was petrified and could barely utter a few words. "How could you come

Figure 23. Traian Popovici, the mayor of
Cernăuți in 1941 (Courtesy of Yad Vashem)

to this, Mr. Governor?" "What could I do?" he said. "It is the Marshal's
order and here are the envoys of the general staff." . . .

I first warned him about the historical responsibility he was taking
upon himself; about the international consequences we will have to bear;
about the difficulties we will face at the final peace conference where
civilized nations will call Romania to account. . . . I spoke about mankind
and humaneness, of the traditional kindheartedness of Romanians, [of]
savagery, cruelty, murder and disgrace. . . . I mentioned the disgrace of Spain
that had never managed to clear its history of the stain of Torquemada's
anti-Jewish persecution of 1492. I said, and I quote: "Domnule guvărnător,
the French Revolution that gave mankind the gift of justice and freedom
took a toll of 11,800 while with the winter coming soon, you are sending
50,000 to their death." . . .

The colonel Petrescu suddenly said: "Who's going to write history,
Mr. Mayor, the yids? I'm coming here to weed your garden and you won't
let me do it?" . . .

On the morning of October 11, a cold wet day, as gloomy as the hearts of so many wretched people, I looked out the bedroom window attracted by the first flakes of an early snow and I couldn't believe my eyes. Out there, a great convoy were going into exile: Old men leaning on children, women with babies in their arms, cripples dragging their mangled bodies, all bags in hand, the healthy ones pushing barrows or carts, or carrying on their back coffers hastily packed and tied, blankets, bed sheets, clothes, odds and ends, all of them heading for the city's vale of tears, the ghetto. . . .

Anyone who was familiar with the topography of Cernăuţi would have grasped from the limits provided in the "notification" what a small area had been reserved for the ghetto. The neighborhood, to which the Jewish population was "invited" to move before 6 PM, or face the death penalty, could not have sheltered more than 10,000 people pressed together like in a bazaar. It had to house 50,000, not to mention the Christian population that was living there. . . .

The accommodation capacity was minimal. Even by huddling up to 30 people or more in what rooms were available, the great majority had to take shelter in corridors, lofts, cellars, barns, or any other shed that would protect them from rain or snow. There were no hygienic conditions to speak about. Drinking water was scant and doubtful; the number of wells was insufficient. Actually, the city had water problems, as two out of three water works had been destroyed. Almost immediately, a combined stench of rank sweat, urine, feces, and mildew extended over the neighborhood, making it distinct from the rest of town. It was exactly the same concentrated smell as that emerging from a pen of sheep in a green pasture. . . .

On the next morning, Sunday, October 12, I was invited to a meeting of all public authorities at the governor's office. We were 18. . . . I was the only one who . . . stood up and spoke at length about the Jewish question in our time and in that climate of racial hatred in which I said we Romanians were a nation too small to engage. I stressed the merits of the Jews, their worthy contributions to the economic development of the country, their achievements in every area of work and culture, and, in my capacity as mayor of the city, I protested against this act. . . .

I asked that those who had devoted their lives to profound culture and fine arts be spared. I asked for the reward of the pensioners, officers, invalids who had earned the gratitude of our nation. I asked if we might keep here professionals in all branches of industry. I asked that foremen in every branch of industry should be allowed to stay. I asked, for the sake of humanity, that doctors be exempted. I argued for keeping back the engineers and architects that would be needed for the work of recon-struction. I pleaded for exempting magistrates and lawyers, showing we owed that much to intellect and civilization. . . . The fact is that the governor partly endorsed my views and publicly authorized me to make a list of who, according to my arguments, were entitled to the gratitude of our nation. I was asked not to exceed a maximum of 100 to 120. . . .

On Wednesday afternoon, October 15, Marshall Antonescu talked with the governor on the phone and agreed to mitigate the deportation measure. Consequently he ordered that up to 20,000 Jews should be exempted, comprising the categories I had mentioned. . . . That's how about 20,000 Jews were allowed to remain in Cernăuți.

On the evening of that very day, October 15, once General Ionescu and I set our schedule for the next day, I took a ride to the Jewish hospital, which was located on a border of the ghetto, on the main street to the station. I had been informed earlier in the day about the outbreak of a typhus epidemic which required some preventative measures that involved the municipality. Besides, I wanted to convey to the community leaders the message that the Marshall intended to spare part of the local Jewry. . . .

The dramatic moments when I broke the hopeful news to them I think have been the most solemn and moving in my life so far. . . .

Old rabbis, intellectuals of all ages, leaders from all areas of social life, merchants, workers, in short, every living soul, burst into soothing tears, went down on their knees blessing their God, thanking heaven for its mercy and the marshal for his favor, and trying to kiss my hands and feet and the tails of my coat. Sometimes even a man must shed a tear. Moved by that natural outburst of gratitude, tears came to my eyes and I, the "father of the city" wept along. . . . That moment we shared the same hope for a better world.[3]

---

"That was on a Wednesday," Carl continued his narrative, standing on what had been the Schulgasse. "On Thursday morning, another piece of news. The ghetto will be expanded beyond the central area of the city and the old Jewish quarter. Some streets in that section had already been evacuated and were closed down, but new streets were opened to accommodate the large numbers of people who were interned. In that new part on the Wojnarowiczgasse [Romanian, Olteniei; now, Fuchika], an uncle of Lotte's lived in a new villa, so on that Thursday the eleven of us moved again, to that uncle Rubel."

"We were also over sixty people there," Lotte recalled, "relatives from all sides of the Rubel family, friends. Blanka Engler and her family also somehow ended up there: we were together again. We slept all over the house. You can imagine the long lines for the toilet." Lotte started laughing. "One day, my aunt really had to go, so she moved to the head of the line yelling, 'I am still the owner of this house!!'"

"We all settled in," said Carl, picking up the story. "We played cards and we waited. Traian Popovici had promised, but we began to have some doubts and worries. So it was Thursday. On Friday I said to Lotte, 'Whatever happens, whether we stay or go, let's get married.' So around 2:00 P.M. on that Friday, I look out the window and there's a rabbi standing outside. So I say to him, 'Can you marry us?' And he says that after 2:00 P.M. on a Friday in late fall it's too late to get married under Jewish law. On Saturday morning, the 18th of October, we go to the commander of the ghetto, a Romanian major and we say, 'Sir, we want to get married.'"

"This was complicated," Lotte chimed in, "because by law you have to post an official 'intention' for two weeks preceding a civil wedding, so we had to get a dispensation from the court."

They were now telling the story together as they had on so many occasions before. It was a story with which I had grown up, one even my children had heard on many an anniversary.

"So the major gave us a soldier as an escort," Carl said, "and we went to the courthouse to get a dispensation so we could get married on that day."

"Actually," Lotte added, "that major called the soldier aside and told him to walk on the other side of the street so it wouldn't be so obvious. But when we got to the courthouse and told the official what we wanted, he said, curtly, 'But how did you leave the ghetto?' So I opened the door and pointed to the soldier and said, 'Under military escort.'" She repeated her gesture of opening the door and of pointing outside, showing us how she maintained her composure through the indignity she was made to suffer.

"We got the dispensation," Carl said, "and in the afternoon we went back to the registry in the city hall again, guarded by that same soldier."

"My sister, Fritzi, and her fiancé, Edi Bong, were allowed to come with us as witnesses," Lotte added, recalling this detail with pleasure.

"When we went to city hall, the registrar who was a professor, received us very warmly and after he married us, he said to me, '*Domnule inginer,* I hope that we will be able to celebrate many other happy occasions with your people here in Romania.' When we went back to the ghetto, Lotte's mother was very surprised and hurt and said, 'No one ever tells me anything.'"

They had left out a detail I had heard before, so I interrupted them here. "But wait, first you went to a Konditorei, a café. Where was that?"

"Yes," my mother was happy to fill this in. "That was Edi's idea. We took our military escort out for a pastry to celebrate. And when we got back to the house, some of the relatives already knew, and they took out whatever bits of food they had left and laid a large and very eclectic table, and we ate and celebrated as best we could."

"That night I slept with my siblings," Carl said, "and Lotte with her family, but the next night they gave us a space in a room with another married couple. We got the spot under the piano. They snored a lot."

"You see, we got married without any rings, without a wedding dress, without pictures. We have no wedding pictures. I remember when I was younger and I saw a bride I would ask my mother, would I have such a dress at my wedding as well. And she assured me that I would, but it was not to be."

"We got these rings years later, in Romania, do you remember?" Carl turned to Lotte and they both showed us their hands.

### TELLING AND LISTENING, 1998

As Lotte and Carl repeated their walk of that day—and as we walked along with them, from the homes they had to evacuate to the house where they first moved to the crossroads where they turned back into the ghetto instead of going to the train station and deportation—they were there with us, but also, at the same time, back in that moment in 1941 when their future was so uncertain. They relived the days of waiting, their wedding at the city hall under military escort, their relief at obtaining exemptions to remain in Cernăuți, the frightening insecurities of the subsequent months. But, owing to our presence perhaps, and through the experience of telling the story to us in all its details and nuances, they could also gain a retrospective distance from that past. They could look back on it with the child who might not have been born had they taken a different turn.

On September 6, 1998, I wrote in my journal: "What's different about hearing the same story, here, in the actual place? Because the stories in fact have not changed, they are still the same. Few new ones have come, a few additional details, maybe. But it is different. This crossroads is so graphic, so immediate, and yet also so symbolic." True: on site, their memories gained substance, dimensionality, texture, and color. Leo and I had visited Terezín, Lvov, and other Nazi-created ghettos; we had seen films and photos, and maps of the ghettos in Warsaw, Lódz, and Cracow. But walking through Chernivtsi with my parents, seeing the houses in which they had been children and grown into adulthood, and having them identify the houses where their various friends and acquaintances had lived, we finally internalized, in a way we never could before, the reality of what we now euphemistically refer to as "ethnic cleansing": the brutality involved in forcing people to abandon their homes, gathering them into one small area, and then, systematically, clearing the city of their presence. We could sense the strange resignation, the compliance with which they must have packed their belongings and lined up for the train station, but also the anger and bitterness that would make Carl want to set the house on fire as he left. We came to appreciate the irony and performative force of my grandfather's invocation of the Declaration of the Rights of Man from the French Revolution at the very moment when he saw himself excluded from citizenship and from humanity.

We could do more than visualize their journey: we could smell and touch that crisp October day in 1941, hear the commotion on the street, the rumors that were flying, participate in the split-second decision that they reenacted at the Springbrunnenplatz as they pointed and turned in the one direction over the other. Suddenly, as we talked and listened, the barricades and rows of soldiers became visible. And as we walked about this landscape of memory, the streets became animated with the presence of people from that past: long-lost relatives, friends, neighbors, Lotte and Carl, young, in their twenties—ghosts emerging from the shadows between the buildings, conjured up by recall and narration, by our being there, by our presence and witness.

"Places," Toni Morrison writes in *Beloved,* "places are still there. If a house burns down, it's gone, but the place—the picture of it—stays, and not just in my rememory but out there, in the world. . . . if you go there—you who never was there—if you go there and stand in the place where it was, it will happen again; it will be there for you, waiting for you."[24] This was indeed the risk of our journey. The location authenticates the narrative, embodies it, makes it real, to the point where it threatens to reengulf those who come to tell and to listen. Our presence there together gave a materiality to those October days of 1941—a substance that they could not possibly attain through a marble plaque mounted on a wall.

And yet, simultaneously, the traffic noises and the people around us, many of them watching as we videotaped Lotte and Carl's testimony, brought us back into the present. Here we found the retrospective vantage point that powerfully confirmed their spur-of-the-moment decision to turn a corner and change direction. But, looking back, we could also see something else that Lotte and Carl had not up until that moment conveyed to us: that this "corner," as they had characterized it, was also a crossing of *many* roads that symbolically reflected the many turns their lives *could have* taken—and that the lives of many of their contemporaries took: emigration . . . exile . . . flight into the Soviet Union . . . deportation . . . Transnistria . . . Bucharest . . . Paris . . . Vienna . . . Tel Aviv . . . New York . . . As absolutely literal as that intersection with the uneven cobblestones on which we were standing was, it also acquired symbolic meaning through *our* contemplation and interpretation—the meaning we were able to find in their narrative. And through this insight that took their journey out of the past into a timeless significance, retrospective witnessing became prospective.

That moment of this insight on the Springbrunnenplatz—and afterwards, when we went back to the Cheremosh Hotel and had a chance to talk with each other, write in our journals, sleep, and dream—produced the link between our generations that compelled us toward this book.

"Niemand / zeugt für den / Zeugen" (No one / bears witness for / the witness), wrote Paul Celan in the 1960s before he committed suicide in Paris, feeling isolated, displaced, and misunderstood.[5] The "listening" he yearned for, which he calls a "bear[ing] witness for the witness" here, he clarifies in another poem by enjoining his listener to "hör dich ein / mit dem Mund" (hear deep in / with your mouth), a deep active listening that leads not just to response but to the listener's own proclamation and even, perhaps, to an act of repair:

The Trumpet Place
deep in the glowing
text-void
at torch height
in the timehole:

hear deep in
with your mouth.

In Biblical terms, Celan calls for a shofar (*Posaune,* trumpet) and a torch to heal the "text-void" (*Leertext*) from which the witness suffers.[6]

Indeed, for Carl and Lotte, our interest confirmed something about their past, its importance, its narrative and its dramatic quality, the need to pass it on. Our challenge was to receive the story from them, and to receive it as active, collaborative "cowitnesses" who could encourage the emergence of the more tentative, fragmentary, and ambiguous—even the more painful and vulnerable—aspects of that past experience, alongside the more positive remembrances of good fortune and community.[7]

This is how we tried to listen. And our retelling, in this book, is the measure of that effort to listen and to read the words and the meanings of testimonies and testaments from this period—indeed, to attempt to bear witness for the witnesses and to respect all that remains incomprehensible and, in Jacques Derrida's terms, untranslatable. Carl and Lotte, Rosa Zuckermann, Matthias

Zwilling, but also Traian Popovici. We listen to them and read them as members of the next generation and as historians, responsible to them and to their story and to the little-known history of the Holocaust in Cernăuți.

We have come to see the Springbrunnenplatz, and the vicissitudes of telling and listening we enacted there, as a figure for our project. For Lotte and Carl—the first generation—that crossroads is a site of nostalgic return because it confirms their good fortune while highlighting their decisiveness and agency. It grounds the enabling moment that set a direction for their subsequent lives in a physical space. Simultaneously, it also concretizes their critical memory—memorializing (in the very physical sense of that concept) their immeasurable loss and their mourning for those thousands of others who were forced to take the other turn. And for us, in the postmemorial generation, this crossroads is—paradoxically—an index for our rootless nostalgia. It is less location than transitional space where the encounter between generations, between past and present, between memory and place, can momentarily, effervescently, be staged.

But it is more: it is an index, as well, for the crossroads that Czernowitz itself has always been—the site of encounters between languages (German, Yiddish, Romanian, Russian, Ukrainian) and cultures (Romanians, Austrians, Jews, Germans, Ukrainians, Hutsuls, Poles, Russians). During the Second World War, as national borders shifted repeatedly in a matter of days or months, its liminal location proved to be decisive for its Jewish population, sending some to deportation and death, enabling others to survive. "We lived on the border," Lotte said to us during our visit to Chernivtsi, "and you could say that that was the root of all our problems. First we were under the Romanians, then under the Soviets, then under the Romanians and the Germans, then under the Soviets again." But in his memoir, Carl underscores their good fortune when he writes, "The threat of the Nazi death camps was as close as the border to Poland, sixteen miles to the North."[8]

### ENCOUNTERS AND FAREWELLS, 1998

On our final morning in Chernivtsi in 1998, the four of us met for breakfast a little later than usual. We had planned to eat, check out of the Cheremosh Hotel, and take a last walk through the city streets. I was determined to look in on Rosa for a last time, to hug her good bye. Even as we were thinking about these farewells, our conversation turned to the next stage of our trip, the two days we had planned to stay in Lviv, the famous Lemberg of my parents' youth, a city they had never visited.

At breakfast, we looked through the Lviv guidebook and discussed our last morning in Chernivtsi. The service was even slower than usual. We had gotten used to the hotel's enormous dining room, its dozens of empty tables covered in not so fresh red-and-white-checkered cloths. Myriads of waitresses circled around, chatted with one another, walked back and forth to and from the kitchen on high heels, projecting an illusion of hurried activity. Yet items appeared on our table one by one, first butter, then some coffee and tea; milk came quite a bit later. One waitress asked if we wanted eggs; another came and offered blinis. We opted for blinis, having tasted them on previous days and found them irresistible. We were decidedly less impatient than we had been when we first arrived; this rhythm had become familiar. Still, our table was crowded with hand luggage and our cameras. We had already moved out of our rooms that morning and were eager to start the day.

Involved in complicated negotiations with several waitresses in the midst of our own plan-making, we were surprised to look up and see a man younger than my parents, informally dressed in pants and a sweater, standing by our table and trying to get our attention. Looking up now, I saw three younger men at his table, also looking over to us. Their resemblance to each other was striking.

"*Entschuldigen Sie,* excuse me," the older man addressed my parents in German, spoken with a distinct Czernowitz lilt, though there was also a slight Hebrew inflection in his voice. "I heard you speaking German with each other. Are you Czernowitzers?"

Carl was still on a mission to get breakfast and move on. "Yes, Hirsch," he said curtly and shook the other man's hand. "And you are?"

"Permit me to introduce myself. Rosengarten. I am here with my three sons." He had barely pointed over to the other table when both my parents began exclaiming.

"Rosengarten! There was an engineer Rosengarten, a close friend," Carl said.

"Come on, now," Lotte almost yelled. "This couldn't be Heinz."

"My name is Andy. Heinz was my older brother." He walked over to my mother, bowed and kissed her hand.

"*Ahi!* Unbelievable!" my parents exclaimed in unison.

At this point, the sons had come over, and we were shaking hands, introducing ourselves in English to them. They were clearly Israeli, but spoke English fluently, with strong Hebrew accents. Both Leo and one of the Rosengarten sons started videotaping this unlikely encounter in the dining room of the Cheremosh.

"This is not such a surprise," said Andy Rosengarten, amused at the excitement of the younger generation. "I am taking my sons on a 'roots' trip. A lot of Israelis do it; it's all the rage. But we have had an amazing stay here these last few days." He used the English word *roots*.

My parents were not ready to hear about his trip; they were too moved to meet the brother of their friend Heinz who, along with his wife Annie, had perished so tragically in Transnistria. "What happened to them exactly?" Carl asked. "How much were you able to find out about it?"

Andy sat down and spoke quietly. "Well, you know that they were deported in 1942 and thus were taken across the Bug River [into German-occupied territory]. The Nazis shot them. That's all I know. You knew them! I was sixteen when I last saw my brother. I was taken to a forced labor camp at the same time."

I studied the four large men whose background was so close to mine. The father's gestures and turns of phrase were utterly familiar, shaped by the lifeways of a city he had left decades before as a teenager, lifeways that themselves had been inherited from the long-since-lost Austrian era of Czernowitz. Bowing, kissing hands—shades of a layered past we all had in common, a shared history and legacy of a world "before," transformed and irremediably shattered by merciless persecution and expulsion. It was a past that continues to haunt in Haifa as much it does in New Hampshire, Vermont, and New York. What did the return to place mean to Andy Rosengarten and his sons? Why did they come?

The ensuing conversation revealed an unmistakable sense of purpose. Beyond taking his sons on the traditional journey of return, Andy Rosengarten had three missions: to visit the graves of his grandparents; to find and again see the houses in which he had lived, particularly the house where his family was interned in the ghetto; and to sit one more time on his high school bench at the Aron Pumnul Gymnasium. He radiated satisfaction, having succeeded in all three. It had taken many hours of working with axes and rakes for the four of them to cut down enough shrubbery to find his grandmother's grave the previous day, they assured us. In addition, Andy had arranged to address the students attending his old school. Sitting on the very same wooden benches that he and his friends had occupied six decades earlier, the students had listened attentively, he reported, as an interpreter translated his account of having attended that school and being chased out, and then, during the war, being interned, deported, and compelled into forced labor. Lastly, he told them of his postwar flight from the Soviet Union.

"You went to Aron Pumnul? Did you by any chance have a teacher named Bong?" Carl asked. Edi Bong was my uncle, Lotte's brother-in-law, a high school teacher of French in Cernăuți and later Timișoara, whose former students I occasionally meet in the United States and elsewhere, and who all seem to remember him vividly.

"Of course. An amazing French teacher, strict, but excellent. I remember everything he taught us. Do you want me to recite the 'Serment de Strasbourg' in old French?"[9] Without waiting for an answer he stood up, really straight, his body remembering the correct posture for recitation, and began to orate the verses breathlessly and eloquently, reciting the first stanza with no hesitation: "*Pro Deo amur et pro christian poblo et nostro comun salvament*. . . . I learned that close to sixty years ago," he insisted, looking around to his sons for approbation.

While our parents continued to exchange news of other friends and acquaintances, the Rosengarten sons talked with us about their impressions.

"It was so amazing to see places you have heard about all your life but that you have never seen before." Each described the special connection he had always felt to Czernowitz that was reinforced and invigorated during this trip. "It is part of us," they emphasized. And they were glad to have made it possible for their father to return and to honor the memory of his forbears. Andy Rosengarten was in the process of writing his memoirs, in Hebrew, for the benefit of his children and grandchildren. As a child survivor, he felt he had a particularly important story to tell.

The remainder of our morning, our last in Chernivtsi with Carl and Lotte, was under the shadow of this chance meeting. The Rosengarten trip made ours at once less unique and more broadly meaningful. Perhaps our multigenerational visits to Czernowitz would have the effect of putting it back on a contemporary map. By bringing our memories and postmemories back here, we were able to move the idea of this city into the present, overlaying, briefly, the place that it once was with a new, altered place, transformed in part by our visit. I thought about the students in the school Andy visited and how they now might have a more concrete sense of history than before, just like the couple living in Lotte's old apartment might now be able to imagine other women cooking in their kitchen, previous residents putting logs in their stove. In spite of the anachronism of the maps we followed, we were, after all, not just living in the past: we were also creating memories in the present. But how interested were we really in the people living here now? How interested were they in us?

We raised some of these questions as we took our last walk down the Herrengasse. My parents fell behind, exchanging impressions with each other. They had said good-bye to Rosa the previous day and did not want to join us in visiting her once again. Did they know that this would be the last time they saw her? "Promise, you won't forget me," she had yelled after them on the previous day. "Call me frequently; you know how hard it is to phone from here."

Leo and I walked quickly along the route we had taken on each of the previous days, down the Franzensgasse to the Pardinigasse. Carrying a small bunch of carnations we had purchased in the market, we rang Rosa's bell unannounced. "Come in, come in!" she exclaimed. "You have to meet my student. She is going to visit Germany and is learning German." We shook hands with a heavy-set young woman, well-dressed by the Ukrainian standards we now knew how to recognize.

"I'm so pleased to see you just one more time. Oh yes, I'm one of the last old Jews here. Soon to be forgotten . . ." Rosa had told us this before, but now she sounded as if she wanted us to reassure her that she was mistaken.

"Masha, show them how well you learned the *Vaterunser*. You'll see, she can recite the Lord's Prayer in perfect German." Rosa smiled: the irony was not lost on her.

"Vater Unser, Du bist im Himmel. Gelobt sei Dein Name," Masha's Ukrainian accent was heavy, the words slow, hesitant, but correct.

And, as we left Rosa's apartment, after several more hugs and promises to stay in touch, the Lord's Prayer, in German, taught to a Ukrainian woman by a Jew who had lost her family to Antonescu and Hitler, was still resounding through the halls of this building, on this street, in this formerly Austro-German city, now in Ukraine.

We met my parents on the old Theaterplatz near the taxi stand that would take us back to the Cheremosh. We were each lost in our own thoughts. My mind was racing with things I had not been able to see, questions about the past I had not been able to resolve. I wished we had a just a few more days. Leo and I held hands; we had become attached to this quiet, rather empty city, to its faded charm, to the past it continued to echo. We had also become attached to the intense conversations we had been having with my parents about their past lives.

"Marianne has no Heimat," my father had said only a week before. Was this city, in any sense, home to me? I considered the question, too tired at the moment to resolve it. I knew that the site of our walks and talks, where the fracture between eras was briefly bridged, could not provide the soil where roots of belonging could ever again take hold. Still, at the crossroads in Czernowitz, telling and listening had become a collaborative endeavor. "It would not have made sense to return except in this constellation," Lotte and Carl said during the taxi ride and later, again and again. "We would not have come without you."

# PART TWO

# The Darker Side
## 2000

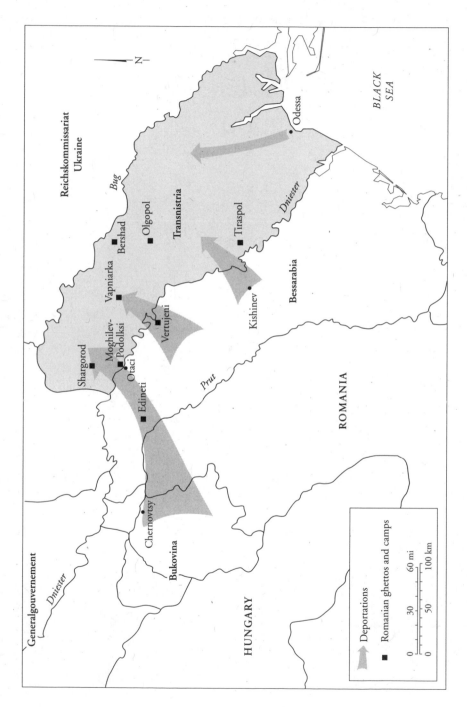

Map 4. Romania with Transnistria, 1941–42 (Based on maps from the United States Holocaust Memorial Museum)

# SEVEN

# Maps to Nowhere

We walked in the direction of Sosnowiec—but WHERE TO GO?!
It was NOWHERE we had to hide.

ART SPIEGELMAN
*Maus: A Survivor's Tale*

PARIS, JULY 1999

When Art Spiegelman, in the first volume of *Maus,* describes his parents'
escape from the ghetto of Srodula to evade the deportations to Auschwitz,
he draws the intersection of several roads in the shape of a swastika. At the
bottom of the image he depicts his parents, Vladek and Anja, two mice walking along an empty road, holding hands, contemplating the different directions they might take. The white paths are set within a desolate landscape.
An ominous black building with four chimneys is visible on the horizon.
"We walked in the direction of Sosnowiec—but WHERE TO GO?! It was
NOWHERE we had to hide," Vladek tells his son. This account of the past
is embedded in the book within a present-day time frame, in a sequence in
which Artie's father is eager to take his son to the bank and give him a key
to the safe deposit box containing the legacy he intends to bequeath to him
upon his death.[1] The box, Artie will soon learn, contains a number of trea-
sures, including a gold cigarette case and a lady's powder case that Vladek
had hidden in a chimney in the Srodula ghetto and, amazingly, had found
again after his return from the camps. Of course, the legacy his son is much
more eager to obtain than these material objects is his father's story, in all its
details.

The crossing of multiple roads in *Maus,* some possibly, but most likely not,

Figure 24. "Nowhere to hide . . .": an image from MAUS I: A
SURVIVOR'S TALE / MY FATHER BLEEDS HISTORY, by Art
Spiegelman, copyright © 1973, 1980, 1981, 1982, 1984, 1985, 1986
by Art Spiegelman. Used by permission of Pantheon Books, a
division of Random House, Inc.

leading to safety, is a perfect visual analogue to the situation of Chernovtsy/
Cernăuţi Jews in the summers of 1940 and 1941. The stories transmitted
to children and grandchildren that have become the legacy of those years
incorporate the feeling of being ensnared within a set of dangerous, if not
lethal, and ultimately unpredictable alternatives. At the same time, like in

*Maus,* these stories emerge within fractured narrative frames; we receive them eagerly, despite their gaps and ellipses.

After returning from our 1998 trip to Chernivtsi, we made it our mission to try to fill in some of the gaps in my parents' stories. Both Leo and I wanted and needed to understand better, and in a broader context, Carl and Lotte's fateful turn back into the Cernăuți ghetto on October 15, 1941. To do so, we first had to backtrack even further in time—to summer, to June 1941, and the retreat of the Soviets in the face of the German and Romanian invasion. Carl had been ready to escape deeper into the USSR together with his family and other friends; the Soviets had allowed civilians to withdraw with them and had made limited transport available for this purpose. Only Lotte's hesitation, her unwillingness to leave her parents behind, held him back. What would have happened to him, to them, had they gone? Here was another turning point that might have resulted in my never having been born.

These questions took us to Paris in July 1999, to speak to Sidy Flexor and to her sons Alex and Peter Flexor about Mischa and Sidy's flight from Chernovtsy during those determining twelve days in June of 1941. The Flexors were Carl's closest friends; had he fled, he might well have shared their fate. Mischa himself had died in Paris a number of years before our visit. Sidy had been ill for a while, and we were not certain whether we would be able to speak with her. But surely their sons (the elder, Peter, was born in Novosibirsk) would know enough about their parents' flight from the accounts they had heard to enable us to imagine, if not reconstruct, this piece of the puzzle we had slowly begun to assemble. Some published memoirs by others who had escaped into the USSR, like Dorothea Sella's *The Ring of Prometheus,* had been helpful to us, but documentary material on this period turned out to be extremely scarce.

"The Soviet army was retreating, the Germans were advancing, and my parents were running." This is how Alex Flexor summed up the days in June 1941 after his parents, along with other Jewish refugees from Chernovtsy and the Bukowina, had made the difficult decision to flee eastward. Unlike Dorothea Sella and others who had joined official student or worker groups and were part of a formal evacuation plan that provided trains and trucks, Mischa and Sidy Flexor escaped without signed authorizations, on foot. "I only know glimpses of their story," Alex told us—and, in the interviews he had audiotaped with his mother in France in the mid-1990s, Sidy also remembered this period in the form of what she called "snapshots" (*Lichtbilder*). The more eager her son had been to establish a clear chronology and map of their flight, the more difficult it had seemed for her to detail the forty days they walked the seven hundred kilometers between Chernovtsy and Poltava in Central Ukraine, where they were able to board the train that would, eventually, take them to Yangiyul, in Uzbekistan. Her tape contains a series of disconnected anecdotes, interrupted, often, by her son's eager questions:

> Your father had learned to draw maps when he was a group leader in the Hashomer Hatzair, and this talent stood us all in good stead. He drew maps on small pieces of paper so we could orient ourselves. There were eight of us, and when we arrived in Moghilev Podolsk, we saw the first casualties on the ground. There was artillery fire, the houses along the way were abandoned. The roads were full of people fleeing eastward with whatever belongings they could carry or transport. Children were looking for their parents, there was confusion everywhere. And then the bombs started falling on us.[2]

We were in Paris, in Alex Flexor's apartment in the 13th arondissement, and we had just finished the meal he cooked for us and his brother, Peter. We opened several histories of the Second World War and studied maps of the rapid Wehrmacht advances in Bessarabia and Ukraine during that period. Arrows and other symbols indicated the shifting front lines: there were four major demarcations covering territorial gains on June 21, July 9, September 1, and September 30. That last line put Poltava on the German side but, by then, Mischa and Sidy were already somewhere beyond the Urals. We counted the days, measured the distances using the maps' scale and a small ruler, tried to imagine the confusion and desperation of the refugees.

We videotaped the brothers' account of what they knew, and together we listened to the interviews Alex had conducted with his mother one summer when he had accompanied her to a sanatorium for the elderly in Evian. She was too ill now to be interviewed, and we were keenly aware of her absence, and of Mischa's. I again thought about how lucky we had been to be able to go to Chernivtsi with my parents; how lucky we were to be able to interview them not only about their own fate but also about the stories of their friends and relatives, of their generation. They had already told us as much as they knew about Mischa and Sidy's flight, to prepare us for the conversations we were having in Paris. The sound of Sidy's voice on the tape, moreover, the anecdotes she related, the pictures of Mischa and Sidy on the wall of Alex's apartment, and the Romanian eggplant salad he had made for us from his mother's recipe keenly evoked for me the presence of his parents as I had known them during my childhood in postwar Romania—close family friends with whom we used to share weekends and vacations. I closed my eyes and could see Mischa and Sidy running across bombed-out villages carrying their rucksacks (as they used to do in our hikes in the Carpathians under such different circumstances): Mischa calm, confident, full of humor and warmth, attentive to everyone's needs; and the diminutive Sidy, less than five feet tall, yet strong, practical, life-affirming. Through the stories we were hearing and the history we were attempting to reconstruct, I wanted Leo, and our son Gabriel, who had come with us to Paris, to know them as I had.

How, we all wondered, did they manage this long and difficult flight with so much going against them? A week or two after escaping into the interior following the retreating Red Army, several Jewish individuals and families returned to Cernăuți under the cover of night, unable to find their way out of German-occupied territories in the surrounding regions. Others were trapped in the attempt and ended up sharing the fate of Jews in Nazi-occupied Poland and Ukraine, becoming victims of the mass killings by the Einsatzgruppen or of brutal pogroms by Ukrainian locals aided by Nazi-organized police units, the Ukrainische Hilfspolizei, or of imprisonment in Nazi concentration camps.[3] Frederic Bernard's memoir *In the Eye of the Storm* does not give any details of his failed attempt to stay ahead of the Wehrmacht and flee into the Soviet interior, but it does relate its aftermath—the months he spent in the ghetto of Koroluvka and the two years he spent with Polish partisans as a fighter in the forests of southern Poland.[4] Carl and Lotte's friend Jascha Stein had been evacuated with Soviet units as far as Kamenetz-Podolsk when, finding himself caught behind German lines, he changed his name to Jakow Andrejewitsch Stejuk and, using false papers, spent two years passing as a Moldavian national. In 1943, after a move to Kiev, he recalls how "so–called 'Ukrainian police'" arrested him and handed him over to the Sicherheitsdienst, the Nazi intelligence and security body. "So began the most terrible period of my life," he relates.[5] Eventually deported to the Siret concentration camp near Kiev, he ended up on a work detail that was ordered to exhume and burn the bodies of the Nazi massacre of Jews at Babi Yar, thus erasing the traces of the atrocity.

Mischa and Sidy Flexor also repeatedly risked falling into Nazi hands during their flight across rapidly shifting territories. Without access to the small maps Mischa had drawn on scraps of paper, it is now impossible to reconstruct the details of their harrowing forty-day walk to Poltava. In Paris, we tried to get as close as was possible to that distant summer and to assess the combination of luck and ingenuity that must have contributed to the ultimate success of their escape. But it was an exercise in speculation and frustration. There was so much we wanted to know—so many details and perceptions we wanted to access—yet so much that the narratives to which we had access left out.

"We had only brought half a loaf of bread with us; we were tired, hungry and frightened," Sidy told her son on the tape. As we listened, Alex described to us the park in Evian where they had had this conversation—a stark contrast to the battlefields of war that Sidy was recalling. "Planes were bombing the roads. After days, we found a Jewish family that took us in for a night. I was able to wash my hair—I really, really wanted to wash my hair. And they gave us a loaf of bread: bread was worth gold. Another time, we went through a village where the peasant women gave some food to the passing refugees. They gave us whatever they had—pickles, some potatoes and bacon. They cooked it for us in a garden. 'Why are you coming here?' they asked us. 'Here there is nothing but hunger, misery and cold.'"

Mischa became known as the man with the lists. Born in the Russian Moghilev, he had grown up speaking Russian and Yiddish. It was only when his family came to Czernowitz in 1917 (when Mischa was four) as refugees from the Revolution, that they learned German. His knowledge of Russian had helped him a great deal during the Soviet occupation of Chernovtsy in 1940–41 and had given him the confidence to escape to the USSR, confidence that also inspired six friends to join him and Sidy in their escape. His language and the camping skills he had acquired in his Hashomer Hatzair days made Mischa the informal leader of their group of eight companions thrown together by a common fate. From our families' hikes and excursions together in the Romanian Carpathians in the 1950s, I could imagine how everyone relied on him for directions and decisions.

As they were advancing east, they encountered many fellow refugees, some of whom had become separated from their families and companions in the confusion. Mischa began writing the names and whereabouts of those they met along the way in the small notebook he carried with him, and people began to seek him out for information. "He was famous, a tool of extreme human value, driven by extreme demand," Alex told us, "though if the lists and his maps had been found, he could easily have been arrested as a spy. He spoke German, after all. He brought the lists back to Romania with him, but they were lost somewhere in our many moves. Later, in Paris, he tried to reconstitute them. He made notes over the years to reconstruct his notebook of that time, hoping to write about it. But he died so soon after his retirement. In fact, he had never told us this story while we still lived in Romania. It wasn't until we arrived in France in the late 1950s that we learned about it."

What was transmitted to Alex and Peter Flexor about their parents' flight and the wartime years they spent as Jewish refugees in the USSR? The missing maps and the missing lists of names for which their father had become renowned in the summer of 1941 can serve as a figure for the sons' fragmentary knowledge. While the sons wanted to connect the points on a rapidly shifting geopolitical map, the parents—one dead, the other ill and forgetful—could provide no more than disconnected glimpses. "Wait," Alex admonished his mother during their interviews, "let me just summarize what you have told me. I don't get a clear picture." And when he tried to tell us what he had learned, he became frustrated by the many gaps in the story he had tried to reconstitute.

Having known Mischa as a prodigious and gifted storyteller, with a flair for the revealing twist in an anecdote and a keen ability to find the irony in a scene, I also find his silence about their escape extremely frustrating. I myself had heard repeatedly that the Flexors had escaped "on foot" while Carl had decided, in a split second, to remain behind. But no one actually seems to have heard the details that would now help us to fill out this tale with texture and color. It is only when we read some accounts by others who attempted this escape—Dorothea Sella's excellent fictionalized memoir, for example—that we saw how much was missing here, how much we had to find between the lines. Of course, Sidy's simple assertions that she "really, really wanted to wash my hair" or that "bread was worth gold" do enough to signal the hunger, the discomfort, and the lice, for example. The story of Mischa's lists evokes the terrifying experience of losing one's travel companions amidst a "storm" of refugees—an experience Sella describes so vividly: "It was not only that we found ourselves in the midst of a devastating storm; we were also in an unimaginable chaos, a chaos of a very special kind. . . . I was seized by an indescribable panic. 'How will we find each other again?' I screamed and with every minute I got more and more nauseous. 'Andi and I are separated forever!' I sobbed. 'This is exactly what we most feared, and now it happened.'"[6]

Unlike the Flexors, Sella had been officially evacuated from Chernovtsy with a group of university students. Unmarried to Andi at the time but pregnant, she gave birth to a baby during the flight. She eventually ended up in Stavropol, in Southwestern Russia and then in Tbilisi, Georgia, before returning to Chernovtsy after the German retreat and Soviet reconquest of the Bukowina in 1944. She lost both her first baby, Ammelie, and then a second, a boy named Viki, in these dire circumstances. She and Andi were separated and reunited on several occasions but, in August 1942, after Ammelie's death and before Viki's birth, the Institute in Stavropol where they were studying was dissolved, Andi was drafted into the Soviet military, and she never saw him again.

On the tape, we could hear the fear in Sidy's voice as well—the need to rely on rumors and the kindness of strangers; the split-second decisions, despair, and loss. In spite of the differences in circumstances, Sella's account helped us imagine what it was like for the Flexors, beyond the few details we could amass from Sidy's recollections.

Together with the two Flexor sons, we tried to understand Mischa and Sidy's initial hopefulness, what Alex called the "enthusiasm," with which they went into the interior of the USSR as confirmed socialists—and the disillusionment with which they returned to Chernovtsy in 1944, as "non-communists," leaving for Romania as quickly as they could in 1945, after the Soviets had again taken control of the northern Bukowina. That profound change, the emotional and ideological backdrop to their story of survival, was even less explicitly transmitted to the two sons raised in communist Romania than the story of their flight. "They did not talk about it a lot because it was dangerous," Alex said. "Only later, in France, did I fully realize how they felt. We met a cousin who had married a French communist. She was outraged by their attitude: 'How can you say these things about the Soviet Union?' she would ask them. 'We know, we were there,' they would answer, and that's how I really knew they were disillusioned. They did not talk about it directly, though I certainly noticed their distance from some of our activities, like our induction into the Young Pioneers when we were in school in communist Romania."

Glimpses, snapshots, innuendos—maps to nowhere. These are the legacies of their flight, and it is no surprise that their paucity leads to some amount of mythification. Two anecdotes in particular have acquired legendary dimensions for Alex. Such myths of origin tend to undergird the identity of children who grow up under the shadows of their parents' stories of survival, transmitted to them in unconnected fragments. As he tells these stories:

> The line of the front was so close that they were sometimes in a no man's land, between explosions and bombings in the east and artillery fire in the west. They were in between. One night, they slept in a bombed-out house, and when they woke up, the rest of their group had left. They were alone. So they started running through some ghost villages, you know, recently abandoned, with the soup still on the stove and a few dogs lying on the street. In one, they met an old man standing by a fence. "Where are you going?" he asked them. "We're running from the Germans," they said. "Then why are you going that way? You're running toward the Germans. You must go this

way," and he pointed in the opposite direction. That is contingency: if they had not met the old man, or if he had been pissing at the moment they were passing by, for example, they would have been killed. That's one of the reasons I am here, because the old man did not piss. . . .

Now they were by themselves, running through villages full of corpses, through fields that were being bombed, like in René Clair's film *Jeux interdits*. Once, when they were lying on their bellies in a field, my father said to my mother, "Let us put our heads close together, because if a bullet hits us, then it will kill us both together." It's a beautiful idea, an indication of their love. If a couple has lived through such a time, their ties are indestructible.

Alex was able to envision their survival by way of a popular war film, René Clair's 1952 *Jeux interdits* (Forbidden Games), a film that inscribes a child's perspective on war. The children in the film enact their experiences through play. They play at death and at love; the two are inextricably connected for them. For Alex, these two anecdotes must have emerged out of fragments he absorbed during his childhood, combined with his childhood fantasies and nightmares, surviving to shape his identity in the present. On the one hand, contingency; on the other, an indestructible love. A crossing of roads, all leading to the unknown, probably all traps, and a chance encounter that miraculously enables them to survive and Alex to be born. It could so easily have gone the other way. In the film, the parents are killed, abandoning their little girl. Alex's parents survived to conceive his brother and then him. But the potential abandonment that precedes his birth nevertheless continued to haunt Alex in Paris some sixty years later.

### FAR FROM THE WAR, 1941–1944

Within a few days after the German invasion, the Soviet government set up the Supreme Evacuation Council, charged with organizing orderly evacuations of important industrial and administrative institutions, along with their employees and their families, into the interior of the Soviet Union. Since there was no unified evacuation plan, so that the relocations were overseen by local authorities under the supervision of the military, and since the Wehrmacht advanced at unforeseen speed through Bessarabia, Ukraine, and Belarus, the first months of the evacuations were extremely disorganized. The confusion was compounded by the large flood of hundreds of thousands of refugees from some of the Soviet-annexed territories in Poland and Romania. These refugees were either Christian communists or Jews, many of whom had already become Soviet citizens under the policy of Sovietization that had been instituted during the Soviet annexations in 1939–41. But even as Soviet citizens, they were considered dangerous and had to face numerous restrictions. They could not live less than one hundred kilometers from the border, for example, or in the large cities. At the same time, many of their compatriots had already been deported into the interior, primarily to Siberia, as politically hostile elements.[7]

When Mischa and Sidy Flexor reached Poltava some forty days after leaving Chernovtsy, they were part of a flood of people who tried to get, as their sons kept repeating, "as far away from the war" as possible. At this point, transports were being made available for the evacuees, but we do not know how Mischa and Sidy acquired the necessary papers. Conditions were terrible and food was extremely scarce, but there was work for the refugees in different regions of the interior. As Westerners, refugees were not drafted until later in the war.

Alex and Peter Flexor did not know how their parents ended up in the Uzbek city of Yangiyul, near Tashkent, except that it was as "far away from the war" as they were able to go. They did know that they went there by train, that it took a long time, that the trains stopped for hours, sometimes for days, along the way. This is as much as Sidy told her sons, but we can find more on the hardships of getting on a train, the hunger and thirst on the journey, the impossible decision about which direction to take given the coming winter and the uncertainty of the course of the war, in Dorothea Sella's harrowing descriptions:

> Never will I forget this fight for a spot the size of a footstep, this pleading for a helpful hand. It's been many decades since I went through this, and even now, when I see a train pull into a station, or a crowd by a trolley car, I reexperience the feelings of those days and start trembling, unable to calm down for a while. . . .
> · While we rushed back and forth, north and south, from train station to train station as though in a trap of three hundred kilometers, we lived through innumerable hours of despair and indecision, of thirst and hunger, of physical and spiritual exhaustion.[8]

We do not know whether Mischa and Sidy's journey was as difficult as Sella's, but they did make it to Yangiyul, where both did agricultural work in a *kolkhoz*, a collective farm. From Sella's description of her own stay in a *sovkhoz* (a state-owned farm) during that same summer, we learn that even though refugees were needed to do farm work in various regions of the USSR, this agricultural work did not promise that there would be sufficient food for them to eat.

By autumn of 1941 the Chernovtsy refugees in the Soviet interior seem to have lost contact with their families at home; later they would find out that their families had believed they were dead. They did not know about the Cernăuţi ghetto and the deportations to Transnistria. When Sella worked on a paper with the title "Homeland" for a course she was taking at the university in Stavropol, she noted that "as I was writing, I thought about my family with great longing, as they were going about the ordinary daily tasks at home that were so familiar to me. I didn't know that thirty-five thousand Czernowitz Jews, among them my family, were deported to the camps in Transnistria during those days [in mid-October]."[9] Similarly, Mischa did not know about the deportation and death of his parents or about the disappearance of his brother Jascha. Later, he would rarely talk about these losses to his sons.

When Alex and Peter tried to understand their parents' next step, the journey to Siberia, they saw it precisely in terms of family relationships and a profound longing for home. "They were so lonely, that they wrote to my father's uncle in Novosibirsk. They were longing for someone familiar, someone to speak with, to speak Yiddish with," Peter told us. Although the official language in Yangiyul, Uzbekistan, was Russian, the local farmers were unlikely to know it, and Mischa and Sidy did not speak Uzbek. Novosibirsk, as distant and cold as it was known to be, at least held out the promise of a familial connection to their lost homeland. Mischa received no reply to his letter, but the couple took the silence for an approval and set out by train to Siberia.

They did find and stay with the uncle, but only for a short time. Yet even though this reunion did not work out well, Novosibirsk did offer them the possibilities for much better jobs than they had in Uzbekistan: Mischa, a textile engineer by training, found work in a textile factory that produced army uniforms, and he eventually came to occupy a high position there as the leader of a production team. Sidy worked in a canteen. She became pregnant, and Peter was born in Novosibirsk in 1943. The changed family circumstances, however, did not provide Mischa with an exemption from the army. Although the textile plant where he worked was considered to be under mobilization, toward the end of the war Mischa, Russian by birth and thus a Soviet citizen, was drafted into the Soviet infantry.

Few anecdotes survived from this period in their lives, few powerful

Figure 25. Mischa Flexor (far left) during his time in the Red Army, toward the end of World War II (Courtesy of Peter and Alex Flexor)

impressions, and the ones that have are strongly inflected by mythic images of a cold, desolate, and dangerous Siberian landscape on the one hand and, on the other, by surprise and delight at the rich Russian cultural and athletic life that Novosibirsk offered even during the war years. Sidy had often told her sons about seeing the unforgettable actor Nicolai Cherkassov, well known from Eisenstein's films, perform at the city theater. Sidy participated in a day-long cross-country skiing competition on the icy river. Leading the group of racers, she suddenly found herself alone in an isolated area. Frightened of wolves, she skied so fast that she ended up winning by many lengths.

Most significantly, there is no narrative explaining the urgency with which the Flexors wanted to leave the Soviet Union toward the end of the war. Presumably, they experienced the repressions for which the regime became known, and in his position of leadership in the factory, Mischa might have felt vulnerable to corruption and denunciation. Did they suffer anti-Semitism as well? Dorothea Sella recounts her own differential treatment as a Jew:

When a woman whom we asked about the room she had for rent asked me my name, I thought it seemed like a good sign and told it to her with joy. Even though it doesn't sound particularly Jewish, she said, "You're a 'Sarotchka' [a little Sarah], isn't that so?" We therefore weren't really surprised that she turned us down and we had to return to the Institute, dejected.

. . . As I stood on the threshold of the semi-dark room, watching how the women and the men gathered around the child, smiling, since it seemed like a miracle in these surroundings, a question arose in me suddenly: How would these people act if they knew that this was a foreign, a Jewish child?[10]

Whether the Flexors' experiences correspond to what Dorothea Sella lived through or not, when the Bukowina was liberated by the Soviets in 1944, they tried everything in their power to return to Chernovtsy, though they no doubt knew full well that a Soviet city could not be home for long. As was also true for many of their contemporaries, their ultimate destination, ironically, would be Bucharest, the place they had left so urgently a mere four years earlier. But, with a small baby and with Mischa in a Soviet uniform, this seemed a distant goal indeed.

### "WITH A CHANGING KEY," 1999

A narrative written from the perspective of the second generation, such as ours is, is necessarily full of unknowns, especially if, as in the case of the Flexors' story of escape, repatriation, and double emigration, the witnesses themselves can no longer speak and the records they left behind are spotty. And yet we believe that the gaps we were unable to fill in connection to the Soviet occupation of Chernovtsy and Chernovtsy Jews' escape into the Soviet Union are due to other, at once more complicated and more particular factors as well. This is certainly one story that corresponds to Paul Celan's well-known poem about silence, and the possibility of unlocking it:

With a changing key
you unlock the house where
the snow of what's silenced drifts.

. . . . . . . . . . . .

Changing your key changes the word
that may drift with the flakes.[11]

It may be that the key to these doors cannot be found now, since the ellipses, or acts of forgetting in narratives concerning the Soviet Union, are related not only to the ideological repressions of the Soviet regime but also to the

Cold War. The latter, especially, may have made certain stories untellable in our present.[12]

How, particularly in the first decade of the twenty-first century, can we describe and motivate what Carl Hirsch called the widespread "sympathy for the Soviet experiment," followed by the ensuing disillusionments? Two memoirs illustrate particularly well how ambivalence can interrupt, even break, this chain of transmission.

Rachelle Rosenzweig's fictionalized memoir *Russische Eisblumen* (Russian Ice Crystals) describes the thirty-five years the author, a doctor born in Czernowitz, spent in the Soviet Union. The book starts with an ellipsis: "It is a cool night in the late fall of 1940. In the Bukowinian border region between Romania and the Ukraine, you can see how a group of Romanian legionnaires [militarized Romanian Fascists] on horseback chased four well-dressed urban civilians with ominous gestures and wild cries. We are the objects of their chase: Suddenly, we find ourselves facing Soviet border guards on horseback."[13] The narrative continues with the arrest of this Jewish family by the Soviets, their internment in the Chernovtsy prison, and their eventual deportation to other prisons and then to Siberia. What were these four people doing at the border between fascist Romania and communist Ukraine in the middle of the night in fall of 1940? Were they escaping from the communists to Romania, afraid of being persecuted by the Soviets as bourgeois property owners? Or were they escaping from Romania into the USSR, afraid of persecutions as Jews? Why does Rosenzweig, whose book is full of anecdotal detail and thoughtful reflection, fail to give the one explanation that would ground her narrative and motivate the actions of her characters?

Fred Bernard's memoir *In the Eye of the Storm* is also based on a narrative ellipsis. Bernard begins his account in the fall of 1942 in the Polish ghetto of Koroluvka, but flashes back to June of 1941 in Cernăuți and the retreat of the Red Army. A general paragraph about the invasion of the Einsatzgruppen and the killings they conducted in the city, aided by Romanian special forces, leads back to Bernard's own story: "Three months later Gusti and I, and a group of six friends, found ourselves in the Ukraine, around 100 or 150 kilometers to the east of the village of Kamenetz-Podolsk.... We were well behind German front lines."[14] Why were they suddenly there? When—and why—did they leave Chernovtsy/Cernăuți, where, Bernard writes, he worked in the Ear, Nose, and Throat Department of the First City Hospital under the Soviets? And, again, why does Bernard, who writes an articulate and detailed memoir about his time in hiding as a Jew in Poland, leave out the crucial motivation for the turn his life took during the war?

Perhaps the ideological clashes of those years, compounded by the intervening political twists and reversals for refugees and émigrés from Czernowitz now in Israel, the United States, Europe, and elsewhere, have invaded and in part obliterated the structures of memory and forgetting, and the textures of logic and narrative. But perhaps, as well, Czernowitz Jews remember themselves as so thoroughly trapped between two corrupt regimes in which they felt equally undesirable—though certainly not equally threatened—that it ultimately matters less why they were on one side or the other than whether, and how, they would manage to survive.

# EIGHT

# The Spot on the Lapel

I come from the war, it is my true origin. But as with all our origins,
I cannot grasp it. Perhaps we never know where we come from; in a
way we are all created ex nihilo.

EVA HOFFMAN
*Lost in Translation*

## THE LITTLE PICTURE

It is the only photograph of my parents taken during the war years and it is
tiny, 2.5 by 3.2 centimeters, about the size of a 35 millimeter negative, with
unevenly cut edges. I have always loved this image of a stylish young couple—
newlyweds walking confidently down an active urban street. The more difficult it was to make out the details of the faded and slightly spotted black-
and-white image, the more mysterious and enticing it became to me over the
years. In it, my mother is wearing a flared, light-colored calf-length coat and
attractive leather or suede shoes with heels, and she is carrying a dark purse
under her arm. My father wears well-cut pants and dark leather shoes, and
a tweed jacket which looks slightly too small. Details of their facial expressions are difficult to read, but their strides appear animated, matching,
their arms interlaced, my mother's hands in her pockets. The picture was no
doubt taken by one of the Cernăuţi street photographers on the Herrengasse
who took the photos that populated my parents' albums and those of their
friends, photos dating from the 1920s and 1930s. This picture's radical difference is marked on the back, however, where my father's handwriting reads
"Cz. 1942."[1]

In 1942 Cernăuţi was again a Romanian city, ruled by a fascist Romanian
government in alliance and collaboration with Nazi authorities. More than

Figure 26. "Cz. 1942": Lotte and Carl in Cernăuți, early in their marriage; the original is 1 x 1.25 inches (Hirsch-Spitzer archive)

half of the city's Jewish population—some thirty thousand persons—had been deported to Transnistria in the fall of 1941. About half of them perished from hunger and typhus during that winter or were murdered either by Romanian gendarmes or Nazi troops. Those, like my parents, who were still in the city, had been issued special waivers to remain by Traian Popovici, the city's mayor, or by Corneliu Calotescu, the region's governor, as Jews who were deemed necessary to the city's functioning. After the ghetto was largely emptied and dissolved by the end of November 1941, they were permitted to return to their own homes, but they were subject to severe restrictions, including a strict curfew, and were obliged to wear the yellow star. Men were routinely taken off the street to do forced labor. By the summer of 1942, my parents would have been vulnerable to a second wave of deportations to Transnistria or further east, across the River Bug into German-administered territories and almost certain death.

Nothing in the picture betrays the hardship of the time. Carl and Lotte are not visibly suffering; they don't look starved, unhealthy, or afraid. The photo is not comparable to pictures of Jews in Warsaw or Lódz streets taken in 1942—images of acute misery and deprivation in ghettos or other restricted quarters.

"Here we are during the war," my parents once said to me, with what I took to be some amount of defiance. This photograph had been a measure for me of the difference between my parents' way of telling the story about their experiences during the war years and the much more dire and frightening narratives we read and collected from other survivors and witnesses. The photo seemed to confirm Lotte and Carl's version of events: what they thought of as their "relatively lucky circumstances" and the youth and young love that helped them to endure and keep up their spirits. Still, I became increasingly puzzled by the little picture's incongruities: by its refusal to testify to what I knew to be true of the context in which it was taken—a time of persecution, oppression, and totalitarian constraints in which photography itself must have taken an ominous turn from a medium of personal and familial remembrance to a threatening instrument of surveillance. Flipping the little photo from front to back, I was unable to get its two sides to match up.

When Leo and I began to write about the wartime in Cernăuţi, this photo was one of very few images we had from there that might supplement the historical analyses, written documents, memoirs, and oral testimonies on which we were basing our understanding of the place and time. However small and blurred, however seemingly incongruous, it was a valuable piece of evidence that, we hoped, would give us some greater insight into the texture of Jewish wartime life here. Eager for it to reveal itself even more to us, we digitally scanned and enlarged it, blowing it up several times, searching to find what might not be visible to the naked eye.

Amazingly, as it came up now at about 10 by 14 centimeters on the screen, the image and the story it told changed dramatically—at least on first glance. All of a sudden, it looked like there *was* something on Carl's left lapel that had not been noticeable before. A bright spot, not too large, emerged just in the place where Jews would have worn the yellow star in 1942. Perhaps the picture was not as incongruous as we had thought: perhaps it would indeed confirm the darker version of the story we had learned and absorbed from so many other accounts. We printed the enlargement, took out magnifying glasses, went up to the window, and used the best lamps in our study to scrutinize the blowup. We played with the enlargement's resolution on the computer in Photoshop, sleuthing like detectives to determine the exact nature of the spot. The spot's edges remained blurry. But didn't their shape suggest points? This *must* be the yellow star, we concluded; what else could he be wearing on his lapel? We blew the picture up even more, then again, even a little more— yes, of course, it had the *shape* of the Jewish star. We began to reread the photograph's content, its message, against Lotte and Carl's facial expression and body language that were now also much more clearly visible. We remembered some of their stories about the star, about how they sometimes went out without it, daring fate to buy groceries more easily, or simply to experience again their former freedom and mobility. The stars in Cernăuţi were not sewn on but affixed with safety pins: young people like Carl and Lotte sometimes wore them on the *inside* of their coats, illegally, but able to show them should

Figure 27. "Blowup . . . ": detail of figure 26, showing Carl's lapel (Hirsch-Spitzer archive)

they be stopped by the authorities. But if that, indeed, explained the seemingly missing star in Lotte's case, wouldn't the couple have been afraid to have their picture taken by a street photographer? The smiles with which they greeted the camera, and the fact that they had stopped to *buy* the photo after it was developed, gave no such impression of fear.

We decided to send the enlarged photo to Lotte and Carl. "There is a small spot on my lapel," Carl wrote in an email, "but it could not be the THE Jewish star. The stars were large, 6 cm in diameter. Maybe I should have written 1943 on the photo. They did away with the stars in July of 1943." "And if that is a star," Lotte wrote, "then why am I not wearing one?" In a later email she said: "Yes, it was definitely taken on the Herrengasse during the war, and to me it looks like a star, but the date is causing us problems."

In fact, we later found two other photos of Cernăuți Jews wearing the yellow star. These photographs are dated "around 1943" and "May 1943," and in them the stars are larger and more distinctive than the spot on Carl's lapel, but they also show people walking through the city—apparently on the onetime Herrengasse—having their picture taken by a street photographer, and evidently purchasing the photo after its development. Like Lotte and Carl's, their stroll also seems "normal," as though the temporal and political moment in which they were photographed and the mark of "otherness" that they were made to display were hardly relevant.

It may not be possible to determine exactly what, if anything, Carl is wearing on his lapel. Perhaps there was no more than some flaw in the pho-tographic process. Whatever the picture says about wartime Cernăuți and about Carl and Lotte's experiences in that city is open to interpretation. It is certain, however, that our reception of this picture says a great deal about *our* interests, as historians and as members of the second generation, and about how different our own interest is from theirs. We look to the photograph for a very different kind of evidence, and our act of enlarging and enhancing it, of zooming in and employing magnifiers, betrays the distinct desire, if not need, to penetrate more deeply into a world that had been opened up to us ever so slightly during our 1998 trip to Chernivtsi with my parents, during the many interviews we conducted before and after, and by our immersion into the city's history through reading and study. Photographs are ultimately flat and two-dimensional, limited by their frame. This one is so small that, in its original form, it defies any real insight. But could the same not be said for our own limited view into the lives of my parents and their generation, into the choices they made and suffered during the fractured history of Czernowitz in the first half of the twentieth century? More and more, we wanted, needed, to get beyond the surface of the tiny picture and to break the restrictions of its frame, to deepen and broaden our knowledge not just about my parents' contemporaries but also about the social, political, and institutional contexts surrounding them.

Figure 28. Stars on the Herrengasse, ca. 1943: Ilana Shmueli and her mother (left); Berthold Geisinger, "Dita," and Heini Stup (Courtesy of Ilana Shmueli and Silvio Geisinger)

The mystery of the spot on the lapel reveals yet another aspect of our curiosity and interest. Listening to Carl and Lotte's stories during our 1998 trip to their Czernowitz, we became increasingly aware of how radically accounts of the past are shaped by the present, by the interaction between speaker and listener, and by the scene of narration. Our "return" journey there together had been affirming and enabling: for them, confirming their choices and good fortune, and for us, inspiring further research and work on this book.

Our decision to return to Chernivtsi in 2000 was motivated by our wish to search for other dimensions of their story, to enhance and enlarge their narratives through our own lenses, however biased by our own interests and interpretations. As it turned out, that trip was a second-generation journey with all of the advantages and disadvantages of this new configuration. It led us to other witnesses and other stories, some of them considerably darker and more frightening than what we had been able to imagine amidst the faded beauty of the Austrian-Romanian-Soviet city that came alive for us through Carl and Lotte's narratives in 1998.

In July 2000, Leo and I were again in the Ukraine, back in Chernivtsi. Without my parents, we were now the main guides through "Czernowitz" for two new traveling companions, David Kessler and Florence Heymann, neither of whom had ever visited the city before. Together we tried to decipher street names and signs with the help of a Russian-English phrase book, having no Ukrainian dictionary with us at the time. By overlaying and matching up our old German-language Czernowitz city map and a Romanian map of the interwar years with a recently issued Ukrainian one of Chernivtsi, we sought to help David and Florence in their search for streets and landmarks they had each carefully identified before we left home as places that were important to them. Although they were total strangers to this place, David and Florence shared with me a frame of reference that had been transmitted to us in our childhood—mine in Romania, theirs in Israel and France, respectively.

We had spent the time on the airplane from Frankfurt to Lviv and in the VW minibus that had taken us from Lviv to Chernivtsi exchanging memories that were not ours. "My father grew up on the Residenzgasse," Florence told us. "I know the house was on a corner. I want to find the apartment. I think I'll be able to. Look," she pulled an old photograph from her bag. "This photo shows a view from their window. If this low building is still standing, I should be able to identify the angle and find the right street corner. It must have been on the second floor. The Herschmanns and the Guttmanns shared the entire building." I was struck by how small the city had in fact been, how closely intertwined its middle-class Jewish residents—and how widely dispersed they had become after the war. Although we had only recently met Florence Heymann at a conference on "Czernowitz as Paradigm" at Tel Aviv University in the fall of 1999, her father's cousin Martha Guttmann Blum, now living in Vancouver, was still a close friend of my parents. Just before this trip I had read Martha Blum's fictional account of Czernowitz and the war, *The Walnut Tree,* a novel she had written when she was already well into her eighties. Florence, a French ethnographer living and working in Jerusalem, had been working on a book about the Jewish identities of Czernowitz for a number of years. This journey was a research trip for her to enable her to complete her manuscript, but it was also a chance to take and collect photographs, documents, and stories about her father's native city—materials she wanted to display in an album that she would present to him on his eightieth birthday. He had declined to accompany her on this voyage—he told her he had no interest in a visit—and she was nervous about how he would receive her gift.[2]

On the drive to Chernivtsi, David Kessler, an optical engineer living in Rochester, New York, showed us some of the photos and documents he had brought along in an impressively organized ring binder. One was of his grandfather, for whom he was named, who had been a well-known rabbi in Czernowitz's large temple. Another was of his father, Arthur, a physician, who was a cousin of my mother's. David had the old addresses of their homes and workplaces neatly arranged on typed lists. He also had brought photos of graves he wanted to visit in the Czernowitz Jewish cemetery. Interested in genealogy, he had carefully researched his family tree. Much of this research was based on family archives that had been passed down to him when Arthur Kessler succumbed to Alzheimer's disease. David, however, viewed this trip to the Ukraine as a further opportunity to fill in missing genealogical and familial information and as a way to make contact with places spoken about so often over the course of his life. For this reason, David had also brought along a great deal of information on Transnistria and the Vapniarka concentration camp to which his father had been deported in 1942. Leo and I had promised to travel there with him if such a trip could be arranged: we ourselves were curious—and also apprehensive—about Transnistria, the much-dreaded region where so many perished and to which my parents had almost been deported in 1941.

Both on our journey there and in Chernivtsi itself, Florence, David, and I continually exchanged stories we had heard growing up, stories set on the Ringplatz, the Herrengasse and its cafés, the Austria-Platz, the Schillerpark, the Volksgarten, on the banks of the Pruth, or in the hills of the Cecina. Bubbling over with references and anecdotes, we talked animatedly as though we ourselves had spent our youths in Czernowitz. Like my own, the nostalgic narratives about Czernowitz that had been transmitted to Florence and David had also always been darkened by the ominous gloom of anti-Semitism, persecution, and displacement. One of the tasks of this visit, therefore, was to sort out these very complicated layers of inherited, as well as self-generated, nostalgia from the competing, and likewise received, negative memories. On the one hand, we were bringing traces of the past back to a place that had shifted nation and generation, a place that had lost most of its own witnesses to Jewish prewar life through death, deportation, or emigration. On the other, we needed to find confirming traces in the city itself—documents, grave markers, addresses. We needed to identify and enter the very houses and apartments where our parents and grandparents had lived, or from which they had been chased out, and we needed to find the evidence of what enabled not only their survival but also the persistence of their memories, however ambivalent.

As we walked around the city together on our first morning, guided by a photocopy of a map that had ceased being valid more than eighty years before, we were hardly conscious of how strange we must have seemed to the local inhabitants. In our mixture of English, French, and Hebrew—with German as our common reference point—we were both of the city and strangers to it, visitors not only from other places but also, in a sense, from another era, H. G. Wells–like time travelers from a past long gone. But we were also very much here in the present, looking to meet present-day Chernivtsi residents and to learn about their lives.

We visited restaurants in search of native specialties—soup with pirogies, sausages, herring, caviar, blyntsi (blini), vodka, local beer. Walking, eating, drinking, talking, we tried to make the present-day city ours, in our own here-and-now, even as we spent days searching for graves and for documents in archives, and tracking down addresses that might open a window or a door to the city's past.

Leo and I noted how significantly Chernivtsi had changed in the two years since we were here. Some buildings were being repainted and fixed up; a few new stores had opened on the Kobylyanska (the former Herrengasse) and the central square; one or two restaurants had English- or German-language menus. Young women in more fashionable clothes were walking in the center and frequenting the bar of the Cheremosh, where we were again staying. A few imported cars could be seen driving through the city center at top speed. The economy had visibly improved, though our hotel rooms had no hot water throughout the week. The water supply, it seemed, was pumped from a centralized source, and the city was saving money during the hot summer months. We had to content ourselves with cold showers supplemented with an occasional visit to the hotel's Turkish-style bath and steam room— utilized separately by men and women on alternate days.

With delight, we introduced our friends to Rosa Zuckermann and to Felix and his wife, Marina. Felix offered to drive us around a bit in the old but meticulously kept Soviet-built Lada automobile that his father had originally acquired in the 1970s. He also offered to help Florence and David with translations. And Rosa, though strikingly pale and suffering from flu, charmed them with the warmth she could nevertheless continue to generate. Between our two visits, Rosa had become a celebrity, the "star" of Volker Koepp's prize-winning documentary of 1999, *Herr Zwilling und Frau Zuckermann,* named after her and the friend she missed so dearly. Matthias Zwilling had been able to travel to Berlin for the film's opening at the Berlin Film Festival in 1999, but had died of a heart attack soon after his return to Chernivtsi. We commiserated with Rosa about his loss and promised to visit his grave.

Rosa was eager to tell us why she disliked the film, in spite of the fact that it had brought her such notoriety, many letters, and numerous visitors from abroad. We agreed with her judgment. This film about present-day Chernivtsi and the remaining traces of its lost Jewish past includes long sequences of the daily visits during which Rosa and Matthias talked about their lives and the world. These are wonderful moments showing how two survivors respond so differently to their fate: Rosa appears as the eternal optimist, Matthias as the dark pessimist, the "knight of the sad countenance," as she often jokingly referred to him. And yet, the film itself is less interested in them as complex individuals than as "last Jews," soon to be extinct, mythic representatives of a lost world. What is more, it fails to explain that world, its particularity and, in the midst of its losses, its vitality.

With Florence, we were also beginning to become a part of a group of colleagues working professionally on the Jewish culture of Czernowitz. In the summer of 2000 in Chernivtsi, we had stimulating conversations and professional exchanges with Peter Rychlo of Chernivtsi's Jurii Fed'kovych University, who had published extensively on the region's German-Jewish literature, and also with two other visitors, Amy Colin, an expert on Paul Celan and Bukowina poetry, and Helmut Kusdat, a scholar from Vienna long interested in the Jewish culture of the region.

### THE ROMANIAN HOLOCAUST IN CERNĂUȚI, 1941–1944

On this, our second trip, Leo and I were most interested in wartime and immediate postwar Cernăuți and in the different fates of the city's Jews in those dark years. What distinguished the Holocaust in this region from other parts of Europe? We wanted to understand the very particular circumstances of the Romanian and the Bukowinian Holocaust and the conjunction of factors responsible for it. How, in particular, did the system of *autorizație* (waivers) work to enable some Jews to survive in the city while others were deported? Besides the accounts in Matatias Carp's Romanian *Cartea Neagră* (Black Book) and fairly recent histories by I. C. Butnaru, Randolph Braham, Jean Ancel, and Radu Ioanid, and some passing comments in the historical and journalistic analyses of Raoul Hilberg and Hannah Arendt, the Romanian Holocaust had received relatively little scholarly attention.[3]

Lotte and Carl's photograph taken on Strada Iancu Flondor in Cernăuţi, Romania, in 1942—or even in 1943—seems to belie the famous statement by Arendt that "in Rumania even the S.S. were taken aback, and occasionally frightened, by the horrors of old-fashioned, spontaneous pogroms on a gigantic scale; they often intervened to save Jews from sheer butchery, so that killing could be done in what, according to them, was a civilized way."[4] Still, the zeal with which Romanian authorities began deporting Jews in the summer of 1941 into German-occupied territories in the Ukraine, without express orders or requests from the Nazis, has become legendary. Unprepared for the masses of deportees, the Germans sent some of them back to Romania and even blocked several bridges on the Dniester to stop the floods that were streaming in from the Bessarabian region of Romania. "German National Socialism was schooled in Romania!" wrote Dr. Nathan Getzler in his wartime diary of Cernăuţi and Transnistria.[5] The Romanian fascist newspaper *Porunca Vremii* presented the Romanian efforts to exterminate the Jews as a model to the rest of Europe as early as the summer 1941: "The die has been cast. . . . The liquidation of the Jews in Romania has entered a final, decisive phase. . . . To the joy of our emancipation must be added the pride of [pioneering] the solution to the Jewish problem in Europe. . . . Present-day Romania is prefiguring the decisions to be made by the Europe of tomorrow."[6] In an address on July 8, 1941, to the Romanian legislature, the interim president of the parliament Mihai Antonescu outlined and justified the plan: "With the risk of not being understood by some traditionalists who may still be among you, I am in favor of the forced relocation of the entire Jewish element in Bessarabia and Bucovina, which must be hurled across the border. . . . It is indifferent to me whether we enter history as barbarians. The Roman empire committed some acts of barbarism and it nevertheless became the vastest and most important political entity of its time. . . . There has never been a more propitious moment in our history. . . . Shoot with machine guns, if necessary."[7]

And yet, despite these "pioneering" efforts, despite an elaborate plan announced in Bucharest in August 1942 to make Romania entirely *judenrein* by sending all Jews to Belzec, and despite a longstanding history of virulent Romanian anti-Semitism, a majority of Jews who inhabited the Romanian Regat—the heartland—survived the war.

The Jews of the border regions, on the other hand, especially those regions like the Northern Bukowina that had been annexed by the Soviet Union under the Hitler-Stalin Pact in 1940–41, suffered a much harsher fate. The Red Army, retreating from Cernăuţi in late June of 1941, had left the Northern

Bukowina to Romanian troops and the ravages of the German Einsatzgruppen C and D. In spite of the fact that, only a few weeks earlier, approximately three thousand Jews had been deported to Siberia by the Soviets as "capitalists" and "social or political undesirables," returning Romanians, inflamed by anti-Semitic propaganda, blamed Jews here especially for facilitating and sustaining the communist regime that had not long ago ignominiously stripped Romania of its territory and national glory. Many of them viewed Jews living in this region as potential, if not active, "communist enemies of the Romanian State" and lashed out against them.

Matatias Carp describes the night of July 6, 1941, shortly after Romanians retook the provincial capital:

> In Chernovitz, individual soldiers and patrols continued to kill Jews at random throughout the night. . . . In less than twenty-four hours more than 2,000 Jews were killed in the streets, yards, houses, cellars or attics, where the unfortunate were seeking refuge.
>
> The corpses were transported in rubbish carts to the Jewish cemetery, and buried in four enormous common graves.[8]

While these murders were carried out, German and Romanian troops set Chernovtsy's imposing Jewish temple on fire, destroying its cupola. Units of gendarmes also scoured houses throughout the city and took some three thousand Jewish men, women, and children to the central police station under arrest. Approximately three hundred from this group, including Dr. Avraham Mark, the chief rabbi of the city, and other Jewish community leaders, were then transported to the banks of the Pruth River and shot.

Hedy and Bubi Brenner, as well as Bubi's mother, Paula, were among those who were arrested during the first days of Romanian rule in July 1941. They had described to us how their entire street was closed off, and all Jews were marched off to the courtyard of the town's army barracks, where the men and women were separated. The men were kept there for several days; some were beaten and humiliated. Both men and women were then moved to the central police station, where they were held overnight with no food or water, surrounded by "hungry cockroaches." The women were freed in the middle of the first night, but not until they were undressed and thoroughly searched and robbed of any valuables that could be found on them. In the process, some of them, including Hedy herself, were sexually groped and molested. Many of the women, Hedy recalled, nevertheless came back the next day with jewelry and cash to bribe police and gain the men's release. Matatias

Figure 29. The temple of Czernowitz burned
by the German and Romanian armies, 1941
(Courtesy of http://czernowitz.ehpes.com)

Carp provides a more specific account of this bribery: "Police commissioner Teodorescu began by taking 60–70 dollars per released prisoner. But later, the price went down to 50 and 40 dollars, and those who had no foreign currency could buy their freedom with various objects of value, a carpet, a clock, a cigarette case, a vacuum cleaner, etc."[9]

"Despite everything," Lotte had told us, "we had to walk out into the streets during those first days after the Romanians came back because both the water and the electricity were off, and we had to try to find some kerosene and something to drink and wash with. One of those times, Carl and I were going to get water from a well, and a non-Jew saw us and warned us that hostages were being taken, so we went right home. There was always danger, and it was a kind of lottery."

Bubi Brenner was arrested again, not long after his initial release, along with three hundred other Jewish men from three centrally located streets. "As we were being walked through the city that second time," Bubi told us, "we met a unit of Romanian soldiers. 'Where are you taking these Jews?'

Figure 30. Hedy and Bubi Brenner, 1939 (Courtesy of Hedwig Brenner)

they asked our guards. 'We can kill them for you right here, and save you the trouble.' We feared the worst since we had already heard about the killings on the Pruth when they shot Rabbi Mark and so many others." In her memoir, Hedy describes the persistence with which she and a group of other wives pursued the men's release from the Romanian Culture Palace on the theater square where they were being held by a German contingent under Obersturmbannführer Finger. In an act of daring, she approached a German lieutenant in the street and asked his intervention on behalf of her husband. Serendipitously in this instance, it turned out that that officer, Klaus Geppert, had studied electrical engineering in the same Prague university

of the public that were free to monitor it as they liked; . . . moreover, it all took place under police and secret police surveillance. . . . The commission's doors, especially the mayor's, were open to anyone.[14]

The days referred to by Popovici in his account appear in great detail, but with divergent emphases, in a number of Czernowitz memoirs by Jews. It was our hope that records at the city archive would clear up some ambiguities and contradictions we had found in written and oral accounts about this distressing time. Accounts by my father, stressing the role of his profession in determining his receipt of the *autorizaţie,* and by Pearl Fichman, who tried to save herself and her family in the absence of such privilege, provide examples of such differences.

As Carl Hirsch tells it:

In the next few days the leaders of the Jewish community prepared lists of the Jewish population arranged by professions, and the Government issued to part of the population authorizations to remain in the city. I got two, one as a civil engineer from the lists of the Jewish community and one as a railway employee, my brother got one as a mining engineer and one from his employment, which having been issued without a first name on it, was used by another Hirsch family. Many got authorizations with bribes that were given to the department heads of the provincial government. Many were not that fortunate and were put into trains to Transnistria, two aunts of ours with their families, my friend Lulziu [Israel] Chalfen who though a doctor did not have the right connections, and many others. . . . Approx. 12 days after we left our homes we returned.[15]

Pearl Fichman's situation seems more chaotic:

Since the Jewish community could not figure out what was intended or who was needed, they started registration of specialists. . . . Everyone was desperate and lists were made of any kind of specialty. I registered wherever they would accept my name. You did not have to show a document, that would come up later. I was on a students list (who needed students?), on a chemists list, nurse, anywhere. I put Father's name on all kinds of lists. . . .

In the meantime, October neared its end, the weather got colder, rains made it very hard to stand for hours and listen for the names of people, who received the permit to return. I went daily to that military station where the lucky ones received the reprieve from concentration camp. Those returned to their apartments in town and those who remained behind felt more and more desperate.[16]

Mrs. N. smiled triumphantly when we returned to the city archive a few days later. She had found nothing concerning Kessler or Heymann, but there were three different items about Carl Hirsch. She did not hand them to us but held on to them. There was no copier here, she said. We would have to make copies elsewhere. She went to get her purse and walked out of the building with me. Leo waited in the archive. Several long blocks away, we found a camera and stationery store where we copied the documents on an old machine that was nearly out of ink. Mrs N. then quickly put the originals back into her purse. We spoke only as we were walking down the street, not when we were within earshot of others. All the while, Mrs. N. cast furtive glances around her. Fear and suspicion did not leave the city with the end of the Soviet Union. I searched for an inconspicuous place where I could put the two twenty dollar bills I had brought into her hand: from the brief and fragmentary conversation we were having about the difficult working conditions and low pay in Ukraine, I knew they would be worth a great deal. We parted outside the Lutheran church after exchanging addresses and some more dollars in the hopes that other documents might turn up. So far they have not.

We rushed back to the hotel where we could study the documents in peace. Mrs. N. had found two lists that contained Carl Hirsch's name: both were informally typed, with some names crossed out and others added in pen or pencil. The first, which had an official stamp, date and signature on it, was a "Table of professional and specialist Jews on forced labor." Dated 22/IX/1842 (an obvious typing error), it could not be the list that was used to authorize remaining in the city during the October and November 1941 deportations, but it could be a later revised version of that initial list. In columns, it contained the names of twenty engineers working for the Romanian railroad, plus the names of their wives and children, their addresses, and fields of specialization, as well as their residence and public labor department registration numbers. The third name on the list was "Hirsch, Carol, inginer, constr."

We can surmise that this was one of the lists used for conscription of Jewish professionals and specialists into forced labor between 1942 and 1944. In his memoir Carl explains that, in December 1941, the Railway Headquarters in Bucharest ordered "to pay us full engineer's wages, retroactively from August" but that, not only were three months' wages immediately withheld from working Jews in Cernăuți as compensation for the military service from which they were excluded, they were also compelled to work one month per

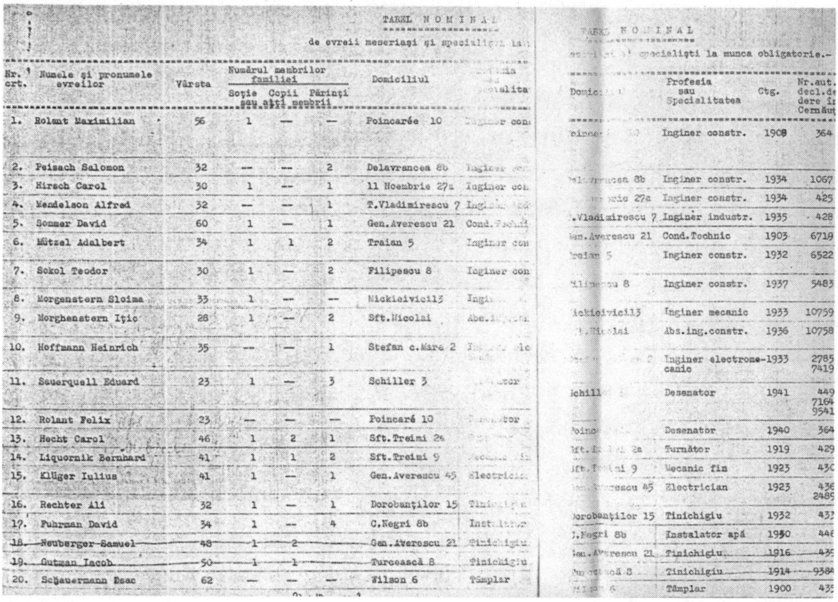

Figure 31. List of Jewish specialists, dated 22/IX/1842 (*sic;* for September 22, 1942) (Courtesy of the Chernivtsi Oblast Archive)

year without pay. It may also have been his registration on this very list of specialists that enabled Carl to return to his engineering work after being taken off the street to do manual forced labor arbitrarily on several occasions—a common experience for Cernăuţi Jews during the war years.[17]

The second list was a document entitled "Descendants of Jewish soldiers on active duty, of widows and orphans of war," and on it were listed Nechume, Lili, Rosa, Iacob Hirsch, and Carol—my grandmother, aunts, uncle, and father. There were two columns for identification numbers, one labeled *autoriz.,* the other, *No. legitim. "L"* (with L. standing for *lucru* or labor). Only Carl (Carol) and Kubi (Iacob), had those numbers, and these corresponded to the numbers on their official identity cards and, in Carl's case to the list from the railway administration.

Later we would find a variety of other lists in the microfilmed documents acquired by the United States Holocaust Memorial Museum, lists of Jewish *bătrini,* or old people, for example. My maternal grandparents and other relatives figured on the old people's lists. Thousands of older people were deported, indicating that these were registration and not exemption lists. How or whether these various lists correspond to the exemption authorizations that were issued in 1941 remains unclear to us. What is clear is that, despite Mayor Popovici's unquestionable integrity and his honorable intentions and despite the fact that he personally assumed, as he stated, the role of last court of appeal in the process, the procurement of exemptions seemed to have been a much more fraught form of selection than he wanted to acknowledge. He admits to responding to all requests by those who received waivers to include their family members, since for him family was a fundamental criterion. Beyond that, he insists, everything was totally above board.

"Who needs students?" Pearl Fichman asks in her memoir, and, on the basis of my father's explanations, I have often wondered how so many in my family (retired lawyers, businessmen, unemployed schoolteachers, unemployed pharmacists, etc.) were exempted from deportation. "You will remember, Carl," Lotte once said, somewhat reluctantly, "that my uncle Kubi Rubel [at whose villa they were all staying] one day took out pencil and paper and made his own list of those who would need *autorizaţie.* Without blinking, he said he would 'take care of' everything." My cousin Beate Schwammenthal, who was a child at the time, also remembers that Onkel Kubi "took care of everything." Rita Pistiner reports that "I was only twenty-one years old, but with money you could do a great deal at the time."[18] Who took the bribes, how members of the Jewish Council might have been involved, how it actually worked, why some doctors and other active professionals were deported while many without "useful professions" were exempted remains veiled in obscurity and suspicion.

By November 15, 1941, the deportations from Cernăuţi to Transnistria stopped. At that point, according to Mattatias Carp's *Cartea Neagră,* about 30,000 Jews from Cernăuţi had been deported, about 15,600 received official exemptions from the selection committee, and the mayor granted the remaining 4,000 or so temporary permits to remain in the city.[19] The latter were referred to as "Popovici authorizations." According to Popovici's account (based on a census carried out for the ministry of agriculture), there had been 49,000 Jews in the city in August 1941. On December 16, 1941, 19,521 Jews remained in Cernăuţi, while 28,391 had been deported. Why did the deportations stop at this point, before resuming again in a more targeted fashion the following July? Why was the ghetto so quickly dissolved? How did such a significant number of Cernăuţi Jews earn the unbelievable good fortune to be spared when in the entire rest of the Bukowina only 182 Jews were exempted from deportation? Some fifty thousand, and perhaps as many as sixty thousand, additional Jews were shipped off the Transnistria from other towns and villages in the Northern and Southern Bukowina.[20] These mysteries are part of the continuing questions surrounding the Holocaust in Romania.

Certainly, the Cernăuţi Jews' worries were not over with the halt of these deportations. "We had barely settled in," Pearl Fichman writes, "when, by the end of November, the governor issued a decree, summoning all permit holders to have them reviewed by a military commission, to have everything documented. That threw a new scare into everybody."[21] This commission had a great deal of power, and its work must have been the source of the numerous categories that can be found on the identification and registration cards that were issued in 1941 and then reviewed again in 1943 and 1944.

Each card was marked with a large yellow star and a stamp reading *evreu* (Jew), as well as with numerous signatures and numbers. "[We were registered] in a large hall with a lot of different tables," Carl told us, "and, listen, this is a good story. I went together with my brother, but it got late and his review was interrupted; he would have to go back the next day to complete his documentation. He came home dejected, in despair. 'Carl, I have to pack for Transnistria,' he told me. What happened? When he was about fifteen years old, he had been arrested one night for passing out communist leaflets. Consequently, on his authorization, which he brought home that night, it said, *provine în liste de securitate* [appears on the lists of the secret police]. This was serious. He was ready to throw in the towel. So you know what I did?" Carl laughed. "I just took an eraser, and I rubbed out that sentence. Just like that. We were lucky it had been entered in pencil. The next day he went back, and—no problem."

When the remaining Jews returned from the ghetto, some found their apartments had been plundered. What belongings they still had would be slowly sold off or traded in exchange for food. Bubi Brenner had a well-known stamp collection. "One day a Romanian knocked on our door and asked to see the collection. 'Aren't you going to sell it?' he asked me. 'Why would I want to sell it?' I said. 'Well, you aren't going to be here long, you'll be sent off sooner or later.' 'Thank you very much for your kind concern,' I said, 'but I'm not selling right now.' And I didn't sell that collection!" Isaak Ehrlich tells of his high school teacher, Professor Mandiuc, who met him on the street one day and told him he was looking for an overcoat: "You will all be deported to the Ukraine, and you will not survive. You must give me your coat, I was your professor."[22] Even Traian Popovici describes the Romanians who bought, plundered, or simply offered to "take care of" the Jews' possessions as "sharks."[23] Nevertheless, Carl was eager to note the friendship and respect he enjoyed at his place of work and how much this meant to him:

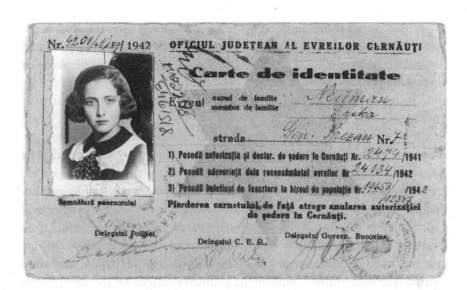

Figure 32. Cernăuți identity cards issued to Jews, with a yellow star as background, 1942 (Courtesy of the United States Holocaust Memorial Museum Photo Archives)

tion about Transnistrian conditions made its way among Jews in the city. As one who had been able to gain an authorization and remain in Cernăuţi, Carl's sister, Lilly Hirsch, was sensitive to this news and tried especially hard, within the restrictive possibilities of wartime, to gain information about the condition and location of relatives and friends who had been deported. She and others found out about Transnistria's camps and urban and rural ghettos—places like Moghilev, where her aunt Fritzi Wurmbrand and her teacher Lydia Harnik were living under appalling conditions and where her cousin Jochanan was doing forced labor in the Jagendorf foundry; Bershad, where Rosa Roth had barely survived the typhus epidemic; and Shargorod, where many of the relatives from villages in Southern Bukowina had been relocated.[25]

But it was not until mid-1943 that it became possible to send small packages, and even money, to surviving relatives and friends in Transnistria by mail. Lilly told us how she sold household goods and other small items so as to be able to send food, clothing, and money to her Aunt Fritzi and cousin Jochanan Wurmbrand, to her cousin Rosa Roth, and to her teacher Lydia Harnik. Yet many others who also had the good fortune to remain in the city were far less concerned or generous than she. Lilly told us that she had gone to see relatives to collect items for Fritzi and her son, and that, while most ignored her or turned her down, one cousin gave her a few clothing items only to have his wife come by the same afternoon to take them back. Being "in the same boat" did not mean that Lilly and other family members would produce recollections that were identical in affect: Lilly's accounts of the war years, like Pearl Fichman's—but generally unlike those of my parents and the Brenners—are often indignant, unhappy, and bitter.[26]

## 1942 DEPORTATIONS

In June 1942, after a seven-month hiatus, deportations from Cernăuţi to Transnistria resumed. For those Jews who had been exempted in 1941, a new period of terror began. Carl and Lotte, now living in Carl's mother's small second-floor apartment on the former Franzensgasse (Romanian: 11 Noembrie; Ukrainian: 28 Tchervnia), together with Carl's siblings and Rosa's husband, Moritz Gelber, were eyewitnesses to selections that were made in the street below. "Each Sunday in June several hundred Jews were gathered here, right in front of the house, and they waited to be sent to the Maccabi-Platz, a stadium, and from there to the train station to board the trains for Transnistria," Lotte had told us in 1998.

"You asked me once for my most powerful memory of those years," said Carl. "There are several, but the first that comes to mind is of our landlord in this house. He was originally from a village near Czernowitz, and in the summer of 1942, when the second set of deportations happened, he was taken away as we were watching. Others stood quietly, but this man cried bitterly and screamed in Yiddish, 'What are they doing to us? Where are they taking us?' I'll never forget that, he cried so bitterly."

Word spread quickly that the so-called Popovici authorizations issued by the mayor in November of 1941 were no longer recognized as valid by the governor of the Bukowina. Popovici, out of favor for his outspoken opposition to the earlier deportations and for his intervention, had been replaced, and the holders of the authorizations he had signed himself (as opposed to those signed by Governor Calotescu) were targeted for deportation to Transnistria in June of 1942. Similarly, some who were considered "politicals," like David's father and Lotte's cousin, Dr. Arthur Kessler, who had been the head of a hospital under the Soviets, were deported later that year. Carl describes his recollections of those fateful Sundays of June 1942 in his memoir:

> The procedure was to pick up the people on Sunday early morning (on 3 consecutive June Sundays), to bring them to an open sports stadium where they were checked in the presence of the Jewish Community, release some who were either needed or taken by mistake, and ship them [the rest] Sunday night to Transnistria. . . . The leaders of the Community used their influence to get the release of some people who had to support their family, and probably for some of their friends who asked to be protected. On the last day too many people were released and in order to fill the quota, the military in charge took a number of people from two streets out of their apartments indiscriminately. . . . Interestingly, some people who knew that they were in danger of being deported went into hiding during these days, and after the deportations were over they came back into the open without being bothered.[27]

One name that comes up quite often in connection to Cernăuți in this period is that of Lieutenant Stere Marinescu, head of the Office of Jewish Affairs II. This man and his coworkers worked under the governor and took massive bribes both locally, from individual Jews, and from Jewish organizations in Bucharest, always promising not to organize further deportations and assuring the safety of Jews remaining of Cernăuți. Many of those who bribed him individually were deported so as not to be able to testify to his corruption. It is possible that Marinescu himself, and no directive from

Bucharest, ordered the June 1942 deportations of those four thousand Jews who only had Popovici authorizations. The deportation orders were signed by the governor, but Marinescu himself carried out the evacuations with great brutality. Matatias Carp cites the war crimes trial records of chief prosecutor A. Bunaciu, regarding the deportations in Cernăuți on June 7, 14, and 28, 1942:

> Marinescu appears in all his inhumanity on the occasion of the deportations of the summer of 1942. At that time Marinescu became the head of the Office of Jewish Affairs II, the one that was in charge of carrying out the deportations. . . . We have a series of witnesses who describe the procedure Marinescu used. . . . The scenes were horrendous. When the inhabitants heard the knock on the door they already knew what was awaiting them. If one had a valid document or authorization exempting him from deportation . . . Marinescu or his people said, "No documents matter here, only money does." Only money had value for him. This is how we can explain . . . the deportation of Polish citizens, of sick people, old people and war invalids.[28]

In a report dated September 7, 1942, and confirmed in a second report of December 12, Governor Calotescu states that 4,094 Jews were deported from Cernăuți during the previous summer.[29] Among them were the parents of Paul Antschel (Celan); Celan himself had gone into hiding during the night that his parents were taken, and his biographers concur that he was never able to get over his guilt at having "abandoned" them. Both parents died in the Mihaelovka camp in Transnistria during the following winter.

In immediate effect, these 1942 deportations were even more deadly than the deportations of 1941 because the majority of deportees were sent to the border of Transnistria adjoining the Bug River or directly across the Bug into German-controlled territory, to Nazi slave labor and almost certain death.

The brutality of people like Marinescu contrasts with the decency of Mayor Popovici, but the fact that local officials had such significant impact on government policy is one of the peculiarities of the Romanian Holocaust.[30] Indeed, throughout the summer of 1942, at the very same time that the Cernăuți deportations were happening, efforts in Bucharest to stop the plan to deport all the Romanian Jews to Belzec (as Marshall Ion Antonescu had been urged to do by his Nazi allies in Berlin) were also under way. The bishop of Transylvania, the Queen Mother Elena (who threatened to leave Romania if her son, the king, went along with the plan), the papal nuncio, the ambassadors of Switzerland and Sweden, and even, indirectly, the U.S. government, all made efforts to intervene and prevent implementation of the plan. Did Antonescu listen to these pleas and arguments? Which made the decisive impact on him? For reasons that remain unclear to this day, in October of 1942, he formed a commission to find a different "solution to the Jewish problem." By then, of course, the Wehrmacht, together with Romanian forces, had already suffered significant defeats on the Eastern front, and the outcome of the war was less certain than it had previously been.[31]

## THE SPOT ON THE LAPEL

According to the notation on the back, the photograph of my parents walking down the former Herrengasse was snapped around the period of the 1942 deportations. We have never been able to resolve the mystery of the spot on Carl's lapel in that photo. When we blew up that photograph to the point where all contrast was gone but that curious spot on Carl's lapel was revealed, we were searching for the confirmation of our own understanding of the past, one that fundamentally contradicted what the picture made visible. We very much wanted to challenge its seeming air of normality—the way it fit like any other everyday snapshot into a page of a photo album without proclaiming the irregularity of the place and time in which it was taken. And, like second-generation artists who reemploy documentary images in their contemporary works, we felt we had to amend and tweak and modify the picture for additional reasons as well. We needed to open up the range of affects and meanings it contained, as well as those we were projecting unto it. Looking at the picture now, we realize that in it Carl and Lotte are *already* survivors, alive within a fortunate minority that had been spared a terrible fate. They are on the former Herrengasse, but, in a sense, they are not supposed to be there; they have outstayed their welcome in this city of their birth. They are looking, shyly, smilingly, toward a future they could not foresee. This is the knowledge a retrospective witness brings to a photograph that, as Roland Barthes writes, "tells me death in the future."[32]

In wanting to restore to Carl and Lotte's photo the hardships it seemed to be eliding, we can now see we adopted the "backshadowing" glance that reads the past backwards through our retrospective knowledge, "judg[ing] the participants in those events *as though they too should have known what was to come.*" Eve Kosofsky Sedgwick has termed this kind of perspective "paranoid reading"—anticipatory, eager to unveil hidden violence and to expose unseen danger.[33] Through our reading of this image, we wanted to find and reveal the negative lurking within and outside the frame of the image and, through our vigilance, somehow, to protect Carl and Lotte, walking down the Herrengasse, from the terrible fate that in hindsight we know could have been—and, in the summer of 1942, could still be—theirs.

But archival photographs also challenge their viewers not to impose retrospection to the point where a photo's own temporality and surface, however delicate and contingent, is erased. While this photo qualifies the grand historical narrative we have of the time, it also requires (again, in Sedgwick's terms) a more generous "reparative reading" than the paranoid scrutiny we initially employed. Such a reading would leave ambiguities unresolved, providing an expanded context for more an affective knowing. Was Lotte and Carl's photo taken in 1942 or 1943? Were they wearing a yellow star, or not? If it was 1942, and they walked on the Herrengasse without it, trying to pass, why didn't they fear a photographic record of their transgression? Why did they stop to buy the photo? Did their purchase accentuate an act of resistance? Alternatively, if they were both, in fact, wearing a star (Lotte, perhaps under a turned-up coat collar), were they humiliated by the photo, yet nonetheless defiant enough to buy it as a record of an outrage Jews were forced to endure? Perhaps, since street photos were printed right onto photo-sensitive paper, without a negative, they were simply buying up the evidence. Or was the inscription on the photo's back indeed an error? Was it taken in 1943—after the stars were discontinued in Greater Romania? The Herrengasse stroll, in that case, would attest to a moment of greater freedom, increased hope, following Carl and Lotte's fortunate evasion of mass deportations. But, if so, then what *is* the spot on the lapel?

By considering, rather than dismissing, these multiple and contradictory readings of Jewish existence during 1942–43, by leaving ambiguities unresolved, we broaden the boundaries of our understanding and tap into a deeper register of intergenerational transmission. We gain an access to what the stories about this past do not readily reveal—the emotional fabric of daily life in extreme circumstances, its aftereffects in the process of survival. If our search was indeed successful in revealing the traumatic wound that seemed so strangely absent from the tiny image in the album, our scrutiny of the picture also reveals the indeterminacy of that wound and the unlocatability of its source. Yet it also reveals that, as much as survival might be a struggle against the recall of trauma, structured by forgetting or denial, the mark is *there,* present, even if it remains submerged, disguised, invisible to the naked eye. Extracting whatever information we can from fragmentary documents, unreadable sources, and blurry, indeterminate spots in a tiny pale image, we also realize that allowing the image to fade back to its initial size, we might be able to make space for the possibility of survival and allow for "life," rather than "death in the future."

Our second trip to Chernivtsi, the search through archives and the opportunity to revisit and to rethink what we had seen and heard from our witnesses previously, involved just such oscillations in our understanding of their past. As their story became our story, more and more, we tried not to assimilate it too easily, thereby smoothing over unanswerable questions. Repeatedly, during those days, we found ourselves in front of Carl and Lotte's former apartments, the places where their families spent the war years in close proximity. It is here that they evaded the 1942 deportations. I went to stand in front of the apartment on the Franzensgasse, in particular, in order to be able to imagine better one story I had heard repeatedly—one that had very much shaped my own view of my family and of myself. That story had always seemed frightening, perhaps because it starts with a phrase that a child of survivors would experience as traumatic: "One night there was a knock on our door."

This was, in fact, one of those darker stories that had inspired this second trip to Chernvitsi. "It was around 2:00 in the morning in June," my father had told us in 1998, though it was a story he had often told before:

That was when they typically came to take people. My brother Kubi quickly slipped under the bed. Well, what was I supposed to do? I went to answer the door. Two gendarmes were outside. "Where's Kahane?" they asked me. "We're looking for the Kahane family." "They're not here," I said to them. These neighbors who lived across the hall had always only had Popovici authorizations, and they knew what was happening so they had gone into hiding somewhere. So the soldiers left. My brother told me his knees couldn't stop trembling. But I went to answer the door.

My father used to tell this story lightly, matter-of-factly, smiling about his brother's fear and about his own courage as he opened the door, and about everyone's relief when they heard that the gendarmes were not looking for them, but for neighbors who were in hiding. I had always been in awe of my father's courage, to the point that, many years ago, when asked to write a short speech about "my greatest quality" in a women's public speaking workshop, I told that story as one that defines me. While others in our group had trouble describing their "greatest quality," I was able, thanks to my father, to speak about myself as the daughter of the man who went to open that door. "My greatest quality is that, like my father, I am a survivor," I said then. Later, when I started studying and teaching the Holocaust, I began to wonder about other aspects of that story. What I now wanted to know is how those few minutes under the bed felt to my uncle. My father did not easily tolerate negativity, let alone what he would consider cowardice. "In June of '43, I got so mad at my brother Kubi that I hit him," Carl once admitted. "I had heard of the German defeats and he, always the pessimist, thought they had gained. I couldn't control myself, I hit him. We depended on hearing good news like that."

In the family account presented by my parents there is little room for pessimism or for that other, less heroic narrative: my parents' construction of their youth shows no marks of the effects or affect of trauma. Carl's account, in particular, has such rhetorical authority, such a sense of closure, that it may become difficult for other memory fragments to surface. Yet, with all I had learned, it became more difficult for me to listen to his version, his sense, always repeated, that it was "not so bad." Were there unprocessed bits of deep memory that neither of my parents could access because of the way in which their "official" family story had been constructed and the ways that familial roles had been allotted? In attempting a corrective reading, at times "paranoid," at others "reparative," Leo and I tried to allow a darker, as well as a lighter, side of the story to emerge. We had come back to Chernivtsi to try to find, and to feel, those other sides of the story. That search would now take us beyond the borders of the city, to the region that was once known, and feared, as Transnistria.

# NINE

# "There was never a camp here!"

## THE ARRESTS, SEPTEMBER 1942

From the memoir of Nathan Simon:[1]

> I was told to get dressed. They handcuffed me and I was forced to face the wall while they searched my room. . . .
>
> In the street I saw that, besides myself, my sister, my brother, two cousins who lived in the neighborhood, and a young woman whom I only knew by sight, had been arrested.
>
> . . . After arriving at headquarters, they led me to a room where the chief of the secret police sat at a table. In a most friendly tone he asked me for a statement and placed a typewritten sheet of paper before me. On it I read a confession: that the signer below, together with a group of Jews, intended to overthrow the Romanian government and to replace it with a communist regime. In a calm voice he advised me to sign: "If you are reasonable and admit these allegations, they will meet you halfway and only penalize you mildly. Otherwise we will resort to more extreme means to extract a confession from you."

From the testimony of Polya Dubbs:

> It was the 6th of September 1942, Friday evening. I was already in bed reading a novel when we heard a loud knock at the door. "Open up, police! Get up. Get dressed. Come with us. Your name is on our list!" I didn't think much of it. My husband, not on the list, accompanied me to the police station. I was on it because I could speak Russian and was employed

by a Russian official during the Soviet year in Czernowitz. People of absolutely no importance were on the list. I thought I would be back home soon.

From the memoir of Arthur Kessler:

There's a big table and at one end sits the chief of the secret police, Cojocariu, the most feared man in the city. The lists are typed, with different rubrics . . . they enter our names here, erase them there. . . . Without judge or trial, years of detention are ordered. . . . The reserved freight car is already standing at the freight railway station. It is night, dark, our guards are standing in groups, smoking cigarettes. . . . We already know that we're not going to a nearby Lager, but across the Dniestr to Transnistria and that this can mean extinction for us.

Nathan Simon, Polya Dubbs, and Arthur Kessler, together with nearly two thousand others from the Bukowina and Bessarabia, were deported to Transnistria soon after their arrests early in September 1942. In Cernăuţi alone, there were several hundred arrests on top of the June 1942 deportations of the several thousand Jews who had procured "Popovici" rather than "Calotescu" authorizations the previous year. Nearly all of the September 1942 deportees wound up at the Romanian concentration camp Vapniarka, which had been newly established for "political" prisoners. Although news from ghettos and camps in Transnistria was beginning to filter back to Cernăuţi, none of the new deportees could imagine what was awaiting them at their destination. But, like a recurring nightmare, Vapniarka would stay with them forever; its memory would envelop their children.

### SHADOW MEMORY

"I knew about this mysterious place called Transnistria, and that there is some place called Vapniarka there, that it was a camp," David, Arthur Kessler's son, said to us in 2000, almost sixty years after his father, a medical doctor, had been imprisoned there:

But nothing specific. You could not not hear about it. There was a string of people coming to our house on crutches. I knew the people. We were surrounded by them. They had special cars, built especially for them. My dad took care of them. It was all part of my surroundings. And my father would say in German, "There are some things children should be spared knowing. One day the story will be told." . . . In my imagination Vapniarka was someplace over there that doesn't exist any more. It was always in black-and-white of course, very unreal, it belonged to the old, old past. It had to do with old people.

Born in Israel, David Kessler had grown up in Tel Aviv with the post-memory of Transnistria and of Vapniarka in particular. After the war, before emigrating from Romania to what was then still Palestine, his father had written a lengthy memoir in German based on his notes as an inmate-doctor in the Vapniarka camp and the Olgopol ghetto in Transnistria. Arthur Kessler's account—typed single-spaced, with occasional handwritten corrections and illustrations—detailed his experiences in both places, but David had been unable to read his father's text. Their language-in-common in Israel was Hebrew. Throughout David's entire childhood and youth, however, Vapniarka's existence had been constituted in numerous other ways for him: through his father's fractured stories, his encounters with other survivors, and through the whispers and silences that had surrounded him and fueled his own fantasies. People on crutches, in wheelchairs and special cars—many came to be treated by Dr. Kessler in Tel Aviv or just to visit him. Vapniarka. The very name sometimes seemed to elicit a shudder in the men and women who spoke about it to his parents. What had happened over there—in that "someplace . . . that doesn't exist anymore"?

After his mother died and his father developed Alzheimer's disease, David began to be the keeper of many items and memorabilia connected to his parents' and grandparents' years in Czernowitz and to his father's deportation—photos, letters and family records, a journal containing Arthur's medical jottings from the camp and from Olgopol, documents written by Vapniarka survivors or concerning them, drawings of the camp produced by inmates, hand-crafted miniature pendants, carvings, and objects made in the camp and dedicated to Arthur, including a leather-covered book, less than an inch in height and width, containing sketches of camp life drawn by several inmate artists. It was to these and to other written accounts and documentary sources—some published, some not—that David turned to learn details of a past experience that had so enveloped him while also remaining so remote.

GOING THERE, 2000, 1942

Over the years, David's wish to travel to Czernowitz and to the places now in the Ukraine and Romania where his family had lived—but especially to what had been Transnistria and to Vapniarka—had intensified. This desire grew

Figure 33. Dr. Arthur Kessler and Judith Kessler in Cernăuţi, late 1930s
(Courtesy of the Kessler archive)

even more powerful when his father's illness worsened and Arthur steadily
lost touch with the world. In some manner, David wanted to witness and
to remember *for* his father, to establish an actual physical connection with
locations that had been so significant in shaping Arthur Kessler's life and
memory, thereby making a pilgrimage that would pay homage to his father's
courage and survival. Thus, he sought to transform shadowy black-and-white
images of childhood remembrance and imagination and to endow them with
color, reality, and concreteness.

For the three of us, companions on this journey, there were other motivations as well. For Marianne, the journey to Transnistria was a journey to the sites of her own childhood nightmares. Her parents had never gone, so, in a sense, she was going there in their stead, to acquire a sense of the fate they succeeded in evading. But Transnistria, and Vapniarka in particular, had also become an important object of study for Marianne and me, a place that would clarify the distinctive features of the Romanian Holocaust and its legacies, as well as its impact on the afterlife of Czernowitz.

---

Leaving Chernivtsi around six in the morning in an old but roomy and well-maintained Toyota van, we reached the Dniester River and the western boundary of what had been Transnistria in a little less than five hours. We were accompanied by Lyuda, a student at the University of Chernivtsi who was to be our translator, and Russlan, our driver. Because we had no transit visas to pass through the newly independent republic of Moldova (the former Bessarabia and the shortest and most direct way to our destination), we had to detour around its northern border—and this had prolonged our journey. The detour road was also bumpier, Russlan complained, uncared for, full of ruts and potholes, uncomfortable, bad for the tires. I could not help but smile when I compared our relatively comfortable drive here by car and the eight-day ordeal in a railroad freight car that Arthur Kessler, Polya Dubs, and other Vapniarka deportees were forced to endure in the midst of battles between Romanian and German forces against the Red Army:

From the memoir of Arthur Kessler:

The hours pass, the train is stationary more than it moves. Here and there a slight snore—restless sleep with chaotic dreams. The light shines through the roof spars of the clanging car. The first needs appear: a piece of clothing is draped across a corner, a piece of paper on the floor, the trapdoor is opened quietly so the sleepy guard on the rear platform won't notice, and out it goes. It's simpler for the men. The carriage doors close badly, the spars leave gaps. . . . We roll on, hear a few words exchanged here and there at a station, but can't understand enough. We are all very quiet. Hunger returns. . . .

We have barely slept for a few hours when it begins. Muffled detonations of exploding bombs, the rattle of machine guns, the boom of antiaircraft guns. A machine gun is mounted on our roof or that of the next boxcar over, the noise is deafening. We open the hatches, no gendarme slams them shut again. We stand on our knapsacks and take turns looking out. Here and there flashes light up the pitch dark night, we see isolated flaming plumes of smoke. Then it is suddenly as bright as day, a strange, colored light. A flare ignites, spreads like a jellyfish and illuminates a large area. The noise of the antiaircraft guns increases, in between again and again single bomb detonations. Suddenly the glaring light is extinguished. Black night, single strips of light, yellow and green. The noise of the guns becomes intermittent and stops. Ten minutes pass, until a broad, smiling face appears in the hatch. Corporal Fanica [one of the guards] tells us: "You're much better off, you can't get out and can sit here quietly. As for me, I didn't know where best to hide, in the garden or the corn field. Do you have any idea how much they were shooting and how dangerous it was?"

. . . Next morning there is a strong jolt. We are keenly sensitive to that by now. It means that we have been reattached and are moving on. . . . Now comes the big bridge, the deciding moment. We cross from our so-called homeland into no-man's-land. Tens of thousands have traveled this way before; none of them has come back. We learned of death from hunger and epidemics. . . . We are afraid of going there, but do not even have the haziest image of the place. Now that we are crossing the broad river, the train travels slowly, as if on unsafe ground. We are all silent. On the other side the same sun. Steppes on either side, fields of grain, sunflowers, corn right up to the train tracks, here and there houses and people. We breathe a little more deeply, one or the other chokes out a word, as indifferent a word as possible. We have not yet become a unit. The concept of fight for survival is still alien. We all exude subjugation, surrender, fear.

On our drive towards the town of Vapniarka, David, Marianne, and I had brought little with us for the journey. We had cameras, a few snacks and water, our passports, and some money. And to help us envisage what the camp might have looked like and, perhaps, to aid us in locating it more precisely as we approached its vicinity, David also brought two visual aids from among his father's possessions: a photocopy of a copy of a detailed German Luftwaffe map of the region that Arthur Kessler had acquired from a historical archive after the war and a photocopy of a photograph of a cardboard model of the Vapniarka camp that had been built from memory by a survivor (and that had been on display at Beit Lohamei Hagetaot in Israel—a kibbutz museum dedicated to the memory of the ghettos and camps).

Traveling without the benefit of survivors as guides, the three of us had to rely on maps and images to help us find the sites we sought in our jour-

Figure 34. Model of the Vapniarka camp (Courtesy of the Beit Lohamei Hagetaot kibbutz museum)

ney. Our photocopy of a photograph of a cardboard model was about as far removed from the "real" as one can get, but we considered it a potentially appropriate guide to identify whatever might remain of the Vapniarka camp, a place to which no survivor seems to have made a recorded visit since its abandonment by the Romanians in 1944. In fact, this mechanically reproduced facsimile seemed to function as both a *vehicle* and a *figure* of the process of postmemory for us: a vehicle to help us search for and locate the site—more useful than we could even have imagined—and a figure for understanding the mediated relationship of a second generation, born elsewhere, to a history that has lost its location through the willful erasures of politics and the inadvertent ravages of time.

### THE ARRIVAL

From the memoir of Arthur Kessler:

> Now we learn our destination . . . the Vapniarka camp. There are nice
> houses there, we imagine wishfully—everything prepared for four
> thousand people, and we'll be fed as well. Vapniarka? Those among us
> who know Slavic languages translate: lime pits. Some draw conclusions

from this: we'll be working in lime pits. I have to write down the name, otherwise I won't remember it.

From Nathan Simon's account:

On the 16th of September 1942 we arrive in Vapniarka. It is a small town, between the Dniester and the Bug, located nearly midpoint on the rail line between Lvov and Odessa.

After everyone has left the train, we are compelled to line up in eight files and placed under the control of Romanian gendarmes. A gigantic human snake, whose tail end I could no longer see, then creeps along the few kilometers separating the train station from the lager. Ukrainian peasants stare at us during that march, and women throw bread into our midst. But these expressions of pity are quickly halted with club and rifle-butt blows from the gendarmes who guard us—by blows and shouts that they also unhesitatingly direct at anyone who, out of wariness or weakness, is unable to keep up with the pace. Faint prisoners have to be carried by others; weak ones, supported by their companions.

In this manner, because we were all nearly totally worn out by hunger, thirst, and the ordeal of our horrendous journey in primitive cattle cars, it takes some hours until we reach the lager. There, outside its gates, we are once again given over to military authorities. A sergeant, sitting by a table, notes down the name, age, and last previous residence of every single one of us prisoners.[2]

From Arthur Kessler:

At the moment the camp is inhabited by only a few people from ghettos in the surrounding area, arrested for diverse violations, and a few hundred Ukrainians. But preparations have been made for the several thousand that are expected. Looking at us, you cannot tell male and female apart, old or young. Nor distinguish our faces. Gray on gray, people and bags, tired bundles of flesh and rags.

·—·—◼◆▤—·—·

The present town of Vapniarka is located some seventy kilometers east of Moghilev, the city on the Dniester River which was both the transit center for many of the thousands of Jews deported to Transnistria during the war and the location of one of the region's largest wartime Jewish ghettos. For us, Moghilev was the entry point into Transnistria. There, overlooking the town, in the midst of a sprawling Jewish cemetery holding the remains of an ancient, sizable, and at one time thriving Jewish population, is a large empty grassy spot, the site of mass graves from the early 1940s. A stone monument, adorned by a large Jewish star and a menorah and a marble plaque in Yiddish and Ukrainian memorializes the years between 1941 and 1944 when thousands of Jews died here, victims of outright killings or of hunger, typhus, and the ravages of freezing winters.

In the center of the town, set unobtrusively on a sidewalk in front of an aging Soviet-built residential block with laundry hanging from its balconies, we found another, smaller, monument, also with a bas-relief star of David, a menorah, and a Yiddish and Ukrainian inscription. Like the monument in the cemetery, this was erected by international Jewish organizations. At its base, inscribed in Cyrillic script, are the names of some of the central deportation sites, ghettos, and camps in Transnistria. "Vapniarka," our intended destination, was carved into the marble there. Next to it, a second monument honors local war heroes and rescuers.

We drove on toward Vapniarka on a road bounded by small houses and sizable farms, some of them still recognizable as old collective *kolkhoz*. Green fields and farm animals were bountiful. It was a quiet summer afternoon—a gloriously warm, sunny day. The entry to the town was indicated by a large vertical signpost mounted on a concrete slab on which the name Vapniarka was spelled in bright red Cyrillic lettering.

We pulled over on the main street and approached a woman, perhaps in her mid-fifties, walking with a young child. Our interpreter, Lyuda, asked her if she knew where the site of the former camp was, and we saw the woman shaking her head and pointing in the direction we had come from. "There was never a camp here," Lyuda translated. "There was a Jewish ghetto in Tomaspol, twenty kilometers away."

We drove further through the town, looking for the buildings on the photocopied image we carried, and we came to a dusty, haphazard, marketplace near the rail terminal. Although it was mid-afternoon by now, people were still buying things from local farmwomen, who spread their wares in a market area on small tables and on the ground. "Where was the old concentration camp in Vapniarka located?" Lyuda asked a number of them, on our behalf. Blank looks, negative head shaking: "What concentration camp?" "Here there was no camp." Somewhat discouraged, the five of us walked over to the only store on the square, a pharmacy.

The pharmacist told us, yes, he was born here and has lived here for much of his life—he knew this place intimately. But when Lyuda, now joined by

Russlan, asked him our question, he also shook his head negatively in what has by now become a familiar shrug. We made out the words "lager" and "ghetto" and "Tomaspol." He waved his hand and pointed a finger in a gesture that implies "outside of the town." When we showed him the photocopy of the model of the camp, he glanced at it briefly, clearly without interest. Dismissively, he told us that we could ask at the militia building across the way if we want. That building, however, was locked. Had we driven here in vain?

We recalled the memoir of Matei Gall, a Vapniarka inmate and, in the 1940s, a Communist: "We are marched through a small town with low, shingle-roofed, farmhouses. The town inhabitants stare at us from their windows and doorways—astonished, but also a bit bored, like people who are used to such spectacles."[3] All along the town's main street, near the railroad terminal, the three of us had been staring at a set of large three-story brick buildings, and we decided to inspect them more closely. They were the only brick buildings in the town. Could the lager have been closer to the town center than the descriptions would lead one to imagine? Could the cardboard model, with its two-story buildings, have been wrong? The memory of the survivor who constructed it could well have been unreliable, recalling two stories rather than three. Should we really trust as accurate evidence the photocopy of a photograph of a model built some time later by someone who had been traumatized in a fascist concentration camp?

In fact, as we soon learned, the three-story brick buildings were built shortly after the war as apartments for older people. A few townsfolk in a group of elderly men and women sitting near the brick apartment houses, under a large walnut tree, tried to be helpful. We asked about the Vapniarka camp and got the familiar head shaking and pointing toward the ghetto of Tomaspol. Yet when we showed them the photocopy of the model, one of them recognized the buildings as former army barracks that had been torn down a few years before. When she gave Russlan careful directions to the site of these former barracks, we realized that without this picture of the camp model we would never have found any traces of the Vapniarka camp in Vapniarka itself. Its memory seemed to have been erased from the landscape and from the memory of its present inhabitants. Even the one old woman who recognized the buildings as "former army barracks" did not associate them with the concentration and punitive labor camp to which they had belonged—with a time of Romanian and German rule, the persecution of Jews and political dissidents; with misery, crippling disease, agonizing death. And now, if the buildings had indeed been torn down, we would at best only be able to find some bricks in a field. Dejected, we returned to our car.

Although Arthur Kessler's memoir describes the "military city" of Vapniarka, we were amazed when our car pulled up at the entrance to what looked like an enormous and still active Ukrainian army training camp, surrounded by a tall fence and a large closed gate with guard post. We parked and decided to leave our cameras in the car, convinced that we were more likely to gain entrance without them. But we brought the photocopied picture of the model along, hoping to find some remains of the former barracks that must be located somewhere behind the gate.

Lyuda and Russlan told the two young Ukrainian guards that we had come from America to find the camp at Vapniarka and showed them the photocopy. Again, much head shaking and pointing toward the former ghetto in Tomaspol. The gate remained locked—this was an army base; we could not go in. We persisted and implored. Finally, they asked us to wait, and they called their superiors.

A short while later two officers arrived by car, listened to our story, shook their heads. There was never a camp here, they claimed. Neither Germans nor Romanians were ever even in this territory. "This was Soviet territory and, in fact, a Soviet army base continuously since 1918," the Ukrainian officer insisted. We respectfully disagreed, pulled out the photocopy of our detailed Luftwaffe map of Romanian-controlled Transnistria, which included the very place where we now were standing. And we showed them the image of the camp model. But we'd given up hope.

And then one of the officers' eyes lit up: he recognized something. Still insisting that no concentration camp had existed here, he nevertheless admitted that, yes, there was one building inside the base that resembled this one, on our photocopy. But the other two had been torn down a few years ago. And suddenly everyone seemed friendlier, less forbidding, more relaxed. We all smiled. But the officers still didn't know whether we could go inside: after all, it was an army base; we were from the United States of America; there might be secret installations we might have to pass by on our way. We agreed to wait by the gate while they went back inside to inquire. But, just in case, we went back to our van to get our video and still cameras.

Only some twenty minutes went by, yet it seemed much longer. Finally the two officers, plus a third one, returned, and we were driven in their jeep into the military base through a back entrance. And then—amazingly—in the midst of a complex of high-rise buildings fronted by lawns, in the vicinity of a children's playground with jungle gyms and clotheslines, we found a large brick building that clearly had been one of three residential structures for inmates in the former Vapniarka concentration camp.

Figure 35. David Kessler in front of the only remaining building of the former Vapniarka camp, now the kindergarten of the Ukrainian military base, 2000 (Photograph by Leo Spitzer)

"This is the kindergarten for our base," one of the officers told Lyuda.

We had to work hard to connect what we'd read and heard about the camp with this place. We were allowed to photograph it and its surroundings, and as we wandered about, under the bemused gaze of the Ukrainian officers, we tried to imagine the site on which we now stood as it had looked some fifty-plus years earlier.

Time and space were out of joint, though David, standing in front of the old camp building, having his picture taken, tried, bodily, to enact a link that had so definitively been severed. Step by step we walked around traces of the demolished foundations of the torn down buildings. We followed what remained of their outlines, and reverently picked up shards from old bricks. We were silent and stared at the ground as if waiting for ghosts to rise from beneath its reddish surface. The day was hazy now in late afternoon. I strained to call to mind an ever more distant 1942.

### LAGER VAPNIARKA, 1942–1943

Vapniarka was first established as a detention camp in Transnistria's Zugas-tru district in the early fall of 1941. It had been located on the grounds of a former Soviet cavalry training base—a place whose structures, furnishings, and equipment had largely been dismantled and taken, or sabotaged and destroyed, when the Red Army withdrew in the aftermath of the July 1941 German-Romanian invasion of the Soviet Union. Despite the ruins and reigning chaos at the site, however, around one thousand deportees were brought there not long afterward: some minor bureaucrats who had been Soviet employees in Odessa and Tiraspol and Jews from Bessarabia and the Bukowina who had failed in their effort to flee to Russia in advance of the German-Romanian onslaught. Within a few months of their arrival, about half of these inmates died from starvation, the freezing winter, and a typhus epidemic. The remaining prisoners were then forced to abandon the camp, marched to the outskirts of the village of Koslova, and shot by Romanian gendarmes.[4] But Vapniarka was again employed not long afterward to imprison individuals accused of various "economic crimes" (such as black-marketeering) and to fulfill what was to become its main purpose: to hold and punish suspected communist sympathizers, Trotskyists, socialists, and political dissidents. Officially, as proclaimed in a decree signed in February 1942 by the governor of Transnistria, Georgiu Alexianu, it was to serve as a "lager for communists of Christian descent," and it was to be set up to receive and house approximately five thousand inmates.[5] Despite this specific religious stipulation, however, the vast majority of persons deported to the camp were Jews. About 20 percent of the inmates were women—among them a few whose children were interned along with them.

In August and September 1942, around twelve hundred Jewish deportees were brought there—from Bucharest and other areas of the Regat, but also from Cernăuţi and the Bukowina region and other areas annexed by Romania.[6] Although for the most part arbitrarily arrested, all these deportees were considered "politicals"—persons who had been active communists or suspected of communist leanings—and among them was Dr. Arthur Kessler, whose "crime" it had been to be the medical director of the Chernovtsy Hospital during that city's year-long spell under Soviet control.

From Arthur Kessler's memoir:

Next morning the doors are opened at dawn, and we take our first look around. There are no soldiers inside the camp compound. The three buildings [in which we sleep] are derelict. There are no window frames or panes, the floors are dirty and defective, some doors are missing and those still in place are without locks. . . . In the small house, opposite the three large ones, that was once a kitchen, big vats remain. But doors and windows, banisters and everything else that is easily removable have disappeared. . . . On the other side of the yard is a latrine, professionally dug and covered with wooden boards, which provides forty holes. There are water pipes in two places in the yard, but no water.

... Summoned for roll call for the first time, we line up somewhat orderly, first women, then men. ... The gate is thrown wide open, and the commandant of the internment area, Colonel Murgescu, appears with a following of officers and noncoms ... In Napoleonic fashion he clutches his right hand between the lapels of his coat and, with feet planted far apart and heavy-jowled head thrown back on a fat neck—a martial specimen, indeed—he turns his attention to us. ... His speech is short: "On the slope behind the camp you can see the graves of 550 people who were in the camp before you. They died of typhus. Try to do better if you can. ... "

From Nathan Simon's account:

As a welcoming speech, Colonel Murgescu hammers us with the rules of the camp, replete with threats, warning us for example that anyone attempting to escape will be executed by firing squad. He finishes with these words: "You entered the lager on two legs. But if you are still alive, you will leave it on all fours!"[7]

The first of the three residential buildings (or "blocks," or "pavilions," as the inmates and camp officials referred to them) housed the women and children on the second floor and the infirmary—of which Dr. Kessler was put in charge—on the ground level. Most of the men who had come on the transport with Arthur Kessler or who arrived in a subsequent transport lived in the smaller rooms and the large dormitory space of the middle building (the one still standing, in whose proximity we now walked). And the third pavilion held some three hundred Ukrainians who had preceded the arrival of the Jewish inmates by a few months—men and women who included partisans, Seventh-Day Adventists, and common criminals among their numbers. The buildings were locked in the evening after the lineup and roll call, and pails were placed near their staircases in each to serve the after-curfew need for nighttime relief. Throughout the night, at regular intervals and from tower to tower, the guards called out to each other in Romanian: "Poooost Number One: Aaall is well ... Poooost Number Two: Aaall is well ..."[8]

But all was clearly not well. "The place looked as though it had suffered through a storm from Hell," Nathan Simon recalled.[9] The pavilions contained neither beds nor chairs, tables, or storage cubicles. For some time after the inmates' arrival in the fall of 1942, cold and wind raged through the paneless window frames. Miraculously, the tile stoves on the end walls of

Figure 36. "Vapniarka, 1942–43," drawing by Moshe Leibel and Ilie; the original is 13 x 9.5 inches (Courtesy of the Kessler archive)

the large rooms in each of the buildings did remain functional. But there was little burnable material to heat them at first, other than what could be salvaged from odds and ends trashed within the buildings themselves. Furthermore, inmates were subjected to extremely harsh forced physical labor and deprivation. Their water supply was shut off at the whim of the camp commander—a single valve controlled the water flow into the two pipes inside the camp grounds. Thirst was inflicted as a punishment.

On a daily basis, inmates carrying whatever containers and implements they could manage to acquire—bowls, small pots, discarded cans, chipped and cracked glass dishes—fetched a thick greenish-yellow soup made from chickling peas (not the same as chick peas, or garbanzos), approximately 400 grams (somewhat more than fourteen U.S. oz.) per person, from the old kitchen building. Each person also received a 200 gram (about seven U.S. oz.) slice of bread made from a mix of barley and moistened straw—bitter tasting, according to Nathan Simon ("soapy," in Arthur Kessler's recollection), and difficult to digest.

The chickling peas used in the soup came from a warehouse that had

totally paralyzed; a number had died. It was Dr. Kessler who deduced that the epidemic was directly connected to the peas in the soup ration:

It is clear that we are in the midst of a mysterious epidemic. But it does not spread through contagion. There are sick Ukrainians and Russians who arrived here before us, as well as Jews from our group, but we have not heard of a single case among the guards and the camp command. It must be brought on by our particular living conditions as inmates, since bacteria do not make exceptions. It can't be the water, because everyone drinks it, nor the bread. We have never encountered a deficiency disease like this one. What distinguishes us, the inmates, from the guards and the command is our fodder-pea nutrition. The afflicted ones among the Russians and Ukrainians have been eating the peas for the longest period and were the first to get sick. In our group, it is the young ones who are first to succumb to the epidemic—the biggest eaters who have come to Vapniarka starving from other prisons and penal camps and who devour all leftovers. Among the women there are fewer and less severe cases. Indeed it seems that the longer and the more a person eats, the worse his condition becomes.

So something in the pea-fodder ration we receive must be the source. We examine the peas for additives, pollution, a mix with other products, black fungus-riddled grains of ergot, and deliberate or random contamination. We find some dark seed grains, plant fibers, small stones, but nothing suspicious. I dimly remember plant toxins in legumes that cause similar symptoms, and try to destroy these by boiling the peas for an additional three hours. But this seems to make no difference. . . .

That leaves the peas themselves. They are of an unusual kind, larger, irregularly shaped, angular—not like our good vegetable pea, *pisum sativum.* [It now seems clear] we are eating poison and will perish from them. Something must immediately be done.

It was subsequently revealed that a steady diet of this particular kind of chickling pea, *Lathyrus sativus,* was known to have brought on paralysis in animals and humans in many areas of the world—and recognition of its toxic hazards was fairly widespread among rural peoples in the regions where it grew. As Kessler later observed: "In Central Europe, reports about stiff legs following the consumption of bread containing flour from the *Lathyrus* pea, and laws to prohibit such adulteration, date back to the seventeenth century. In India, North Africa (Algier), and in Southern Russia, larger epidemics of lathyrism have regularly been observed amongst the poor in times of famine. . . . Malnutrition and low temperatures favored the onset of the disease."[11]

Figure 37. "Infirmerie," drawing by Moshe Leibel and Ilie; the original is 13 x 9.5 inches (Courtesy of the Kessler archive)

It is significant to stress that neither Vapniarka's Romanian camp officers nor its military guards ate the toxic peas—only the inmates. Yet when Dr. Kessler and other leaders among the prisoners appealed to the camp command to change their diet and to be given medical supplies to treat the sick, they were ignored. "Captain Buradescu [the new commander] listens quietly with a pinched face," writes Kessler in his account, "and after I am through pleading, curtly limits his reply to these words: 'What makes you think that we are interested in keeping you alive?' That concludes our hearing."

The situation in the lager continued to deteriorate. It had grown extremely cold during the winter months. In the large hall of the infirmary, those who could still move sat around its small tin stove, holding out their hands to the heat, their legs jerking with unrelenting tremors. They leaned on sticks when they tried to walk, fell, and tried again. Many showed new symptoms: dark blisters on their toes, heels, the sides of their feet. They developed fever, extreme pain. Their legs turned pale, cold, losing all feeling. Gangrene set in, and some had to have toes or legs amputated. "It is a hellish, unimaginable scene," Kessler observes, "hundreds sick and paralyzed, gangrenous legs, loss of urine before they can reach the pails, distorted posture caused by muscle spasms in their arms, back, belly, and legs.... Treating a stinking, gangrenous leg, keeping a cold, bloodless, extremity warm, maintaining a paralytic and keeping his bunk free of excrement are insoluble problems."

And yet, through inmates in the laboring groups that worked outside of the camp and by means of bribes and the hushed cooperation of guards and soldiers, and of civilians with whom they occasionally came into contact, the doctors and leaders among the prisoners did manage to send appeals to the outside world—some even reaching Jews in their hometowns, as well as Jewish community officials in Bucharest. Moreover, not long after the onset of the mass paralysis and the realization it came from the fodder-pea soup, Vapniarka's inmates embarked on what Dr. Kessler described as "not a hunger strike but the highest degree of abstinence."

Having undertaken this course of action, they would no doubt have been forced to make the "choiceless choice" between paralysis and poisoning or starvation had the camp not received an inspection in mid-January 1943—routine, it seems—from a Romanian government doctor from Odessa checking the region for safeguards against the recurrence of a typhus outbreak.[12] This visit was followed by one from a neurologist two weeks later, by a medical investigative commission in late February 1943, by clerical visitors, and even by one from Georgiu Alexianu, the governor of Transnistria. Each time the visiting officials arrogantly dismissed the diagnosis connecting the strange mass paralysis and suffering to the pea-soup diet. Instead, they maintained that it was the result of a viral infection or that it was a type of inflammation of the bone marrow or spinal column (myelitis) that had spread from person to person or, in the most bizarre explanation, that it had resulted from the body fluids of inmates who were schizophrenic—it being a "fact of science," they argued, that such fluids were toxic and thus virulent when transmitted through contact. Overtly they did not acknowledge the obvious counterarguments from the inmate physicians: that any viral or otherwise contagious disease could not possibly have been contained so thoroughly so that the camp guards, officers, and non-inmate population with whom the prisoners came into contact every day would not be infected by it. There was certainly no official recognition—and no acknowledgment or admission—that the pea fodder that was being fed the inmates had any relevant connection to the epidemic in the camp. But, in fact, while not stopping and withdrawing the soup as the daily staple for the prisoners, the Romanian authorities in late January 1943 began to send dried fruit and moldy pig-fodder potatoes as a supplement to the peas, and also designated forty old or crippled packhorses for slaughter and consumption within the camp.[13]

It now seems clear that the decision to feed Vapniarka's inmates the toxic pea fodder in the first place was made for both practical and ideological reasons. At a time when large amounts of food supplies were being diverted to the Romanian military for campaigns against the Red Army in the Soviet Union, the ready availability of the chickling-pea fodder for use in the inmates' food would have seemed like a windfall and a logical allocation of resources. But since it also seems to have been known by some Romanian officials that the pea fodder was toxic for human consumption (hence, their withholding of the pea-soup diet from the camp guards and officers), feeding it to the imprisoned Ukrainian partisans, religious sect members, Jews, communists, and other "politicals," did in fact conform to official and unofficial directives from the highest authorities in Bucharest itself. These, in the Romanian version of the Final Solution, had mandated the elimination of such "enemies of the state."[14] The induced lathyrism epidemic in Vapniarka is perhaps one of the clearest manifestations of the exterminationist aspects of the Romanian Holocaust.

By the beginning of spring 1943, however, as the war in Eastern Europe turned increasingly against Germany and the Romanian military suffered massive casualties in the Soviet campaign, Romanian authorities began to reevaluate their support of the Third Reich and to moderate some of their policies against Jews and their political enemies on the left. Although at this point General Ion Antonescu and his leading advisors still refused to repatriate Jews and others who had been sent to Transnistria, a decision to hedge their bets in the alliance with Germany seems to have been made relatively soon after the devastating losses sustained by the Romanians at Stalingrad during the winter months of 1942–43. For Vapniarka, this hedging was manifested in the slight relaxation in controls restricting the ability of camp inmates to communicate with outsiders, as well as in the allocation of the supplementary food for inmate consumption.

Eventually, by the end of March 1943, as the lathyrism epidemic was brought under some control—or at least claimed no additional victims—and a commission in Bucharest held that some 440 of Vapniarka's inmates had been sent there without "just cause," Romanian authorities decided that Vapniarka would be closed down altogether.[15] Dr. Kessler and other surviving inmates, including Polya Dubbs and Dr. Moritz from Cernăuţi, as well as Nathan Simon, and Matei Gall, then began to be released from Vapniarka, either immediately or in the course of the next few months. But even those who had been officially acknowledged as having been unjustly arrested and imprisoned were not permitted to return home. Instead, they were placed in ghettos or in alternate camps in other parts of Transnistria. These shifts in policy in response to the progress of the war are also distinctive aspects of the Romanian Holocaust.

RESISTANCE

What no doubt contributed immensely to the ability of Vapniarka's inmates to resist and to survive the deprivations of the camp and the epidemic that threatened them with paralysis and agonizing death was the effectiveness and power of their internal organization. Unlike in the German-run concentration camps in Poland and elsewhere in Eastern and Central Europe, no *kapos* or other privileged figures were chosen from among the inmate population by the camp authorities. The camps and ghettos of Transnistria were essentially self-administered. In Vapniarka, the spokespersons officially recognized by the Romanian camp command for the "decimal divisions" (the groups of ten inmates) and for the "sections of a hundred" into which the prisoners were arranged were nominally in charge. But an underground political committee composed of former activists and communist leaders in effect ran a significant segment of the camp in a *sub rosa* manner, instituting measures to distribute food fairly, control against lice and the reappearance of typhus, staff the makeshift infirmary, and repair the broken-down inmate residential buildings. Indeed, largely because so many of the camp's inmates *were* political prisoners—communists and others who had once been active in underground activities and who were highly educated, politically and academically—it was perhaps easier for them to organize within the camp and to maintain discipline among their fellow prisoners.

In Vapniarka, thanks to the suggestions of the camp physicians, for example, the underground leadership insured that each group of ten prisoners selected a hygiene supervisor from among themselves to oversee a strict delousing inspection shortly after wake-up and before night curfew. Twice daily, every article of clothing, every shirt and piece of underwear, as well as every personal crevice and every cranny in the residential buildings, was closely scrutinized by the inmates and by the hygiene supervisor. Difficult as this was to carry out in all of the three residential pavilions in the camp, lice infestation was virtually wiped out by early 1943, and the threat of typhus was eliminated.

The underground command also organized a variety of work details within the inmate ranks—as much as was possible—taking advantage of skills and specializations that prisoners had brought to Vapniarka. A tailor-group and a cobbler-group thus emerged, each somehow managing to acquire at least a few of the essential tools of their craft, enabling them to sew and repair clothing and to resole and mend shoes—essential practical functions that helped prisoners survive the freezing snow and numbing cold temperatures of the winter months. There were also plumbers and pipe-fitters who repaired the wood-stoves and main kitchen oven, and the on-again, off-again water line. But the largest laboring detail, consisting of skilled workers and specialists who had been carpenters, woodcrafters, and builders, was focused on rebuilding the devastated structures in which the inmates were initially housed. These workers cleaned the ground of rubble and ruin, gathered whatever discarded materials they were permitted access to within the compound of the old Soviet cavalry school, and used these to rebuild or replace stairs, frames, cracked doors—even the broken or missing glass panes in the windows of the buildings in which they slept. Using pieces of planks that they managed to salvage from horse stalls and storage sheds, they built wooden bunks for the large dormitory spaces and smaller rooms of the residential pavilions. They consequently saved themselves and their fellow inmates from the only option that had been available to them when they first arrived in Vapniarka: to lie in misery and bone-chilling discomfort on the buildings' cold floors.

Most importantly, the underground leaders (or, as Arthur Kessler referred to them, "the members of the Black Hand") used bribes, payments, promises, perhaps even intimidation, to build up a network of communications and exchanges involving inmates and a few of the (perhaps more corruptible, perhaps more sympathetic) camp guards and officers. They were thus not only able to get word out about the paralysis that afflicted so many camp inmates and about the need for additional food and medications, but also, by early 1943, were themselves able to receive bits of news from the war front and from the world at large.[16] Certainly, when small supplies of additional food did manage to pass into Vapniarka on occasion (other than the supplements and staple changes authorized by the camp command), it was the underground leadership who seem to have enabled its entrance and controlled its distribution.[17]

Overall, the internal organization of Vapniarka camp and its effectiveness attest to the fact that even in a case of extreme physical and mental brutality and danger such as this one, disciplined resistance by inmates could in some rare instances break through the walls of despair and depression within which their captors attempted to crush them. And yet, as Marianne, David, and I realized during our visit there, such acts of collective resistance did not engender any sign of public recognition nowadays at the site where they had taken place. Given our experience with the dearth of on-site memorials in Chernivtsi, we should perhaps not have been surprised that they had been largely forgotten or suppressed from memory even within the communist state that evolved from the movement of which so many inmates had been a part. And yet, in truth, we were. All that remains of the inmates' experiences are a few memoirs, a few oral recollections from survivors—and some ephemera. But these are rich ephemera.

### THE LITTLE BOOK

Among the objects that David Kessler inherited from his father, the most remarkable is one of several presents Arthur received from his patients before he left the camp for the Olgopol ghetto—a tiny book, one inch high, about two-thirds of an inch wide. Bound in leather and held together by a fancifully tied but simple rope, it immediately betrays its handmade origin. Elegant raised lettering graces the cover: "Causa Vapniarka, 194 . . . "—the last number is missing, the decorations at the top hard to make out, the word *causa* not quite comprehensible in Romanian. The title page, in purple lettering, is less a title than a dedication: "To doctor Arthur Kessler, a sign of gratitude from his patients." Its forty-some pages contain a series of drawings by seven artists: each begins with a signature page, followed by several pages of storyboard drawings, a few with labels, one page of writing. While the drawing styles range from simple black stick figures to sophisticated watercolors, the subjects depicted and the stories that are told through them are remarkably uniform. The tiny drawings, some horizontal and others vertical, necessitating that the book be turned, feature scenes of camp life. Some depict cooking, food delivery, the exterior of the camp buildings, the interior of the bunks. All of them represent the infirmary and one or several figures on crutches. And most end with a scene of liberation, either as in the pages by Ghiţă Wolff, a figure throwing away the crutches and going through the gate toward a space labeled "liber," or by Gavriel Cohen, a train with a large question mark above it, or by "Romăşcanu" (this and some other names are not fully legible), a train labeled *spre libertate* (toward liberty), or simply, as in the series by "D.B.," a dancing stick figure.

Tiny in size, the little book is rich in meaning, a testimonial object for those who want to know more about Vapniarka and its remarkable history. As a book, it promises insight, exposure, but opening this book and "reading" its pages is not so much an act of revelation as it is an acknowledgment of an ultimate impenetrability. We find a series of names and drawings that

Figure 38. The little book (Photograph by Leo Spitzer)

seem to tell the same story, through the same bare-bones, minimalist plot, repeated seven times, with slight variations.

For Arthur Kessler, the little book was no doubt a sign of gratitude, a form of recognition of his remarkable work as a physician. It was a lovingly made gift that shows, as he writes in his memoir, the patients' talents, not just for drawing, but also for ingenuity in finding the materials, their skill in bookmaking, their ability to collaborate and create beauty in circumstances of extreme mistreatment and deprivation. It is a testament to him and to them, to their relationships and sense of community. It is also, of course, a souvenir of sorts, triggering memory and connecting it indexically to a particular place and time. As a souvenir, the little book imagines a moment in the future when the camp experience will be recalled and thus it expresses a sense of reassurance, a will to survive.

In the context of postmemory, however, the little book is more than all that: it is a valuable testimonial, a record of experiences subsequent generations can barely imagine. Like the elaborate woodcuts and drawings made by camp artists like Moshe Leibl and Aurel Mărculescu, it provides an account

Figure 39. (Here and overleaf) The pages in the little book, with drawings by "Romășcanu," Ghiță Wolff, "Avadani," Jeșive, Aurel Mărculescu, "D. B.," and Gavriel Cohen (Courtesy of the Kessler archive)

curge apa!

Omul
sfințeste
locul
—.—
Locul
sfințeste omul
—.—

of small details of the camp itself and of camp life. It testifies to Arthur Kessler's role in the camp; to the inmates' primary preoccupations: food, water, the disease and the crutches, the desire for freedom. But it speaks also to their courage and their spirit of community and collaboration, their ingenuity and resilience.

A testimonial object, the little book is bound, carefully assembled. Much effort clearly went into making it beautiful. It is indeed a work of art—a testimony to the lively cultural and artistic life that survived in the camp even at its worst moments. In his memoir, Matei Gall evokes the determination with which the artists worked in the camp:

> One day I saw a man who held a nail in his hand and tried to flatten it, to refigure it so as to create a kind of chisel; this seemed unusual if not somewhat suspicious. I continued to observe him. From somewhere— maybe from a fence, or from his bunk, I don't know—he got a piece of rotting wood; he looked at it, tried to make it smooth, found a place in the courtyard of the lager and started working on that piece of wood, to chisel it. . . . A few days later the men who unloaded coal at the railway station brought him something he mixed to create a kind of ink. Now he had color! With a brush made out of some remnants of rags he began to color his piece of wood and he pressed the damp surface unto a sheet of paper. The carving became a work of art: In front of me I saw an engraving that represented our pavilion. It is only then that I learned that this carver was a well-known and talented artist, a master of woodcuts, engravings and lithography who had worked at a number of magazines.[18]

Along with the other drawings and woodcuts that were produced—and carefully preserved by Arthur Kessler—the little book enables us to imagine what we know from the Vapniarka memoirs and testimonies: that, during the period when Kessler was interned in the camp and until the camp's closing in late December of 1943, inmates did manage to engage in a variety of cultural activities during the evening hours. Every evening after darkness began to set in, gendarmes locked the inmates into the three pavilions housing them. Rather than sleeping after long hours of slave labor, however, the inmates often stayed awake and engaged with each other intellectually and artistically. This occurred even during the most miserable months in the camp—during the epidemic, when Murgescu and Buradescu were its commanders—and continued in a much less inhibited fashion during the period in 1943 when the more liberal, and culturally more sensitive, Colonel Hristache Popovici (no relation to Traian) was Vapniarka's commander.

The professional and amateur artists, musicians, and theatrical persons who had come to the camp played a particularly significant role in these after-lock-up doings. On a regular basis someone in the group would narrate a story—either one recalled from a novel or book of tales, or made up on the basis of lived and imaginary experience. One inmate, a refugee from Germany, recited fragments of Goethe's *Faust* from memory. Occasionally such a story would elicit discussion and analysis by listeners, sometimes even lively debates in which differences of opinion emerged. At other times, one of the academically trained inmates—or one who was perhaps more knowledgeable about political history and theory—would present an informal lecture. Andrei Bernath, who had been a member of the central committee of the Romanian Communist Party, spoke to the group about the Revolution of 1848 and its history. Marxism, fascism, the causes of the war: he and others would lecture about these topics and engage in debate. Judaism and Jewish subjects were by no means concealed or kept in the background: someone gave a talk about the Macabee uprising; someone else, about Jewish resistance against the Romans; another, about early Jewish history. Rabbi Wilner, the only rabbi in the camp, set up a small corner on the second floor of the second pavilion for inmates wishing to worship together.

Music was another staple during the evening hours. Inmates sang, whistled, and hummed songs in groups or for each other. They remembered tunes and lyrics from their homes and taught them to their companions. They composed and made up songs in German or Romanian, a number about the very place where they were imprisoned:

> Im fernen Wapniarka,
> Wo so bitter die Not,
> Schmerzt mich Sehnsucht nach Freiheit,
> Sehnsucht nach daheim . . .[19]

> *In the far-away Vapniarka,*
> *Where such bitter misery is found*
> *I suffer, yearning for my freedom*
> *Yearning for return to home . . .*

The little book the inmates made for Arthur Kessler can certainly enable us to imagine a dimension of the cultural and artistic vitality that constituted their spiritual resistance. Moreover, its most distinctive aspect, its miniature form, specially relates to and provides a graphic analog for another incident of miniaturization discussed in several of the Vapniarka memoirs: the elaborate communal letters the inmates composed and smuggled out with the help of Colonel Popovici. Here is Matei Gall's account:

> What are our letters like? An ordinary sheet of paper was folded so as to produce twenty-four squares of one centimeter each. Every square was numbered front and back, each one of us received a code number that corresponded both to the number on one of the squares and to the number of our respective family. I for example had the correspondence Number 14. Once the courier arrived safely with the folded and well-hidden sheet of paper, the letter was cut into the respective squares, and everyone received the correct message.[20]

And yet the miniature book is more than one of these letters. Certainly the materials—leather, paper, string, pens, and watercolors—must have been hard to come by, so we could speculate that the miniaturization attests to their scarcity. The small size also reflects the minimalism of the master-plot that we find in the little book's seven narratives. Perhaps, paradoxically, it is only through minimalism that the prisoners could express the enormity of their experience. Each tiny drawing in stick-figure form represents individualized experiences of unprecedented suffering and survival, even as it underscores the inadequacy of this or any other idiom for its expression.[21] Although it was collectively made, we can see the book as an expression of the subjective interiority that is most assaulted and threatened by the structure of the concentration camp, of its persistence against all odds. Whatever the practical reasons for the book's miniature status, they need to be supplemented with an understanding that by giving Arthur this tiny object, the patients were giving him the most precious gift they could bestow—the small bit of privacy and interiority, of depth and subjectivity they had been able to preserve. With a miniature that is handmade, they are sharing with him, and through him and his son, also with us, their signature and bodily marking.

But its small size also makes the book difficult to decode. It took bright lights, magnifying glasses, and a great deal of persistence, for example, for us to decipher its full title. *Causa,* it turns out, was not meant to be Romanian at all, since, before some of the letters faded, the cover actually meant to say "Dr. Honoris Causa, Vapniarka, 1943." Amazingly, with this gift the patients are bestowing an honorary doctorate from a concentration camp on Arthur Kessler! Or do they mean the title to express that he himself was an honorable physician, a doctor in the cause of honor? That in addition to his medical doctorate, a doctorate of honor had to be awarded to him for his extraordinary service?

The little book's Latin title, the conjunction of artists within its pages, the communal effort that went into its production, all present us with an incredibly fruitful and suggestive source to contextualize Vapniarka within Transnistria and the larger Romanian Holocaust. Certainly, there were moments of inmate strife, mostly provoked by camp guards or brutal commanders. But the little book's very existence attests to the fact that there were times in Vapniarka (as, undoubtedly, in other places in Transnistria) when deportees of different backgrounds and, in this case, ethnicities, succeeded in living and functioning together in a multicultural mix reflecting some of the best traditions of communal tolerance that had also existed in prewar Bukowina, Bessarabia, and other parts of Romania.

### A JOURNEY OF RETURN

For us, the drive back from Vapniarka toward Chernivtsi was full of mixed emotions. We were excited by our adventure, by the impression that we might have been the first to visit this place since the war, and by the sense that we might well be the last outsiders to see the one remaining building that housed the former concentration camp. This structure, the three of us agreed, will surely also be demolished in the not too distant future. And yet our ability to locate that last standing Vapniarka building, and to gain admission to what had been the camp itself, clearly filled us with a sense of satisfaction, if not elation. We had traveled there; we found the place; we saw it, and we touched it.

It did not take long, however, before an ironic postscript to our journey was revealed to us as our driver, Russlan, stopped in the center of several small towns so that we could photograph the enormous monuments that dominated them. Everywhere in what had been Transnistria, Soviet memorials commemorating the Soviet heroes who died in the battles of the Second World War were prominently displayed. For Ukrainians in their now-independent republic, these Soviet memorials are surely remnants of a history to be backgrounded, if not suppressed or forgotten. Within the context of local economic resources, however, they are also too expensive to be removed from their central locations. For the three of us, on the other hand, these memorials highlighted the vicissitudes of memorialization and forgetting. The enormous efforts and sacrifices made by the Soviet Red Army in driving back and defeating Nazi and fascist forces certainly deserved recognition, we concurred. But in light of Vapniarka and our knowledge of the dark history of this region, we also felt that the presence of these enormous memorial structures and the general absence of any others glorified military history to the detriment of all else. We had, of course, found plaques commemorating Transnistrian ghettos when we first stopped in Moghilev. But elsewhere, at the sites where they had taken place, where were the markers to remind us of the sufferings, persecutions, and murder of thousands of Jews? Where were the monuments commemorating acts of resistance by Jewish and non-Jewish antifascist political prisoners? Vapniarka, it seemed, was a case study in strategic forgetting, or, at the very least, in simple neglect.

When we returned home to the United States not long thereafter, we began to wonder what our trip had actually accomplished. In visiting the region that had been Transnistria, we had intended to connect memory to place. But we visited places so emptied of memory that our objective seemed a failure. No one we encountered during that entire afternoon in Vapniarka asked us anything about the history of the Vapniarka concentration camp. The Ukrainian officers accepted our gift of the photocopy of the Luftwaffe map for the army base museum, but they were remarkably uncurious about the details of a past whose existence they were still reluctant to acknowledge. At best, we might think of our appearance as an intervention, an act of witnessing in retrospect. If through our visit, we brought the memory of its past back to the place, then that return is as evanescent as that hazy summer afternoon. It is an act, a performance that briefly, fleetingly, re-placed history in a landscape that had eradicated it. But would that one-time act in itself be remembered? Does our telling the story, writing about it, confirm and concretize that encounter and memorialize it?

Photography helped us to perform and carry out such memorial work. We recorded our visit in still image and video. Even when the last remnant of the camp is removed, our pictures, together with a version of this account will serve as testimony to the lives of those who were interned there and to our own effort to understand and transmit their stories. Our photos and videos, however flat, partial, and fragmentary, record and memorialize the fleeting reconnection that transpired between memory and place. They provide some small compensation for those images that could never have been taken of the camp itself.

And yet, for us, this was not enough.

Upon leaving Vapniarka each of the three of us—David, Marianne, and I—took a stone along. Now two of those stones from one of the demolished buildings of the camp sit on our desks in our apartment in New York

City, and another is in David's house in Rochester, New York. We did this unthinkingly, and now, writing this chapter, we ask ourselves what this gesture meant to us. When Jews visit a gravesite they customarily place a small stone on it. Symbolically, this is meant both to help the dead to rest by aiding their return "to dust" and to mark the fact that someone *has been there, someone remembers.* In our case, instead of leaving a marker of our visit, we carried a fragment of the place away with us. If through our fleeting presence there we could not hope to *re-place* its history into the landscape, we made a gesture to *displace* it. We brought a physical fragment from the demolished camp back to our present world as concrete evidence—substantiation both of a particular past and the place where it had occurred that we wanted to memorialize and of our own efforts to locate and to bear witness to that past. This physical testimonial fragment reflects our transformation into co-witnesses, carriers of a memory we have adopted—a memory we ourselves will now transmit and hope to pass down.

# TEN

# "This was once my home"

The gentle, the German, the pain-laden rhyme

PAUL CELAN
"Nearness of Graves"

When the mother tongue came to serve his mother's murderers, a pall fell across it.

JOHN FELSTINER
*Paul Celan*

REPATRIATION, 1944

It was the middle of the night when we returned from Transnistria, exhausted by the physical hardships and the intense emotions of the day. We had intended to spend the night in Moghilev, but the only hotel we could locate was so unprepossessing that we preferred to brave the long drive back. The three of us slept through the latter part of the bumpy journey, grateful to Russlan, our driver, for bringing us safely back to the Cheremosh, where a night guard let us in. Those hard mattresses had never seemed so comfortable.

The next morning, we retraced our steps to the northern entrance to Chernivtsi and to the old bridge crossing the Pruth River. We had asked Rosa Zuckermann to accompany us, so that we might hear about her return to Chernovtsy from Bershad in Transnistria after her liberation in the spring of 1944. In 1998 a new, wider bridge had been inaugurated over this part of the river, mainly for auto and bicycle traffic, and the old one, directly alongside and slightly lower in height, was now reserved entirely for pedestrians. With its rusty iron railings, cracked asphalt, and peeling paint, it clearly showed its age, and we had heard rumors that it might be dismantled in the near future. But for us, and for many Jews from this city, this bridge was an important historical and emotional landmark.

By the time we reached it with Rosa and walked to its midpoint, it was late morning, and few other pedestrians were in sight. We were there on a misty day, and other than tree-thick hills rising to urban terraces, not much of Chernivtsi itself was visible to us. The beautiful Habsburgshöhe park and the imposing former seat of the Bukowina Metropolitan, now the main site of the city university, lay just beyond the crest of the hill that we had descended to reach the river. In 2000, that park, which the Romanians had renamed Princess Elena Park and which present-day Ukrainian residents merely referred to as "the area adjacent to the Jurii Fed'kovytch Park, next to the university," was also still home to a small bust of the emperor Franz Josef and a bas-relief plaque for his beloved spouse, Princess Sissy.[1] Most impressively, however, the park offered the most expansive view in the city of the hills and villages surrounding Chernivtsi, and so we were surprised not to be able to see it from below.

We had stopped by the Pruth River in 1998 with Carl and Lotte, to look at the beaches they had told us so much about: the Volksbad (People's Beach), where Romanians, Poles, and ethnic Germans used to go; and the choice of local Jews, the Gänsehäufl, where they had spent many leisure hours sunning, swimming, socializing. These beaches were later renamed by the Romanians: Venezia, and Mamia after the most beautiful Romanian beach on the Black Sea. Lotte loved to reminisce about the Gänsehäufl (literally, pile of geese, named for a famous beach area outside Vienna on the banks of the Danube), where young people flirted and occasionally fantasized about far-off lands. Couples, especially, she confided, liked to swim to one of the Pruth islands they called Africa, where a grove of willow trees provided them with some privacy. One had to be a good swimmer to negotiate the rapids of the Pruth, wide near the bridge, with broad banks, a few small islands, and numerous grassy groves surrounded by weeping willows. Lotte and Carl's generation observed the development in gender relations on these beaches, where swimming was initially gender-segregated and where bathing costumes evolved, in a few short years, from full-length dresses to fashionable, if scant, two-piece suits. In the early decades of the twentieth century, Czernowitz/Cernăuţi, like other cities in Western and Central Europe, exhibited its modernity in its leisure time activities.

Standing on the far side of the bridge with Rosa Zuckermann in July of 2000, we did have the chance to appreciate the city's modernization. It is next to the river that the early industries had sprung up in the late nineteenth

Figure 40. The old bridge over the Pruth, now used only for pedestrian traffic, 2007 (Photograph by Leo Spitzer)

and early twentieth centuries: a large beer brewery, a beet sugar factory, and a lumber mill, all powered by steam engines and generators drawing power from the river. Other, more recent and distant industrial installations, however, were barely visible through the mists and bends in the river.

Yet, as Marc Sagnol has written, a century ago the Pruth represented a very different kind of threshold: "The Pruth was the symbolic border for the Jews of Bukowina, a border between the *shtetl* and the big city, between tradition and assimilation, between Yiddish and German."[2] Traditional observant Jews from the surrounding villages could expose themselves to the promises and the risks of assimilation and modernity by crossing the bridge into Czernowitz. In Karl Emil Franzos's 1906 novel *Der Pojaz* (The Clown), the young Sender, a would-be actor, comes to the city with his friend Schmule to see his first theater performance. As soon as they cross the bridge, Schmule begins to scream that he "wants nothing to do with that unholy place where Jews speak Hochdeutsch and eat pork."[3] Sender, on the other hand, is pulled by the lure of modernity and assimilation.

But toward the end of the Second World War, the Pruth marked a different kind of frontier. Rosa explained to us that in the spring of 1944, returnees from Transnistria, exhausted, ill, dirty, carrying their meager belongings in small bundles, came back to the Bukowina by the same road on which we had returned from Moghilev. Survivors reached Chernovtsy after harrowing journeys, mostly on foot, through a war-torn landscape with shifting borders between battling armies. Most had been liberated by the Red Army and had waited for an end to the fighting before braving the journey back home. Under the Soviet reoccupation of this region, however, their return home was only slightly less fraught than under the retreating Romanians. No one was allowed to travel in the Soviet Union without a *propusk*—a travel permit—and proper identification papers. Yet most returnees had been robbed of their identification papers during their deportation, which made their transit through the numerous checkpoints they had to pass extremely precarious.

At the bridge where we were now standing, survivors were stopped by Soviet authorities and asked for identifications attesting to their former residence. Unable to prove their birthplace or abode before deportation, many were turned away from Chernovtsy when they tried to enter.

"They stopped me right here," Rosa told us. "I was worn out, helpless. Acquaintances passed me and promised to get word to my family. Eventually, many hours later, your father and Kubi waved to me from the other side of the guard post." Carl's memoir corroborates her story:

> Within a few days after the takeover by the Soviet army in late March and early April, the survivors from Transnistria started to come back, among them my aunt Fritzi Wurmbrand (her son Jochanan was retained there for the time being by the new Soviet authorities as a worker in a military supply plant). The Soviet authorities were not very helpful in this repatriation effort; for instance, they sometimes closed the entrance to the city from the North (the bridge over the River Pruth) for people without passes. One day we were told that our cousin Rosa was barred from crossing the bridge. My brother and I went to bring her across into Czernowitz with my credentials as railway engineer. When I tried to get across to find her, an officer stopped me and said "NKVD, your papers, please." When I showed him my ID, he let me cross the bridge and come back with her.[4]

Rosa evoked for us the crowds and the chaos, but she expressed no anger at being turned away from her native city. Three years in the Bershad ghetto in Transnistria and the multiple losses she had suffered had taught her resignation. "Your grandmother took me in," she said, "she fed me, made me a bath, gave me some clean clothes. I had left with my parents, my husband and child. I came back all alone. They all took me in, gave me a home."

Later, Carl and Lotte described to us how emaciated, how gray and exhausted Rosa looked on that day. "As soon as they walked in, Carl's mother heated the bathroom stove with wood and filled the tub," Lotte recalled. "We were all in the other room, silent, wondering how she felt seeing us all together like that. And then—I will never forget that—a wailing emerged from the bathroom such as I've never heard, before or since. It lasted and lasted, it didn't sound like it came from a human being. All that had happened, all she had lost, all was in that scream, and it didn't stop. That scream, more than the stories people told later, gave me a sense of horrors of Transnistria."

"When I remember Rosa's return to Czernowitz," Lilly Hirsch once told me in Düsseldorf, "I can still visualize her first bath. She shut herself into the bathroom, and she let out this incredible scream. I will never be able to forget it. And she continued crying, for weeks. And then, over the next months, in bits and pieces, she told us how her parents died, and her husband and her little boy. And how she lived there after."

Survivors who managed to gain admission returned to a city whose central buildings had suffered relatively little physical harm during the war years. The water and electricity works were severely damaged during the Romanian evacuation, and Chernovtsy would remain without power or running water and without public transportation for many months in 1944–45. The more serious damage, however, was the irreparable assault—both material and spiritual—on the Jewish community. "There were just a few of us Jews left in the city," Moritz Gelber writes. "Of the beautiful people that the Romanians had chased out of our beloved Bukowina in 1941, only a sad remnant was left."[5]

The shifting front, the end of Romanian rule, and the retreat of the German and Romanian military had been terrifying for that "sad remnant." As Carl writes in his memoir:

> The last day was the most unpleasant with rumors that the Germans were taking Jewish men as hostages. Lotte and I went to hide with friends. . . . It occurred to us that that we shouldn't have left our families without protection. When we came back, neighbors told us that Lotte's sister Fritzi was taken hostage by the Germans. . . . She had been locked into an empty room, and when we returned, German soldiers came in with her, threatened us with shotguns, but finally took only our watches and left. It was an unpleasant experience to have a German gun pointing to your face. Next day (March 27) Soviet soldiers were back on the streets of Czernowitz.[6]

Indeed, Jews were again caught in the crossfire. Some, like Carl, exhilarated by Soviet victories, were cautiously optimistic. Hedwig Brenner writes:

"Without the yellow star we were equal again, no longer inferior second-class citizens. That is what we thought."[7] The written and oral accounts of this period exhibit what to us, reading in the broader context of what was happening in Europe in 1944, might appear surprising: a great suspicion of the liberators based on previous experiences with Soviet rule, fears of Soviet anti-Semitism, and ill-treatment of Jews during the liberation. Pearl Fichman writes: "The Russian military, in pursuit of the retreating Germans, were angry, aggressive and contemptuous of the local population. The ubiquitous question: Why did they kill all the other Jews and left you alive? . . . The anti-Semitism of the Russians surfaced glaringly. It soon became all too clearly apparent that the liberators hated us as much as the Germans did."[8] Paul Antschel (Celan), recently repatriated from forced labor details in Romania, later described this to a friend as "anti-Semitism Soviet-style."[9]

The returnees from Transnistria, approximately half of the thirty-four thousand who had been deported from Cernăuţi, found their houses occupied, their belongings plundered and stolen.[10] But those Jews who had managed to stay behind in Cernăuţi also had few remaining possessions. Most had had to sell their goods and valuables—furniture, dishes and silverware, and even clothes—or barter them for food and firewood during the previous harsh winters. There was little left to share with returning family and friends and little to live on. Although the American Joint Distribution Committee did contribute financially to help in the repatriation to the Northern and Southern Bukowina and the Regat, the general economic hardship produced tensions and exacerbated the enormous psychological gap between Transnistria survivors and those who had remained behind.[11]

Klara L. describes her and her son's repatriation to Chernovtsy from the deadly forced labor quarry at Cariera de Piatră, where she had lost her husband:

> It was not a comfortable feeling when the Russians came. We had suffered a great deal under the Russians, and we surely would have ended up in Siberia [if the Soviets had not left in 1941] since we had the passports #39. All the men were mobilized by the Russians, but we pulled ourselves together to go home. The journey took several weeks. I said to myself, "When I reach Czernowitz, I'm going to kiss the pavement. I'm going home! Will I see my mother, my father again?" People there were well-dressed. Everyone wanted to hear something, and I thought they would help me. I was coming from the lager. They listened, but soon they turned their backs. That was the first disappointment. . . . My parents were still alive, but they were living in such poverty. Everything was gone from the house, there were no curtains, no

rugs. My son ran to the cupboard as soon as he walked in, but there were no toys there; the cupboard was empty, except for a few odds and ends. "Perhaps the people took them," I said to him. He was crushed. . . . Those who had stayed behind avoided us; they were afraid of disease. They all complained about how much they had suffered. Even with my own brother, I could find no language in common.[12]

Although the war ended in the Bukowina in March 1944—more than a year earlier than in most of occupied Europe and six months before the rest of Romania—and although Bukowina Jews were visibly relieved that they had survived the immediate dangers posed by the Nazis, those with whom we spoke about this period invariably, and to us shockingly, remembered 1944–45 as the bleakest of the "war" years in the city. "Life continued to be brutally hard, sullen and joyless," Pearl Fichman writes. People were hungry and cold; almost nothing was available on the market: "Except for bread, which was rationed and available, everything else was scarce and if available, people stood in line for hours, sometimes days. The bread was baked from a mixture of grains and maize and the cobs ground in. A kilo bread (over two pounds) was a small loaf, heavy as a rock. You could not bite the bread, only gnaw."[13] Since older people could not digest this bread, the only option was to buy more expensive and better quality loaves for them on the black market. But few had any money for such "luxury" transactions; whatever people could earn they had to spend on bare essentials. Clothes were also unavailable. Hedwig Brenner describes the cottage industry she started: "Once in a while I found a few minutes to manufacture some sandals. I covered a cardboard sole with a brightly colored ribbon. I bought some wooden heels from a cobbler, covered them with glued-on fabric remnants, and sewed on some pieces of rope that I acquired from a rope maker. I attached two straps made out of old belts, then an insole, also brightly covered, and the sandals were ready to be sold. People practically tore them from my hands. It was a good way to make a little extra money."[14]

Worse than the material deprivations, however, was the constant danger of mobilization into the Soviet military or conscription for mine labor in the Don Basin. Men and women, young and old, were taken out from their homes or rounded up in the streets and, if they did not have valid work papers, they were mobilized. Fichman and other women hid out for weeks and months. "The first night while I stayed at the office, Cossacks had come to our house, in the middle of the night, and poked with bayonets into the beds; made crippled Mrs. Kreisel stand up to see if she was fit for military service, and then left."[15] Women who had no steady work faced the most immediate danger, and, indeed, a number were conscripted and placed on a train marked "Prostitutes." "Your parents helped me hide and thus saved me from going to the mines," Rosa Zuckermann told us as we now walked back across the bridge. "Rosa Gelber and I hid together in a basement for many days."

Those who were picked up could sometimes be rescued through bribes. "Bribes and barter worked," Carl told us. "The Soviet personnel, who themselves suffered deprivation, were mainly interested in their personal well being. At the railroad administration, where I continued to work, we had a running joke about the Soviet economy. It operated by barter, but since all we had to barter with were rails, we were left out of the transactions."

Carl was indeed lucky to have been able to keep his job at the railroad. After the Romanian officials left the city, he and his Jewish coworkers had decided to return to work and to wait for Soviet officials to arrive. After a few days of waiting, they were rehired to repair and maintain the tracks. The job, despite its minimal pay, protected Carl from mobilization. Many of his friends and acquaintances were less fortunate and had to go into hiding or devise alternatives to conscription.

Moritz Gelber was one of many Jewish men who were drafted by the Soviets:

Men up to the age of 50 were mobilized. I was a fit young chap. All the work I had done for my company did me no good. I was called up on April 30, 1944. We were told to pack some things and to report at 6 A.M. the next day. It was May 1. I was in the first row and when I saw my wife hanging out of the window of our apartment, I knew she would come along with other women who followed our huge convoy, but only to the bridge crossing the Pruth. That's the last many were to see of their wives. We were taken to a hillside where several officers were gathered. One addressed us in Russian and told us that we were now part of the Soviet army which meant that we must follow all orders and instructions. Another officer outlined the exact state of the front, which I knew very well, and we marched on over Sadagora and several other villages on the banks of the Pruth.

We then traveled by train to Kiev where we spent a few beautiful days. But then we were off to the station again, they put us in cattle cars, to go where? No one knew. A long journey began now; there were some stops, we were amazed to see an enormous river; I said, hey, that's the Volga. There we were taken to a large army camp, told to bathe, and given uniforms. Next, we were registered, I as a sergeant because of my rank in the Romanian army before the war, and we were then inducted into an enormous regiment. Our training began. It lasted fifteen days. I did well, but it was exhausting. . . . Suddenly, the commander called me to his room and said to me, "I hear you're a tailor." "I'm even a very good tailor," I responded. "Good. You'll work for me. I will need a coat and other items. There's a house in the neighborhood where a woman lives alone. Her husband was a tailor but he's been gone for a while, so you can use all his equipment. He has everything you'll need." . . . I finished his coat in a few days and it fit him perfectly. It was a pleasure to see it. Soon the commander's girlfriend came by. She was the doctor for the entire regiment. She asked me to make her a stylish blouse, and I said I'd start on it next week. It was now mid-August and our company had completed its training, received new uniforms, and was certain to be sent to the front. . . . The girlfriend of my commander praised my work and also my singing. She heard me sing Russian songs when I was working. I told her I was a violinist, and it turned out she played piano at home. She told me she liked my work. "You and the others don't know it yet, but you're about to leave here within a few days for the front. I'm going to keep you here. If that doesn't work I'll have you sent home. You are suffering from abdominal pains. I will give you the necessary certifications." I thanked her and promised her some other items of clothing. I knew she wanted a riding outfit and other things. . . . I came before the commission with my doctor and another woman doctor of higher rank. . . . It worked. On September 26, I was on my way home. But I was 9,000 km away; it was no fun to travel by train in those days.

Moritz returned to Chernovtsy on October 4. His new coat, part of his uniform, was taken from him on the train by thugs who almost threw him off the train because he was a Jew. In Chernovtsy, friends advised him to maintain his sick leave certification to avoid being sent back. Moritz spent the next months in a hospital bed, "sick." "We were really lucky in so many ways," Moritz writes. "I was also fortunate that there was another Gelber in that hospital, someone suffering from insanity," Moritz writes, "and so by means of forged records, and in the general confusion, I was able to pass the frequent inspections and to be recertified as 'sick.' Of course, we had to find money for all that. And, all the while, my wife spent a lot of time hiding in a kitchen closet so she wouldn't be sent to the Don Bass [Basin] mines."[16]

Naftali Hertz Kon, sent by the Moscow Jewish Anti-Fascist Committee to report on Jewish resistance fighters in the Bukowina, found he had to report on the deplorable conditions of Jews in Chernovtsy as well: "On my arrival, I found the population traumatized and in difficult circumstances. . . . They were being seized on the street, or at night in their apartments, or near police stations, where they stood in line to register, and taken to the county administration buildings, kept there as prisoners, with no food or adequate clothing, and then sent to the Urals and later on to Don Bass. . . . During the capture people were treated brutally. . . . When a woman presented a document certifying her employment or a document of exemption from mobilization, the document was either confiscated or torn to pieces." Along with the city's intelligentsia, Kon speculated that "the mobilization was a scam . . . to alter the Czernovitsy demographics." Stressing that Transnistria survivors, especially, were in atrocious condition and too weak for heavy labor and that some people who had been mobilized for labor to Sverdlovsk, for example, wrote to their relatives that they had been released there to find work on their own, Kon and others surmised that Soviet authorities wanted to reduce the Jewish population of the city so as to use the housing and food freed up for the incoming Soviet population.[17]

Chernovtsy's liberation enabled many of those who had survived their flight into the Soviet Union during the German invasion in 1941 to attempt to return as well. Although they were traveling within territory that was again part of the USSR, their journeys home were not much easier than those of the repatriates from Transnistria nor was their entrance to the city less difficult. In *Der Ring des Prometheus,* Dorothea Sella describes her seemingly endless train journey from Tbilisi. On the last leg she traveled with her old friend Martha and a young Ukrainian woman named Mascha:

> Mascha, who heard us call out the German street names, was amazed that we were not using the Romanian names from 1919–40 or the Ukrainian ones from 1940–41. We explained to her that the German names were familiar to us from our homes, and that the Romanian names had been largely unknown to us. As for the Soviet year, it was too short for us to have memorized the new names introduced at that time. "From now on you will have to remember the Ukrainian names for life; this city will never be anything but Soviet," Mascha replied in an earnest tone, and we assured her that we had no doubts about that either. . . . No sooner had Mascha, Martha, and I gotten off the tram, than a militia man blocked the way and proceeded to interrogate not Mascha, who was from Kiev, but Martha and me, the returnees to our home city. . . . Who are you? Where are you coming from? Where are you going? What is your occupation? What is the purpose of your coming here? As he was studying our identification cards with a grim look and keeping them much too long, Martha and I went pale with fear, even though we had nothing to hide. I then expected him to examine Mascha's papers as well. The war is not yet over, I said to myself, it's his duty

to check everyone's travel permits. But no, Mascha had gone ahead a few steps and he left her alone. How did he know she was Ukrainian? And why was it so obvious for him that she belonged here, and not Martha and I, though Czernowitz was our native city and not hers. . . . Is that how my Czernowitz greets me? I thought, sadly.[18]

Sidy Flexor applied to the authorities in Novosibirsk in the spring of 1944 for a travel pass to return home to Czernowitz. This was a dangerous undertaking; some people were deported to labor camps for such requests: "'What do you mean, you're Romanian?' they said to me. 'We're all Russians here.' I persevered and got permission to visit my family in Chernovtsy with my one-year-old baby. But Mischa had been drafted by then, and he had to stay in Siberia." At first, the refugees to the USSR had been considered foreigners and were exempt from military service, but by 1944 all able-bodied men had been mobilized. It was not until a year later, in spring of 1945, that Mischa was granted a brief furlough to visit his wife and child, who had remained in Chernovtsy after their return. By the time he arrived there, after another long and difficult journey, the war was over, and talk of demobilization had begun. Nevertheless, Mischa was in uniform and due to report back to his unit in Siberia. Not to go back meant desertion; to do so meant that he would perhaps be permanently separated from his family. His parents had perished on their way to Transnistria; his only brother Jascha had disappeared without a trace, somewhere in Poland or the Soviet Union. He was determined to stay with his wife and son at any cost. He and Sidy contacted everyone they knew and, succeeded, through one of these contacts, in bribing a Soviet official who issued an affidavit affirming that Mischa was needed for work in Chernovtsy. But their goal, like that so many others, was to move south to Romania and, eventually, as far beyond the sphere of influence of the Soviet Union as possible.

## BEFORE "AFTER AUSCHWITZ," 1944–1945

"When did you know that you had to leave Czernowitz?" we asked every one of our interviewees during the course of our research. "Weren't you afraid to go to Romania after all you had experienced of Romanian anti-Semitism and collaboration?" Mostly, their initial response was to laugh. Carl was more direct in an email: "a pretty naïve question," he let us know, having made the decision of whether to entrust his fate to the Soviets or the Romanians on several excruciating occasions during the early 1940s. In March 1944, many Ukrainian and Polish intellectuals from Cernăuţi fled south with the retreating Romanians, and a number of Jews, disillusioned by their memories of Soviet rule in 1940–41, joined them as well. Decades later, Carl and Lotte would still argue about their decision not to leave Cernăuţi at that time. As on previous occasions, they had to make a choice overnight, in the absence of crucial information: "We were in a dilemma: to stay with the Soviets or leave with the Romanians into Romania proper still facing the danger that the Germans might enforce their rule in Romania as they did this same month [March 1944] in Hungary. . . . Lotte would have preferred to leave, and I was rather undecided."[19] Eventually, Carl came to feel that the likelihood of survival would be greater in Soviet Chernovtsy and, given the massive Hungarian deportations to Auschwitz in 1944–45 and the months of continuing war and uncertainty in Romania, his instinct certainly seems warranted in retrospect. It was not until August 23, 1944, that Marshall Antonescu, who had been unwilling to agree to a cease-fire with the Soviet Union, was arrested in Bucharest; not until September 12 did Romanian King Mihai sign a cease-fire with the Allies. But by that time, when the war in Romania had ended, the borders of the USSR were closed, and possibilities of emigration from Soviet territory became much more difficult, if not impossible.[20]

Was it this sense of blockage in 1944–45 that caused the intense feelings of hopelessness among Czernowitz Jews? Material deprivations and dangers of conscription and mobilization under Soviet rule do not in themselves explain why this "liberation" seemed to turn into a demoralizing imprisonment, to be escaped at any price. For us, in retrospect, knowing what occurred in 1944–45—the deportation and extermination of Hungarian Jews, the death marches across Poland, Austria, and Germany, the devastating battles and massive bombing in Western Europe, and the death of so many civilians—the despair in Chernovtsy seems out of scale. This is so even when we consider the traumatic losses of family and friends that had to be absorbed, and the radical changes brought about by Sovietization.

And yet, as we read and listened to the stories of Czernowitz Jews, we came to understand how a sense of future could shut down so definitively, even for those who had been fortunate enough to survive immense dangers. As Carl writes, "It was not the miserable life we went through during this war year, with most essentials missing, but mainly the fact that the Soviet Union under Stalin was a closed country with an ideology stronger than any fundamentalist church. Any deviation from this ideology was punishable by prison or death."[21] Demoralization, fear, scarcity of food and basic necessities, and a general feeling of exhaustion punctuate their narratives. "Everyone walked hunched over; no one ever smiled," Hedy Brenner recalled. Dorothea Sella highlights this despair in entitling a chapter of her book "This Was Once My Home." For native-born Jews, the sense of dispossession from a place they had still wanted to call Czernowitz and home was now radical and definitive. Ostensibly citizens of the Soviet Union, the Jews in the city felt marginalized, unaccepted.

Once again, their language, the German they continued to speak, somewhat fearfully perhaps, had been declared illegal as part of Sovietization.[22] And yet, once again, German persisted. "The main thing is to get away from here," Paul Celan is said to have insisted to his friend Ruth Lackner. "Where one winds up is irrelevant, so long as there's freedom there. How would it be, for instance, to arrive in Jerusalem, to go to Martin Buber, and to say to him: 'Uncle Buber, here I am, here you have me.'"[23]

Celan had returned from the forced labor camp run by the Romanian army in combination with Todt Organization and German military engineers in Tăbăreşti, near Bucharest, in the spring of 1944, just two months before Alfred Kittner and Immanuel Weissglas, fellow poets, were repatriated from their deportation to Cariera de Piatră and later to the Obodovka ghetto in Transnistria. They all met again at Rose Ausländer's house and exchanged their war experiences and poems they had written during forced labor, ghetto life, and deportation. It was there also that Celan found out more details about his parents' fate in the Mihaelovka camp on the German side of the river Bug, where many of the 1942 deportees were sent to do forced labor on military roads and bridges for the Todt Organization.[24] Celan's father died of typhus during this ordeal, and his mother, too exhausted to continue laboring, was shot by the Nazis. Celan's cousin, the young poet Selma Meerbaum-Eisinger, deported on the same transport as his parents, also died of typhus shortly after her arrival in Transnistria.

To save himself from mobilization, Celan found work as an aide in Chernovtsy's psychiatric hospital. In September, he resumed his university literary studies, specializing, this time, in English. He also earned some money by doing translations from Romanian to Ukrainian for a local newspaper. Awaiting a chance to leave the Soviet Union, he continued adding to the handwritten collection of approximately ninety German-language poems he had written in the early 1940's and in Tăbăreşti—poems he hoped to publish as a book.

It was during this time that Celan composed some of his early "postwar" poems, including the emblematic "Todesfuge" (Death Fugue). The ambiguity surrounding the date of this poem is significant, perhaps as clearly indicative of the complicated history of this liminal moment in Chernovtsy as of the moment "After Auschwitz" with which it is usually associated.

Schwarze Milch der Frühe wir trinken sie abends
wir trinken sie mittags und morgens wir trinken sie nachts
wir trinken und trinken
wir schaufeln ein Grab in den Lüften da liegt man nicht eng

*Black milk of daybreak we drink it at evening*
*we drink it at midday and morning we drink it at night*
*we drink and we drink*
*we shovel a grave in the air where you won't lie too cramped*[25]

The poem's memorable imagery of "black milk," of the "grave in the air," of the orchestra playing while Jews shoveled their own graves, as well as its searing indictment of traditional German literary motifs ranging from Goethe's *Faust* to Bach, Wagner, and Heine, and the repetitive and rising rhythm building this fugue of death have become universal signifiers of the horrors perpetrated by the Nazis. These horrors were revealed to a dumbstruck world when the death camps were liberated by the Allies in the first half of 1945. But Alfred Kittner remembers hearing a version of his friend's poem "not long" after his own return from Transnistria in spring of 1944. "[O]ne morning, outside the iron railing of Czernowitz's archdiocesan cathedral in Siebenbürger Street, . . . he read me the 'Todesfuge' written shortly before."[26] Other friends, among them Immanuel Weissglas, also place the date of this poem in 1944, but for a 1962 anthology in which it was republished, Celan dated it 1945, and later located it "Bucharest, 1945."[27]

The date is important insofar as it might indicate when Bukowinian Jews found out about the Nazi concentration and extermination camp system with its gas chambers and camp orchestras. The smoke and the grave in the air in the poem could, of course, refer to Kristallnacht in 1938 which Celan barely missed on his journey back through Germany from France to Cernăuți, or to accounts of the 1941 brutal pogroms in nearby Bessarabia that reached wartime Cernăuți by way of a few surviving refugees. In August 1944 Celan might have read a widely publicized pamphlet on Maidanek, titled "The Lublin Extermination Camp," in which a Soviet officer who had liberated Maidanek in July reported that prisoners played foxtrots and tangos at camp functions. It was not until March 1945 that survivors of Auschwitz reached Chernovtsy. Hedwig Brenner describes her first encounter with four of these survivors: "I was putting my groceries . . . into my shopping bag when the door opened . . . and four miserable creatures who barely looked like women entered the grocery store. They were dressed in rags, on the back of their threadbare coats one could make out a black and white striped spot, the mark of Cain of the Lager. . . . I invited the four to my house to serve them tea and bread with jam. . . . The three who came along were all Dutch Jews. . . . We could hardly believe their stories, they sounded totally unreal to us—us who had deplored our own fate during the war."[28]

The details of persecution and dehumanization evoked in "Todesfuge" might well seem incongruous, given when and where the poem was apparently written. But the ambiguity surrounding Celan's knowledge can tell us a great deal about the tenuous status of what is generally referred to as "After Auschwitz,"[29] and thus about the very particular Holocaust experience of Bukowinian Jews. The brutal murder of his parents, the shame and guilt of his survival, his own experiences of forced labor and dispossession, all reach across the experiences of Jews in occupied Europe. But, as Hedwig Brenner writes, those who survived in Romania, as Celan did, still found the stories of the death camps "totally unreal." "Todesfuge" emerged from this continuity and from this gap. It emerged from the moment, 1944–45, when the war was over for some but not for others, but when Jews all across Europe found they had nowhere to turn. This is the moment *before* "After Auschwitz." Most searingly, the poem emerged from the moment before Celan fully acknowledged the irrevocable loss of language and homeland, or, more precisely, from the moment before he realized that language, the German that was his mother tongue and his literary language, had become the "language of the murderers." How to write in it nevertheless? This would occupy the rest of his oeuvre. As he said publicly in 1958, on the occasion of receiving a literary prize in Bremen: "Reachable, near and not lost, there remained in the midst of the losses this one thing: language. . . . But it had to pass through its own answerlessness, pass through frightful muting, pass through the thousand darknesses of deathbringing speech. . . . Passed through and came to light again, 'enriched' by all this."[30] If Celan later repudiated "Todesfuge," it may be because its language had not yet passed through these deadly losses and transformations so that it could be spoken and written again, but differently.

This struggle with language occupied all the surviving poets and writers of the interwar generation. In Rose Ausländer's late poem "Mutterland" (Motherland), German survives the destruction and disappearance of her native fatherland:

Mein Vaterland ist tot
sie haben es begraben
im Feuer
Ich lebe
in meinem Mutterland
Wort

*My fatherland is dead*
*they have buried it*
*in fire*
*I live*
*in my motherland*
*the word.*[31]

But Ausländer, Alfred Kittner, and especially Paul Celan, also began to fracture and to challenge the comfortable way in which Bukowina writers had always aspired to inhabit the German language. In Alfred Kittner's 1945 poem "Die Schule des Todes" (The School of Death), the German language is broken down into its most basic components: "Als mich der Tod zur Tafel ruft / Das A ist Grab, das U ist Gruft" ("When death calls me to the board / A is grave and O is tomb").[32] Kittner's regular meter and rhyme only makes his point more devastating, his irony more biting. In his 1944 rhymed poem addressed to his mother, a victim of the Transnistria camps, "Nähe der Gräber" (Nearness of Graves), Paul Celan asks: "Und duldest du, Mutter, wie einst, ach, daheim, / den leisen, den deutschen, den schmerzlichen Reim?" ("And can you bear, Mother, as once a time, / the gentle, the German, the pain-laden rhyme?" Note that due to the rhythm of the line, the poet's word "daheim" [at home] has had to drop out of the translation.)[33] For Celan, not only German but language and reason itself had become irrevocably tainted, and his poetry became a struggle at once to reach and to avoid silence. It may well be significant that the culture that engendered Paul Celan—whose name and poetry are virtually synonymous with the *Sprachlosigkeit*, the loss of language and reason that has been seen as emblematic of postwar European thought—is the distinctive "Czernowitz" culture with its ambivalent adherence to a deterritorialized German that had become unspeakable while still being spoken.

After 1945, the German-language culture associated with Czernowitz and the Bukowina continued to thrive in the diaspora. It now came to center in Romania, where Alfred Margul-Sperber became a prize-winning state poet; in Israel, where a German-language Bukowina newspaper, *Die Stimme*, continues to be published to this day and where Bukowina writers are an important component in active German-language literary associations; and in Germany, which recognizes the poetic talents of Rose Ausländer and counts Celan as one of its major twentieth-century poets (despite the fact that he lived and wrote in Bucharest, Vienna, and Paris until his suicide in 1970). Assessing the significance of this literary-cultural dispersion, the literary critic Peter Stenberg noted: "There is perhaps no better indication of what German culture has lost than the realization that Czernowitz—the easternmost urban outpost of that language and the capital city of Bukovyna—must have produced proportionately more major twentieth-century writers whose native language was German, than any other city. . . . The fate of the Jews and Germans of Czernowitz, and of the Yiddish and German languages in that German-speaking city of only half a century ago, serves as something of a microcosm of what was about to happen throughout Eastern Europe."[34]

"THE MAIN THING IS TO GET AWAY FROM HERE," 1945

In March of 1945, the Soviets began to issue travel permits to Romania for Jews originating in the Southern Bukowina who had survived Transnistria but had only been able to travel back as far as Chernovtsy when Soviet borders were closed in 1944. A Soviet-Romanian agreement signed in June 1945 allowed several thousand additional Jews to relocate from North to South Bukowina.[35] Pearl Fichman writes: "When the news first spread that people could apply at the militia, to leave for Romania, many careful people could not believe it. They feared that it was a ruse, a trick, a way to show up people as unpatriotic. They feared that if one applies to leave for the West, they would put you on a train going East, to Siberia. The very careful ones are still in Czernovitz."[36]

Certainly, those who applied for a *propusk,* many falsely claiming Southern Bukowinian roots and thus Romanian nationality, knew they might be expelled from their jobs or university studies if they were denied the permit. They were willing to take significant risks for the possibility of "freedom" in a Romania that was not yet out of the war but was turning to the Allied side, or for the possibility of using Romania as a springboard for further emigration.

Fichman and Hausleitner speculate that these permissions were issued in order to facilitate Soviet Ukrainianization. Indeed, the future of Soviet Bukowina was still uncertain prior to the end of the war in Europe. Before 1940, the Northern Bukowina had never been part of the Soviet Union, and the Soviets had no historic claim on it. The rumor circulating in Chernovtsy was that at the end of the war the Allies might demand a plebiscite to decide whether the Northern Bukowina would be Soviet or Romanian. The presence of Southern Bukowinians in Chernovtsy, it was believed, might weaken Soviet support and endanger a Soviet victory in the plebiscite. The repatriation of Romanian Jews to Romania thus appeared to serve the Soviet authorities well.[37] With Russians and Ukrainians flooding the northern region, moreover, there were also enormous housing shortages, and rooms vacated by repatriated Jews—even those occupied by recently returned Transnistria survivors—were highly valuable resources.

As soon as the possibility was offered, Lotte and Carl applied for travel documents twice, once under their own name and the second time under an assumed name, in both cases claiming family ties to Suceava in Southern Bukowina. Friends and family began to leave, and they started to lose hope. Securing a *propusk* was a two-stage process: after people were notified at the militia that they had received the authorization, they had to pick up the document itself at a window where names were called out and applicants had to provide proof of their identity. Since people tended to apply under multiple names, they sometimes received more than one authorization, and, indeed, it was through friends who had received two authorizations (one for a family named Sachter who had been killed in Transnistria and whose identity documents they had in their possession) that Carl and Lotte succeeded in leaving. These friends gave Mr. Sachter's birth certificate to Carl so that he could memorize the relevant information. That afternoon, when Carl went to the window where the *propusks* were being handed out, he waited anxiously, and listened carefully: "To this day, I don't know how I was able muster the presence of mind to raise my hand when I heard the official call out in Russian pronunciation 'Shachtior,'" Carl told us. "Date of birth!" the official called out impatiently. "Father's first name! Grandfather's first name!" Carl had memorized the answers and was able to rush home with his *propusk*.[38] The possession of this document engendered a renewed if-cautious sense of hope:

> Around the age of 35 I had two memorable days to remember, one was
> June 30, 1940, when I entered Czernowitz, which had been occupied
> two days earlier by the Soviets, full of hope that communism will bring

better days for mankind, and thankful to have escaped the anti-Semitic regime that had taken hold in Romania, and the other was April 24, 1945, when we were able to leave the Soviet Union and its drab unfree life, with the hope that after the end of the European war we would have better opportunities outside. We thought that even if the Communist party dominates the government in Romania, it would be different from what we had experienced in the Soviet Union. Little did we know.[39]

For Lotte too that day is fixed in memory, and when we were in Chernivtsi together in 1998, she had described it in detail:

> I remember so vividly that last day, the day we left here forever. I washed some underwear in the afternoon, and we hung it in the dining room so that neighbors wouldn't suspect anything. I slept for only a few hours, in my black slip, so I could put on my clothes quickly at dawn when we would be picked up by the truck we had arranged to take us to the border. I cried and cried all night, since we were leaving my parents and sister behind, as well as Carl's mother, sister, and brother. We had no way of knowing if we'd ever see each other again. At previous such moments, I had always chosen to stay with them, but this time we were *really* desperate.

In reconstructing their flight, their voices expressed their own amazement at having pulled it off. "But we didn't even have enough money to pay for our part of the truck a friend had arranged to share," Carl noted. "We borrowed 1,000 rubles from Lotte's father, or, rather, I traded him a sports jacket for it which he later actually sold for 1,000 rubles. We had to leave at dawn and get to the border fast. I never told anyone at work about it, and by 10 o'clock they sent someone over to the house to see why I had not come to work that morning."

"When we walked out the door at dawn," Lotte added, "a few Soviet officers were waiting to claim the rooms or apartments of Jews who were being repatriated. I'm not sure whether they knew about us, or whether they were simply walking the streets at dawn, waiting for people with luggage. One rushed into the building just as we walked out. 'Please, Comrade,' I said to him as we passed, 'be kind to my parents.' And, actually, he was very helpful to them. He lived together with my parents and with my sister and brother-in-law for another eight months. Then, a year later, in another wave of emigration, they were allowed to leave for Romania as well."

Listening to Lotte's account, I began to think about how few objects from my childhood had come from Czernowitz. As if reading my thoughts, she continued:

You see, we had to leave in a big hurry, and we didn't even have any luggage. We made some bags out of sheets and blankets and put in a few items. We had so little anyway, but we brought our birth certificates, diplomas, marriage license, work certificates—whatever we had by way of documents—and some photographs, clothes, and books. Carl had bought some German-language engineering books from ethnic German colleagues who fled from the Soviets in 1940, so we took those along. Since it was April, I left my heavier coat behind—a nice coat with a fur collar, I really could have used it—and I wore my light spring coat. I froze the whole way on that open truck. When we got to the border, a woman guard looked through our stuff and asked, 'Why are you so poor?' Later, the next year, when the rest of the family was able to join us in Romania, Lilly brought my warmer coat along for me, and my parents brought a few other objects I still have—a hat brush in the shape of a question mark that my father had brought back from Vienna in 1918 and Fritzi's opera glasses, also from Vienna. Imagine: that's what they thought to bring with them.

"And they brought us the rest of our books," Carl added, "Thomas Mann, Stefan Zweig, Heine, Jakob Wassermann, and many others. Each contained an official Soviet stamp on its title page. The departures in 1946 were much more carefully supervised; they checked every item."

"Our departure was so much more dramatic than yours," Bubi Brenner told my parents when we interviewed them together in Vermont in 1990:

I'm not sure I told you everything when we met up in Dorohoi in late April of '45. Who had time to go into details then? First, I had to argue and pay a bribe for the *propusk* I was able to secure. They interrogated me at the militia. "Why do you want to leave the Soviet Union?" they kept asking, and I knew well that this was a trick question. Any wrong answer could land you in Siberia. I said I was Romanian, but they didn't buy it. So I tried another line: I wanted to go to Palestine to the homeland of my people. They badgered me for half an hour. Finally, I bribed them, and it worked.

But wait, it gets worse. We were leaving with Hedy's mother, and we packed three trunks. We brought everything we could fit into them, our clothes, books, household items. Hedy was pregnant so we arranged for a good truck to take us to the border. I got scared when a militia officer climbed on the truck with us and when, suddenly we took a turn and drove back into the city. Sure enough, we stopped at the NKVD headquarters: we had been denounced by someone, but I really couldn't figure out why.

Bubi went into great details about the harrowing interrogations they each had to undergo separately. Every departure from Czernowitz was an adventure, an act of outwitting an arbitrary system based on suspicion, intimidation, and punishment, carried out by officials who themselves oftentimes did not believe in the laws they were supposed to enforce. Corruption was rampant, bribes tended to work, but one had to develop an instinct for how and when to offer them. A wrong move could result in imprisonment or deportation without appeal.

Bubi enjoyed fleshing out the details of their departure for us, building suspense, conveying a disdainful sarcasm and a sense of retrospective bemusement, even as he placed himself back into the fears and frustrations of the time:

> I was interrogated by three officers; they brought one trunk upstairs and asked if anything was hidden in it. Dollars? Jewels? I was ready to sign an attestation; as far as I knew there was nothing there. Well, what do you know? They took everything out, dismantled the trunk and there was a secret compartment with about $100 or $200 in gold pieces. My mother-in-law had it built without telling anyone: the only person who could have denounced us was the carpenter himself. That was it. They assured me I'd get ten years in Siberia at least and made me confess to my guilt and sign everything over to the Soviet state. I had to do it to protect my mother-in-law.

Lotte and Carl had not heard this story before. And yet, the elements were familiar to them, the sense of triumph about overcoming enormous obstacles and successfully leaving the USSR are profoundly shared. Bubi continued: "I had already admitted to everything when a Jewish officer of the NKVD comes into the interrogation room and speaks to me in Yiddish: 'Why are you so sad?' he asks me, and reassures me after I tell him all my woes. 'Don't worry so much! Your stuff has already been distributed among these officials; they're going to let you go. But, listen carefully: let me give you some advice. Don't stay in Romania. We will soon be there too!'"

Such moments of human connection with Soviet officials were possible only at the point of leaving. Sympathy with these ordinary Soviet citizens was modulated by disdainful anger, sometimes expressed as cultural chauvinism, directed at those who exercised their authority over Czernowitzers in the city that was once their home. When, at the Soviet-Romanian border, a female guard threw Bubi Brenner's German books into the mud exclaiming that they were "books by our enemies," Bubi said, "I had to give her a gold ring I had hidden. . . . I didn't want to leave my German library in that hell-hole." With that gesture, exchanging gold for books, Bubi asserted a sense of cultural values that enabled him to preserve an identity threatened by yet another deadly assault.

German classics, my grandfather's hat brush, my aunt Fritzi's opera glasses from Vienna . . .

Pearl Fichman's volume of Shakespeare and English dictionary, her parents' Chanukah menorah, their kiddush cup and Pessach plate . . .

Objects such as these contained within them whatever small lines of continuity with a former Czernowitz that could be salvaged from the devastating ruins of persecution and displacement. Potent carriers of culture and meaning, these items maintain their power through the years.

Faded smells, distant memories, ghosts of home . . .

From the memoir of Pearl Fichman: "The night before we left, all three knapsacks ready, we looked around the house: the furniture in the dining room and bedroom, all brought by my parents from Vienna, the beautiful grandfather clock that had to be wound once a month—all these were part of our lives. Father, without saying a word, opened the clock, cut through the spring, took the beautifully engraved, gilded weights and threw them in the garbage. He did not want anybody to enjoy that clock that was brought from Vienna in 1918 and was chiming the quarter, half and the hours for our entire life, in good times and bad."[40]

From Dorothea Sella's *Der Ring des Prometheus:* "During the long ride through the streets of the city, I silently bade farewell to the Czernowitz of the present that we were now leaving forever. But the Czernowitz of old, the city in which I was born and grew up, that I took along with me."[41]

### BUCHAREST: MAY 1, 1945

It was again time to say goodbye to Rosa Zuckermann who, during this trip, had shown signs of failing health. Would we see her again? "I am the last real Czernowitzer *now,*" Rosa said to us once more. "When they all left, in 1945 and again in '46, I stayed. I waited for my brothers." Rosa's brother Muniu came back from Transnistria a few weeks after she did. He, also, had been deported with a young wife and he came back alone. Then, after Rosa had begun to lose hope, her brother Paul returned a year later, in 1945, from his flight into the Soviet Union. But Rosa continued to wait for her other brother, Arthur, who had also miraculously survived the war by passing as German in Yugoslavia and Austria and who, bypassing Chernovtsy, eventually made his way to Southern Bukowina. It was there that Carl, arriving in 1945, had to tell him about the death of his parents in Transnistria. "I stayed here because I wanted to reassemble whatever family I had left," Rosa continued. "When Jews left for Israel in the 1970s and 1980s, I stayed behind again to be with my son. And now you are leaving too." As on our previous visit, we promised to be in touch, to send books, and to phone frequently. We did not know if we'd be back.

On this second trip, we had decided to leave Chernivtsi by way of Romania. Our return flight was booked through Bucharest, but beyond that we made no firm plans. Certainly, I was curious, but also quite hesitant, to revisit some of the scenes from my own childhood, in Cîmpulung, Southern Bukowina, where my aunt and uncle, Rosa and Moritz Gelber, and their three daughters had lived through the 1950s and where my paternal grandmother was buried, and in Bucharest where I grew up and went to elementary school. We wanted to see the beautiful painted churches in the Northern Moldavian region of Romania. But we were also eager to leave Chernivtsi by the same route that repatriated Jews had taken in 1945 and, even if only in a retrospective gesture of imagination, accompany them across that momentous frontier.

The Romanian border was less than an hour by car from Chernivtsi. We hired a taxi to drive us across it, and on the advice of friends from Chernivtsi, we hired a guide who would, they assured us, facilitate the formalities that could otherwise take many hours. On the other side of the boundary, another car would pick us up to drive us to Suceava, the largest city in Southern Bukowina, where we had reserved a hotel room.

It was a cold, bleak, and wet July morning, and the rain increased in intensity as we drove toward the border. Our guide seemed annoyingly officious and self-important, and we wondered why we had bothered to bring him along. No doubt, the fear of border guards is something that had been passed down to me and that I remembered from my own childhood behind the Iron Curtain. Visas, passports, travel permits, customs inspections were part of the idiom and the imaginary of my childhood—their mention alone can revive a bodily fear of arbitrary authority. Sure enough, once we reached the wooden hut that was the Ukrainian check point, and the corresponding hut on the Romanian side, his presence enabled us to sit in the car, watching the rain, while he rushed around, bribed various guards with the bills he had extracted from us, and finally, after what seemed like hours, transferred our luggage to the Romanian taxi waiting for us. I had heard enough stories about this border on the other side of the River Sereth, to realize how privileged we were in our uneventful journey.

"It was May 1, 1945," writes Carl Hirsch in his memoir. "We arrived in Bucharest's main railway station late that evening and saw many banners and other signs of the May Day celebration around the station. The railway workers' unions had been in the hands of the Communists before the war, so it is no wonder that they were solidly led by the now legal Communist Party. . . . The day before we had gotten the news of Hitler's suicide, which meant that the war will be over in a few days. Bucharest looked to us like a city that had not suffered from the war at all. We walked around in amazement. . . . After what we had gone through, it was unbelievable."[42]

They had no real plans, Carl writes. Was Romania a way station for them, a gateway to a firmer sense of freedom, stability and, yes, home? Or did Bucharest itself offer the possibility of reconstituting some of the sense of community that they had lost? My childhood there in the 1950's had some elements of both. But after the Communist takeover in Romania in 1947, there was no longer a real choice: the Romanian border was closed, as the Soviet one had been earlier. Emigration, a daily topic of conversation and debate, became possible only during a few brief periods in the late 1950s and early 1960s, and then only under danger of unemployment and imprisonment if one applied and failed.

I grew up in Bucharest surrounded by Czernowitz friends and Czernowitz stories. Rarely did my parents socialize with Bucharest Jews or gentiles, though my father did rekindle connections with a few friends from his university days and from the period he spent working in the Regat. But my playmates were the children of the Flexors, the Brenners, the Singers, and the Blums, all from Czernowitz. We spoke German of the Czernowitz sort: Romanian was our second language, and some of us spoke it with an accent. We went to the German-language school in Bucharest, where our teachers were either Czernowitz exiles or ethnic Germans who had remained behind after the war. Our Romanian classmates were sent to the school by ambitious parents leery of the Communist regime. Our German-language education reinforced our status as outsiders in Romania, but, for our parents, it offered the passport to a life somewhere beyond the Iron Curtain. We did not read German classics in school; we read Alfred Margul-Sperber who, in an effort at integration, had begun to write German poems in the accepted patriotic style and to translate Romanian poets into German.

When we went to the Black Sea and the Carpathian mountains in summer, on hikes in the Carpathian foothills in the fall, and on Sunday excursions to nearby lakes, we were always in the company of Czernowitz friends. Czernowitzers were our doctors, our pharmacists, my parents' bridge partners. At our get-togethers, we ate Nusstorte, Schmettentorte, or Palatschinken made from Czernowitz recipes, avidly exchanged by our mothers. Czernowitz jokes punctuated these meetings and would often reduce our parents to uncontrollable fits of laughter. We sat and listened to their reminiscences, and their stories became ours.

At the same time, we lived in Bucharest, a bustling capital that offered the attractions of Romanian culture in which we also participated, but always with an eye toward a past and a future elsewhere. Was this resistance to Romanian identity something our parents had brought with them from their youth in Cernăuți—their way of living in Romania without becoming Romanian—that they were now passing down to us who were born in Bucharest or Timişoara or Ploeşti? Or was integration into Romanian culture precluded by the anti-Semitism and the social and political exclusions to which Jews who did not join the Communist Party were subject in 1950s Romania? As Jews who spoke German, who were professionals rather than workers, and who had voluntarily left the USSR, our parents were under constant suspicion. Incentives to settle down lessened steadily through the 1950s, as restrictions increased and political pressures to join the party and work for the *Securitate* mounted. Stalin's death in 1953 offered a moment of hope, but the brutal repression of the Hungarian revolution in 1956 clarified our fate. In 1958, as soon as it became possible for Jews who could claim family ties to Israel (and later also to Western Europe), my parents, along with many other Czernowitz friends and relatives, began to line up, under the cover of night, to apply for passports to leave Romania. My family was among the relatively small number who succeeded. In 1961, we were the proud owners of a travel document.

Meanwhile, Czernowitz itself, or Chernovtsy, had become a distant memory. Just a few kilometers north of the Romanian border, yet out of reach. Even letters from Rosa and her brother Paul took a long time to reach us, and I knew little about this branch of the family. Rosa and Felix came to Bucharest for a brief visit in the late 1950s. To me, the city in which they lived and that they described to us seemed totally unrelated to the idea of Czernowitz my family and friends evoked in the reminiscences that shadowed my childhood.

# PART THREE

# Ghosts of Home
## 2006

Figure 41.  Deportees at the Dniester, 1941, and the Dniester at sunset,
2006 (Courtesy of the United States Holocaust Memorial Museum
Photo Archives and Yad Vashem Photo Archives [1941 photo] and Leo
Spitzer)

# ELEVEN

# The Persistence of Czernowitz

You must never undertake the search for time lost
in the spirit of nostalgic tourism.

GREGOR VON REZZORI
*The Snows of Yesteryear*

MOGHILEV, ON THE DNIESTER, SPRING 2006

The Dniester flows quietly this late afternoon beneath the white concrete outlook terrace adjacent to a small, well-kept park in Moghilev, Ukraine, where we had arrived a few hours earlier. Everyone in our Transnistria group is scheduled to gather for dinner soon in a nearby restaurant, but while we await their arrival, the two of us, together with David Alon and his adult son Danny from Israel, stand near the terrace edge looking at the dark green waters of the river and at the landscape on both of its banks. We've walked to this outlook after checking into our overnight lodging and exploring the town together—a lengthy stroll—and I am happy to have a short respite. But the view is captivating. The Dniester is wide here and seems ominously deep. Yet without a noticeable breeze at this hour to highlight its flow and disturb its surface, it appears glass-smooth, stunningly beautiful. My glance repeatedly falls on the opposite shore—nowadays part of the Republic of Moldova—at fields and houses in Otaci, the crossing point to Transnistria for so many tens of thousands of Jews from the Northern Bukowina and Bessarabia in 1941 and 1942. No matter how much I try to push my imagination, however, I am unable to reconcile the view before my eyes with the squalor and mud that is so evident in the black-and-white photos I have seen of the masses of deported Jews waiting on the river's bank to cross. Today has been a brilliant, warm late spring day, with only an intermittent light cloud cover. Now, at this hour, the rapidly setting sun colors the sky in a rich burnt orange that reflects and sparkles like glowing coal in the river's darkening waters.

Near us on the terrace, small children play and eat ice cream while their parents watch and converse, a young couple embraces, teenagers chat and smoke cigarettes, two old men on a bench doze. I remain immersed in my thoughts. Suddenly, Danny Alon takes a cell phone out of his pocket, dials it, and within a short while, begins to speak with someone animatedly, in Hebrew. The conversation continues for some time, and when he is finished, I ask him curiously about the call. "I was talking with my grandfather in Israel," he responds. "He was deported from Czernowitz to Transnistria through Moghilev, over the Dniester. Somehow I wanted him to be here with me. That was impossible. He did not want to set foot here ever again. So I wanted to let him hear my voice and some of the sounds by this river, and to let him know that here I am, his grandson, standing with his son, my father, in that place that he had often talked about with so much revulsion. I wanted to let him hear, directly from this spot, that despite it all, we have survived it."

## THE WEB AND THE "REUNION"

"We often visited my mother's exceptionally close and German-speaking family," wrote David Glynn from London in his "personal introduction" to subscribers to the Czernowitz-L internet mailing list, "and to me Czernowitz has always been a familiar concept, but I knew absolutely nothing about it. And I could find out nothing about it, since no books in England seemed to make any reference to [it] . . . at all. It was only with the advent of the internet that Czernowitz began to take a concrete shape in my mind, and I have been amazed by the flood of information to be found there. I am looking forward to the reunion, my first visit to Czernowitz, as an opportunity to understand more of the context from which the family came."[1]

The afterlife of Czernowitz on the web: transgenerational and virtual. David Glynn's observation that "it was only with the advent of the internet that Czernowitz began to take a concrete shape in my mind" and his eager anticipation of "the reunion" were shared by many on that same mailing list. Indeed, what Czernowitz-L subscribers in 2005 voted online to call the "Czernowitz Reunion" emerged from the phenomenally increased availability of the internet worldwide over the course of the last decade and its greatly expanded use as a source of information and vehicle of communication.

Initially, it was an interest in genealogy and a search for family connections and roots relating to the Jewish community of Czernowitz and the nearby Hassidic center of Sadagora that had led to the formation of an informal internet mailing list "Sadagorans United" in 1997. In 2002, thanks largely to the efforts of Bruce Reisch, a professor of genetics at Cornell University whose paternal family originated in the Bukowina, that mailing list formalized and expanded into a moderated listserv, Czernowitz-L (or Czerno-L, for short). We joined the list at that point. Indeed, in the years since its formation, list membership came to include many (perhaps a majority) whose connection to Czernowitz derived only through parents or grandparents. By 2003, as interest in Czernowitz-L increased further and individual membership subscriptions to it grew, Jerome Schatten—a U.S.-born Canadian resident whose grandparents, father, and uncle had emigrated from Czernowitz to America in the first decade of the twentieth century—created a website for the group (czernowitz.ehpes.com).

This website quickly became an invaluable digital repository for articles, photographs, postcards, maps, family histories, documents, and bibliographic materials related to Czernowitz and the Bukowina—all made easily accessible on a worldwide basis. It became a dynamic, "living," and steadily growing virtual archive. Available to anyone at any hour using a computer connected to the internet, it provides browsers and interested researchers public entrée, for the first time, to an immensely rich trove of visual, testimonial, and documentary resources—to a broad range of uploaded informative materials that had been amassed over the years in previously unknown or hard-to-access private holdings and family collections.

The site was set up to satisfy a number of different purposes and to address the interests of diverse users. To meet the genealogical interests of some of its users, the site provided access to a periodically updated "Czernowitz Family Finder" listing family surnames, their city of residence in the Bukowina (if not Czernowitz), and names and email addresses of interested researchers. A "Czernowitz Jewish Cemetery" link was added in 2003, after the Jewish Genealogical Society of Ottawa coordinated a project to digitally photograph the graves in the Jewish cemetery and to link the images to the burial registers they were able to acquire from the caretakers of the Chernivtsi Christian cemetery located across the street. Volunteer list members immediately began to create a searchable database that would make graves findable by name, death date, location, and image. Volunteer translators have begun to translate the register into English. Cemetery maps are available on this link, with both old and new parcel numbers. In addition, a "Help Identify/

Find" link is available on the site, containing requests for information about relatives or other persons from Czernowitz or its environs—some depicted on posted old photographs—as well as appeals for translations into English of letters, postcards, or documents written in Romanian, Russian, or Yiddish. But predominantly, the site features scanned postings, largely supplied by list members, that contribute to significant, complex, virtual representations of Czernowitz/Cernăuţi/Chernivtsi and its inhabitants—to historical, geographical, cultural, political, and personal renderings in which both the city, over time, and its people become visible and, in varying degrees, comprehensible to casual surfers or more serious systematic researchers.

It is this latter functionality of the website that David Glynn and others—children, grandchildren, and more distant relatives of Czernowitz/Cernăuţi-born persons—think of when they credit the internet for helping to give Czernowitz "a concrete shape" in their mind. Website postings provide them with a variety of reference tools: a lengthy, albeit critically incomplete, reading list; a table of "Notable Czernowitzers," women and men who were themselves born or resided in the city or whose families originated there, including Otto Preminger, Edward G. Robinson (born Emanuel Goldenberg), the economist Joseph Schumpeter, the poets Rose Ausländer and Clara Blum, and the singer Joseph Schmidt; a "Czernowitz Address Finder," listing Czernowitz/Cernăuţi ancestors of listserv subscribers, their relationship, and their last known residence address (an address invariably cited with its German, instead of Romanian or current Ukrainian street name); and a "Czernowitz Street Name Translator," allowing users to identify the city's streets by their Romanian, German, or Ukrainian names.

The site also offers users access to an open archive of pictorial materials which enables the viewing, downloading, and printing of a variety of images: detailed, high-resolution, pre–First World War maps of the Austro-Hungarian empire and the Bukowina province; several excellent maps of Austrian Czernowitz, with German street names; of Romanian Cernăuţi, with streets in Romanian; of Cernăuţi in 1941, displaying a German military map, with some street and institutional names again in German; and of present-day downtown Chernivtsi, a pictorial map with street names in Ukrainian (but displayed in Latin characters). A large collection of low- and high-resolution postcards of the city and its surrounding region during the Austrian, Romanian, and Soviet eras shows photographic images of streets, monuments, stores, and street vendors, close-up details of the Temple, the Café Habsburg and the Europa, the Hotels Bristol and Schwarzer Adler, the Pilsner-Bierhalle, and many other public and commercial buildings.

It is, however, through the hundreds of photos of people and places in Czernowitz/Cernăuți from the years before 1945, submitted to the website from family albums and private collections of Czernowitzers and their descendants around the world, that one gains the fullest sense of how Czernowitz, the city and its people, is shaped in cyberspace. Browsing through these, and connecting what they seem to show with other information passed on to us, we can better understand how Czernowitz persists as image and idea in the mind of its present-day surviving exiles and their offspring across generations.

To be sure, given the fact that most subscribers and contributors to the Czerno-L discussion group and website are Jews, it is largely Jewish Czernowitz—and to a significant extent bourgeois, German-speaking Jewish Czernowitz—that is transmitted in this manner. And yet, not surprisingly, attesting to the present-time diasporic identities of these subscribers and contributors and to the North American nationalities of the listserv moderators and webmasters, the lingua franca of the virtual cyberspace in which they now communicate is English, not German. The Czerno-L website, of course, does provide links to other sites in several other languages—many of which, in turn, offer additional links. One of these links is to "Czernowitz/ Bukowina: Wo Menschen und Bücher lebten" [www.czernowitz.de], an elegant site in German established and maintained by Othmar Andrée, focusing largely on the cultural, intellectual, and literary dimensions of pre– Second World War Czernowitz and Bukowina Jewish life. Andrée, our travel partner in 1998, is an independent scholar living in Berlin who is neither Jewish nor with family connections to the city, but he is one of a number of German and Austrian intellectuals for whom Habsburg-era Czernowitz represents a highpoint of multicultural urbane tolerance, vitality, and creativity. Regarding that "German-language Jewish city" as a "home of the German-Jewish symbiosis" ("Heimstätte jüdisch-deutscher Symbiose"), Andrée has himself written a book and many essays about Jewish lifeways in Czernowitz and its vicinity, and has translated Yiddish and Hebrew works concerning Czernowitz into German.[2] Most of these works, as well as many by other writers and scholars writing in German, are posted on his site, intended for a German-speaking audience interested in learning more about a place that, in his estimation, serves as a positive model for present-day Jewish-German cultural interaction.

Several other significant links are also available: to a rich and detailed archive of materials about the 1908 Yiddish language conference (czernowitz .org); to the lively exhibits on Czernowitz on www.museumoffamilyhistory .com; to a post–Second World War gallery of city and area photographs (www.cv.ua); to official as well as unofficial contemporary City of Chernivtsi webpages (in Ukrainian as well as in English; www.komkon.org/~sher/chern/hist.html); and to the official website of the Israeli-based World Organization of Bukovinian Jews (www.bukowina.org.il/). The site www.bukovina jewsworldunion.org originally in Romanian, German, English, Hebrew, and Yiddish, but now primarily in Hebrew, offers book reviews, news about notable Bukowinians, and an online edition of the German-language Bukowina newspaper *Die Stimme,* a publication that has now added some pages in English. In addition, a lively group posts pictures and engages in conversation in Ukrainian on a livejournal blog, and French-speaking Bukowinians can log on to bukovine.com for news and postings.

Altogether, the various portals and web pages establish a matrix—a series of chronologically, spatially, and linguistically interconnected and linked digital pathways that carry and convey a tremendous amount of cultural and historical information about Czernowitz and its iterations. Simultaneously, they reinforce the sense that significant traces of the city's pre–First World War cultural and physical identity continue to persist over time and are still accessible in the present. And in the present they also mark generational shifts: German no longer dominates but has given way to English and Hebrew, the languages most commonly spoken by the second and third generations of Czernowitz descendants. For those descendants to have access to the world of their parents and grandparents, documents, memoirs, and literary works have to be translated, and the websites offer volunteer translators a grateful readership. At the same time, only readers of Ukrainian can tap into the exchanges taking place on the various Ukrainian sites and blogs the reflect present-day concerns.

Despite their vast informative power, however, and the fact that many posted materials can be downloaded, printed, and viewed "offline," they do remain in the realm of the virtual. They lack the smells, scale, and tactile physicality of the "actual," certainly, but also of the analog "originals" from which they were generated. They are generally also without the context in which their originals were first collected and displayed in family albums and communal archives. Web photos especially, scanned from such originals, lose the connection to the "real" that Barthes had so aptly termed as the "ça a été," or "having-been-there," of the photograph.[3] Furthermore, as Svetlana Boym notes, "computer memory has no patina of history, and everything has the same digital texture."[4] Digitized images and documents posted on the web, combining private and familial with public holdings, *seem* to offer more immediate access and breadth of detail than materials in traditional archives.

But in the process of their web-based dissemination and circulation, these resources—often compressed, cropped, and attenuated—remain frustrating simulacra. As rich and varied data in a vast and interchangeable digital archive, they stimulate more desire than they are able to satisfy—a desire for the "actual" and "original" that is further compounded and intensified by what we would call the "communal aspect" of internet communication.

In effect, internet-subscriber mailing lists, more so, perhaps, than lists and sites open to random browsers, tend to foster a sense of community and a shared intimacy based on common interest in a topic and/or, as in our case, a common origin. These screen communities, however—whose individual subscribers know little, if anything, about each other's real-world lives—are ultimately also only virtual and disembodied. Their members usually remain faceless to one another and, where identified by screen pseudonyms only, nameless as well.

It was, no doubt, a feeling of frustration with the intangibility of cyberspace and the illusory sense of community that led a number of Czernowitz-L subscribers to consider organizing a real, rather than virtual, gathering of their group "somewhere in the world." This idea grew out of an animated exchange of mailings in which list subscribers discussed and shared recipes for favorite foods associated with Czernowitz and the Bukowina that they and their families continue to enjoy. Most of the discussions had centered on recipes passed down within families from mothers, grandmothers, senior cousins, and other relatives; one even came from acquaintances of the one-time owner of "the famous Friedman Restaurant" in Cernăuți. At length, and with some passionate disagreements about ingredients and details of preparation, recipes were posted on the list for "Czernowitz versions" of Austro-Hungarian favorites—*Zwetschkenknödel* (plum dumplings), *Kaiserschmarrn* (Emperor's fluffy omelet), *Gefüllte Paprika* (stuffed peppers), *Krautfleckerl* (noodles with cabbage), *Busserl* (almond cookies), *Schmettentorte* (sour cream cake)—or for Romanian-Balkan-Jewish inspired versions of *Mamaliga* (cornmeal polenta), *Vinete/Pătlăjele* (eggplant salad), *Ghiveci* (vegetable mix or stew), *Haluschken* (*Holishkes:* stuffed cabbage leaves; *Sarmale* in Romanian), *Totzc* (flour/potato kugel), and many others.

These postings led to the creation of the Bukowina Cookbook Project—an ongoing compilation of posted recipes in a "Cookbook" on the Czernowitz-L website. But perhaps more significantly, this passionately shared interest, heightened by nostalgic memories of past meals and the preparation of Czernowitz and Bukowina recipes, also stimulated list subscribers to try to enhance their communication with each other. In the early summer of 2005 one list member, "Malvina M.," from Melbourne, Australia, proposed that they organize "a reunion"—meaning, of course, an *actual, embodied* get-together of people connected to Czernowitz and its surrounding region.

Many list members responded enthusiastically to this idea. But when would such a reunion occur? And where? Correspondents agreed that sometime in mid-2006 was a realistic goal—that would be during the summer (in the Northern hemisphere) and far enough in the future for a meeting to be adequately planned and prepared. And the place? "Malvina M." suggested that it be held in Vienna because, in her opinion, Vienna had been the metropolitan "cultural core" for Czernowitzers. An optional visit and tour of "Czernowitz," for those interested, might then follow the Vienna gathering, she wrote, even though the Austrian capital "will certainly be more fun than the Ukraine!" But Miriam Taylor voiced emphatic negative feelings about Vienna: "For us to have a reunion there, would be to say the least, a slap in the face of those of us who suffered the consequences of German and Austrian anti-Semitism and those members of our families who lost their lives because of it." Bruce Wexler emphatically urged, "GO TO CZERNOWITZ! I urge you to consider having this reunion on the streets where our ancestors lived."

In the end a majority of participating list members agreed on Czernowitz—or, more accurately, on present-day Chernivtsi—as the site for a reunion in mid-May of the following year. With this choice made, they elected an organizing committee online to address the practicalities of group tourism in the Ukraine and to plan communal activities, talks, and acts of commemoration on behalf of the reunion group. The event itself quickly acquired characteristics of a group pilgrimage—a journey addressing both secular and religious desires. It served the need, as the anthropologist Jack Kugelmass has indicated about all pilgrimages, "to peer behind surface representations to *re-experience* culture as fully three-dimensional, as real."[5] It promised them a sense of elation from the in-the-flesh encounters with physical and cultural sites that some had remembered from their youth and others had only imagined.

In the course of the planning for this gathering, however, one fundamental question did not arise. What did their decision to hold "a reunion" actually mean? Given the generational, geographical, national, linguistic, political, and even religious differences among subscribers, who (or what community or group) was in effect reuniting? A number of list subscribers had of course been born in Cernăuți in the interwar years and had left the city or region as children or young teenagers after surviving the war. Conceivably, those belonging to this group might wish to reunite in the place of their birth. But the majority of other list members were only indirectly connected to the city, through parents, relatives, or research interests—and, for them, the notion of "reunion" was hardly applicable.

——— ◄✦► ———

No matter. The "Czernowitz Reunion 2006" did, indeed, take place during the week of May 18–25, 2006. Sixty-eight participants from nearly a dozen countries in Europe, the Americas, and the Middle East convened in Chernivtsi at the now partially renovated Hotel Cheremosh, where the majority had booked rooms, and where all group events took place.

We too flew into Chernivtsi, through Kiev, to attend the gathering— our first, and rather nerve-wracking, arrival in the city by air, on an ancient Antonov-24, a small twin turbocraft Soviet-era aircraft built around 1960. When we landed, we were happy to be met at the airport by cousin Felix Zuckermann.

Felix looked well. He came to fetch us in the same ancient but immaculately preserved Lada car that he had been driving when we first met him in 1998 and in which he drove us on a few occasions in 2000. He was nattily dressed in a jacket, shirt, and pressed blue jeans—clothes that visibly contrasted with the grungy outfits we were wearing after our lengthy overnight flights from New York. But even though he was clearly very happy to see us again, the effect of the death of Rosa, his mother, in 2002 was also immediately evident in his face and demeanor. "I miss her so profoundly," he said to us soon after we drove off towards the Cheremosh. "I wish she could have welcomed you again and been part of this event." We felt Rosa's absence as keenly as that of Carl, who died in the fall of 2004, only a few months after his sister Lilly. It felt good to reminisce about their extraordinary lives with Felix and to console one another on their loss.

Chernivtsi, we all observed as we drove toward the hotel, had become a more bustling city in the six years since we were last here—a reflection, perhaps, of benefits it had derived from the Ukraine's emerging free market economy and the generally positive growth in the country's gross domestic production. Cars were numerous on the road from the airport and on city streets, and they included many late-model luxury Mercedeses and BMWs. Many new stores, including supermarkets displaying a wide selection of national and international foods and brands, were evident as well. And they did not seem to lack customers. Everywhere we looked, private houses and larger commercial buildings were under construction or reconstruction.

"The place has changed and grown a lot," remarked Felix, "but the old center, as you will see, is still very much as it had been. Many buildings there have been renovated and painted. It's all busier now, and there are more stores and new restaurants and discos—and slot machines. Nowadays, more people can afford these. Some people have become very rich, and there is a growing middle class. But there are also still many, many very poor people struggling to make do."

We arrived at the Cheremosh in the late afternoon, eager to continue the conversation and our own family reunion, but we took temporary leave from Felix, arranging to get together with him and Marina, his wife, for dinner and a much longer visit the following day. We then checked-in to the hotel, which indeed had spiffed-up a number of its guest floors and rooms, and began to meet other Czernowitz Reunion attendees—almost all of whom we had only encountered before as names on the internet and web. David Glynn and Miriam Taylor, two of the reunion organizers, Gabriele Weissmann, Charles Rosner, Berti Glaubach, Abraham Kogan, "Arthur von Czernowitz," and Yehudit Yerushalmi-Terris: all previously only cyberspace correspondents from within our listserv greeted us, shook our hands, and became real. Our friend Florence Heymann, with whom we had traveled in 2000, had come again as well, this time with her husband, Jacky, a gerontologist. Further personal introductions and longer conversations with reunion participants continued during a group dinner that evening and at breakfast next morning.

It soon became quite clear to us that within our group of participants there were at least three slightly different agendas motivating interest in the gathering.

For the half-dozen or so participants of the older generation—those born in the 1920s or early 1930s in Romanian Cernăuţi, like Berti Glaubach, Abraham Kogan, Hardy Breier, Fred Andermann, Alexander Raviv, Max Reifer, and Karla Kahane—it provided a late-life opportunity for a return-visit-to-place, either by themselves or with their spouses and/or children and grandchildren. Like Carl and Lotte in 1998, these returnees also sought to re-trace, re-visit, and touch places they associated with their past life in the city, and to transmit accounts of that past, on site, to their offspring. They did so, generally, in Hebrew or English—the languages of the countries where they now resided. But, not surprisingly, everyone in this group could still easily switch into what one of them referred to as "the home language of our youth"—German.

German came less easily to the larger component within our group that belonged to what Susan Suleiman has referred to as the "1.5 generation"—

in our gathering, those who were born in Cernăuți or nearby villages in the late 1930s or early 1940s and who were young children during the war: Arthur Rindner, Asher Turtle, Yehudit Yerushalmi-Terris, Peter Medilanski, Miriam Taylor, Wolfgang Schaechter, Charles Rosner, Miriam A., and Batia Reifer (Max's wife) among others.[6] These participants had spent only a few years in the city. Some were deported to Transnistria with their families. The more fortunate evaded deportation. All subsequently fled or emigrated to new sanctuaries in Europe, Palestine, or the Americas. For those in this cohort, the Chernivtsi gathering enabled a search for material roots. Some had lost one or both parents during the war and had come back to look for gravestones or markers in the cemeteries of Chernivtsi or in Transnistria, to which they also planned to travel. The trip permitted them to rediscover vaguely remembered or subsequently learned-about childhood sites: family residences, neighborhoods, streets, schools, parks and playgrounds that contained something of the world "before" the enormous losses they suffered at a young age. And it allowed them to search for and reclaim personal documents that had been lost or never formally acquired—birth certificates, certificates of marriage of parents or grandparents, residential or property records. In so doing, it made it possible for them to certify, in concrete fashion, both to themselves and to others, an identity that had been severed from its foundation through expropriation and displacement. Arthur Rindner, who with his family had been deported from Cernăuți to Transnistria when he was a very young boy and who, in his many communications with members of Czernowitz-L had always identified himself as "Arthur von Czernowitz," was so overjoyed after a clerk at the city registry helped him to find and get a duplicate of his birth certificate that he kissed her. He did not mind that his birth certificate was in Ukrainian. For him, and for others in this group, the retrieval of documents and addresses momentarily compensated for the vagueness or insufficiency of memory.

The reunion, however, also included a sizable contingent of second- and third-generation participants who were born *after* the war and *after* parents, grandparents, or other relatives had left the city. Unlike those who still had direct memories of this place, this group belonged to the generation of postmemory. Among others, it included David Glynn from England, Rita Margalit-Shilo and her sister Monika, Florence Heymann, and David Alon and his son Danny, all from Israel, Gabriele Weissmann from Berlin, Joe Poras from Boston, Renée Steinig from New York, Simon Kreindler and his daughter Lisa from Toronto, Veronica Ellran and her brother Bernardo Stein from Colombia, as well as Mark Heckman from California. As had been the case with us when we first traveled here in 1998, people in this group viewed the Chernivtsi trip as a chance to "return" to a world they had never actually known personally. Their "return" promised to help transform *virtual Czernowitz,* built and detailed from a seemingly limitless digital archive, into a three-dimensional, tactile entity. Through their direct encounter with the city, the narratives and images that had been conveyed to them, first by parents and grandparents and subsequently by the internet and web, could be given physical reality. Strolling about on the Herrengasse, Ringplatz, Theaterplatz, and in the Volksgarten, Jüdisches Haus, Gymnasia, and university—places they knew from images and descriptions, and usually only by their German names—they could situate these in actual space, in proper scale, concretely and in color, textured by smells and surrounding sounds. And when they visited these sites with people in the reunion group who had grown up in the city, something else would happen as well. As had been true with us when we first traveled here with Lotte and Carl, by listening to the on-the-spot narratives of these elders and witnessing their "at the place" performance of bodily practices and deeply absorbed habits of long ago, aspects of the affective qualities of daily life as it once had been resurfaced and were conveyed to them.

The organizing committee had planned a variety of events for the reunion. Besides a city tour emphasizing the sites of Jewish Czernowitz and a literary-cultural tour of the city and nearby Sadagora led by Peter Rychlo, professor of German-language Bukowinian literature at the Jurii Fed'kovych University in Chernivtsi, there were lectures, panel discussions, and photo presentations by participants scheduled on a daily basis in a large hall in the Cheremosh Hotel. Their object was to fill in a history of the city's Jewish community and to give group members the chance to share stories and reminiscences with each other. Many of the speakers had done research into topics like "Jewish Immigration into Bukowina in the Late Nineteenth Century" or "Cultural and Educational Institutions in Czernowitz," but by far the most moving presentations were the personal and familial ones: Charles Rosner's account of his mother's life in the Cernăuți ghetto when he was a small baby (later published in his book *Émancipation: Êtes-vous [aussi] de Czernowitz?*); David Glynn's reading of a memoir piece his mother Erika (who could not accompany him) had written for the group; or Rita Margalit-Shilo's powerful rendering of her father's first-person recollection of the war years. Each of these, it seemed to us, were moments in which these absent elders were vividly recalled and given substance in the very city from which they had once been evicted and displaced.

Figure 42. Images from the "Czernowitz Reunion 2006" (Courtesy of http://czernowitz.ehpes.com)

But even though the reunion did enable all this, it was much less successful in establishing the communal identity among participants that the gathering was intended to affirm. Pre-trip emails had already begun to reveal disturbing fissures. Some, for example, had wanted to limit participation only to "*Jewish* Czernowitzers and their descendants." Spouses of the latter were to be included, even if not Jewish, but when a non-Jewish Romanian scholar writing a book about Jewish Czernowitz asked to join the trip, one of the organizers vociferously defended denying access to "outsiders." We were not "objects of study," one organizer insisted, nor would we want onlookers when we might be "moved to tears" at the experience of our "common" past or, especially, during our scheduled memorial service at the Jewish cemetery, when we would surely "bare our soul" remembering our loved ones and their suffering.

Despite this controversy, the Romanian scholar did come along to Chernivtsi, joining friends she already had among the participants. But the divisive, nasty, exclusionary conflict around her presence continued throughout our stay. She became a scapegoat for the objectors, a representative of

Romanian anti-Semitism that our ancestors had experienced, a catalyst for the expression of what, after all, were very divergent interests and investments in the trip. Arguably, in our interpretation, at least, the discord that brewed around her participation was a symptom of the tenuousness of our connection with one another and of the desire of a few to define themselves as "real Czernowitzers" by excluding an "alien other" who was not.

The relation to present-day inhabitants of Chernivtsi, both Jewish and non-Jewish, also divided the group. Beyond collecting donations for a Jewish communal and medical organization, most participants in our trip showed little interest in the lifeways and situation of Jews *now* living in the city, almost all of whom had resettled there from other parts of the former Soviet Union. The planned memorial service at the cemetery, to which local Jews were invited, for example, yielded little opportunity for interaction. As visitors, we had a different relationship to the cemetery service than did the local residents. They, like us, had come to mourn loved ones lost in the Holocaust—deaths, in their case, in Poland, Bessarabia, or in other places in the Ukraine or Eastern Europe where their families had originated and where so many had perished. They also came to remember more recently deceased relatives who are buried in this cemetery. We wished to memorialize violent deaths and deportations of family members who had once resided in this city. In a significant difference, moreover, some in our group—those who had been born in this city—also considered this service as a symbolic recognition and ritual mourning for the loss of home. "I took part in the memorial service," one person later remarked. "I said kaddish and marked my presence with a small stone. Yet, for me, the service also acknowledged that I no longer belong here."

In addition, we, unlike the local Jews, wished to identify the burial sites of long-ago-deceased relatives who were interred here. Most of us had prepared for this visit with the help of the cemetery registers now posted on the website. We came already knowing the exact location of the graves we were researching. On our visit in 2000, Marianne and I had finally succeeded, with a great deal of local help, in locating the immensely faded and almost unrecognizable grave of Marianne's grandfather Markus Hirsch. Now, in 2006, we managed to make our way through the brambles and to find the graves of Marianne and Felix's great-grandparents, Yochanan and Chaja Wurmbrand as well. The cemetery was no less overgrown and impenetrable, but the maps we had downloaded were of such immense help that locals working in the cemetery asked us for copies that would enable them to help future visitors to indentify graves.

The brief connections with local Jews we made during the cemetery service were hardly sustained, however. Later in the week, when our participants collectively invited the Chernivtsi Jewish community to the Cheremosh for an evening of refreshments and dancing to the music of a local Klezmer band whose authenticity was tenuous at best, our two groups interacted little, each tending to sit at separate tables or cluster together without much of a mix. The cheery Klezmer music and the jokes, mainly told in English—even the relatively inexpensive vodka—did not help to create an atmosphere for closer mingling. At one point many from both groups did join a circle to dance a hora. But its aftermath, marked by a seemingly uncomfortable milling around and a quick return to previous seats, indicated that the significant cultural, experiential, and economic differences between us had hardly begun to be bridged.

In part, of course, our communication was greatly impeded by language. Local Jews have Ukrainian, Russian, Polish, and Romanian backgrounds and know one or more of these languages. Members of the older generation still feel most comfortable using Russian but some also speak to one another in Yiddish. Children born after the independence of Ukraine in 1991 are most fluent in Ukrainian. Only two or three Chernivtsi Jews—like Felix Zuckermann, the offspring of "old Czernowitzers"—speak German, and only a few speak a very rudimentary English or French. In our group, only a relatively few among our oldest members could communicate in languages other than Hebrew, English, French, or Spanish. Conversing with Chernivtsi Jews in a meaningful way was thus certainly problematic.

An attitudinal element, however, was perhaps even more impeding than language. The fact, of course, was that the vast majority of persons in the reunion group came to present-day Chernivtsi to see *old Czernowitz*. The actual encounter with the living city did not significantly alter the mythic ideas and images that returnees had brought with them and that the internet had helped to circulate and enhance. Like other Jewish visitor-tourists to places in Eastern Europe from which Jews had been displaced or eliminated during the Second World War and its aftermath, the primary focus during our short stay in Chernivtsi was not on the living but on the dead.[7] Not surprisingly, therefore, in the course of city strolls, members of our group liked to visit the newly opened Café Vienna in the former Herrengasse. With its excellent coffee, its delicious Torten and Strudel served with whipped cream, its comfortable wicker chairs and beautiful pots filled with pansies, the Café Vienna tapped into nostalgic sentiments and made Chernivtsi feel like what many imagined Czernowitz of old might have been like. Present-day residents in Chernivtsi imparted services—in the hotel and restaurants, in shops, as taxi or bus drivers, occasional tour guides and informants, and as providers of access to documentation and other archival resources. But, as Sergij Osatschuk, a Ukrainian Fellow in the Bukowina Research Institute in Chernivtsi, observed about "returnee" visitors to the city more generally, in privileging what he calls "Mythos Czernowitz," many in our group treated the city's current inhabitants as interlopers in the urban space. Visitors exclaimed positively at the survival of so many Habsburg-era buildings and spaces. Yet, beneath this awe lurked a consistent critique of the present. Osatschuk identifies it well: "the stage set remains, but the actors are no longer present."[8]

Indeed, a few persons in our group even regarded non-Jewish residents in the city with a mixture of apprehension and unease. Because of personal experiences in a few cases or a more general acquaintance with stories about pogroms, intense anti-Semitism, and the wartime displacement and murder of Jews with the acquiescence or participation of people in the local population, for some in the reunion group Ukrainians and the Ukraine, like Romania, still bore a reputation as untrustworthy and potentially dangerous. In a couple of instances, participants expressed a long-internalized anger in denunciatory outbursts during our group sessions or tours. A Ukrainian priest, long-dead, was thus publicly berated by one participant for his collaboration with Romanian fascists and Germans in the Transnistria deportation that this person had survived. Besides the quest aspect involved, or the desire to restore graves, or the wish to concretize long-carried images in three-dimensional space, some journeys of return also contain the fantasies of settling old scores.

### RETURN TO TRANSNISTRIA

The reunion schedule had been planned so that most mornings were left free to permit participants, on their own or in small groups, to explore places in the city or nearby towns and villages where relatives had been born or been buried. From the start, a group of participants had also planned for a two-day bus trip to Transnistria.

Why organize a side trip to such a devastating site of trauma? What did this small group of reunion participants hope to find there? Much has been written about such visits from memorial and anthropological perspectives—the Jewish nationalist, exclusivist, character of pilgrimages like March of the Living, for example, or the tourist industry evolving around journeys to Auschwitz, or the packaged tours retracing the steps of Oskar Schindler in

Cracow. Unlike these, the Transnistria trip was planned as a simple memorial undertaking: as an opportunity to visit a few of the towns and villages beyond the Dniester where some of the participants or members of their families had survived the 1941–42 deportations, or where their parents, grandparents, siblings, and relatives had perished.

The two of us, veterans of our brief visit to Moghilev and Vapniarka in 2000, were well aware of the practical hardships and discomforts involved in making this journey. From that occasion, we knew the difficulties in finding traces—or even any acknowledgement—of the Jewish wartime suffering in this region. Despite our misgivings, however, there was no question that we would join the Transnistria group. We both wanted to go to Bershad, where Rosa Roth Zuckermann had been confined in the ghetto during the war. In 2000, we did not have time to drive to this town near the banks of the River Bug in the northeastern part of Transnistria. Although Rosa herself had always been reluctant to speak about the horrors of her survival there in any detail, we had read Ruth Glasberg Gold's powerful memoir of the years she spent in the ghetto orphanage set up by the Jewish community in Bershad, as well as many other accounts and documents about this place.[9] Of the more than one hundred camps and ghettos for Jews in Transnistria, Bershad had been the second largest after Moghilev. It had been a town notorious for its nearly unbearable conditions, its immense death toll from typhus, hunger, cold, and the brutality both of its Romanian administrator, Florin Ghineraru, and the Germans who culled its wretched inmates for forced labor in areas under their control. Our visit to Bershad, in the company of a few of Rosa's fellow survivors, was intended to honor Rosa's courage and dignity and to pay tribute to her memory.

But, in truth, we had other motivations as well. The two of us, there for the second time, now thought of ourselves as observer-witnesses on this Transnistria-bound trip rather than as personally affected participants. In our teaching and writing, we had begun to study return visits to sites of trauma, to wonder what memory they hold, what they might reactivate in the survivor returnee or in his or her descendants. Transnistria's lack of an institutionalized culture of remembrance that we had encountered in 2000, the destruction of its large prewar Jewish population by Einsatzgruppen, and the apparent local lack of interest in, if not submergence of, the history of the thousands upon thousands of Jews who were deported there by the Romanians promised to make this visit particularly interesting for our research. And yet, the observer stance we tried to adopt and the emotional distance that we had intended it to protect vanished less than two hours into the journey.

Very early in the morning of May 23, twenty of us, including a driver and two translators, Natasha and Lyuda (not the same young woman who accompanied us in 2000), boarded an old German bus owned by the Ukrainian tour company that had been hired to organize our outing and began our journey. In exchanging stories we discovered that five in our group were Transnistria infant or child survivors and one had survived as a teenager. Of these six, two had lost one parent during their deportation and one had lost both. The others in our group, like us, came to trace the Transnistria histories of their parents and other close relations. No one seemed to know exactly what to expect there, but everyone expressed some apprehension about the feelings that the journey might activate or provoke.

Indeed, not long after our bus journey began, we realized that it would be long and difficult. Because of the driver's unfamiliarity with the route and (once again) our lack of transit visas through the Republic of Moldova, which lay directly east between Chernivtsi and our destination, he took us by way of a very lengthy detour northeastward, hoping also to avoid heavy truck traffic and the worst of badly worn and potholed roads. In fact, however, we encountered not only many bumps, twists, and turns, but also numerous delays where the bus literally inched along, impeded either by trucks and cars that prevented our passing or by herds of cows or goats or flocks of geese.

As the hours of travel passed, the outside temperature steadily rose as well. The air-conditioning in the old tour bus stopped working by late morning when the drive belt to its generator snapped—a belt, alas, that could not be replaced anywhere during the remainder of our journey—and the temperatures inside the bus climbed to nearly 100 degrees Fahrenheit. We also soon discovered that the on-board toilet, a feature many in the group had insisted upon because of the anticipated lack of adequate facilities on the way, was non-functional. The driver made pit stops every once in a while by the side of the road to compensate for this problem, providing opportunities for us to use the woods for relief and to cool off slightly in the shade. But, as a consequence, the journey time increased even more and seemed to become endless.

Many hours later, we crossed the Dniester River and entered what had been Transnistria. Here the scenic countryside became overwhelmingly beautiful. I was once again astounded, as I had been six years ago, by the rich black soils and the acres upon acres of planted grains and oilseed buds that emblazoned the fields in a carpet of yellow. The incredible contrast between the splendid scenery and the horrors that had occurred here sixty years ago underscored the immense perceptual gaps that visits to former sites of trauma can make so palpable.

Despite the external beauty—or perhaps because of the incongruities it revealed—passengers became surprisingly argumentative as the trip progressed. Tensions mounted, apprehensions increased. The warmer it became, and the longer the trip lasted, the more did conflicts and irritations surface within the group.

By mid-afternoon, some eight hours after our departure, our bus stopped in the shade near a tree-lined square bounded by flowerbeds in the small town of Shargorod. In 1941, a ghetto demarcated by barbed-wire barriers was established for Jews in a section of this town, and some seven thousand deportees, mainly from Bessarabia but also from the Bukowina, were squeezed into it and compelled to seek shelter wherever they could find it. Yehudit, one of our fellow passengers, had been one of them. Together with her mother and father, she had survived the ghetto as a young girl, but both of her maternal grandparents died here from typhus during the epidemic in the winter of 1942. For a long time after the war, she said to the group, her parents told her stories about Czernowitz—nostalgic stories about their youth, their marriage, and her birth there—but they refused to talk at all about Transnistria. Yehudit's own childhood memories of this place had been repressed as well until, many years later in Israel, through the survivor organization AMCHA, she joined a child survivors' therapy group in which details of her own experiences began to surface, as did those of her fellow members. Over time those details were fleshed out by her own efforts to research and contextualize this traumatic episode in her life history. When the opportunity to visit Transnistria arose, Yehudit particularly wanted to go to Shargorod to try to find the grave of her grandparents which, she told us, had been dug and marked, despite the deeply frozen ground and miserably cold temperature, because of her mother's steadfast insistence (and, no doubt, bribery of the diggers) at the time. She also hoped that being back in the place itself would open up the past in new ways for her, allowing her to access some of the scenes she had long repressed.

When we walked through a town she hardly recognized, however, the resistances to remembrance did not easily dissipate. Nor was she able to find her grandparents' burial site. Other than the three or four gravestone tips that still remained visible above an inaccessible brush-covered field at the edge of town, there was no visible trace that a Jewish cemetery had ever existed here. There was also no evidence—or memorial indication—of the mass graves that had been dug in the early 1940s for the numerous victims who had perished in this town. Nonetheless, Yehudit did find something totally unexpected in Shargorod, and perhaps even more consequential.

It happened not long after our arrival, on the town's main square. Our two translators had left our group to search for someone local who might direct us to the site of the old Jewish quarter. They returned a short while later with four casually but neatly dressed men, one of whom—in his late forties, with cropped silver-gray hair, blue eyes, and a friendly smile—was introduced to us as the mayor of Shargorod. The mayor, after a brief statement welcoming us to the town, told us that one of his companions would show us the site of the old ghetto and the Jewish cemetery, as well the town's main synagogue. Then, however, the mayor did something surprising for a town official. Yehudit had told him that she had been in the ghetto here, as a child, with her parents. She wanted to let him know that she and her parents had managed to stay alive due to the charity of local Ukrainians who gave them food and who, at one point and at great risk to themselves, protected her and her mother during a roundup by Romanian gendarmes. She wanted to acknowledge them publicly because she would forever be grateful to these kindhearted and brave local farm people whose names she had probably never known. The mayor, looking primarily at her, was visibly moved. "Shargorod is a small town," he said in Ukrainian, while Natasha translated. "Still, before the war, some four thousand Jews lived here. Their persecution and suffering is a stain in our memory. I acknowledge that suffering for which we Ukrainians also share responsibility. Now, only some thirty Jews remain here. The absence of Jews is our loss for which I am truly sorry."

For me, this was a powerful moment. Even though, as we subsequently learned, the ancient and beautiful Jewish synagogue here had been transformed into a winery, and few physical traces of the Jewish past were visible in the town, the mayor had acknowledged the lengthy historical presence of Jews in Shargorod as well as Ukrainian complicity in their wartime persecution and suffering. This very understated on-site human exchange between him and Yehudit, witnessed by all of us and bystanders from the town, created a reparative atmosphere that seemed like a good beginning for our time in Transnistria and augured well for what lay ahead.

When we got back on the road, however, the good feelings dissipated rather quickly, and conflicts again came to the fore. When the trip was being planned, we had been asked about places in Transnistria to visit that were personally most important to us, and Shargorod, Moghilev, Bershad, and Budi were submitted to the tour company as primary goals. Arthur Rindner, who with his family had been deported from the Bukowinian town of Storojinetz

Figure 43. Yehudit Yerushalmi-Terris (center) and the mayor of Shargorod (back to camera), with Greta Rindner, Rita Shiloh, Marianne Hirsch, and Leo Spitzer (from left), 2006 (Courtesy of Gideon and Rita Shiloh)

to Bershad as a small child, was the only group member who wanted to stop in Budi, where his mother had perished during their forced march east. Arthur's request was certainly reasonable even though driving to Budi would entail a detour. But a few persons aboard the bus, primarily one or two of the other child survivors and their spouses, began to challenge the "extra stop" in Budi. How was he so sure his mother had died there, in that particular place, one asked him? He had, after all, been less than five years old at the time: why should his memory be trusted?

Despite the fact that we were not scheduled to be in the Budi area until our second day in Transnistria, the skepticism about Arthur's request was expressed impatiently, as though we had to decide then and there if the detour was going to be made. Arthur's hurt and indignation were immediately discernible. Why would anyone want to challenge his recollections? For most of his life, he said, he had been haunted by flashbacks of his mother lying next to him, cold, dead, when he woke up in the morning in a cowshed where he and his parents had found shelter during their time in Budi. His memories of this period came back to him in black-and-white, "like a movie, but with some scenes cut out, missing," he told us. "I want to go back to Budi, fill in some of those missing pieces. And say kaddish for my mother. Maybe that can help to bring some closure."

As we moved forward toward particular sites within Transnistria, not only Arthur but the other child survivors on the bus began nervously to draw into themselves and to shrink physically. Their faces reflected an overwhelming sense of anxiety. At the same time, however, the strife and negativity continued. Why did we stop for lunch so early? Why were we stopping at every cemetery, some asked? And when were we going to see the cemetery in Bershad, others insisted? Nothing was right. Where we had expected solidarity and mutual sympathy, a sharing of past experiences, a feeling of community, we found wrangling, competition, bickering.

We were, of course, conscious of the fact that a number of our travel companions had suffered severe trauma as young children. And we were sufficiently familiar with the literature on childhood trauma to know about some of its recurring manifestations. Dori Laub, a psychoanalyst who was, himself, a child survivor of the deadly camp at Cariera de Piatră in Transnistria, describes his own heightened awareness of details from that time—a precocious remembrance of events that seemed "far beyond the normal capacity for recall in a young child." Yet he also notes discontinuities in memories of childhood trauma indicating that, in his own case, "these memories are like discrete islands of precocious thinking and feel almost like the remembrances of another child, removed, yet connected to me in a complex way."[10] When we discussed our trip with him after our return to the United States, he told us that he never wanted to go back to Transnistria, fearing perhaps what we had the occasion to witness on our journey—the loss of the doubling and projection, of the protective shield that locates the trauma outside himself, in the persona of "another child."

At last we arrived in Moghilev, where we visited several sites, all had dinner together at a local restaurant, and then spent the night in the less than adequate local hotel. Next morning we set out early. As we neared the village of Budi, a short detour off the main road to Bershad, Arthur requested that we all permit him and his wife, Greta, to descend from the bus by themselves and that we return to fetch them again a while later. Normally genial and talkative, he had become quiet as we neared Budi, focusing his glance out of his window. At one point, he asked the bus driver to slow down so he could snap a photo of one of the cowsheds we passed. "In Budi, in a cowshed similar to that one, we spent our first winter in Transnistria," he said. "All these sheds have only one story, but ours had two. It looked a little bit like this one, but it was different." He addressed this comment to no one in particular before lapsing back into solitude and silence.

Shortly thereafter we approached a cluster of modest, well-kept houses of fairly recent vintage and a signpost reading "Budi" on a small grass-covered circular island that divided the road. No people, stores, or even cars were visible. Placing a *kipa* on his head and carrying a small prayer book, Arthur got off the bus there with Greta and walked to the sign. It was clear that he was about to fulfill what he had set out to do—to say the mourner's kaddish for his mother. But since he had absolutely no knowledge of where in this village his mother's burial site was located, he stood at the entrance of Budi, at the post that marked its physical location. When we returned, we saw Arthur take some photographs and place a stone by the "ВУДИ" sign to mark his visit.

The change in Arthur's countenance and mood after this was remarkable. He began to brighten up, to tell stories and converse in a good-humored way. He felt lighter, he told us, as if some weight had been removed from his chest. He became an engaging adult once again. He noted that he was beginning to feel as though he might be able to attain some closure on a traumatic past. And, he told us with a smile, a powerful image fragment that had once meant so much to him as a child in Transnistria had suddenly again flashed before his eyes as he looked out of the bus window after leaving Budi. Outside now, like then, sunshine had broken through overcast clouds. It reminded him of a late winter day in the Bershad ghetto, to which he and his father were forced to move after Budi and where they had survived the war years under great duress. One day, he told us, on a snowy tree branch illuminated by the sun's rays, he saw a beautiful scarlet-colored bird. Instantly he knew that this was a good omen, a sign that spring was coming, that the war would end, and that they would be liberated and allowed to return home. And now, again, he sensed the promise of renewal and release—this time, however, less physical and more psychological if not spiritual. Perhaps, he said, it was a signal to let go and move on.

Late that morning we arrived in Bershad, a surprisingly traffic-busy and bustling mid-sized town with a central avenue and tree-lined sidewalks on which many recently built and renovated buildings and stores were evident. In our group, besides Arthur and his father, Rita Margalit-Shilo's parents and grandparents had been interned in its ghetto, as had David Alon's father and his family, and also Batia Reifer who, as a small girl, had been left in an orphanage run by the ghetto's Jewish communal organization that Ruth Glasberg Gold describes in her memoir.

When we reached the ghetto area, we began our walk on an unpaved road, deeply rutted from the weather and without sidewalks, which was lined with small grayish brick and clay wood-trimmed cottages with corrugated metal roofs. Most of these seemed to be inhabited by impoverished Ukrainians, Roma, or recent immigrants from the Indian subcontinent and elsewhere. Almost all the houses we passed were in a state of disrepair, with broken windowpanes, rain gutters, and stairs, rust-eaten roof panels, peeling paint, collapsed walls and ceilings. Their small yards were covered with overgrown grasses, gnarled bushes, and fallen branches.

The Bershad Jewish ghetto had consisted of approximately twelve narrow roads like the one we were on, two wider main streets, and slightly more than three hundred cottages like the ones we were viewing. In the autumn of 1941, it had been the destination for more than twenty-five thousand deportees from Northern and Southern Bukowina who were forced to find some space within it—a virtually impossible ordeal, since many of the houses had already been plundered and destroyed when the Einsatzgruppen made their killing raids through the area a few months earlier. The deportees gathered in windowless huts, in cowsheds, pigsties, and haylofts. In the ensuing harsh winter months, in which the temperature in the region occasionally plunged to minus 40 degrees centigrade and a typhus epidemic raged, thousands died here: Rosa Zuckermann's parents, husband, and son were among them, as was Batia Reifer's mother. Their bodies, left unburied because of the frozen ground and the lack of sufficiently healthy workers, remained piled in the snow for weeks before they could be taken away. Eight months later, in May 1942, only some ten thousand deportees remained alive in this place.[11]

"This is very, very similar," Arthur suddenly said to me, stopping near the entrance of one of the cottages that we were passing. His voice, interrupting my videotaping and my efforts to imagine this place many decades ago, reminded me that he was searching for the house where he and his father, and a score of others, had lived after his mother's death in Budi.

"But it is not our house because our house was right near the entrance of the main square. Exactly like this one, it had slats going off from the door. The windows there were just like the windows here, on this one. Very, very similar. But this cannot be it." Arthur's comment reflected our visit to Bershad. Nothing we found corresponded to what people in our group were actually searching for. And yet, unquestionably, for many on this journey, being *in the place* activated deep, embodied trauma.

Certainly, without a knowledgeable guide, there was no hope of identifying the actual location of the Bershad orphanage building that Batia had been seeking. She had survived in it as an infant after her mother's death

Figure 44. Bershad: old ghetto street and synagogue, 2006 (Photographs by Marianne Hirsch)

and her father's murder on the other side of the Bug River until, in 1944, she and several thousand other orphans left Transnistria following an agreement between Romanian officials and international Jewish rescue agencies willing to pay for their release. Batia was subsequently transported over land and by ship to Palestine where she was adopted by Aliyat Hanoar, a Zionist organization aiming to integrate children and young refugees into a new homeland.[12] Like Arthur before the stop in Budi, Batia had also displayed many different emotions during our long bus journey—in actions that ranged from small outbursts of annoyance and frustration about the trip, the heat, and the translators, to competitive challenges about stops that some members of our group had requested to make. She, too, at moments, had revealed a kind of petulant anger that was then modulated by periods of quiet and withdrawal—reenactments, perhaps, of childhood trauma that the visit to Transnistria, and to Bershad in particular, had stirred up.

We left the ghetto area after a brief stop in what had been its ancient synagogue—a once imposing but now extremely neglected whitewashed building that brought on a particularly strong sense of desolation within me. Its doors were unlocked by a very old hunched-over man, one of the last Jews still alive in the ghetto area, the synagogue's watchman. In exchange for a tip he allowed us to wander about its dark and damp interior with its collapsed floors, broken pews, and walled-off women's prayer area. What layers of memory did this spooky place hold, I wondered? Survivor memoirs mention the hundreds of frozen bodies awaiting burial that had been piled up in the synagogue yard at the height of the typhus outbreak in the winter of 1941–42. But this place had a history before that horror. What had the people that worshipped in this synagogue been like? Was anyone interested in retrieving anything from that past?

For many participants in our group, the Bershad cemetery promised to offer a more definitive sense of personal closure than the former ghetto. While being driven to it on the outskirts of town, on our bus, I took out Ruth Gold's memoir from my backpack and reread two sections she wrote about this cemetery—the first, about sneaking off in the spring of 1943 with a group of other orphans to search for the resting places of their parents and other relatives, and the second, relating a brief return visit to this cemetery in 1988. Recalling the 1943 incident, she wrote:

> Trembling with fear, I looked around. . . . But there wasn't a single sign to indicate the last resting place for the thousands of victims who had perished during the devastating winter of 1941–42.

Suddenly I made a grisly discovery. Scattered throughout the whole area were entire, unburied skeletons and individual bones—human bones that covered the soil like shells on a beach.

... Momentarily it occurred to me that among these bones might also be those of my family.[13]

The Bershad Jewish communal organization that ghetto inhabitants had created decided to use some of the funds they were able to receive from the "outside" in 1943–44 to build a monument in the cemetery for local victims buried in the cemetery's mass graves. Amazingly, that monument was quickly erected—a five-sided prism topped by a Star of David, whose sides, on marble plaques, bore the names of many of the thousands of Bershad victims as well as a Hebrew inscription by Rabbi Berl Yasser of Briczine.[14] When Ruth Gold visited this cemetery in 1988, determined to find the names of her parents and relatives on the monument, she was greatly disappointed. Apparently the memorial, quickly built in 1943, using inferior wartime materials, could not survive decades of harsh weather and had crumbled:

> Utterly frustrated, and with a sunken heart, I gave up my search. . . . I badly needed a moment of meditation, some spiritual contact with my loved ones to let them know that I had come back to pay tribute after all these years. But where could I do that? Accidentally, I located a small, weathered monument, still bearing a few names of people from towns near Czernowitz. Its sight was pitiful, yet it bore the only testimony to that time of infamy. I leaned on it and poured out tears of sadness I had accumulated over the last forty years. Then it was time to leave.[15]

Our own search through the cemetery was also extremely frustrating and emotionally unsettling. We all—and especially the child survivors in the group—were upset about our inability to locate these monuments, or even a plaque or any other indication of a mass grave where we could commemorate the deaths of relatives that we had come here to mourn. We had collected small stones to leave behind as symbolic markers of our visit but found no suitable spot to place them. Still, it also became clear to a number of us that the general sense of disappointment and weariness that pervaded the group was overshadowed by Batia's apparent agitation about her failure to find the burial site where she could mourn and say kaddish for her mother. Without saying anything, we all intensified our search, winding our way across sunken and unmarked graves, toward a clearing where a number of gravestones from the 1940s and a newer monument with some inscribed names could be seen.

It corresponded neither to the description of the 1943 monument nor to the old weathered one Ruth Gold had found: it was larger, square, and had apparently been erected quite recently by an international organization to honor the victims. We were relieved to locate it, read some of the inscriptions, and then most of us moved away to make space for Batia who stood by it, silent, next to her husband. Had she in any way found what she was looking for? She never said, and, in fact, she never communicated a sense of closure. Just unending sadness and despondency.

## MEMORY AND COMMEMORATION

Over the course of our work on this book and our trips to the Ukraine, the curious coexistence of nostalgia and negative, traumatic memory that shaped the relationship of displaced Czernowitzers to the city and region of their childhood and youth had increasingly intrigued and troubled us. Our research into the details of this city and its history was clearly motivated by our desire to find the sources of both the deeply positive associations many carried with them and the traumatic experiences that could not erase or even strongly modify the persistent "idea of Czernowitz."

The 2006 Reunion brought us into contact with a younger generation of Czernowitzers than the one to which Lotte and Carl belonged: with people whose physical connections to the city had been much briefer and who had experienced and suffered the effects of anti-Semitism, persecution, and expulsion more pervasively and personally. On the trip to Transnistria, we became cowitnesses to the childhood trauma of some of our fellow travelers and its powerful aftereffects—emotions that touched us profoundly. For much of the two days we spent on the grueling bus trip and in our searches through towns and villages, the positive associations with the old, idealized Czernowitz seemed distant indeed.

And yet, even the child survivors of the Transnistria horrors had initially been attracted to make this trip to the Ukraine by the appeal of a gathering and visit in "beautiful Czernowitz." They too held on to a notion of Czernowitz that they had acquired and that had been reinforced in them over the course of their lives—an idea of place that had shaped their identity. Although some of them had been orphaned as children and had spent only very little time in Romanian Cernăuți or Soviet Chernovtsy—and that during the years of intensifying persecution when the city had become inhospitable to Jews—they had all maintained a surprising attachment to the place and its surrounding region, an interest that seemed to us more intense than the affect associated with the proverbial search for roots.

The journey of return to "Czernowitz," however, elicited different psychological responses than the return to Transnistria—different ways of engaging and addressing the layered memories of the past. There were moments during the Transnistria trip that upset that tipping point between positive and traumatic recall we had previously observed during our many hours of work with survivors of persecution and displacement. Both on our journey there and in Transnistria itself, traumatic recall certainly predominated. Being with this group of child survivors, we finally came to understand and sense the affect of a bereavement so intense that neither narrative history nor memory or testimony can adequately convey or transmit it; of a loss so deep that it remains forever incarnate, and forever uncommunicable, within the survivor.

The moments of despair and regression that we witnessed were certainly exacerbated by the paucity of on site memorials. There were a few exceptions. In Moghilev, our bus group did visit the monument to Transnistrian ghettos and camps, as well as the monument to rescuers in the center of the town, and the cemetery's mass-grave memorial that the two of us had previously encountered on our way to Vapniarka with David Kessler in 2000. We also visited a new, small, and very touching museum that the head of the local Jewish community unlocked especially for us in early morning after our overnight's stay in town. Its holdings were modest and largely handmade: a large and very complete map of Transnistria with all the 1940s camps and Jewish ghettos marked; photographs and names of Moghilev natives who had been killed by the Nazis; some letters and other documents relevant to the period, mainly in Russian but also in Romanian, set in makeshift display cases; a rudimentary and unintentionally comical "eternal" torch animated by an electric fan blowing on a red crepe-paper cutout, creating the illusion of a flame. All the displays were dusty, cluttered together, and located in small exhibition rooms whose street entrance seemed to be unmarked by any identifying sign. Did local people visit this place? Did Moghilev's inhabitants know any more about the wartime history of this town than the present-day residents of Vapniarka, who had largely seemed clueless about its local past?[16]

We left the museum glad that it existed yet saddened by the fact that it was such a minor memorial undertaking, so seemingly out of public view, impoverished, and insufficient as acknowledgment of the deportations, killings, and deaths from starvation, disease, and cold that had taken place in this town and throughout Transnistria. Individual gestures of commemoration such as Arthur's kaddish to his mother, or Yehudit's encounter with the mayor of Shargorod, or Max Reifer's compulsive account of his deportation experiences and Transnistrian ordeals to local Ukrainians at the Moghilev hotel: all these seemed much more powerful to us than the monuments or museum we had seen. And yet, inadequate as these memorials may be, at the very least, they existed.

### "JUST MORE QUESTIONS"

On our long drive back to Chernivtsi from Bershad, Jacky Heymann suggested that everyone in the group use the vehicle's intercom system to share impressions of the trip. Bad idea, I initially thought: too much exhaustion, too many resentments and disagreements. But amazingly, the contentiousness that had disrupted the group was submerged by the intense emotions that our visit had stirred up in all of us. Surprisingly, almost everyone on the bus—all currently residents of Israel, excepting the driver, our translators, and the two of us—did speak, and their voices, resonating in lively Hebrew and translated for us in a whisper into French by Florence, have remained among the most vivid legacies of this return journey for me. Each account reflected the struggle to extract some personal meaning, some reparative possibility, from the devastating sadness we had all witnessed and, to some degree, briefly shared. Natasha and Lyuda spoke movingly as well, in English and German. They had learned more about the history of the region of their birth in these last two days, they said, than in many years of schooling. Lyuda was studying Hebrew, she told us; she wanted to learn more about Jews and their history.

A desire for transmission, communication, and engagement—with all of us on the bus and with children and grandchildren who were not present—characterized all of the brief comments. Here are a few excerpts:

*Miriam:* I did not know what to expect. I was very, very small when I was here. I don't like opening my wounds, but today I did, I picked my scabs. I am in shock. I don't know how this trip will affect me. I am strong, I didn't sink into depression, I have enjoyed life all these years.

I saw during this trip that some of us did not understand each other. We each have a big wound, and some did not empathize with the other one's wound. That was really sad for me, really awful, after all we've been through. . . .

I also want to say something personal to all of you that will shock you. My bladder betrayed me twice on this trip. I am not sure if this is due to the shock or to my age, but I remember the first moment we came back from this pit [when I was a child]. The same thing happened. I tried to hide it then, but now I am not ashamed: it's what happened. I am wet now.

I hope to come back from this trip with my sanity and with the ability to laugh and be happy again. But I don't know what this will do for me in the future. All I want is to transmit this to my children. How I will do that, I don't yet know.

*Danny:* I always knew that one day I would go to visit Czernowitz. I've had trouble defining my origins: my parents said they're from Romania, but this is Ukraine. And they spoke in German. I tried to explain this in the Roots paper that all Israeli children write in seventh grade, but I couldn't. My interest intensified when my grandfather was hospitalized last year. I realized I would lose him and there would be no one to ask. I am happy to have come here with a group. The only way to make Czernowitz alive again is with a group such as this one and I am grateful to all of you.

Transnistria was always a synonym of hell for me, so when we started the ride yesterday, I felt that everything around me, the Ukrainian villages, the landscape I saw, was irrelevant. Today I feel a big change in me. Something momentous moved inside me on this trip. I felt like I could connect to the stories I had heard throughout my life. I spoke to my grandfather from Moghilev on my cell phone. And I called my grandmother's sister in Israel from the former ghetto in Bershad. She was so excited to hear my voice, and she said, "Danny, when are you coming home?" I said, "Tomorrow." I could tell her I'd be back tomorrow. I am not taking this return for granted, and I know I come back from this trip a more complete person.

*Asher:* For me this is only the beginning. I was born in 1941 shortly before my family was deported to Transnistria. When I was nine, I moved to Israel and I acted like a complete *sabra*. But I do not belong anywhere. I've researched Czernowitz for fifteen years, collecting a lot of information, but a trip like this always seemed a distant dream. I had so many questions. What would have happened, I always wondered, if the Holocaust had not happened? What would my life have been like? I came to Czernowitz to find answers, but I did not find any, just more questions.

# TWELVE

# The Tile Stove

My emotions peaked when I approached the tile stove, next to
which my divan once stood. It was a kind of upright floor-to-ceiling
ceramic tile stove, the same one where Papa used to warm the
eiderdown to cover me on cold winter nights.

    I opened the creaky iron door. To my astonishment inside was
a gas burner instead of the coal or wooden logs we used in my time.
Still caressing the cold tile stove, as if merely by touching it I could
reproduce the feelings of a pampered and sheltered infancy, I collapsed into a nearby chair. The river of tears would not stop flowing
for several minutes, overwhelmed as I was by this physical contact
with my past.

    I stared lovingly at the French crystal-paned doors and the parquet
floors we used to walk on. I could almost see Mama meticulously
polishing it with the two brushes mounted on her shoes. . . . I got
goose bumps as I touched the horizontal iron bar on which everyone
used to beat the dust out of the rugs and on which we children
exercised our athletic prowess.

RUTH GLASBERG GOLD

*Ruth's Journey*

WHAT IF?

"What if the Holocaust had not happened? What would my life have been
like?" Asher asked this question again when we saw him in Jerusalem in 2007.
Although not an academic, he attended every session of an international conference on Transnistria organized by Florence Heymann at the Centre de recher-
che français de Jérusalem, the first scholarly conference on this subject. Asher
came with Yehudit, Rita, and Arthur; they were joined by their spouses. He still
had more questions than answers, he told us. His research was not complete.

Is Asher's question the one that preoccupies all survivors and their children?

Is this what we want to find out in our journeys of return? Perhaps one of the motivations for "traveling back" to the past is to imagine alternate trajectories leading out of it—perhaps even a different future. What if Europe's Jewish worlds had not been annihilated? What if our parents had been able to remain in Czernowitz, if we had grown up there ourselves? Even as I try to imagine this possibility raised by the nostalgic reminiscences of Czernowitz exiles all over the world and by the role that a Habsburg-ruled Czernowitz has come to play in contemporary discussions as a "paradigm" of multicultural tolerance and understanding, other voices undercut such musings.[1] "I always wanted to leave Czernowitz," Lotte often says. "It was small, provincial. When I visited my uncle in Bucharest in the late 1930s, I loved the liveliness of the big city. And my parents and sister always fantasized about their time in Vienna." Hedwig Brenner, evoking the year of her baccalaureate exam, 1935–36, writes about her classmates: "Every single one of us had future plans. Most wanted to study abroad—Paris, Vienna, Prague—many planned on medicine, a few were interested in humanities. No one suspected that it would all turn out differently."[2] And when we met Lotte's cousin Martha Rubel Gordey in Sydney, Australia, and showed her pictures we had taken in Czernowitz during our trips there, she surprised us by voicing a positive dislike of her native city: "I could not wait to be old enough to leave. It was not to happen until after the war, but we traveled a great deal during my youth, and after visiting Vienna, Paris, and Berlin, Czernowitz seemed like a backwater." Even by the mid-1930s, in fact, Carl and many of his friends had left to study and work in Romania. Would they have returned had the war not broken out? Perhaps the "idea of Czernowitz" which is, after all, largely an effect of its loss, tells only one side of a much more contradictory story.

The writings of Aharon Appelfeld offer a very different perspective on the world of the Bukowina than the narratives on which we have focused in this book. Appelfeld is one of those orphaned child survivors of Transnistria like the ones we met on our reunion trip. Born in 1932 and raised in Cernăuți speaking German, he nevertheless adopted Yiddish and later Hebrew as his languages. For him, German, "the language of home," was, in Sidra deKoven Ezrahi's terms, "not simply forgotten, having fallen into disuse—it was denied."[3] This denial, not only of the language but also of the lost world of the former Austro-Hungarian Empire, suffuses Appelfeld's writings.

"A wonderful gift and a relentless curse," Appelfeld called the memory by which Czernowitz descendants are haunted in the essay on his own return journey in the late 1990s with which we began this book. If his writings return to the lost world of Czernowitz, and they do so repeatedly, though rarely explicitly, it is to point to the false lures of its appeal. Thus, in his novels and stories the "relentless curse" may seem more evident, as he highlights the traps of assimilation and the anti-Semitism that ends up annihilating the Jews who buy into its promises. Invariably, Appelfeld's characters either lose their soul by converting to Christianity or are brutally maimed and killed as Jews. As an alternative to the dangers of assimilated Jewish life—and he does not distinguish between assimilation and conversion—Appelfeld invokes a premodern rural, maternal world in the countryside, the Yiddish *shtetl* life of his grandparents that offers warmth and joy, and a small degree of protection from the ruins of the cosmopolitan diaspora that surround his child protagonists. Still, even here, his characters ultimately find little solace. It is no accident that Michael-André Bernstein finds in Appelfeld's work the paradigm for the notion of backshadowing: his characters' journeys are indeed haunted by the catastrophe that is to come and the multilayered present of his narratives is always infused with the inevitability of that future: "We know they are doomed," Bernstein writes; "they stubbornly refuse to know it."[4] One wonders whether Appelfeld has inherited the "idea of Czernowitz"—the multicultural and cosmopolitan humanism that defines the assimilationist aspirations of Czernowitz Jews—only to the extent of exposing the false sense of promise to which Jews have turned out of naiveté, perhaps, or out of ignorance. As Ezrahi points out, when Appelfeld's characters return to the landscapes of Habsburg Europe after the war, they find them not destroyed but eerily preserved down to the smallest flowerpot, strangely unmarked by the absence of Jews.[5]

Why return? What, indeed, is the "wonderful gift" Appelfeld so hauntingly opposes to the "relentless curse?" Is it the search for home that mythically suspends his writings, in Ezrahi's terms, "between Czernowitz and Jerusalem"? Or is it writing itself, writing in a tradition that, in a different language and a different register, he has indeed inherited from the Austro-German world of Franz Kafka or Joseph Roth?

Reading these detracting voices does not, cannot, minimize the power of the "wonderful gifts" that Czernowitzers have brought into exile with them from their youth or the depth of their loss. "Is it wrong to love my birthplace, my native land, even though I was cruelly deported from it?" Ruth Glasberg Gold asks in her memoir of survival in Transnistria.[6] That love clings to the world of "before" that she revisits in the space of her old apartment when she touches the tile stove by which her father used to warm an eiderdown for her.

By reconnecting with that past world, with its qualities and ideals, returnees hope not just to recover some of what they or their parents have lost, but also, counter-factually, to be able to imagine what might have been, if . . .


## THE TILE STOVE

When we walked through their Czernowitz with Carl and Lotte in 1998, we were at first struck by how predominant critical and traumatic memories had become for them in the long period of their displacement and emigration.[7] Our visits together to the public squares and central streets of the city enabled broad historical narratives to emerge. Even though they had come on this return trip with powerful attachments and nostalgic reminiscences of the city in which they had spent their childhood and youth, in the place itself they were time and again drawn to the sites where the Jewish community suffered humiliation and persecution. And we, as well, encouraged the visits to these sites, eager to deepen our own historical knowledge of the war period in Cernăuţi with on-site evocations.

But when we walked along the city's streets toward the houses in which they had spent their childhood and youth, when we entered the apartment building where Lotte had lived the first twenty-seven years of her life, and where, except for the brief period in the ghetto, she and Carl had survived the war, the two of us also expected to hear their more unambiguously positive recollections of home, friendship, and community that had provoked their return trip in the first place. Lotte had described this apartment in detail over many years and had made it clear that loving memories of home and family life were associated with its spaces and the objects it had contained. Our visit there was one of the highlights of our trip with them: we were as eager to enter the apartment itself as to witness Lotte and Carl's reactions as they rediscovered, touched, and smelled the spaces and objects of their youth.

On a sunny day in September 1998, the second day of our visit, beckoned by Lotte, we walked into the dark and spacious hallway of the apartment building on the former Dreifaltigkeitsgasse 41, with its beautiful, if somewhat chipped and neglected tile floors and curved cast iron staircase. The present occupant of the second floor apartment, a tall, arresting Ukrainian woman in her mid-forties introduced herself to us as Nadja, and was welcoming when, in halting Russian, Lotte, helped by Rosa and Felix, explained her desire to revisit her childhood home. "Somehow it was much more beautiful," Lotte whispered to us in German as she walked through the rooms, finding familiar spaces, pointing out differences. Under her breath, she recalled some of the objects she remembered vividly and pointed to where they used to be—the large blue Smyrna carpet, the brown leather couch and chairs in the sitting room, the walnut dining table. We learned from Nadja that the apartment had been subdivided for two families during the Soviet period after the war. The old dining room had been split up into two rooms, and an extra wall had been built there—a disorienting change for Lotte. Recently, Nadja and her husband, Yuri, and their two sons had been able to reunite the two units.

Lotte walked from room to room trying to find her bearings. Two large tile heating stoves—*Kachelöfen,* one white in the bedroom and one green in the former dining room—stood out amidst the unfamiliar furnishings. "They're the same," Lotte smiled, as she bent down to open the two small hinged-doors of the white one to peek inside. "When the bad times came," she told us, ignoring the change to gas burners that were clearly visible behind the open door, "this stove was heated with wood, and when the fire was going out, cakes were baked here." She was eager to translate this story for Nadja and called her into the room to show her where this had taken place.

When refugees and exiles return to a past "home"—to the interior spaces where they went about their daily lives—they attempt to make contact with and to recover the qualities of that dailiness. "Habit," Paul Connerton writes, "is a knowledge and a remembering in the hands and in the body, and in the cultivation of habit it is our body which 'understands.'"[8] By means of the material objects associated with former homes, the displaced can recover habits and embodied practices along with incorporated knowledge and memory. In bourgeois turn-of-the-century apartment houses in Eastern and Central Europe, like the one in which Lotte grew up, several spaces and objects can provide striking continuities across the span of decades. When Lotte put her finger on the old doorbell, turned the external doorknob, when her hands ran over the indentations of the wooden banister and the cast iron decorations of the staircase, when she touched the iron rod in the back yard where carpets were beaten and children used to swing and play, when she walked up the well-trodden stone stairs, and when she opened the doors of the two Kachelöfen, she reanimated body memories—deeply absorbed habits of long ago.

Objects and places can function as triggers of remembrance that connect us, bodily and thus also emotionally, with the physical world we inhabit. Memory can function as a system of potential resonances, of chords that, in the right circumstances, can be made to reverberate.[9] One might say that the returning body itself is open to the resonances it can generate with the objects and places it reencounters, and the body thus becomes a vehicle of emotional as well as of cognitive memory. In the case of massive historic fractures and dispossessions, such as the ones introduced by the Holocaust, however, places change, objects that are found again upon return were used by other, perhaps hostile enemy owners, and can just barely approximate the objects that were left behind. And yet, return can provoke the kind of spark that is created when the two parts of a severed power line touch ever so briefly. This kind of spark erupted when Lotte opened the small door of the tile stove in her former home.

But unlike many other such objects of habitual use, the white tile stove in which cakes were baked "when the bad times came" is overdetermined. It possesses historical, as well as memorial, and postmemorial, dimensions. And it carries powerful symbolic associations as well. Energy-efficient Kachelöfen (long used in the Central European Germanic world for heating) became popular in Czernowitz in the nineteenth century.[10] Heated with wood or coal, and later with gas, the stoves' richly colored exterior tile—the *Kachel*—generally reflected the fashion of the period of their creation; they could be gothic, rococo, Biedermeier, art nouveau, or modernist in style. Almost always custom-built, their aesthetic appearance and size were indicative of class background and affluence. Their built-in permanence, moreover, enabled them to endure through historical continuities and radical discontinuities: changes in family life, furniture fashion and decor, to be sure, but also, more significantly, the political shifts that led to the persecution, the deportation and displacement of German-Jewish and Romanian populations in the 1940s, and their replacement with Soviet and Ukrainian ones after the war. Their endurance even to this day testifies to the minimal modernization undertaken during Soviet and now Ukrainian rule in cities like Chernivtsi.

If the Kachelöfen can mediate the memory of returnees, they do so not only through the particular embodied practices that they re-elicit. They also act as a medium of remembrance by invoking primal associations with home, comfort, security—with a childhood world of familial warmth and safety, of privacy and interiority. These associations persist, or perhaps even increase, when war and deprivation interrupt familial life and break bodily practices. Lack of heating materials during wartime did change the habitual functionality of the stoves: in Lotte's case the dying embers in the bedroom stove had to be used for cooking and baking. But as Lotte's apartment visit and reverie shows, returnee journeys can recover and convey the duality of nostalgic and negative associations through the imbrication of deeply ingrained habits with the fractures of extraordinary circumstances. In telling her story, Lotte used the German impersonal pronoun *man* to describe what took place in the room—"man hat Feuer gemacht," "man hat Kuchen gebacken" (in effect, "fire was made," "cake was baked")—eschewing agency, and thus allowing the ghosts from the past to drift into the present room like gentle spirits. Conjuring up the smell of cake and the fading fire in a wartime of want also enabled her to overlay conflicting memories onto an alienating present, without resolving the contradictions among them. As she walked through the apartment searching for the remnant traces of past lives and for cues to remembrance, she recovered body memories both of comfort and warmth and of extreme scarcity and threat. And amidst these contradictions, she found resilience, adaptability, and small pleasures—ingredient elements that enabled survival. It's not so much the "what if..." that she found and was able to transmit to us, as that kernel in the past that could not be destroyed by the overwhelming events that definitively changed the course of their lives. And as we listened to her, she was able to transmit this kernel of resilience to us, reinforcing the legacies that had provoked our common journey in the first place.

For returnees, making contact with spaces and objects of their own past provides a means of working through the multiple and discordant layers of lives interrupted by war, genocidal threat, displacement, and emigration. But what kind of past is created by journeys and narratives of "return" for those in subsequent generations? Will sparks (re-)ignite for them?

---

Traveling in the company Lotte and Carl in 1998 allowed the two of us to face up to the sharp edges of ambiguity and to modulate our need to separate out a safer world "before" in which the Holocaust had not yet intruded. But in 2000, during our second journey to Chernivtsi, this time without parents but with other second-generation travel companions, Florence Heymann and David Kessler, that need became more dominant and pervasive, and the objects that provided clues to the "before" more necessary. Florence and David, too, were especially eager—even, perhaps, compelled—to identify and enter the very houses and apartments where their parents and grandparents had lived. By enabling them to imagine and to inhabit the textures, smells, sounds, of their parents' and grandparents' daily lives there, these past dwellings promised to provide a way of dealing with their own mixed feelings. The childhood house became for them the imaginary container of the good that had to be separated from the bad, and thus it promised to provide the space in which to soften the contradiction between the need for a sense of *Heimat* and the reality from which our parents fled or were deported.

When we began to search for Florence's and David's addresses, however, we found that not only had street names changed and houses been renumbered but that multiple entrances to apartment buildings also confused easy access. In the absence of parental guides, we became engaged in a kind of detective work using flimsy clues. Here again, tile stoves came to play a powerful mediating role—but this time in a postmemorial dimension. For descendants of refugees and emigrants who had been able to bring only very few objects along with them to their new homes, the discovery of solid, deeply resonant, and long-enduring objects like tile stoves in the very places where they presumed their families to have lived could potentially have tremendous reparative value.

In her journal from this trip, Florence Heymann writes:

I remember a photo taken from a window in the apartment from which the house across the street is visible. I think I recognize it. The Residenzgasse is now the University Street. . . . I feel that I have discovered the right house. I have a curious feeling of familiarity. A very strange impression for a place that is totally phantasmal to me. . . . The second floor has three apartments. . . . We ring on the right and a young Ukrainian woman in a pajama top answers the door. . . . "Of course, come in."

The apartment, if it is the right one, probably does not have a great deal in common with the one where my father spent his childhood. In one room, the green tile gas stove is probably of recent vintage. . . . But, in the other room, another white ceramic one is older. . . . In the garden, the walnut tree that Martha wrote about.[11] From that I deduce that I am in our familial home . . . Later I will see that other very similar gardens are adjacent to many other houses, and that the city is full of walnut trees.

The Ukrainian furnishings do not stop me from imagining another apartment, another stairwell. . . . I imagine my father as a child in these rooms, coming home from school and going up the stairs two by two or four by four, his brother Leopold going down to meet his friends on the square in front of the temple or in one of the cafés on the Herrengasse. . . .

I feel myself both excited and at peace. The children play hula hoop in the yard and wonder why this stranger is filming and photographing their house.[12]

Florence's account demonstrates that her desire to find the actual place was so strong as to circumvent contraindications or present-day appearances. She could screen out the furnishings and the sounds and smells of the present, the changes and doubts. She zeroed in on the older of the tile stoves. As the only object likely to have survived the ravages of time, it not only offered the most direct palpable connection to the familial past, it also functioned, once again, as a synecdoche of home. It could effect what she most wanted: her reanimation of this alien place with the spirits of long ago—her father as a child, her uncle as a young man.

Her "feeling" of being "at home," however, could only barely submerge her nagging doubts. How did she allay them? For her, as for David, photography and video served as prosthetic devices substantiating a tenuous intuition about "home." For second-generation "returnees" encountering places and objects associated with their familial past, still and video cameras are vehicles of choice for knowledge, documentation, and memorial transmission. "I film and I photograph," Florence writes. She filmed and had herself photographed in front and inside of the apartment she believed to have been the one in which her family had lived. David was equally eager to have his picture taken in what, on fairly thin clues, he deduced to have been his parents' first apartment and his grandparents' home. Triumphantly, he too posed in front of their impressive tile stove.

The impulse to frame a scene through the viewfinder and to freeze such a moment of encounter in a photograph can certainly be understood, especially since photographs can easily be transported back. Even in miniaturized, two-dimensional form, these photos, like other souvenir images, could serve as a proof of the visit and the quest ("I was there" and "it was there"). But, given the uncertainty about what they depict, the photos' content still demands confirmation that "it was *it*." For most descendants, such an imprimatur of authenticity is not available. And yet, highly *symbolic* and thus interchangeable objects like tile stoves might still generate the evocation of mythic worlds of origin even without particularized authentication. Florence makes this clear when she concedes that many Czernowitz buildings have walnut trees in their yard, and tile stoves are equally ubiquitous, signifiers of generality, not particularity.

While for Lotte the living room stove contained both memories of want and the smells of cake, for Florence and for David, these interior spaces become objects to be photographed in the search for knowledge, illumination—the reanimation of ghosts of home, the fantasy of a "what if . . ." But this mythic "home" is *constructed* in their layered postmemory more than

Figure 45. David Kessler in what he believes is his family's old Czernowitz apartment, 2000 (Courtesy of the Kessler archive)

actually *found* through less than conclusive clues. Although it is concretized in film and photographic images, neither the uncertainties nor the ambivalences surrounding it can ultimately be assuaged. Dominated as our narratives are by our own second-generation, backshadowing glance, they easily lose the modulations and ambiguities of survivor accounts such as Lotte's. For second-generation returnees, the parents' former home remains in the realm of the general and the symbolic, it cannot be fully particularized or fleshed out.

And yet second-generation returnees do bring their own embodied knowledge with them when they "return." Along with stories, behaviors, and symptoms, parents also transmit parts of their relationship to places and objects from the past to children raised among material objects in different and distant familial spaces. Descendants bring that knowledge with them and connect it to what they find there, on site. The spaces they encounter are then modulated and informed by what is being brought to them.

Massive stationary objects that refugees and exiles leave behind, like the tile stove, cannot be bequeathed from their owners to their descendants. The moment of transmission occurs through the testimonial encounter such as the one we experienced in 1998 or through encounters like our "return" visit of 2000. Less clearly authentic, less verifiable, that encounter was nevertheless *also* a result of inheritance and transmission: Florence and David came to find the quality of "home"—and the effects of its shattering—that our parents had brought along with them and had, through narrative, affect, or behavior, transmitted to us as we were growing up. We all came to re-discover and to confirm those kernels of the past that had not been destroyed by the massive historical fractures that propelled our families across the world. We went there to attempt to connect to the courage that enabled survival and the moments of chance, or luck, to which we owe our very existence. Perhaps, it is that quality, and not at all a counterfactual and ultimately unimaginable "what if . . . ," that each of us was seeking as we opened the little doors of the tile stoves in Chernivtsi, Ukraine.

When we returned to Chernivtsi in 2006, I badly wanted to touch the tiles of the white stove in Lotte's apartment one more time and to open that little door for clues to my remaining questions. In fact, our strolls through the city, whether by ourselves or in the company of other reunion participants, seemed to draw us back to the former Dreifaltigkeitsgasse and to the building where my mother had lived. In a moment of courage, I walked up to the entrance, eager to climb to the second floor and to ring the bell of the apartment on the right. But the entrance door was locked. A new set of security doorbells had been installed. We did not know Nadja and Yuri's last name. Would they have been home? And would they have buzzed us in if we had rung the right bell? The moment passed, we walked on, caught up in conversation and plans for the evening. "I'll try again next time," I told myself.

# Epilogue
## 2008

Figure 46. Chernivtsi night, 2008 (Photograph by Leo Spitzer)

# Chernivtsi at Six Hundred

If you go to the City Jubilee in October to join the celebration
remember this:

The festivities are to be held from October 4 to 10.

The following day is the 11 of October which for us, the Jews
of Czernowitz, has a very special significance.

On this day, 67 years ago, the Jewish Ghetto was established.
It was a Saturday. Many of the Jews that left their homes were not
to see them again.

For the Czernowitzer Jewry this was the final chord. . . .

This day of infamy should be remembered.

If not by others then by us, the survivors.

If you are in town for the Jubilee, where there will be no mention
of the Jewish story, stay one more day for the Ghetto Day.

Start the day by going down the Russischegasse or the
Hauptstrasse or the Hormuzakigasse in the footsteps of tens of
thousands of our brethren on their way into the Ghetto.

When you reach the Alte Shil on the Synagogengasse, in the heart
of the Ghetto, think of all those who perished and thank God that
you were fortunate to survive.

HARDY BREIER

Czerno-L posting, September 2008

On October 8, 2008, the city of Chernivtsi celebrated its six-hundredth anniversary. Major planning for the commemorative events was several years in
the making. Residents of the city might well associate the anniversary with
the date of the actual foundation of the city. But in fact October 8 merely
recalls the date when the first written mention of "Chern" was recorded in
a manuscript presented in 1408 by the Moldavian prince Alexander Dobryl

(the Good) to merchants from Lviv. For Chernivtsi's current municipal administration, however, the months leading up to this six-hundredth anniversary, and the October 4–10 celebration itself, provided opportunities to gain publicity for the city, attract tourists to its historic sites, bring about corporate and private investment and funding, and support Chernivtsi's social and economic development and well-being. Major renovations in the city center were undertaken with the hope of having the area declared a UNESCO Heritage Site—they continued more slowly, and under greater financial duress, when the application was denied because original windows on the old façades had been replaced with double-paned glass. For a year preceding the anniversary, the city's ambitious official website, in Ukrainian and English, made clear that, like all such celebrations, this one was primarily intended to consolidate a Ukrainian national and a commercial agenda. Not much was said there about a desire to highlight key moments in the city's layered multiethnic history or to commemorate population groups, such as Jews, that are not currently in the majority.

This absence was not lost on members of the Czerno-L discussion group. As early as spring of 2007, members began to wonder how Jews—referring primarily to "old Czernowitzers"—would be included in the six-hundredth anniversary celebration, and whether the city planned to renovate important and neglected Jewish sites, particularly the temple and the cemetery. Members made ambitious proposals with requests (some termed them "demands") that were discussed and then collectively sent to the mayor. As the weeks passed and nothing but a form letter arrived in response, the tone of list communications became more imperative and more indignant, self-righteous, even downright proprietary. Since they or their ancestors had been driven from their homes there, list members felt justified in drawing attention to their contribution to the city and to their claim to be known and commemorated by those who replaced them.

Those in the group who had visited Chernivtsi in recent years were keenly aware that the memory of the city's rich prewar Jewish culture, and of the multiethnic character of the city more generally, had largely been forgotten or erased from the present landscape. To be sure, architecturally, the city bears witness to its layered past. As a memorial space, however, present-day Chernivtsi was, in 2007, still remarkably monolithic, mainly Ukrainian in focus. The transnational memory culture that has so thoroughly transformed cities like Cracow, Budapest, Prague, or, perhaps most significantly, Berlin, seems to have had little effect so far in Chernivtsi. Even today Chernivtsi has not yet fully shed the traces of the intended homogenization and Sovietization of public spaces undertaken by Soviet authorities in the regions they ruled or of their erasure of the diverse histories associated with past dwellers in the buildings they occupied.

And yet now, after Ukrainian independence and the removal of the Lenin and Freedom statues that dominated the city center for a half-century, these suppressed histories are, gradually and selectively, beginning to be recalled and reinscribed. Thus, throughout the central core of the city, a growing number of marble plaques identify the birth houses of notable writers, artists, and intellectuals, the majority of these Ukrainian, as one would expect, but with a scattering of Jews and Romanians among them. Statues celebrating prominent Ukrainians also exist, as well as one memorializing Paul Celan and another, the Cernăuți-educated Romanian national poet Mihai Eminescu. But in 2007 no memorial marker identified the Jewish temple, now a cinema and thriving amusement arcade. One could also easily miss the two small, almost invisible plaques we found in 1998, commemorating the Cernăuți Jewish ghetto. And it takes ingenious detective work (in the neighborhood of Bila) to locate a recently erected memorial in the woods above the banks of the Pruth River commemorating the shooting of three hundred Jews by Nazi troops and Romanian gendarmes in July of 1941.

How then, given the realities on the ground, could the multidimensional richness of the life of Jews here and their relations with other ethnic populations, as well as the brutality of their persecution and mass displacement, be memorialized more extensively and visibly on site? How could this forgotten world be best included in the anniversary celebration and granted the importance and recognition, the proportionality, it deserves?

After repeated efforts and no small amount of discouragement, the Czerno-L group did receive a response to its requests from the Office of the Mayor. Maita Prout, an American Peace Corps volunteer in Chernivtsi working with city officials, wrote to ask whether some of the visual materials on the Czerno-L website could be made available for display. She announced that Natalya Shevchenko, a Chernivtsi museologist, had been made executive director of a small museum project on the Jewish history of the Bukowina, to be housed in two rooms of the former Jüdisches Haus.

Members of Czerno-L rallied to the opportunity for direct involvement in the museum planning and began corresponding with Natalya Shevchenko and Josef Zissels, a leader of the Jewish Confederation of Ukraine in Kiev, who was taking the lead in conceptualizing, overseeing, and funding the project. Though communication was slow and made cumbersome by the need for translation from and to Ukrainian, it soon became evident that

Figure 47. The former Moorish-style Jewish temple, now a cinema and arcade, colloquially referred to as the "Kinagogue," 2008 (Photograph by Leo Spitzer)

the planners had decided to feature Jewish life in the region only until the beginning of the Second World War and not to include the Holocaust in the exhibit, so as not to "focus on death." List members were outraged by what they perceived as the city's intent to show "pictures of family reunions, weddings, smiling faces" and to exclude "shootings, deportations and mass emigration—the most fateful aspect of our history." Another spate of protest emails, and the collective refusal of members to allow any of their images to be used in any exhibition that restricted its focus to pre-Holocaust times, resulted in a concession by Zissels and the local planners: yes, one of the museum's twelve wall display cases would be on the Holocaust and one other, similar in size, would feature the Soviet year, 1940–41. That the two events were thus made to appear equivalent did not seem to engender hesitation on the part of the planners, but, in response to Czerno-L postings, the museum designers invited emissaries from the list to travel to Chernivtsi to consult with them on the exhibition. That is how the two of us, along with Florence Heymann and Dr. Cornel Fleming, born in Cernăuţi but now living in London, found ourselves in Chernivtsi once again in May 2008.

What were our stakes in this project? In the terms of the memory theorist Jan Assmann, it takes three generations (about eighty years) for "communicative" memory, handed down in embodied form, through families and communal groups, to be transformed into what he terms "cultural" memory, institutionalized in archives and museums.[1] Czernowitz was at this juncture, we thought. And creative museums find ways to reembody archival memory, engaging visitors in affective and not just conceptual ways.

In preparation, we corresponded with Natalya Shevchenko and began to think about the challenges faced by museum designers. What kind of exhibition, we wondered, might interest today's Chernivtsi residents in the city's and region's Jewish and multiethnic past? How might the restorative desires of Jewish survivors and their descendants living throughout the world be addressed and reconciled with the interest and receptivity of the city's present-day inhabitants, especially its Ukrainian majority? And how might Jews avoid becoming ethnographically frozen artifacts in glass cases of Judaica placed under the sign of loss? Certainly, we hoped that the museum would be enlivened by monitors on which the faces and voices of Jewish survivors narrating their accounts of the past could be seen and heard in the original language and in Ukrainian translation.

And, inspired by postmodern memorials and countermemorials in cities like Berlin, Buenos Aires, Cape Town, and Washington, we initially set our sights high. Ideally, it seemed to us, the exhibit would call attention to multiple sites throughout the city in a dynamic rather than passively received manner, revealing the largely unnoticed and unrecognized layers of memory that remain present in the urban landscape. Such an exhibit, combining a visit to an interactive museum display with a map-guided stroll through the city's core to specific locations, would involve residents and tourists in an appealing and potentially instructive pilgrimage. In the evenings, it would use sound, light, and the projection of images onto the façades of buildings directly associated with events in the Jewish past, transforming them momentarily to illuminate their histories. Each building or stopping-point—the synagogues, the Musikvereinssaal, the Toynbeehalle, the schools and university, the site of the Jewish hospital, the cemetery, the houses where prominent Jewish Czernowitzers used to live and work—could thus open a window or doorway to the city's Jewish and multiethnic past. The embodied, participatory spectatorship elicited in a directed walk, supplemented perhaps with audio or video commentary downloadable to iPods or other MP3 players (lent or rented to participants), might thus be able to effect a powerful excavation, activation, and performance of memory on site. It might spur and provoke remembrance instead of—as we feared a museum alone risked doing—consolidating forgetting.

We were aware, of course, given the very limited resources available in Chernivtsi, that the implementation of our concept was a fantasy. And yet we strongly felt that it was imperative that any temporary or permanent exhibition about the Jewish past intervene perceptively in the contemporary life of the city in order to restore some of the history that was erased—and it had to do so in a way that would acknowledge both the pastness of the past and the vitality of the city's present. But through what kind of realistically implementable multisite exhibit might this past best be integrated into the contemporary historical consciousness of Chernivtsi's inhabitants and visitors? As far as we knew, nothing but the museum was planned.

These were some of the questions with which we arrived in Chernivtsi on May 27, 2008. We also brought along several CD's with high-quality scans of images and documents donated by list members, as well as a few original postcards and objects we were willing to donate to the museum. We had booked rooms in one of the new small hotels that had sprung up in the city center since our last visit and therefore felt much more mobile and independent than at the distant Cheremosh. What is more, the new hotel, perhaps looking ahead to the anniversary celebrations, offered a transliterated Ukrainian map of the inner city, and for the first time we were actually able to recognize and learn Ukrainian street names.

The new museum was only a few blocks away from our hotel, and we rushed over early on our first morning, eager to see its space and to begin our work with Natalya Shevchenko and Josef Zissels. Chernivtsi was glistening in the morning sun, and the mood was more festive than we had ever seen it. It was the last day of school—"Last Bell Day" as locals referred to it—and different school classes were doing public performances, having group photos taken, and parents and children, in fancy dress, were going out to celebrate. While we waited for our hosts in front of the Jüdisches Haus, we watched little girls and boys in regional garb performing folkloric dances in front of the municipal theater as they were being televised. Anxious mothers were cheering from the sidelines, snapping photos and making videos of their daughters' and sons' beautifully executed steps and twirls.

When we subsequently left the sunshine and entered the Jüdisches Haus, our eyes required some adjustment in its dark corridors. But the images of the children outside and the sounds of those performing to loud music in the recital halls on the third floor of the building stayed with us as we tried to envision future local audiences for the Bukowina Jewish Museum of History and Culture, as we were told it would be called.

To reach the third floor and the two rooms that housed the Jewish Community offices and the preparatory workspace for the museum, we ascended the stairway that contains one of the most interesting memorials in the city. In its original form, when the building was indeed the Jüdisches Haus and devoted solely to Jewish organizations, this stairway had been decorated with gold-painted cast iron stars of David. During the Soviet period when such signs of religion were frowned upon, two corners were sawed off each star to create an abstract decoration of a series of quadrilaterals. In the mid-1990's after Ukrainian independence, the missing corners were carefully reattached, although a few of the Soviet-era shapes remain and an explanatory plaque relates the history of these emblematic decorations. This kind of layering seemed like an ideal model for a museum hoping to display the complexities of Chernivtsi's history.

When we met Natalya Shevchenko, we immediately hit it off. An energetic, tall, gray-haired woman in her sixties with piercing green eyes and an amiable smile, she had recently retired from her position in Chernivtsi's regional museum. Her palpable warmth made us feel welcome and instantly included, and her evident expertise and passion for the project inspired confidence. Clearly, she had a vision for the museum design and was eager to explain it to us and to ask our advice on several important issues. But we soon came to recognize that complicated and contradictory agendas were driving the project, and, sadly, none of them seemed to correspond to our own understanding of Jewish Czernowitz.

The actual space devoted to the museum is small indeed. When Natalya took us to see the two rooms on the ground floor of the building that had been allocated for it, they had already been freshly painted and twelve arches were marked out in reserve for twelve displays that would organize the exhibit. In addition, several empty glass cases would be installed, lit, and filled with exhibition materials. Natalya also proudly showed us the large photos in three-dimensional wooden frames that would be mounted above the wall displays to form a frieze depicting various Bukowina synagogues as well as a few significant secular structures.

"This first room is devoted to Jewish traditions," Natalya said while Ulyana, a student from the university studying English, translated. "We begin with general information on the community during two hundred years of its history and display maps and documents about Jews under the Habsburgs. We then want to represent Rabbinical Judaism and the important Hasidic dynasties— the Khager dynasty from Vishnitz, the Fridman dynasty from Sadagora, and the Boianer Rebbe—each will have one of the twelve wall displays. The last display in this room will exhibit Jewish folk traditions, particularly grave markers.

Figure 48. The metal railings in the Jüdisches Haus in Chernivtsi, decorated with Stars of David; one star is a restoration of the original, and one is still missing two corners, sawed off during the antireligious Soviet era (Photograph by Leo Spitzer)

And in the corner there, we want to set up a typical Sabbath table, and we've collected some ritual objects to display on it." Seeing our raised eyebrows, she added: "Museums need objects. We want to make the past vivid to our visitors. And Jews are very dramatic. See how the displays will be draped by blue and white fabric? These are meant to recall *tallith* [prayer shawls], but they are also like stage curtains. We want all this to be like a performance."

The second room, brighter and more expansive, was dominated by a beautiful large window. Through its beveled glass, we could make out the Theater Square, teeming with festive activity. "How perfect," I exclaimed. "I always thought that the city should be part of the display. This window connects the museum to the city. It's ideal."

"No, the window is our big problem," Natalya said sadly. "We have to cover it. Ideally, we would have a wall with a mural there or a work of stained glass—a symbolic representation, not a view of the city. But we're short on funds, so a thick curtain will have to do. Certainly, we do not want visitors looking out the window: we want them to concentrate on the exhibits."

This was far from our only substantive disagreement. As Natalya explained the model of the Czernowitz Temple that would be in the center of this room and spoke about the wall displays devoted to the history of the 1908 Yiddish conference and the cases devoted to artistic, cultural, and political life before the Second World War, we increasingly came to feel that much of what we considered characteristic or distinctive about Jewish Czernowitz, and the Bukowina more generally, was missing from the planned set-up or had faded into the background. When we returned to the first room and viewed the last two empty cases to be set aside for displays—one for the Soviet year, the other for the Holocaust—this impression was confirmed.

It was not until Josef Zissels and Natalya took us on a tour of Jewish Chernivtsi, however, that we began to understand the differences between their, or perhaps especially Josef's, interpretation of this history and ours. Our group, led by Natalya who is an expert in local architectural history, visited three synagogues, only one of which is still functional today.[2] We met the new Chabad rabbi, sent to Chernivtsi to rebuild a small synagogue on Sadovskogo, the former Sankt Nikolausgasse (across the street from where Carl had lived as a young boy and where his grandfather used to pray) and to install a large new religious school and Jewish cultural center there.[3] And we visited the present Jewish school in Chernivtsi where local Jewish—but also non-Jewish—children were instructed and, among other topics, were taught Hebrew and Jewish history and literature.

"Do the children study local Jewish history as well?" we wanted to know.

"The older ones can do projects on it, but our focus is on ancient history and Hebrew culture," the history and literature teachers explained, "not the Yiddish and certainly not the German-Jewish history of Bukowina."

"Josef made all this possible," the principal continued. "He is our biggest supporter, our benefactor. All this would not be possible without him." While we talked, Josef Zissels was on his cell phone, which rang constantly. On his monthly visits to Chernivtsi, he had a lot to do. Having just returned from New York and Tel Aviv, he was on his way to Warsaw, by way of his home in Kiev. A native of Chernovtsy and a dissident who had spent several years in Soviet prisons on two separate occasions, Josef Zissels told us that the museum had been a dream of his for many years. Over the last century there had been several plans afoot, he told us: one in the 1920s under the Romanians, the second in the late 1990s spearheaded by the local Eliezer Shteynbarg Jewish Society under Yevgenia Finkel. But they never went anywhere. He was visibly proud of the progress he had been able to make. "This is only the beginning. We want to install a library and a research center upstairs on the third floor of the Yiddishes Haus as well, and I've spoken to Felix Zuckermann about beginning with our beloved Rosa's library. It's still intact in her apartment, you know."

"It's pretty clear what the underlying agenda is," Florence said when we walked to dinner at Café Vienna that night to meet Felix Zuckermann and Florence's son Elinadav, who had decided to join her on this trip and to take photos of the city to which his mother had devoted her career and so much passionate interest. "The museum is part of a larger movement to revitalize Jewish life in Ukraine and, in view of the tiny present population of Jews in the city [about three thousand at its highest count, based on the Israeli law of return which counts non-Jewish spouses of Jews], the only way they can imagine doing that is through religion. The museum, like the Chabad center, is meant to connect Chernivtsi to a larger religious Jewish world abroad, not to highlight its particular history. But even as far as religion is concerned, I want to urge them to display items that are *distinctive* of *local* practices, not Judaica that can come from anywhere."

It was the ultimate irony, we agreed. The unique Jewish culture of Czerno-witz was erased one more time, squeezed between Ukrainian national agendas that continued to blame Jews for their allegiance to German—the language associated with the Nazi invaders—and former Soviet Jews, descendants of Yiddish speakers and orthodox in practices, who had little interest in the assimilated secular German-Jewish culture, or its multiethnic connections, that we associated with the idea of Czernowitz.

"The Holocaust and the Soviet year are our most delicate topics," Natalya

Figure 49. Natalya Shevchenko (seated) shows plans of the Bukowina Jewish Museum of History and Culture to Leo Spitzer, Florence Heymann, Natalie Dudnitska, and Cornel Fleming (from left); Marianne Hirsch is at the computer (Courtesy of Elinadav Heymann)

announced when we met again the next morning in the museum offices. She had just spent some time showing us all the objects she had available for display—a few books, one by Nathan Birnbaum on Yiddish, some documents, a few items of Judaica. She again pleaded with us to ask list members for additional donations.

We were joined by Oleg Surovtsev, a historian at the university. "Oleg is in charge of the Holocaust display," Natalya indicated, "but we don't have a historian who could work on the Soviet year. I don't know how we will present it and what it will show. The archives contain very little material, indeed."

"Isn't there a risk of equating the Soviet occupation with the Holocaust, by allotting one display case to each?" Leo asked.

Oleg agreed but, clearly, the choice was not up to him. "The Holocaust display will have three parts," he told us through our second translator, Natalie. "We begin with the summer of 1941, the Einsatzgruppen killings in the villages, the shootings by the Pruth, the yellow star. Then we have the Chernivtsi ghetto and the deportations. And then life in Chernivtsi between 1942 and 1944. We plan to show one or two deportation photos but Transnistria will not be included."

Natalya wanted to explain the delicate issues and sought some advice about how to deal with them. "First, we have the issue of Ukrainian collaboration. How much of that do we need to show? It's not something people want to see." Leo argued that self-critical displays are morally and rhetorically the strongest and gave examples of the Washington and Berlin Holocaust Museums. But were Ukrainians ready? She thought not.

"Then we have Traian Popovici, in whom you are all so interested," Natalya continued. "What are we supposed to do with him? Was he a Wallenberg or a Schindler? I think he sold the permits to stay in the city for a lot of money. I suspect he was a pragmatist, not a humanitarian. And that brings us to the third problem, Jewish collaboration and the Jewish councils. Should we represent them? How?"

We shared with Oleg and Natalya some of the evidence we had, and they showed us theirs—primarily the introduction written by Yevgenya Finkel to *Juden aus Czernowitz,* the five-volume collection of testimonies she edited, in which she claims that all authorizations to remain in the city in 1941 were sold.[4] Clearly, we had different interpretations of limited sources. It was not likely we would come to an agreement on the character of Traian Popovici. Natalya was cynical. Oral sources, memoirs—she did not give them much credit, and yet she chose to believe Finkel's account.

Oleg continued to show us a few documents that would be in the display cases: a ghetto ordinance, some identification cards with the yellow star. "What about the photos of Jews on Kobylanska in 1942–43?" Leo asked. "See, here are two of them. [See figure 28.] The stars are very visible. We find these fascinating testaments to the will to normality in times of extremity. I'm sure your visitors will be moved as well."

It was hard to read Natalya's expression as she shook her head, hurriedly searching through her files. She pulled out a picture of a young man with a depressed look in his eyes, dressed in torn and patched clothing, wearing a large yellow star. The background was blank but the image, which we knew well since it was taken from Hugo Gold's *Geschichte der Juden in der Bukowina,* was labeled "Return from Transnistria."[5] "This is the one we must show," she said. "Look at the others—they are smiling. They give the wrong impression."

Figure 50. "This is the one we must show":
a photograph from Hugo Gold, ed., *Geschichte
der Juden in der Bukowina* (Tel Aviv: Oleamenu,
1962), vol. 2, plate 4

We left our meetings with Natalya glad that a museum was being installed, though chastened by the constraints to which the project was so evidently subject. We were also chuckling at the elaborate exhibition plans we had sketched out before we arrived in Chernivtsi and which now seemed positively fantastic. But we took solace in recognizing that, even though we may not have had much influence on the museum's mission or design, we ourselves gained a great deal during this trip. Working on the museum led us to think about the city's present and future even while contemplating how these might most effectively incorporate significant dimensions of its past. For the first time, we made close Chernivtsi friends with whom we shared interests and who were willing to include us in local debates and engage us in their own concerns. These, we knew, were relationships that would endure.

Figure 51. Photograph of the installation in room two in the Bukowina Jewish Museum of History and Culture, now open to the general public (Photograph by Natalya Shevchenko)

We did not attend the October celebrations. The event, by all reports, was generally predictable: festive marches, distinguished guests including the president of Ukraine, fireworks, laser shows, and performances by brass orchestras and school choirs. There were a few surprises, however. There was a folk festival in which the city's minority cultures (Romanian and Polish but also Jewish and Austro-German) presented their "culture and cooking." There was a concert commemorating the music immortalized by Josef Schmidt. And the museum did open, though to this date, no sign indicates its presence on the outside of the building. As far as we can tell from installation photos, the displays are varied, beautifully installed and lit, yet also conventional and limited. The city's Jewish history still remains contained, encased behind glass in two rooms of the former Jüdisches Haus.

The Czerno-L list members who attended the anniversary celebrations wrote enthusiastic reports about their experiences to the list. In their photos, the city is filled with people, lively and exuberant. Although they seemed to have felt included in the general festivities, they did heed Hardy Breier's challenge and spent October 11 on the ghetto walk, as an alternative and private commemoration ritual. And they checked on the progress of the plaque that, after great effort on the part of Miriam Taylor and other list members, would soon be installed on the house of Traian Popovici, to honor this Romanian mayor for saving some twenty thousand Jews from deportation and death. List members planned to return to Chernivtsi for the plaque's installation.

—⊷ ⋈⊹⋈ ⊶—

Our flight home was scheduled to leave on Sunday morning, June 1. But it turned out our travel agent had made a mistake, and we found ourselves with an extra day in Chernivtsi. I asked Felix if he could go with us to my mother's old apartment, Bogdana Khmelnitskogo 63. We had had little time for family reminiscences during this trip. And even less for unfinished business.

"I want to see and to touch the tile stove in the apartment again. Could you translate for me and explain to Nadja and Yuri why we're intruding on them?" I asked. I thought that touching the stoves would connect me again to my parents, bring them back to this place.

"Oh," Felix replied. "I forgot to tell you. I run into Nadja occasionally, and she always asks about you. We usually chat for a few minutes. A couple of years ago, I met her on the street and she asked me if I knew anyone who might want to buy tiles. 'Why?' I asked her. 'Because,' she told me, 'we finally dismantled the tile stoves in the apartment. We installed more modern radiators. But I don't know what to do with the tiles.'"

# NOTES

## PREFACE

Epigraph: Aharon Appelfeld, "Buried Homeland," trans. Jeffrey M. Green, *The New Yorker,* November 23, 1998, 61.

1. Paul Celan, "Speech on the Occasion of Receiving the Literature Prize of the Free Hanseatic City of Bremen," in *Selected Poems and Prose of Paul Celan,* ed. and trans. John Felstiner (New York: Norton, 2001), 395.

2. Handwritten document in the Franzos archive at the Wiener Stadt- und Landesbibliothek, cited in Ernest Wichner and Herbert Wiesner, eds. *In der Sprache der Mörder: Eine Literatur aus Czernowitz, Bukowina. Ausstellungsbuch,* (Berlin: Literaturhaus Berlin, 1993), 31.

3. The 1910 census of the region—the last under Austrian rule—counted 102,919 Jews in the Bukowina, 13 percent of the total population of the province. See, "Bevölkerungsentwicklung," in Albert Lichtblau, ed., *Als hätten wir dazugehört: Österreichisch-jüdische Lebensgeschichten aus der Habsburgmonarchie* (Vienna: Böhlau, 1999), 43–45.

4. See Stefan Zweig, *The World of Yesterday* [*Die Welt von gestern*], trans. Eden and Cedar Paul (New York: Viking Press, 1943).

5. Svetlana Boym, *The Future of Nostalgia* (New York: Basic Books, 2001), xiii.

6. See Florence Heymann, *Le Crépuscule des lieux: Identités juives de Czernowitz* (Paris: Stock, 2003).

7. Marianne Hirsch and Leo Spitzer, "Testimonial Objects: Memory, Gender, and Transmission," *Poetics Today* 27, 2 (summer 2006): 353–83.

8. We use this notion, "points of memory," as an alternative to Pierre Nora's well-known, but more nationally based *lieu* or site of memory. See Pierre Nora, *Realms of Memory: Rethinking the French Past,* ed. Lawrence D. Kritzman, trans. Arthur Goldhammer (New York: Columbia University Press, 1996).

9. James Young, "Toward a Received History of the Holocaust," *History and Theory* 36, 4 (December 1997): 21–43.

## ONE. "WHERE ARE YOU FROM?"

Epigraph: Benno Weiser Varon, cited in Volker Koepp's film Herr Zwilling und Frau Zimmermann, 1999. See also Benno Weiser Varon, *Professions of a Lucky Jew* (Cranbury, NJ: Associated University Presses, 1992), 17–19.

1. Eva Hoffman, *After Such Knowledge: Memory, History, and the Legacy of the Holocaust* (New York: Public Affairs, 2004), 25.

2. Leo Spitzer, *Hotel Bolivia: The Culture of Memory in a Refuge from Nazism* (New York: Hill and Wang, 1998).

3. Hoffman, *Lost in Translation, A Life in a New Language* (New York: E. P. Dutton, 1989), 84.

4. Marianne Hirsch, *Family Frames: Photography, Narrative, and Postmemory* (Cambridge: Harvard University Press, 1997).

5. For this pun we thank Florence Heymann.

6. For an earlier version of this description of Rosa's bookshelf, see Marianne Hirsch, "Editor's Column: Uprooted Words on a Bookshelf in Chernivtsi," *PMLA* 121, 4 (October 2006): 1400–1402.

7. Ilana Shmueli, "Über mein Czernowitz erzählen (1924–1944)," in Cécile Cordon and Helmut Kusdat, eds., *An der Zeiten Ränder: Czernowitz und die Bukowina* (Vienna: Theodor Kramer Gesellschaft, 2002), 166.

8. "Wo / in der österreichlosen Zeit / wächst mein Wort / in die Wurzeln / Ans Buchenland / denk ich / entwurzeltes Wort." (Where / in the austrianless time / does my word grow / become rooted / I think of / the Buchenland / uprooted word); Rose Ausländer, "Das Erbe," in Amy Colin and Alfred Kittner, eds., *Versunkene Dichtung der Bukowina* (Munich: Wilhelm Fink Verlag, 1994), 203.

## TWO. VIENNA OF THE EAST

Epigraph: Aharon Appelfeld, *The Story of a Life,* trans. Aloma Halter (New York: Schocken, 2004), 6.

1. On the Czernowitz Jewish Cemetery, see Alti Rodal, "Bukovina Cemeteries, Archives, and Oral History," *Avotaynu* 18, 3 (fall 2002): 9–15. Also see Othmar Andrée, *Czernowitzer Spaziergänge: Annäherungen an die Bukowina* (Berlin:

Rose Ausländer-Stiftung, 2000), 38–47, for a fascinating account of Andrée's walk through the Chernivtsi cemetery.

2. This information comes from Iuriy Prestupenko, a burial register assistant at the Chernivtsi cemetery. Also see Manfred Reifer, "Die Aera der moldauischen Fürsten (1360–1774)," in Hugo Gold, ed., *Geschichte der Juden in der Bukowina* (Tel Aviv: Olamenu, 1962), vol. 1, 10; and Rodal, "Bukowina Cemeteries."

3. N. M. Gelber, "Geschichte der Juden in der Bukowina (1774–1914)," in Gold, *Geschichte,* vol. 1, 57.

4. For a comparative overview of this discussion, see Leo Spitzer, *Lives in Between: The Experience of Marginality in a Century of Emancipation* (New York: Hill and Wang, 1999), chaps. 1–4. Also see Lichtblau, *Als hätten wir dazugehört,* chaps. 1–2; Oleksandr Masan, "Czernowitz in Vergangenheit und Gegenwart," in Herald Heppner, ed., *Czernowitz: Die Geschichte einer ungewöhnlichen Stadt* (Cologne: Böhlau Verlag, 2000); Emanuel Turczynski, *Geschichte der Bukowina in der Neuzeit: Zur Sozial- und Kulturgeschichte einer mitteleuropäischgeprägten Landschaft.* Vol. 14 of *Studien der Forschungsstelle Ostmitteleuropa an der Universität Dortmund* (Wiesbaden: Harrassowitz, 1993).

5. See Jean Ancel and Theodore Lavi, eds., *Encyclopedia of Jewish Communities: Romania* [translation of *Pinkas ha-kehilot: Romanyah*] (Jerusalem: Yad Vashem, 1980). The Sadagura entry is reproduced online at www.jewishgen.org/yizkor/pinkas_romania/rom2_00469.html.

6. Gelber, "Geschichte der Juden," 47–50; Hermann Sternberg, "Zur Geschichte der Juden in Czernowitz," in Gold, *Geschichte,* vol. 2, 31–33.

7. For a comparative perspective: the population of Jews in Vienna in 1910 was 175,318 out of 2,083,630 Viennese inhabitants—11.8 percent.

8. See, in Gold, *Geschichte,* Gelber, "Geschichte der Juden," vol. 1, 45–63; Sternberg, "Zur Geschichte der Juden," vol. 2, 29–38; and Leon Arie Schmelzer, "Die Juden in der Bukowina, 1914–1919," vol. 2, 67–68.

9. The *Reichsvolkschulgesetz,* 1869, and the *Landesschulgesetz für die Bukowina,* March 2, 1873. These were later modified and reduced, making attendance mandatory between the ages of seven and thirteen. See Hannelore Burger, "Mehrsprachigkeit und Unterrichtswesen in der Bukowina, 1869–1918," in Ilona Slawinski and Joseph P. Strelka, eds., *Die Bukowina: Vergangenheit und Gegenwart* (Bern: P. Lang, 1995), 97–98.

10. Paraphrased in Jakob Katz, *From Prejudice to Destruction: Anti-Semitism, 1700–1933* (Cambridge: Harvard University Press, 1980), 265–66.

11. Ibid., 266.

12. Poale Zion was the worldwide Marxist-oriented Jewish labor organization that worked to establish a model Jewish socialist republic in Palestine.

13. Kurt R. Grossmann, ed., *Michael Wurmbrand: The Man and His Work* (New York: Philosophical Library, 1956), 13, 121–23.

14. Heymann, *Le Crépuscule des lieux,* 19–43.

15. See Fred Sommer, *"Halb-Asien": German Nationalism and the Eastern European Works of Emil Franzos* (Stuttgart: Akademischer Verlag Hans-Dieter Heinz, 1984), 60–62.

16. The others were: Catholic and Protestant Austrians and Germans, Eastern Orthodox and Greek Catholic Ruthenians and Romanians, and Catholic Poles. According to the 1910 census, in which persons were asked to identify the "national group" to which they belonged, there were 26,618 Jews, 15,254 Ruthenians (Ukrainians), 14,893 Poles, 13,440 Romanians, and 12,747 Germans. Masan, "Czernowitz in Vergangenheit und Gegenwart," 26–30.

17. Aharon Appelfeld, "A city that was and is no longer," *Haaretz,* March 6, 2008.

18. Gregor von Rezzori, *The Snows of Yesteryear: Portraits for an Autobiography,* trans. H. F. B. d. Rothermann (New York: Vintage International, 1991), chap. 1, "Cassandra."

19. Oleksandr Dobrzans'kyj, "Czernowitz und die Ukrainer," in Heppner, *Czernowitz,* 45–51.

20. For examples, see von Rezzori, *Snows of Yesteryear.*

21. Amy Colin, *Paul Celan: Holograms of Darkness* (Bloomington: Indiana University Press, 1991), Introduction; Peter Rychlo, "Ukrainische Motive in der deutschprachingen Lyrik der Bukowina," in Cordon and Kusdat, *An der Zeiten Ränder,* 325–36.

22. See Valentina Glajar, "From Halb-Asien to Europe: Contrasting Representations of Austrian Bukovina," *Modern Austrian Literature* 34, 1/2 (2001): 1–20.

23. Karl Emil Franzos, *Aus Halb-Asien: Kulturbilder aus Galizien, Südrussland, Bukowina und Rumänien* (Leipzig: Verlag von Dunder un Humblod, 1876). See also Marianne Hirsch and Leo Spitzer, "Die Sprachen der Czernowitzer Juden: Zwischen Assimilation und Widerstand," in Amy D. Colin, Elke V. Kotowski, and Anna D. Ludewig, eds., *Spuren eines Europäers: Karl Emil Franzos als Mittler zwischen den Kulturen* (Potsdam: Moses Mendelsohn Zentrum, 2008); Winfried Menninghaus, "'Czernowitz/Bukowina' als Topos deutsch-jüdischer Geschichte und Literatur," *Merkur* 3, 4 (1999): 345–57; Sommer, *"Halb-Asien";* Carl Steiner, *Karl Emil Franzos, 1848–1904: Emancipator and Assimilationist* (New York: Peter Lang, 1990).

24. David Sha'ari, "The Jewish Community of Czernowitz under Habsburg and Romanian Rule," *Shvut* 6, 22 (1997): 165.

25. The nationalist-exclusivist view looked to the writings of Wilhelm Schlegel and J. G. Fichte for its philosophical underpinnings. See C. A. Macartney, *National States and National Minorities* (London: Oxford University Press, 1934), 98–99.

26. Schmelzer, "Die Juden in der Bukowina," 91–92, 95.

27. See Max Weinreich, Zalmen Reyzen, and Khayim Broyde, eds., *Die Ershte Yidishe Shprakh-Konferentz: Barkhtn, dokumentn un opklangen fun der tscherno-*

*vitser konferents, 1908* (Vilna: YIVO, 1931); see also Joshua A. Fishman, "Attracting a Following to High-Culture Functions for a Language of Everyday Life: The Role of the Tschernovits Language Conference in the 'Rise of Yiddish,'" *International Journal of the Sociology of Language* 24 (1980): 43–73.

28. For a brief but excellent overview, see "Hasidism," in Gershon David Hundert, ed., *The YIVO Encyclopedia of Jews in Eastern Europe* (New Haven: Yale University Press, 2008), vol. 1, 659–81.

29. Joshua A. Fishman, *Ideology, Society, and Language: The Odyssey of Nathan Birnbaum* (Ann Arbor: Karoma Publishers, 1987), 38, 43–54; Emanuel S. Goldsmith, *Modern Yiddish Culture: The Story of the Yiddish Language Movement,* expanded ed. (New York: Fordham University Press, 1997), 41; Dovid Katz, "Language: Yiddish," in Hundert, ed., *The YIVO Encyclopedia of Jews in Eastern Europe,* vol. 1, 979–87.

30. Albert Lichtblau and Michael John, "Jewries in Galicia and Bukovina," in Sander Gilman and Milton Shain, eds., *Jewries at the Frontier* (Champaign: University of Illinois Press, 1999), 80; Robert D. King, "The Czernowitz Conference in Retrospect," in Dov-Ber Kerler, ed., *Politics of Yiddish: Studies in Language, Literature, and Society* (Walnut Creek: Altamira, n.d. [c. 1998]); Ruth Kaswan, "Yiddish Language Conference in Czernowitz" (http://czernowitz.org/kaswan-ch2.html), 4 (Joseph Kissman [1889–1968], Ruth Kaswan's father, was one of the youngest participants in Czernowitz Conference).

31. At the time of the Yiddish language conference, Birnbaum's spoken Yiddish was still weak, and he largely continued to communicate in his native German—much to the chagrin of a number of attendees and amusement of Yiddish-language journalists. See King, "The Czernowitz Conference in Retrospect," 42.

32. Ibid., 43–45; Goldsmith, *Modern Yiddish Culture,* 200–208.

33. The Bund (Algemeyner Yidisher Arbeter Bund or Jewish Labor Bund of Russia, Poland, and Lithuania) was a socialist worker's organization created in 1897 in Vilna. It took hold in Romania in 1922 and became particularly popular in Bessarabia and the Bukowina. The Bund opposed Zionism and placed its hopes in the success of a proletarian revolution to obtain rights for Jews in the countries in which they resided. See Daniel Blatman, "Bund," trans. David Facher, in Hundert, *The YIVO Encyclopedia of Jews in Eastern Europe,* 274–80. See also Heymann, *Le Crépuscule des lieux,* 239–40; Joseph Kissman, "Zur Geschichte der jüdischen Arbeiterbewegung 'Bund' in der Bukowina," in Gold, *Geschichte,* vol. 1, 144.

34. *Die Ershte Yidishe Shprakh-Konferentz,* 82, cited in Goldsmith, *Modern Yiddish Culture,* 213.

35. For Peretz's entire proposal, see Goldsmith, *Modern Yiddish Culture,* 195–96.

36. See Fishman, *Ideology, Society, and Language,* 55; Goldsmith, *Modern Yiddish Culture,* 236.

37. Heymann, *Le Crépuscule des lieux,* 183–84.

38. See Goldsmith, *Modern Yiddish Culture,* 217–21.

39. David G. Roskies, *A Bridge of Longing: The Lost Art of Yiddish Storytelling* (Cambridge: Harvard University Press, 1995), 233.

40. Schmelzer, "Die Juden in der Bukowina," 67.

41. Cited in Carola Gottzmann, ed., *Unnerkannt und (un)bekannt: Deutsche Literatur in Mittel- und Osteuropa* (Tübingen: Francke Verlag, 1991), 209.


### THREE. STROLLING THE HERRENGASSE

Epigraph: Michel de Certeau, *The Practice of Everyday Life,* trans. Steven Rendall (Berkeley: University of California Press, 1984), 108.

1. Hermann Mittelmann, *Illustrierter Führer durch die Bukowina, 1907* (Czernowitz: Verlag der Buchhandlung Schally, 1907–8; republished by Helmut Kusdat, Vienna: Mandelbaum Verlag, 2001).

2. Raimund Lang, ed., *Czernowitz: Ein historischer Stadtführer* (Innsbruck: Traditionsverband "Katholische Czernowitzer Pennäler," 1998), 25–26.

3. Günther Zamp Kelp and Julia Lienemeyer, eds., *Czernowitz Tomorrow: Architecture and Identity in the Surge of Central Eastern Europe* (Düsseldof: Institut für Aussenwirtschaft, 2004), 50; our translation from the German in this bilingual edition.

4. Portions of the rest of this chapter appear in an article, Marianne Hirsch and Leo Spitzer, "Incongruous Images: Before, During, and After the Holocaust," *History and Theory* 48, 4 (December 2009).

5. For explanations of the technology of street photography see "Scott's Photographica Collection," Chicago Ferrotype Company / Mandelete Postcard Camera at www.vintagephoto.tv/index.shtml. See also the exhibition on "The Photographic Studios of Eastern Europe," www.museumoffamilyhistory.com.

6. Roland Barthes, *Camera Lucida: Reflections on Photography,* trans. Richard Howard (New York: Hill and Wang, 1981), 76–77.

7. See the excellent analysis of this process by Mariana Hausleitner, *Die Rumänisierung der Bukowina* (München: R. Oldenbourg Verlag, 2001). See also Carol Iancu, *Jews in Romania 1866–1919: From Exclusion to Emancipation* (Boulder, CO: East European Monographs, 1996), 173–82.

8. The baccalaureate exam had been given for many years under the Austrian regime, but was discontinued in 1908. It was reinstituted in 1925 as a way to screen high school seniors for entrance to universities. Critics, justifiably, saw the reintroduction of the test, and its administration largely by government-appointed examiners willing to use it against students belonging to minority nationalities in the newly acquired provinces, as blatant state-supported discrimination against them. See Irina Livezeanu, *Cultural Politics in Greater Romania: Regionalism,*

*Nation Building, and Ethnic Struggle, 1918–1930* (Ithaca, NY: Cornell University Press, 1995), 79.

9. See ibid., 80. Also see Berthold Brandmarker, "David Fallik," in Gold, *Geschichte der Juden in der Bukowina,* vol. 2, 174–75.

10. Totu was then active in the proto-fascist Brotherhood of the Cross. Some years later, after receiving a law degree from the University of Iași, he became a leader in the fascist Romanian Iron Guard. He fought in the Spanish civil war on Franco's side. See Livezeanu, *Cultural Politics in Greater Romania,* 85.

11. Brandmarker, "David Fallik," 174–76; Josef Ebner, "Aus der Welt von Gestern in der jüdischen Renaissance-Bewegung," in Gold, *Geschichte,* vol. 2, 128; Radu Ioanid, *The Holocaust in Romania: The Fate of Jews and Gypsies in Fascist Romania, 1940–1944* (Chicago: Ivan R. Dee, 2000), 17; Livezeanu, *Cultural Politics in Greater Romania,* 86; Romanian Ministry of Foreign Affairs Archives, RG 25.006M, roll 4, "Chronology of Anti-Semitism in Romania, 1926–1927," 18 (on microfilm, U.S. Holocaust Memorial Museum).

12. Pearl Fichman, *Before Memories Fade* (n.p.: Booksurge Publishing, 2005), 15.


FOUR. THE IDEA OF CZERNOWITZ

Ilana Shmueli, "Über mein Czernowitz erzählen," in Cordon and Kusdat, eds., *An der Zeiten Ränder,* 166.

1. Livezeanu, *Cultural Politics in Greater Romania,* 70.

2. Ibid., 58–60; Hausleitner, *Die Rumänisierung der Bukowina,* 175–76. Also see Heymann, *Le Crépuscule des lieux,* 233–71.

3. Mariana Hausleitner, "Juden und Antisemitismus in der Bukowina zwischen 1918 und 1944," in Krista Zach, ed., *Rumänien im Brennpunkt: Sprache und Politik, Identität und Ideologie in Wandel* (Munich: Südostdeutsches Kulturwerk, 1998), 155.

4. Hausleitner, *Die Rumänisierung der Bukowina,* 141. As Livezeanu, *Cultural Politics in Greater Romania,* 65, indicates about the effort to displace the use of Ukrainian and German: "An ordinance in spring 1927 ... demanded that all advertisements, posters, cinema, theatre, and concert programs be published either in Romanian or bilingually."

5. In Livezeanu, *Cultural Politics in Greater Romania,* 271.

6. Despite the citizenship rights and protection clauses included in the new 1924 constitution, many Jews in the Northern Bukowina who could not provide the required documentation proving residence continued to be recognized only as "subjects," not as enfranchised citizens.

7. For Codreanu and the Iron Guard, see Corneliu Zelea Codreanu, *For My Legionaries (The Iron Guard)* (Reedy, WV: Library Bell Publications, 1990); Armin Heinen, *Die Legion "Erzengel Michael" in Rumänien: Soziale Bewegung*

*und politische Organisation* (Munich: R. Oldenburg Verlag, 1986); Radu Ioanid, *The Sword of the Archangel* (Boulder, CO: East European Monographs, 1990). Also see Zvi Yavetz, "An Eyewitness Note: Reflections on the Rumanian Iron Guard," *Journal of Contemporary History* 26 (1991): 597–610. For a contemporary eyewitness report on the situation for Jews in Romania in the late 1920s, see The Joint Foreign Committee of the Board of Deputies of British Jews and the Anglo-Jewish Association, *The Jewish Minority in Roumania: Correspondence with the Roumanian Government Respecting the Grievances of the Jews. Presented to the Board of Deputies of British Jews and the Council of the Anglo-Jewish Association, June 1927,* 2nd ed. (London: Joint Foreign Committee of the Board of Deputies of British Jews and the Anglo-Jewish Association, 1928). For excellent accounts of Romanian anti-Semitism, see Alexandra Laignel-Lavastine, *Cioran, Eliade, Ionesco: À l'oubli du fascisme, Trois intellectuels roumains dans la tourmente du siècle* (Paris: Presses Universitaires de France, 2002); Mihail Sebastian, *Journal, 1933–1945: The Fascist Years,* trans. Patrick Camiller (Chicago: Ivan R. Dee, 2000).

8. In the summer of 1930, a fire that destroyed practically all of the houses on the main street of Borşa where most of the town's Jews resided was viewed by many as an act of arson instigated by anti-Semitic agitators. Fortunately no one died in this affair. See Hausleitner, "Juden und Antisemitismus," 157; Hausleitner, *Die Rumänisierung,* 220–24; Livezeanu, *Cultural Politics in Greater Romania,* 287, 291–94.

9. Hausleitner, *Die Rumänisierung,* 266–75.

10. Livezeanu, *Cultural Politics in Greater Romania,* 276–77; Paul A. Shapiro, "Prelude to Dictatorship in Romania: The National Christian Party in Power, December 1937-February 1938," *Canadian-American Slavic Studies* 8 (spring 1974): 45–88.

11. From the German by Hermann Sternberg: "man müsse behutsam und zielsicher vorgehen 'um den Juden allmählich das Brot aus dem Munde zu nehmen.'" See Sternberg, "Zur Geschichte der Juden in Czernowitz," in Gold, *Geschichte der Juden in der Bukowina,* vol. 2, 40. After completing his stint in the Liberal government, Nistor was appointed rector of the University in Cernăuţi. Also see Hausleitner, "Juden und Antisemitismus, 158–59.

12. The definition of *Romanian* in this measure was left ambiguous—not clearly specifying whether ethnicity or citizenship was the applicable category of identification. But the political intention of the Liberals was clear: to undercut extreme advocates of Romanianization for whom Romanian citizenship belonged only to those with "Romanian blood." Hausleitner, "Juden und Antisemitismus," 158–59; Joshua Starr, "Jewish Citizenship in Rumania (1878–1940)," *Jewish Social Studies* 3 (1941): 68.

13. Heinen, *Die Legion,* 309.

14. Shapiro, "Prelude to Dictatorship," 46.

15. Ibid., 72–73.

16. Hausleitner, "Juden und Antisemitismus," 160–61; Starr, "Jewish Citizenship in Rumania," 57–58, 72–80.

17. Shapiro, "Prelude to Dictatorship," 81.

18. Alfred Kittner, *Erinnerungen, 1906–1991,* ed. Edith Silbermann (Aachen: Rimbaud, 1996), 41–42.

19. Shapiro, "Prelude to Dictatorship," 68–69, 73–74.

20. Carl Hirsch, "A Life in the Twentieth Century: A Memoir," unpublished manuscript (Leo Baeck Institute, New York, 1996, www.ghostsofhome.com), 54. See also Israel Chalfen's account of the Antschel (Celan) family's deliberations: Paul Celan's father suggested Paul interrupt his studies in 1938 so the family could buy visas to South America, but Paul insisted on traveling to Germany and then Paris because he did not agree with the need to emigrate. Israel Chalfen, *Paul Celan: A Biography of His Youth,* trans. Maximilian Bleyleben (New York: Persea Books, 1991), 89.

21. On these movements, see, in Gold, *Geschichte,* Chaim Ehrlich, "Zur Charakteristik der Zionistischen Bewegung in der Bukowina zwischen beiden Weltkriegen," vol. 2, 133–56, and M. D. Beinisch, C. Ehrenkranz, N. M. Gelber, "Die Hebräische Sprachbewegung in der Bukowina," vol. 2, 163–64; Heymann, *La Crépuscule des lieux,* 221–32.

22. Hirsch, "A Life in the Twentieth Century," 13, 16.

23. While the First Aliyah to Ottoman Palestine followed the pogroms in Czarist Russia in 1881–82, the Second Aliyah occurred between 1904 and 1914, following a series of pogroms and other anti-Semitic outbreaks in Russia and Poland, notably the Kishinev pogrom in Bessarabia in 1903 and the pogroms following the Russian revolution of 1905.

24. Jaakow Polsiuk-Padan, "Die Geschichte des 'Haschomer Hazair' in der Bukowina," in Gold, *Geschichte,* vol. 1, 145–52.

25. The first members of Hashomer Hatzair to move to Palestine went with the Third Aliyah (1919–23), and established their kibbutzim there starting in 1927.

26. On Betar, see below. Blau-Weiss (Blue-White) was the first Jewish youth movement established in Germany. Active from 1912 to 1929, it advocated emigration to Palestine, manual labor, and rural settlement. These and other Jewish youth organizations were active in the Bukowina in the interwar years. On Jewish youth groups in Cernăuți, see Zvi Yavetz, "Youth Movements in Czernowitz," in Gerd Korman, ed., *Hunter and Hunted: Human History of the Holocaust* (New York: Viking, 1973), and Heymann, *Le Crépuscule des lieux,* 221–32.

27. See Jakob Schieber and A. Liquornik, "Der Jugendbund 'Betar,'" in Gold, *Geschichte,* vol. 2, 176–77; "Betar," in *Encyclopedia Judaica* (Jerusalem: Ketar Publishing House, 1972).

28. Hirsch, "A Life in the Twentieth Century," 39, 41.

29. Rose Ausländer, "Erinnerungen an eine Stadt," in Wichner and Wiesner, eds., *In der Sprache der Mörder*, 33. On Bukowina German, see also Georg Dorzdowski, *Damals in Czernowitz und rundum: Erinnerungen eines Altösterreichers* (Klagenfurt: Verlag der kleinen Zeitung Kärnten, 1984), 69–77; Edith Silbermann, "Deutsch—die Muttersprache der meisten Bukowina Juden," in Cordon and Kusdat, *An der Zeiten Ränder*, 39–44; Emanuel Hacken, "Das Czernowitzer Deutsch," http://czernowitz.ehpes.com.

30. Zvi Yavetz, *Erinnerungen an Czernowitz: Wo Menschen und Bücher lebten* (Munich: C. H. Beck, 2007), 200.

31. Drozdowski, *Damals in Czernowitz*, 14; Yavetz, *Erinnerungen an Czernowitz*, 201; Czernowitz-L posting by Hardy Breier, July 2, 2008.

32. Czernowitz-L posting by Hardy Breier, June 26, 2008.

33. Vera Hacken, *Kinder- und Jugendjahre mit Eliesar Steinbarg* (Israel: J. L. Peretz Verlag, 1969), typescript translated from Yiddish into German by Othmar Andrée, 13, 14.

34. See Livezeanu, *Cultural Politics in Greater Romania*, 267–68, on other student disruptions of Jewish cultural events in Romania during the early 1920s.

35. Yavetz, *Erinnerungen an Czernowitz*, 175, 179.

36. Cited in Hilde Bechert and Klaus Drexel's documentary about Paul Celan, *Erst jenseits der Kastanien ist die Welt* (Arte, 1994).

37. Andrei Corbea-Hoisie, ed., *Jüdisches Städtebild Czernowitz* (Frankfurt am Main: Jüdischer Verlag im Suhrkamp, 1998), 20–23.

38. Karl Kraus, the noted Viennese satirist, had a great following in Czernowitz, even though he disappointed Jewish intellectuals when he left Judaism and was baptized as a Catholic. Although he eventually also left the Catholic Church, he notoriously failed to repudiate Hitler.

39. The proposed anthology "Die Buche" formed a centerpiece of the 1993 Literaturhaus Berlin exhibition "In der Sprache der Mörder: Eine Literatur aus Czernowitz, Bukowina." The following account is based on the materials published in the exhibition catalogue, Wichner and Wiesner, eds., *In der Sprache der Mörder*. Parts of this account appeared in an earlier version as Marianne Hirsch, "1945: An official Soviet stamp permits the exportation of cultural documents including a draft version of *Die Buche*, a never-published anthology of German-Jewish poetry from the Bukowina found in the estate of Alfred Margul-Sperber," in Sander L. Gilman and Jack Zipes, eds. *Yale Companion to Jewish Writing and Thought in German Culture, 1096–1996* (New Haven: Yale University Press, 1997), 627–33.

40. Wichner and Wiesner, *In der Sprache*, 182–84.

41. These letters are cited in ibid., 189–99. In some of the final drafts of the "Buche" anthology, the very poets who initially declined, like Victor Wittner, are amply represented. Evidently, they had changed their minds, out of an ambiva-

lent attachment to an idea of a city that was to survive even further political and ideological assaults.

42. Ibid., 199. Margul-Sperber's estate contains three handwritten and typed versions of the anthology, the third including poems written during and after the Second World War as well; see Amy Colin, "Introduction," in Colin and Kittner, eds., *Versunkene Dichtung*, 14. Significantly, a poetry anthology did appear in Czernowitz in 1939. This work, entitled *Bukowiner deutsches Dichterbuch* (German Poetry Book of the Bukowina), did not include a single Jewish writer. Not until 1991 was an anthology of Bukowina German and German-Jewish poetry (though one not at all based on the selections of "Die Buche") to appear in Germany; this is Klaus Werner's *Fäden ins Nichts gespannt: Deutschsprachige Literatur in der Bukowina* (Threads Stretched into the Void: German-Language Literature of the Bukowina). Finally, in 1994, sixty years after the original project, the heavily revised version of the long-forgotten anthology appeared as *Versunkene Dichtung der Bukowina* (Submerged Poetry of the Bukowina), edited by Amy Colin and Alfred Kittner and dedicated to the memory of Alfred Margul-Sperber. The original manuscript was significantly supplemented with additional selections by Kittner, who dedicated his postwar life to this project but who died before its publication. *Versunkene Dichtung der Bukowina* contains the work of non-Jewish German writers, as well as Jewish ones. Appearing in Germany in the 1990s, however, this volume certainly has a very different meaning than the drafts on which it is based.

43. Wichner and Wiesner, *In der Sprache*, 110–15.

44. Colin and Kittner, *Versunkene Dichtung*, 294.

45. Cited in Colin, *Paul Celan*, 20.

46. Colin and Kittner, *Versunkene Dichtung*, 189, 187.

47. See Colin, *Paul Celan*, 20–22, 39–40; Andrei Corbea-Hoisie, "Deutschsprachige Judendichtung aus Czernowitz," in B. Hain and H. Gaisbauer, eds., *Unverloren—trotz Allem* [Not Lost, After All] (Vienna: Mandelbaum Verlag, 1999); and Menninghaus, "'Czernowitz/Bukowina' als Topos," 356–57.

48. Itzik Manger, *The World According to Itzik: Selected Poetry and Prose*, trans. and ed. Leonard Wolf (New Haven: Yale University Press, 2002), 236–37.

49. Yitskhok Niborski, "Shteynbarg, Eliezer," trans. Yankl Salant, in Hundert, ed., *The YIVO Encyclopedia of the Jews in Eastern Europe*, ed. Gershon David Hundert (New Haven: Yale University Press, 2008), 1739–40. Arthur Kolnik, "'Der jüdische Schulverein' in Czernowitz," in Corbea-Hoisie, ed., *Jüdisches Städtebild Czernowitz*, 181–90; Ruth Wisse cited in Roskies, *A Bridge of Longing*, 235.

50. Roskies, *A Bridge of Longing*, 233.

51. Alfred Kittner, "Erinnerungen an den Poeten Itzik Manger," in Corbea-Hoisie, ed., *Jüdisches Städtebild Czernowitz*, 198.

52. Hacken, *Kinder- und Jugendjahre*, 16, 17.

# FIVE. "ARE WE REALLY IN THE SOVIET UNION?"

Epigraph: Carl Hirsch, "A Life in the Twentieth Century," 63.

1. Dorothea Sella, *Der Ring des Prometheus: Denksteine im Herzen. Eine auf Wahrheit beruhende Romantrilogie: Stawropol, Tbilissi, Czernowitz* (Jerusalem: Rubin Mass Verlag, 1996), 13.

2. Hedwig Brenner, *Mein 20. Jahrhundert* (Brugg, Swizerland: Munda, 2006), 134–38.

3. Carl Hirsch, "A Life in the Twentieth Century," 55.

4. George F. Kennan, *Russia and the West under Lenin and Stalin* (Boston: Little, Brown and Co., 1960), 332.

5. Ibid., 332.

6. The secret protocol was modified in September 1939 to include Lithuania in the Soviet sphere. In return, the Germans received a larger portion of Poland.

7. Quoted in Nicholas Dima, *Bessarabia and Bukovina: The Soviet-Romanian Territorial Dispute* (Boulder, CO: East European Monographs, 1982), 27.

8. Quoted in David J. Dallin and Leon Dennan, *Soviet Russia's Foreign Policy, 1939–1942* (New Haven: Yale University Press, 1942), 237–38.

9. Dima, *Bessarabia and Bukovina,* 28–30; Kennan, *Russia and the West,* 339–40.

10. Dallin and Dennan, *Bessarabia and Bukovina,* 239; *New York Times,* June 30 and July 1, 1940.

11. Hirsch, "A Life in the Twentieth Century," 57.

12. Manfred Reifer, "Ein Jahr Sowjet-Rußland," in Corbea-Hoisie, ed., *Jüdisches Städtebild Czernowitz,* 243.

13. Hirsch, "A Life in the Twentieth Century," 58.

14. Heymann, *Le Crépuscule des lieux,* 272.

15. Hirsch, "A Life in the Twentieth Century," 58.

16. Reifer, "Ein Jahr Sowjet-Rußland," 243; Fichman, *Before Memories Fade,* 57.

17. Reifer, "Ein Jahr Sowjet-Rußland," 244.

18. Fichman, *Before Memories Fade,* 61.

19. Hausleitner, *Die Rumänisierung der Bukowina,* 363; Dov Levin, "The Jews and the Inception of Soviet Rule in Bucovina," *Soviet Jewish Affairs* 6, 2 (1976): 55.

20. Hausleitner, *Die Rumänisierung der Bukowina,* 358; Levin, "The Jews and the Inception of Soviet Rule," 60; Reifer, "Ein Jahr Sowjet-Rußland,"245.

21. Manfred Reifer, "Geschichte der Juden in der Bukowina (1919–1944)," in Gold, *Geschichte,* vol. 2, 12; Levin, "The Jews and the Inception of Soviet Rule," 57.

22. Hausleitner, *Die Rumänisierung der Bukowina,* 357, 358.

23. Chalfen, *Paul Celan,* 111.

24. Lilly Hirsch, interviews in Düsseldorf, Germany, October 1998.

25. Levin, "The Jews and the Inception of Soviet Rule," 62–63.

26. For an account of Stalin's national policy regarding Jews, Yiddish, and the

Jewish national Oblast (province) in Birobidzhan, see Robert Weinberg, *Stalin's Forgotten Zion* (Berkeley: University of California Press, 1998).

27. Hardy Mayer, "Czernowitz and Yiddish—random reminiscences of a budding septuagenerian," http://czernowitz.org.mayer.html.

28. Levin, "The Jews and the Inception of Soviet Rule," 65, quoting "Di oyspruvn in di shuln fun tsofn Bukovine—muter shprakh," *Der Shtern*, June 15, 1941.

29. Fichman, *Before Memories Fade*, 59.

30. Ibid., 63. NKVD is the acronym for what translates as the People's Commissariat for Internal Affairs, the Soviet "internal security" agency. Later the NKVD became the KGB, the Committee for State Security.

31. Yavetz, " Youth Movements in Czernowitz," 138–39.

32. Sella, *Der Ring des Prometheus*, 19.

33. Yavetz, "Youth Movements in Czernowitz," 138.

34. Hirsch, "A Life in the Twentieth Century," 65.

35. Hausleitner, *Die Rumänisierung der Bukowina*, 366.

36. Levin, "The Jews and the Inception of Soviet Rule," 62; Fichman, *Before Memories Fade*, 60.

37. Hirsch, "A Life in the Twentieth Century," 67.

38. Among the memoirs recounting the experiences of these deportations, see esp. the two by Margit Bartfeld-Feller, *Dennoch Mensch geblieben: Von Czernowitz durch Sibirien nach Israel, 1923–1996* (Constance: Hartung-Gorre Verlag, 1996) and *Nicht ins Nichts gespannt: Von Czernowitz nach Sibirien deportiert. Jüdische Schicksale* (Constance: Hartung-Gorre Verlag, 1998).

39. Levin, "The Jews and the Inception of Soviet Rule," 59. See also Hausleitner, *Die Rumänisierung der Bukowina*, 363–66.

40. Fichman, *Before Memories Fade*, 66, 67.

41. Reifer, "Ein Jahr Sowjet-Rußland," 251, 252, 254.

42. Levin, "The Jews and the Inception of Soviet Rule," 59.

43. Paraphrase of oral accounts by Lilly Hirsch over many years.

44. Paraphrase of oral accounts by Lotte and Carl Hirsch over many years.

45. Excerpted from Sella, *Der Ring des Prometheus*, 27–29.

46. Excerpted from Fichman, *Before Memories Fade*, 68–69.

47. Paraphrase of accounts by Alex and Peter Flexor, Paris, July 1999.

48. Paraphrase of oral accounts by Carl and Lotte Hirsch and from Hirsch, "A Life in the Twentieth Century," 70.

### SIX. THE CROSSROADS

Epigraphs: Paul Celan, "Aschenglorie," in Felstiner, *Paul Celan*, 260–61; Jacques Derrida, *Sovereignties in Question: The Poetics and Politics of Witnessing*, ed. Thomas Dutoit and Outi Pasanen (New York: Fordham University Press, 2005), 67.

1. An earlier version of this account appeared as Marianne Hirsch and Leo Spitzer, "'We would not have come without you': Generations of Nostalgia," *American Imago* 59, 3 (fall 2002): 253 -76; reprinted in Kate Hodgkin and Susannah Radstone, eds., *Contested Pasts: The Politics of Memory* (London: Routledge, 2003), 79–96.

2. See Matthias Zwilling's brief account in Jewgenija Finkel and Markus Winkler, eds., *Juden aus Czernowitz: Ghetto, Deportation, Vernichtung, 1941–1944, Ueberlebende berichten,* trans. (from Russian into German) Kateryna Stesevych (Constance: Hartung-Gorre Verlag, 2004), 105–7.

3. Traian Popovici, *Spovedania Testimony,* ed. Th. Wexler, trans. Viviane Prager (Bucharest: Fundația Dr. W. Filderman, 2001), 76–90.

4. Toni Morrison, *Beloved* (New York: Alfred A. Knopf, 1987), 36.

5. Paul Celan, "Aschenglorie," in Felstiner, *Paul Celan,* 260–61. See Derrida's extensive discussion of these lines in *Sovereignties in Question*, chap. 2.

6. Paul Celan, "Die Posaunenstelle," in Felstiner, *Paul Celan,* 360–61. See Felstiner's reading of this poem's Biblical sources and meanings, 271–73. In the bibliography, Felstiner translates "Pausane" as "Trumpet," which we prefer. A shofar is a trumpet made of a ram's horn which is traditionally sounded in the synagogue during the high holidays.

7. For a discussion of the useful notion of cowitnessing, see Irene Kacandes, *Talk Fiction: Literature and the Talk Explosion* (Lincoln: University of Nebraska Press, 2001), 95–140.

8. Hirsch, "A Life in the Twentieth Century," 84.

9. "Le Serment de Strasbourg" is the oath sworn by Charles the Bald and Louis the German against their third brother, the Emperor Lohair I, in 842, prior to the 843 treaty of Verdun in which the three divided the kingdom of their grandfather, Charlemagne. The oath is thought to exemplify one of the oldest known written versions of French.


SEVEN. MAPS TO NOWHERE

Epigraph: Art Spiegelman, *Maus: A Survivor's Tale,* vol. 1 (New York: Pantheon, 1986), 125.

1. Ibid.

2. Sidy Flexor, audiotaped interview by Alexandre Flexor, Evian, France, c. 1995; translated from German; tapes held by Alexandre Flexor.

3. See Patrick Desbois, *The Holocaust by Bullets: A Priest's Journey to Uncover the Truth Behind the Murder of 1.5 Million Jews* (New York: Palgrave Macmillan, 2008).

4. Frederic L. Bernard, *In the Eye of the Storm: Surviving in Nazi-Occupied Poland, a Memoir* (Sarasota, FL: Frederic L. Bernard, M.D., 1995).

5. Jakob Stejuk, "Flucht" [Flight], in Finkel and Winkler, *Juden aus Czernowitz,* 108, 109.

6. Sella, *Der Ring des Prometheus,* 71, 76, 77.

7. "The Soviet Union," *Encyclopedia of the Holocaust,* ed. Israel Gutman (New York: Macmillan, 1990), 1387.

8. Sella, *Der Ring des Prometheus,* 70, 72.

9. Ibid., 108.

10. Ibid., 91, 128.

11. Paul Celan, "With a Changing Key," in Felstiner, *Paul Celan,* 73.

12. Only recently, for example, have historians begun to study seriously the experiences of survivors who spent the wartime in the Soviet Union. As Atina Grossman has argued, the Jewish historical commissions collecting testimonies after liberation focused specifically on the experiences of the camps, of hiding, passing, and partisan warfare rather than on survival in the Soviet Union—this in spite of the fact that most Jews who survived the Second World War did so in the USSR. See Grossman, *Jews, Germans, and Allies: Close Encounters in Occupied Germany* (Princeton: Princeton University Press, 2007).

13. Rachelle Rosenzweig, *Russische Eisblumen: 35 Jahre in sowjetischer Unfreiheit* (Frankfurt am Main: Haag and Herchen Verlag, 1993).

14. Bernard, *In the Eye of the Storm,* 9.


EIGHT. THE SPOT ON THE LAPEL

Epigraph: Hoffman, *Lost in Translation,* 23.

1. For an earlier and fuller discussion of this photograph in the specific context of the use of archival images in second-generation literature and art, see Marianne Hirsch and Leo Spitzer, "What's Wrong with This Picture? Archival Photographs in Contemporary Narratives," *Journal of Modern Jewish Studies* 5, 2 (July 2006): 229–52; also translated as "Erinnerungspunkte: Schoahfotografien in zeitgenössischen Erzählungen," *Fotogeschichte: Beiträge zur Geschichte und Ästhetik der Fotografie* 95 (2005): 29–44.

2. For Florence Heymann's diary of our trip, initially presented to her father along with photos she had taken in Chernivtsi, see *Le Crépuscule des lieux,* 359–386. In the book she does not write about how her father received this gift, but she does end her book with a haunting dream: "my father comes to visit me. Where am I? I don't know but I am surrounded by my family and friends. I walk up to my father who opens his arms to embrace me and seems so happy to see me. '*Come,* he says, *let's talk. We have so much to say to each other.*' But he remains stubbornly silent, and as he looks for a place to sit he almost falls into the void. With horror, I realize that he is blind" (390–91).

3. See Matatias Carp, *Cartea Neagră: Suferinţele Evreilor din România.*

vol. 3 (Bucharest: Editura Diogene, 1996; orig. pub. 1946–48) and *Holocaust in Rumania, Facts and Documents on the Annihilation of Rumania's Jews, 1940–44*, abridged trans. of *Cartea Neagră* by Seán Murphy (Budapest: Primor Publishing, 1994); I. C. Butnaru, *Waiting for Jerusalem: Surviving the Holocaust in Romania* (Westport, CT: Greenwood Press, 1993); Randolph L. Braham, *The Destruction of Romanian and Ukrainian Jews during the Antonescu Era* (New York: East European Monographs, No. 433, 1997); Jean Ancel, ed., *Documents Concerning the Fate of Romanian Jewry during the Holocaust*, 12 vols. (New York: Beate Klarsfeld Foundation, 1986); Radu Ioanid, *The Holocaust in Romania;* Raul Hilberg, *The Destruction of the European Jews*, vol. 2 (New York: Holmes and Meier 1986); Hannah Arendt, *Eichmann in Jerusalem: A Report on the Banality of Evil* (New York: Penguin, 1994).

4. Arendt, *Eichmann in Jerusalem*, 190.

5. Nathan Getzler, "Tagebuchblätter aus Czernowitz und Transnistrien (1941–1942)" [Diary Pages from Czernowitz and Transnistria], in Gold, *Geschichte der Juden in der Bukowina*, vol. 2, 55.

6. Cited in Ioanid, *The Holocaust in Romania*, 122, 123.

7. Carp, *Cartea Neagră*, vol. 3, 96.

8. Ibid., 251–52.

9. Ibid., 35. Also see Brenner, *Mein 20. Jahrhundert*, 173–76.

10. Brenner, *Mein 20. Jahrhundert*, 177–88.

11. Carp, *Cartea Neagră*, vol. 3, 989.

12. For more on the yellow star in Cernăuţi, see Ioanid, *The Holocaust in Romania*, 141–42.

13. Getzler, "Tagebuchblätter aus Czernowitz und Transnistrien," 55.

14. Popovici, *Spovedania Testimony*, 90–92.

15. Hirsch, "A Life in the Twentieth Century," 76–78.

16. Fichman, *Before Memories Fade*, 75–76.

17. Hirsch, "A Life in the Twentieth Century," 79.

18. Rita Pistiner, cited in Gaby Coldewey, et. al., eds., *Zwischen Pruth und Jordan: Lebenserinnerungen Czernowitzer Juden* (Cologne: Böhlau Verlag, 2003), 43.

19. Carp, *Holocaust in Rumania*, 285.

20. Popovici, *Spovedania Testimony*, 97. In all probability, of course, the numbers of Jews in the city after the 1941 deportations was higher. Popovici writes: "By my own estimates, their [the Jews'] number must have ... topped 20,000. It is a noted fact that many Jews, for reasons that are not hard to figure, eschewed both the census and the sorting process and preferred never to ask for ration tickets" (98).

21. Fichman, *Before Memories Fade*, 78.

22. Interview with Bubi and Hedy Brenner, Norwich, Vermont, 1990; Isaak Ehrlich, cited in Coldewey, *Zwischen Pruth und Jordan*, 42.

23. Popovici, *Spovedania Testimony*, 83.

24. Hirsch, "A Life in the Twentieth Century,"78.

25. See esp. Julius S. Fisher, *Transnistria: The Forgotten Cemetery* (Cranbury, N.J.: Thomas Yoseloff, 1969) and Siegfried Jagendorf, *Jagendorf's Foundry: A Memoir of the Romanian Holocaust, 1941–1944*, ed. Aron Hirt-Manheimer (New York: Harper Collins, 1991).

26. "Life was an unending stream of hardships," writes Fichman, *Before Memories Fade*, 82.

27. Hirsch, "A Life in the Twentieth Century," 80.

28. Carp, *Cartea Neagră*, vol. 3, 251, 252.

29. Ioanid, *The Holocaust in Romania*, 173.

30. Mayor Traian Popovici was recognized as one of the Righteous Among Nations by Yad Vashem in 1969. There was no recognition of the role he had played as a rescuer of Jews in present-day Chernivtsi until 2008–09 when people who owed their survival to him, as well as children and grandchildren of such survivors, all now living in various countries throughout the world, collected funds and commissioned a Popovici memorial plaque for display outside of the house where the mayor had lived in Cernăuți. In August 2007 Theodor Criveanu, a lawyer from Brashov, who had been sent to Cernăuți in 1941 by the Romanian government to implement the establishment of the ghetto, was also honored in the Garden of the Righteous in Yad Vashem for his role in secretly handing out work permits—and thus permits to escape deportation—to Jews who were, in fact, not essential to the workforce.

31. Ioanid, *The Holocaust in Romania*, 238–48; Hausleitner, *Die Rumänisierung der Bukowina*, 402–3.

32. Barthes, *Camera Lucida*, 96.

33. The useful term "backshadowing" is Michael André Bernstein's in *Foregone Conclusions: Against Apocalyptic History* (Berkeley: University of California Press, 1994); quote at 16. On "paranoid" and "reparative" reading, see Eve Kosofsky Sedgwick, *Touching Feeling: Affect, Pedagogy, Performativity* (Durham, NC: Duke University Press, 2003), 123–51.

NINE. "THERE WAS NEVER A CAMP HERE!"

1. This chapter relies substantially on and cites from the typescript memoir by Dr. Arthur Kessler, "Ein Arzt in Lager: Die Fahrt ins Ungewisse. Tagebuch u. Aufzeichnugen eines Verschickten," based on notes taken in the camp and written not long after the war (Kessler archive, unpaginated); translations modified from a draft version by Margaret Robinson. We also gained detailed and insightful information from our lengthy videotaped interview with the camp survivor Polya Dubbs in Rehovot, Israel, in September 2000, and the memoirs of Matei Gall, *Finsternis: Durch Gefängnisse, KZ Wapniarka, Massaker, und Kommunismus. Ein Lebenslauf in Rumänien, 1920–1990* (Constance: Hartung-Gorre Verlag,

1999), and Nathan Simon, *". . . auf allen Vieren werdet ihr hinauskriechen!": Ein Zeugenbericht aus dem KZ Wapniarka* ["On all fours you will crawl out!": An eyewitness report from the Vapniarka Camp] (Berlin: Institut Kirche und Judentum, 1994; quote here at 18–20). In addition, we relied on microfilm testimonial transcripts from the trials of Romanian officers accused of crimes in Târgu Jiu and Vapniarka; see Romanian Intelligence Service (SRI)-RG-25.004M, reels 20, 21, and 26, in United States Holocaust Memorial Museum. Artwork included in the chapter is from David Kessler's archive; the artists' names are not always legible or known. Parts of this chapter were previously published in different form. Our description of our trip to Vapniarka appeared as Marianne Hirsch and Leo Spitzer, "There Was Never a Camp Here: Searching for Vapniarka," in Annette Kuhn and Kirsten McAllister, eds., *Locating Memory* (New York: Berghahn, 2006), 135–54. A much fuller theoretical analysis of the little book appeared as Marianne Hirsch and Leo Spitzer, "Testimonial Objects: Memory, Gender, Transmission," *Poetics Today* 27, 2 (summer 2006), 353–84; and was reprinted in M. Baronian, S. Besser, and Y. Janssen, eds., *Diaspora and Memory* (Amsterdam: Thamyris, 2006).

2. Simon, *". . . auf allen Vieren,"* 63.

3. Gall, *Finsternis,* 111.

4. Ibid., 119–20. According to Simon, *". . . auf allen Vieren,"* 64, they were shot by members of a Nazi Einsatzkommando.

5. G. Alexianu, Decree Nr. 0607, 13 Feb. 1942, quoted in Gall, *Finsternis,* 121.

6. Simon puts the number at eleven hundred; Kessler and Gall at twelve hundred; and Dubbs at fourteen hundred.

7. Simon, *". . . auf allen Vieren,"* 63–64.

8. Gall, *Finsternis,* 112–14; Simon, *". . . auf allen Vieren,"* 65. Kessler and Dubbs also mention this.

9. Simon, *". . . auf allen Vieren,"* 66.

10. Ibid., 67.

11. Arthur Kessler, "Lathyrismus," *Psychiatrie und Neurologie* 112, 6 (1947): 345–76.

12. The term *choiceless choice* is Lawrence Langer's; see his *Holocaust Testimonies: The Ruins of Memory* (New Haven: Yale University Press, 1991).

13. Kessler, Dubbs, Simon, and Gall all present similar versions of this account. Simon was himself struck with lathyrism.

14. See Gall, *Finsternis,* 127–29; Ioanid, *The Holocaust in Romania,* 110–75, See also Felicia Steigman Carmelly, ed., *Shattered! Fifty Years of Silence: History and Voices of the Tragedy in Romania and Transnistria* (Scarborough, Ont.: Abbeyfield Publishers, 1997), 138.

15. Gall, *Finsternis,* 153–55; Simon, *". . . auf allen Vieren,"* 90–92.

16. Information about the camp organization and leadership derives from Kessler and Dubbs. Also see Gall, *Finsternis,* 122–23, 126, 129–30; Simon, *". . . auf allen Vieren,"* 66–69.

17. Gall, *Finstneris,* 127, suggests that the inmate leadership had managed either to build a radio receiver or to smuggle one into the camp. But while other testimonies attest to the communications that were established between inmates and persons outside the camp, no one else mentions a radio.

18. Ibid., 150.

19. Polya Dubbs sang, and we recorded, the Vapniarka song when we interviewed her in the year 2000. Also see Gall, *Finsternis,* 151.

20. Ibid.

21. On the miniature, see Susan Stewart, *On Longing* (Durham, NC: Duke University Press, 1993), xii.

## TEN. "THIS WAS ONCE MY HOME"

Epigraphs: Celan, "Nearness of Graves," *Selected Poems,* 11; Felstiner, *Paul Celan,* 24.

1. This monument has since been vandalized and, other than its supporting pedestal, largely destroyed.

2. Marc Sagnol, "Aux Confins de la culture allemande: Czernowitz près de Sadagura," *Les Temps modernes* 60,3 (March-April 1999): 50–51.

3. Franzos, *Der Pojaz* (Frankfurt: Athaneum Verlag, 1988), 54.

4. Hirsch, "A Life in the Twentieth Century," 85. The remarkable report by the Russian Yiddish-language writer Naftali Hertz Kon corroborates these accounts of Soviet mistreatment of Jewish deportees returning from Transnistria. The Russian translation of the Yiddish original of Kon's report was published by Lev Drobyasko in *The Holocaust and Modern Times* 2, 8 (March-April 2003). The Russian version was then translated into English by Kon's daughter, Ina Lancman, and distributed on the Czernowtiz-L listserv.

5. Moritz Gelber, "Reminiscences," handwritten manuscript in German, unpaginated, 2000, Beer Sheva, Israel.

6. Hirsch, "A Life in the Twentieth Century," 83.

7. Brenner, *Mein 20. Jahrhundert,* 214.

8. Fichman, *Before Memories Fade,* 89.

9. Celan, letter to Harald Hartung, 4 December 1958, *Park* 14–15 (1982): 7, cited in Felstiner, *Paul Celan,* 24. Antschel (in Romanian, Ancel) changed his surname to its anagram, Celan, in 1947 while living in Bucharest. For more on the name change, see Felstiner, *Paul Celan,* 46.

10. Our figures for the deportations and returns are estimates based on somewhat divergent figures in the accounts of Traian Popovici, Radu Ioanid, and Jean Ancel. Thus we estimate that between sixty thousand and seventy thousand Jews inhabited Cernăuți at the start of the Second World War in 1939. Popovici

names the number at over fifty thousand when he came to the city in August 1941. About thirty thousand were deported in October and November 1941, and about an additional four thousand were deported in 1942, which leaves approximately sixteen thousand Jews in the city after the 1942 deportations. Popovici uses census and ration card figures but estimates that a small additional number of Jews remained in the city unofficially, without permits or ration cards. As we mention, over 90 percent of Jews from small towns and villages in Northern and Southern Bukowina were deported. By all estimates, about half of those who were deported survived. Survivors either made their way back to their hometowns, or went directly to Bucharest and further, illegally, to Palestine. Those attempting to return to their Southern Bukowinian home towns (now belonging to Romania) were forced to remain in Soviet Chernovtsy until the borders were opened for them in 1945.

11. See Chaim Gelber, "Die Repatriierung der Bukowina Juden in den Jahren 1944–1946," in Gold, *Geschichte,* vol. 2, 79–80.

12. Klara and Dori L., Holocaust Testimony (HVT-777), Fortunoff Video Archive for Holocaust Testimony, Yale University archive (our translation from the German). For "passports" 39, see chapter 5.

13. Fichman, *Before Memories Fade,* 95.

14. Brenner, *Mein 20. Jahrhundert,* 216.

15. Fichman, *Before Memories Fade,* 91.

16. Gelber, "Reminiscences."

17. See Kon in Lev Drobyasko, *The Holocaust and Modern Times.* Kon's report was scathingly repudiated by regional party and Soviet officials as "ranting" and "crafty slander," but written and oral testimonies confirm his observations. Kon was arrested as part of the persecutions of the Jewish Anti-Fascist Committee leaders in 1949. On Kon, see Karen Auerbach, "The Fate of a Yiddish Writer in Communist Eastern Europe: The Case of Naftali Herts Kon in Poland, 1959–1965," *Polin: Studies in Polish Jewry* 21 (November 2008): 307–28.

18. Sella, *Der Ring des Prometheus,* 425.

19. Hirsch, "A Life in the Twentieth Century," 83.

20. Hausleitner, *Die Rumänisierung der Bukowina,* 428–29.

21. Hirsch, "A Life in the Twentieth Century," 89.

22. Interestingly, Naftali Hertz Kon supported this move when he suggested to Soviet authorities that, to ease conditions and clear up misunderstandings, they meet with members of the Jewish population, in "their native language"—Yiddish.

23. Chalfen, *Paul Celan,* 179.

24. The Todt Organization was a German civil engineering company employing forced labor to build roads and bridges during the German military invasion of the Soviet Union.

25. Paul Celan, "Todesfuge," in *Selected Poems and Prose,* 30–31.

26. Kittner, *Erinnerungen,* 218; also cited in Felstiner, *Paul Celan,* 27.

27. Felstiner, *Paul Celan,* 27.

28. Brenner, *Mein 20. Jahrhundert,* 233–35.

29. In *Paul Celan,* for example, Felstiner entitles his chapter on "Todesfuge" "Fugue After Auschwitz."

30. Celan, "Speech on the Occasion of Receiving the Literature Prize of the Free Hanseatic City of Bremen [1958]," in *Selected Poems and Prose,* 395.

31. Colin and Kittner, *Versunkene Dichtung,* 203.

32. Ibid., 249.

33. Celan, *Selected Poems and Prose,* 10.

34. Peter Stenberg, *Journey to Oblivion: The End of Eastern European Yiddish and German Worlds in the Mirror of Literature* (Toronto: University of Toronto Press, 1991), 42.

35. Hausleitner, *Die Rumänisierung der Bukowina,* 428.

36. Fichman, *Before Memories Fade,* 97.

37. Ibid., 100, 101; Hausleitner, *Die Rumänisierung de Bukowina,* 428.

38. See Hirsch, "A Life in the Twentieth Century," 90, 91.

39. Ibid., 92.

40. Fichman, *Before Memories Fade,* 98.

41. Sella, *Der Ring des Prometheus,* 453.

42. Hirsch, "A Life in the Twentieth Century," 93.


ELEVEN. THE PERSISTENCE OF CZERNOWITZ

Epigraph: Gregor von Rezzori, *The Snows of Yesteryear,* 290.

1. David Glynn, http://czernowitz.chpcs.com: Postings from 2006: Introductions.

2. See, for example, Andrée, *Czernowitzer Spaziergänge.*

3. Barthes, *Camera Lucida: Reflections on Photography,* trans. Richard Howard (New York: Hill and Wang, 1981), 96.

4. Boym, *The Future of Nostalgia,* 347.

5. Jack Kugelmass, "The Rites of the Tribe: American Jewish Tourism in Poland," in Ivan Karp, Christine Mullen Kreamer, Steven D. Lavine, eds., *Museums and Communities: The Politics of Public Culture* (Washington, D.C.: Smithsonian Institution Press, 1992), 401–3.

6. On the "1.5 generation" see Susan Suleiman, *Crises of Memory and the Second World War* (Cambridge: Harvard University Press, 2006).

7. Kugelmass, "The Rites of the Tribe," 396.

8. Sergij Osatschuk, "Czernowitz heute und der Umgang mit dem gemeinsamen kulturellen Erbe," paper for the conference Mythos Czernowitz, sponsored by the German–East European Cultural Forum, Potsdam, September 17–19, 2004, http://www.czernowitz.de/index.php?page=seiten&seite=55.

9. See Ruth Glasberg Gold, *Ruth's Journey: A Survivor's Memoir* (Gainesville:

# SELECTED READINGS

Following is a list of sources on Czernowitz, the Bukowina, and the Romanian Holocaust. Many of these sources are also cited in the notes.

Ancel, Jean. "Antonescu and the Jews." *Yad Vashem Studies* 23 (1993), 213–80.

———. "The Romanian Way of Solving the 'Jewish Problem' in Bessarabia and Bukovina, June-July 1941." *Yad Vashem Studies* 19 (1988): 187–232.

———. *Transnistria, 1941–1942: The Romanian Mass Murder Campaigns,* 3 vols. Vol. 1: *History and Document Summaries;* Vols. 2 and 3: *Documents.* Translated by R. Garfinkel and Karen Gold. Tel Aviv: Goldstein-Goren Diaspora Research Center, Tel Aviv University, 2003.

———, ed. *Documents Concerning the Fate of Romanian Jewry during the Holocaust.* 12 vols. New York: The Beate Klarsfeld Foundation, 1986.

Ancel, Jean, and Theodor Lavi, eds. *Encyclopedia of Jewish Communities: Romania [Pinkas ha-kehilot: Romanyah].* 2 vols. Jerusalem: Yad Vashem, 1980.

Andrée, Othmar. *Czernowitzer Spaziergänge: Annäherungen an die Bukowina.* Berlin: Rose Ausländer-Stiftung, 2000.

Appelfeld, Aharon. "Buried Homeland." Translated by Jeffrey M. Green. *The New Yorker,* November 23, 1998, 48–61.

———. "A city that was and is no longer." *Haaretz,* March 6, 2008.

———. *The Story of a Life.* Translated by Aloma Halter. New York: Schocken, 2004.

Ausländer, Rose. *Mother Tongue / Rose Ausländer.* Translated by Jean Boase-Beier and Anthony Uivis. Todmorden, U.K.: Arc Publications, 1995.

———. "Mutterland Wort: 1901–1988." Üxheim/Eifel, Germany: Rose-Ausländer-Dokumentationszentrum, 1996.

Bartfeld-Feller, Margit. *Dennoch Mensch geblieben: Von Czernowitz durch Sibirien nach Israel, 1923–1996.* Edited by Erhard Roy Wiehn. Constance: Hartung-Gorre Verlag, 1996.

———. *Nicht ins Nichts gespannt: Von Czernowitz nach Sibirien deportiert. Jüdische Schicksale, 1941–1997.* Edited by Erhard Roy Wiehn. Constance: Hartung-Gorre Verlag, 1998.

———. *Wie aus ganz andern Welten: Erinnerungen an Czernowitz und die sibirische Verbannung,* Edited by Erhard Roy Wiehn. Constance: Hartung-Gorre Verlag, 2000.

Bartov, Omer. *Erased: Vanishing Traces of Jewish Galicia in Present-Day Ukraine.* Princeton: Princeton University Press, 2008.

Benditer, Ihiel. *Vapniarca.* Tel Aviv: ANAIS Ltd., 1995.

Bernard, Frederic L. *In the Eye of the Storm: Surviving in Nazi-occupied Poland, a Memoir.* Sarasota, FL: Frederic L. Bernard, M.D., 1995.

Blum, Martha. *Children of Paper.* Saskatoon: Coteau Books, 2002.

———. *The Walnut Tree.* Saskatoon: Coteau Books, 1999.

Böttiger, Helmut. *Orte Paul Celans.* Vienna: Zsolnay Verlag, 1996.

Braham, Randolf L. *The Destruction of Romanian and Ukrainian Jews during the Antonescu Era.* New York: East European Monographs, No. 433, 1997.

———, ed. *The Tragedy of Romanian Jewry.* New York: Columbia University Press, 1994.

Brenner, Hedwig. *Leas Fluch: Eine Familiengeschichte, 1840–2003; Ein Zeitdokument.* Brugg, Switzerland: Munda, 2005.

———. *Mein 20. Jahrhundert.* Brugg, Switzerland: Munda. 2006.

Brown, Kate. *A Biography of No Place: From Ethnic Borderland to Soviet Heartland.* Cambridge: Harvard University Press, 2004.

Burger, Hannelore. "Mehrsprachigkeit und Unterrichtswesen in der Bukowina, 1869–1918." In *Die Bukowina: Verganenheit und Gegenwart,* edited by Ilona Slawinski and Joseph P. Strelka. Bern: P. Lang, 1995.

Butnaru, I. C. *The Silent Holocaust: Romania and Its Jews.* Westport, CT: Greenwood Press, 1992.

———. *Waiting for Jerusalem: Surviving the Holocaust in Romania.* Westport, CT: Greenwood Press, 1993.

Carmelly, Felicia Steigman, ed. *Shattered! Fifty Years of Silence: History and Voices of the Tragedy in Romania and Transnistria.* Scarborough, Ont.: Abbeyfield Publishers, 1997.

Carp, Matatias. *Cartea Neagră: Le Livre noir de la destruction des juifs de Roumanie, 1940–1944.* Translated, annotated, and edited by Alexandra Laignel-Lavastine. Paris: Denoël, 2009.

————. *Cartea Neagră: Suferinţele Evreilor din Romănia.* Vol. 3. Bucharest: Editura Diogene, 1996; orig. pub. 1946–48.

————. *Holocaust in Rumania: Facts and Documents on the Annihilation of Rumania's Jews, 1940–1944.* Abridged translation of *Cartea Neagră* by Seán Murphy. Budapest: Primor, 1994.

Celan, Paul. *Selected Poems and Prose of Paul Celan.* Edited and translated by John Felstiner. New York: Norton, 2001.

Chalfen, Israel. *Paul Celan: A Biography of His Youth.* Translated by Maximilian Bleyleben. New York: Presea Books, 1991.

Coldewey, Gaby, et al., eds. *"Czernowitz is gewen an alte jidische Schtot . . . ": Jüdische Überlebende Berichten.* Berlin: Heinrich-Böll Stiftung, 1999.

————. *Zwischen Pruth und Jordan: Lebenserinnerungen Czernowitzer Juden.* Cologne: Böhlau Verlag, 2003.

Colin, Amy. "An den Schnittpunkten der Traditionen: Deutsch in der Bukowina u.a." *Neue deutsche Hefte* 30, 4 (1983): 739–69.

————. *Paul Celan: Holograms of Darkness.* Bloomington: Indiana University Press, 1991.

Colin, Amy, and Alfred Kittner, eds. *Versunkene Dichtung der Bukowina: Eine Anthologie deutschsprachiger Lyrik.* Munich: Wilhelm Fink Verlag, 1994.

Colin, Amy D., Elke V. Kotowski, and Anna D. Ludewig, eds. *Spuren eines Europaers: Karl Emil Franzos als Mittler zwischen den Kulturen.* Potsdam: Moses Mendelsohn Zentrum, 2008.

Corbea-Hoisie, Andrei, ed. *Jüdisches Städtebild Czernowitz.* Frankfurt am Main: Jüdischer Verlag im Suhrkamp, 1998.

Corbea, Andrei, and Michael Astner, eds. *Kulturlandschaft Bukowina: Studien zur deutschsprachigen Literatur des Buchenlandes nach 1918.* Iaşi: Editura Universităţii Alexandru Ion Cuza, 1990.

Corbea-Hoisie, Andrei, and Alexander Rubel. *"Czernowitz bei Sadagora": Identitäten und kulturelles Gedächtnis im mitteleuropäischen Raum.* Iaşi: Editura Universităţii Alexandru Ion Cuza; Constance: Hartung-Gorre Verlag, 2006.

Cordon, Cécile, and Helmut Kusdat, eds. *An der Zeiten Ränder: Czernowitz und die Bukowina.* Vienna: Theodor Kramer Gesellschaft, 2002.

Dallin, David J., and Leon Dennen. *Soviet Russia's Foreign Policy, 1939–1942.* New Haven: Yale University Press, 1947.

Desbois, Patrick. *The Holocaust by Bullets: A Priest's Journey to Uncover the Truth behind the Murder of 1.5 Million Jews.* New York: Palgrave Macmillan, 2008.

Dorian, Emil. *The Quality of Witness: A Romanian Diary.* Translated by M.S. Vamos. Philadelphia: Jewish Publication Society, 1983.

Dorzdowski, Georg. *Damals in Czernowitz und rundum: Erinnerungen eines Altösterreichers.* Klagenfurt, Austria: Verlag der kleinen Zeitung Kärnten, 1984.

Felstiner, John. *Paul Celan: Poet, Survivor, Jew.* New Haven: Yale University Press, 1995.

Livezeanu, Irina. *Cultural Politics in Greater Romania: Regionalism, National Building, and Ethnic Struggle, 1918–1930*. Ithaca, NY: Cornell University Press, 1995.

Macartney, C. A. *The Habsburg Empire, 1790–1918*. London: Wiedenfeld and Nicolson, 1969.

———. *National States and National Minorities*. Oxford: Oxford University Press, 1934.

Manea, Norman. *The Hooligan's Return: A Memoir*. New York: Farrar, Strauss and Giroux, 2003.

Manger, Itzik. *The World According to Itzik: Selected Poetry and Prose*. Translated and edited by Leonard Wolf. New Haven: Yale University Press, 2002.

Meerbaum-Eisinger, Selma. *Harvest of Blossoms: Poems from a Life Cut Short*. Translated by Jerry Glenn and Florian Birkmayer, with Helene Silverblatt and Irene Silverblatt. Evanston, IL: Northwestern University Press, 2008.

———. *Ich bin in Sehnsucht eingehüllt: Gedichte*. Edited by Jürgen Selle. Hamburg: Hofmann und Campe, 2006.

Melzer, Jacob. *Jankos Reise: Von Czernowitz durch die transnistrische Verbannung nach Israel*. Edited by Erhard Roy Wiehn. Constance: Hartung-Gorre Verlag, 2001.

Menninghaus, Winfried. "'Czernowitz/Bukowina' als Topos deutsch-jüdischer Geschichte und Literatur." *Merkur* 3, 4 (1999): 345–57.

Mittelman, Hermann, ed. *Illustrierter Führer durch die Bukowina, 1907*. Czernowitz: Verlag der Buchhandlung Schally, 1907–8. Republished by Helmut Kusdat; Vienna: Mandelbaum Verlag, 2001.

Nagy-Talavera, Nicholas. *The Green Shirts and the Other: The History of Fascism in Hungary and Rumania*. Stanford, CA: Hoover Institution Press, 1970.

Ofer, Dalia. "Life in the Ghettos of Transnistria." *Yad Vashem Studies* 25 (1996): 175–208.

Osatschuk, Sergij. "Czernowitz heute und der Umgang mit dem gemeinsamen kulturellen Erbe." Paper for the conference "Mythos Czernowitz," sponsored by the German–East European Cultural Forum, Potsdam, September 17–19, 2004. http://www.czernowitz.de/index.php?page=seiten&seite=55.

Pachet, Pierre. *Conversations à Jassy*. Paris: Maurice Nadeau, 1997.

Palty, Sonia. *Jenseits des Dnjestr: Jüdischer Deportationsschicksale aus Bukarest in Transnistrien, 1942–43*. Constance: Hartung-Gorre Verlag, 1995.

Pollack, Martin. *Nach Galizien: Von Chassiden, Huzulen, Polen und Ruthenen. Eine imaginäre Reise durch die verschwundene Welt Ostgaliziens und der Bukowina*. Vienna: Christian Brandstätter, 1984.

Popovici, Traian. *Spovedania Testimony*. Edited by Th. Wexler. Translated by Viviane Prager. Bucharest: Fundaţia Dr. W. Filderman, 2001.

Porat, D. "The Transnistria Affair and the Rescue Policy of the Zionist Leadership in Palestina, 1942–1943." *Studies in Zionism* 6, 1 (1985): 27–52.

Ranner, Gertrud, Axel Halling, et al., eds. *"... und das Herz wird mir schwer dabei"*: Czernowitzer Juden erinnern sich. Potsdam: Deutsches Kulturforum, 2009.

Roberts, Henry L. *Rumania: Political Problems of an Agrarian State*. New Haven: Yale University Press, 1951.

Rodal, Alti. "Bukovina Cemeteries, Archives, and Oral History." *Avotaynu* 18, 3 (fall 2002): 9–15.

Rosenzweig, Rachelle. *Russische Eisblumen: 35 Jahre in sowjetischer Unfreiheit*. Frankfurt am Main: Haag und Herchen Verlag, 1993.

Roskies, David G. *A Bridge of Longing: The Lost Art of Yiddish Storytelling*. Cambridge: Harvard University Press, 1995.

Rosner, Charles. *Émancipation: Êtes-vous (aussi) de Czernowitz?* Ventabren: Les Éditions CZ, 2007.

Rostoş, Ioana. *Czernowitzer Morgenblatt: Eine Monografie*. Suceava, Romania: Editura Universităţii Suceava, 2008.

Rothschild, Joseph. *East Central Europe between the Two World Wars*. Seattle: University of Washington Press, 1974.

Rudel, Josef N. *Das waren noch Zeiten: Juedische Geschichten aus Czernowitz und Bukarest*. Edited by Erhard Roy Wiehn. Constance: Hartung-Gorre Verlag, 1997.

Rychlo, Peter, ed. *Europa erlesen: Czernowitz. Texte über Czernowitz aus dem 19. und 20. Jahrhundert*. Klagenfurt: Verlag der Kleinen Zeitung Kärnten, 2004.

Safran, Alexandre. *Resisting the Storm, Romania 1940–1947: A Memoir*. Jerusalem: Yad Vashem, 1987.

Sagnol, Marc. "Aux Confins de la culture allemande: Czernowitz près de Sadagura." *Les Temps modernes* 603 (March-April, 1999): 50–51.

Schectman, Joseph B. "The Transnistria Reservation." *YIVO Annual* 13 (1953): 178–96.

Scherzer, Julius. *While the Gods Were Silent: Growing Up under Fascists and Communists*. Baltimore: Public America, 2005.

Schultz, Deborah, and Edward Timms, eds. *Arnold Daghani's Memories of Mikhailowka: The Illustrated Diary of a Slave Labour Camp Survivor*. Edgeware, U.K.: Mitchell Vallentine, 2009.

Sebastian, Mihail. *Journal 1935–1944: The Fascist Years*. Translated from the Romanian by Patrick Camiller. Chicago: Ivan R. Dee, 2000..

Sella, Dorothea. *Der Ring des Prometheus: Denksteine im Herzen. Eine auf Wahrheit beruhende Romantrilogie: Stawropol, Tbilissi, Czernowitz*. Jerusalem: Rubin Mass Verlag GmbH, 1996.

Sha'ari, David. "The Jewish Community of Czernowitz under Habsburg and Romanian Rule." *Shvut* 6, 22 (1997): 150–83.

Shachan, Avigdor. *Burning Ice: The Ghettos of Transnistria*. Translated by Shmuel Himelstein. Boulder, CO: East European Monographs, 1996.

Shapiro, Paul A. "Prelude to Dictatorship in Romania: The National Christian Party in Power, December 1937-February 1938." *Canadian-American Slavic Studies* 8, 1 (spring 1974): 45–88.

Shmueli, Ilana. *Ein Kind aus guter Familie: Czernowitz 1924–1944.* Aachen: Rimbaud Verlag, 2006.

Simon, Nathan. *". . . auf allen Vieren werdet ihr hinauskriechen!": Ein Zeugenbericht aus dem KZ Wapniarka.* Berlin: Institut Kirche und Judentum, 1994.

Sommer, Fred. *"Halb-Asien": German Nationalism and the Eastern European Works of Emil Franzos.* Stuttgart: Akademischer Verlag Hans-Dieter Heinz, 1984.

Starr, Joshua. "Jewish Citizenship in Rumania (1878–1940)." *Jewish Social Studies* 3, 1 (1941): 57–80.

Steinberg, Arieh. "Underground Activity of the Halutz Youth Movements in Romania." In *Zionist Youth Movements during the Shoah,* edited by Y. C. Asher Cohen. New York: Peter Lang, 1995.

Steiner, Carl. *Karl Emil Franzos, 1848–1904: Emancipator and Assimilationist.* New York: Peter Lang, 1990.

Stenberg, Peter. *Journey to Oblivion: The End of Eastern European Yiddish and German Worlds in the Mirror of Literature.* Toronto: University of Toronto Press, 1991.

Sternberg, Hermann. *Zur Geschichte der Juden in Czernowitz.* Tel Aviv: Olamenu, 1962.

Teich, Meyer. "The Self-Administration of Jews in the Shargorod Ghetto." In *Studies of Heroism in the Holocaust Period,* edited by S. Esch. Jerusalem: Bialik Foundation, Yad Vashem, 1959.

Turczynski, Emanuel. *Geschichte der Bukowina in der Neuzeit: Zur Sozial- und Kulturgeschichte einer mitteleuropäischgeprägten Landschaft.* Vol. 14 of *Studien der Forschungsstelle Ostmitteleuropa an der Universität Dortmund.* Wiesbaden: Harrassowitz, 1993.

Turczynski, Emanuel, and Gerhard Grimm. *Von der Pruth-Ebene bis zum Gipfel des Ida.* Vol. 10 of *Studien zur Geschichte, Literatur, Volkskunde, und Wissenschaftsgeschichte des Donau-Balkan-Raumes: Festschrift zum 70. Geburtstag von Emanuel Turczynski, Südosteuropa-Schriften.* Munich: Südosteuropa-Gesellschaft, 1989.

von Rezzori, Gregor. *Memoirs of an Anti-Semite.* Translated by Joachim Neugroschel and Gregor von Rezzori. New York: Vintage International, 1991.

———. *Mir auf der Spur.* Munich: C. Bertelsmann Verlag, 1997.

———. *The Snows of Yesteryear: Portraits for an Autobiography.* Translated by H. F. B. d. Rothermann. New York: Vintage International, 1991.

Weißglas, Isak. *Steinbruch am Bug: Bericht einer Deportation nach Transnistrien.* Berlin: Literaturhaus, 1995.

Werner, Klaus, ed. *Fäden ins Nichts gespannt: Deutschsprachige Dichtung aus der Bukowina*. Frankfurt am Main: Insel Verlag, 1991.

Wichner, Ernest, and Herbert Wiesner, eds. *In der Sprache der Mörder: Eine Literatur aus Czernowitz, Bukowina. Ausstellungsbuch*. Berlin: Literaturhaus Berlin, 1993.

Winkler, Markus. *Jüdische Identitäten im kommunikativen Raum: Presse, Sprache und Theater in Czernowitz bis 1923*. Bremen: Editions Lumière, 2007.

Yavetz, Zvi. "An Eyewitness Note: Reflections on the Rumanian Iron Guard." *Journal of Contemporary History* 26 (1991): 597–610.

———. *Erinnerungen an Czernowitz: Wo Menschen und Bücher lebten*. Munich: C. H. Beck, 2007.

———. "Youth Movements in Czernowitz," in *Hunter and Hunted: Human History of the Holocaust*, edited by Gerd Korman. New York: Viking, 1973.

## USEFUL WEBSITES

http://bukowina.info/index.html
http://czernowitz.ehpes.com/
http://ghostsofhome.com
www.bukovinajewsworldunion.org/
www.city.cv.ua/
www.czernowitz.de
www.geocities.com/zaprudol/
www.jewishgen.org/yizkor/bukowinabook/Bukowina.html
www.museumoffamilyhistory.com/

# INDEX

Italicized page references indicate illustrations.

Hirsch, Markus (Meilech), 20, 25, 36, 47–49, 179, 272

Hitler-Stalin pact (Ribbentrop-Molotov Nonagression pact), 81, 102–3, 107, 114, 115, 172

Hoffman, Eva, 9, 11, 162

Hofshteyn, Dovid, 113

Holocaust, in (Romanian) Cernăuţi: archival documentation of, 177–81, 183–84, 184, 312–14, 315; and arrests, 173–74, 197–98; and deaths, 163, 173; and deportations, 102, 125, 128–32, 131, 134–35, 163, 184–86, 189–92, 198, 338n10; and forced labor, 163, 183–84, 188; and ghetto, 122–25, 126–27, 128–32, 129, 134–38, 178, 185, 188; and identity cards, 186, 187; and Jewish star, 163, 164–67, 167, 173, 186, 187, 188, 189, 194; and restrictions, 163, 176, 177; and waivers (authorizations), 171, 180–82, 185, 191, 192, 198

Holocaust, in Transnistria. See Transnistria

Holocaust Memorial Museum, Washington, D.C., 61–63, 64, 65, 70, 184

Hungarians, in Romania, 75

Hungary, 243, 256

identity documents, 111, 115, 186, 187, 235

Iron Guard, 77, 78, 93, 325n10

Israel, 25, 141–43, 259, 260, 288

Israeli literature, 18

Jabotinsky, Ze'ev (Vladimir), 87

Jewish Councils, 63, 124, 128, 131, 185, 314

Jewish Genealogical Society of Ottawa, 261

Jewish refugees in Soviet Union, 149–60, 158, 241, 242, 333n12

Jewish residents of Austro-Hungarian Czernowitz: and anti-Semitism, 34–35, 41–42; assimilation of, 27–28, 35–43, 234; civil rights of, 26–28, 30, 33, 34, 41; economic activity of, 30–33; education of, 27, 34, 58; and ethnic diversity, 38–39; and German language, 26–28, 30, 33–34, 37, 39–43; gravesites of, 22–23, 25–26, 28–30, 47–48; and Hebrew language, 43, 45, 46; and social class, 22, 23, 28, 68; social mobility of, 27–28, 32, 33, 40; and street

photos, 65, 68, 69; and Yiddish language, 27–28, 32, 33, 40, 41, 43–47

Jewish residents of Romanian Cernăuţi (1918–1940): and anti-Semitism, 69–70, 79, 80, 82, 101, 102, 326n8; and civil rights, 69, 80, 325n6; and education, 58, 69–70, 72–73, 75–76, 88–89, 101–2; and ethnic diversity, 38, 89, 95; and German language, 51, 70–71, 74, 75, 82, 85, 88–92; and German literature, 91–98; and Hebrew language, 82–83, 84, 85; and leftist politics, 87–88; and Romanianization, 73, 74–82, 88, 90, 91, 325n4, 326n12; and social class, 58, 68, 74, 89, 92; and Soviet occupation, 98, 99–100, 101; and street photos, 63–71, 66–67; and Yiddish language, 46, 59, 83, 89, 90, 91, 92, 96–98; and youth organization, 83–87

Jewish residents of Romanian Cernăuţi (1941–1944): archival documents relating to, 177–81, 183–84, 184, 312–14, 315; and arrests, 173–74, 197–98; deaths among, 163, 173; and deportations, 102, 125, 128–32, 131, 134–35, 163, 184–86, 189–92, 198, 338n10; and forced labor, 163, 183–84, 188; and ghetto, 122–25, 126–27, 128–32, 129, 134–38, 163, 178, 185, 188, 303; and identity cards, 186, 187; and Jewish star, 163, 164–67, 167, 173, 186, 187, 188, 189, 194; and restrictions, 163, 176, 177; and waivers (authorizations), 171, 180, 185, 191, 192, 198

Jewish residents of Soviet Chernovtsy (1940–1941): and civil rights, 115; and deportations, 112, 116–17, 160; and economic relations, 110–12; and education, 113–14; and identity cards, 111, 115; and leftist politics, 106–9, 110–11, 114–15; and Russian language, 20, 111, 115; and Ukrainianization, 104, 110–11; and Yiddish language, 20, 112–13

Jewish residents of Soviet Chernovtsy (postwar era): emigration of, 248–53; and German language, 244; return of, 232–42; and Sovietization, 243–44; and Soviet reoccupation, 236–42

Jewish residents of Ukrainian Chernivtsi, 14–19, 20, 71, 143–44, 170–71, 232–33, 253, 267, 311

| | |
|---:|:---|
| Text: | 11.25/13.5 Adobe Garamond |
| Display: | Adobe Garamond |
| Compositor: | BookMatters, Berkeley |
| Indexer: | Andrew Joron |
| Cartographer: | Bill Nelson |
| Printer and binder: | Thomson-Shore, Inc. |